HABITATS OF
NORTH AMERICA

HABITATS OF NORTH AMERICA

A Field Guide for Birders, Naturalists, and Ecologists

Phil Chaon | Iain Campbell
Photography by Ben Knoot

Special contributors
**Giselle Velastegui, Mike Parr,
David Wiedenfeld, Christopher Tracey,
Regan Smyth, and Pablo Cervantes**

PRINCETON UNIVERSITY PRESS
PRINCETON AND OXFORD

Published by Princeton University Press
41 William Street, Princeton, New Jersey 08540
99 Banbury Road, Oxford OX2 6JX

press.princeton.edu

All Rights Reserved
ISBN (pbk.) 978-0-691-24506-5
ISBN (e-book) 978-0-691-24516-4

British Library Cataloging-in-Publication Data is available

Editorial: Robert Kirk and Megan Mendonça
Production Editorial: Karen Carter
Jacket/Cover Design: Ben Higgins
Production: Ruthie Rosenstock
Publicity: Caitlyn Robson-Iszatt and Matthew Taylor
Copyeditor: Amy K. Hughes
Typesetting and Design: D & N Publishing, Wiltshire, UK

Cover Credit: Cover images by Christine Elder

This book has been composed in Cambay Devanagari

Printed in China

10 9 8 7 6 5 4 3 2 1

CONTENTS

LIST OF FIGURES AND SIDEBARS

FIGURES

SIDEBARS

INTRODUCTION

GENESIS OF THE HABITATS OF THE WORLD BOOKS

The authors of *Habitats of the World*, the global field guide in this series, have had a lifelong fascination with biogeography and wildlife ecosystems. Like the vast majority of other passionate traveling naturalists, we are most consistently interested in birds and larger mammals, while also paying some attention to reptiles, amphibians, butterflies, and other groups, especially in places where they're conspicuous. We have all been frustrated by the approach to habitat/ecosystem classification used in most books and the complete absence of habitat information in many vertebrate field guides. The creation of *Habitats of the World*, although limited in scope with enough space for just 189 habitats to be delineated and described, showed the great interest and need for a set of habitat descriptions that could be used by ecologists and naturalists. So, employing this common language, we set about producing a series of regional books that break down the habitats at a finer resolution than the original book, with each habitat based on floristics, forest structure, and bird assemblages, along with other wildlife to a lesser degree. In this book, we present our view of North American wildlife habitats (ecosystems). We have also created online resources, such as a bird-assemblage habitat database, listing all global habitats along with the indicator bird species, which will allow people to search via birds or habitats to find and understand their relationships (www.habitatsoftheworld.org/birdassemblages).

There are innumerable lenses through which planet Earth's habitats can be assessed. Geology, geography, and botany are all critically important. But we don't view any of them as the final word on habitats, and much of what these models prioritize is of little immediate relevance to traveling naturalists or ecologists. A specialist in entomology or herpetology will apply a different, and fascinating, lens to the world. Our reason for prioritizing the bird (and to a lesser extent mammal) "lens" is that we look at the world primarily through this lens, and so do the vast majority of the world's traveling naturalists. A handful of specialists seek out moths in the Yucatán, whereas millions of tourists visit Yellowstone to see big mammals and glamorous birds, or flock to birding migration hot spots such as High Island on the upper Texas coast or Magee Marsh in nw. Ohio. Our presentation at first glance may lack the clarity of a botanical approach to the world's habitats, but by using bird assemblages in conjunction with botany, we provide truly ecological mapping of habitats. At the scale we present it, our classification has far greater utility to most world travelers, regional ecologists, and conservationists than any other previous perspective on habitats.

In its attempt to cover the wildlife habitats of the entire continent of North America, this is an ambitious book, in which hard decisions had to be made about what to include and exclude based on botanical and bird assemblages. We freely admit that deep oceanic habitats, and to a lesser extent surficial aquatic habitats, are worthy of far more detailed coverage using fish and invertebrate assemblages than we have given in this volume; we will get around to filling in these gaps in a global marine and aquatic volume once the terrestrial and surficial habitats are described. At this time, the habitats are almost all based on surficial botany and aquatic habitats as they relate to birds and mammals. Our approach is certain to alienate some, but we firmly believe it will be both enjoyable and useful to other ecologists, conservationists, and global naturalists like ourselves.

WHAT DO WE COVER AS A DISTINCT HABITAT IN THIS BOOK AND HOW DID WE MAKE THE MAPS?

We use the word *habitat* as a synonym for *ecosystem*. We understand that anywhere an animal exists is its individual "habitat," but we refer to broadly similar ecosystems with similar animal assemblages as habitats.

The habitat delineation was done in collaboration with the American Bird Conservancy and NatureServe by combining bird assemblages and existing vegetation mapping. The mapping, done by NatureServe using our criteria, allows us to use the very detailed mapping employed by the International Vegetation Classification (IVC) system (explained in the next section). By assigning the IVC system's 218 "Macrogroups," encompassing NatureServe's 800-odd "Groups," to 84 North American habitats based on bird assemblages, we were able to make habitat maps much more efficiently than if we had started from scratch, reinventing the wheel. As with the *Habitats of South America* and *Habitats of Africa* books, we are using the IVC Macrogroups as the starting point for our analysis. If the existing IVC Macrogroups (with all their contained Groups) match bird assemblages, we use those as our base. If multiple Macrogroups have the same bird assemblages, we combine them, and if a Macrogroup contains habitats with different bird assemblages, we break it down and assign the Groups to different habitats.

We evaluate habitats based on two main criteria: (1) Their visual distinctiveness, which can be easily assessed by a casual observer and usually relates to the types of structure (forest vs. shrubland) and the species of plants present, which is a very similar approach to other ecosystem-mapping systems; and (2) their assemblage of wildlife, primarily birds—but we also considered other vertebrates, in a massive departure from any existing global or regional ecological mapping system. Each habitat is described with a suite of obligate and indicator bird species, available online at www.habitatsoftheworld.org/birdassemblages. An example is Jack Pine Forest, which is quite distinct in appearance from other coniferous habitats and supports a fairly distinctive set of wildlife, including breeding Kirtland's Warbler, restricted to this habitat. But in some cases, one or the other criterion is of predominant importance. Except to the eye of a trained botanist, Pacific Chaparral is not very different from other Mediterranean-climate woodlands around the world, but the bird assemblage there is very different from analogous habitats in Europe or Chile, so it is considered a distinct habitat. An example of the opposite case is Bald Cypress–Tupelo Gum Swamp. This habitat is characterized by the dominance of Bald Cypress and tupelo trees, which are very distinctive and easily recognizable, even as it lacks a bird assemblage very different from surrounding deciduous forests. Some species such as Prothonotary Warbler are more common here, but a bird list alone cannot easily distinguish this environment. Having said that, the (very valid) case can be made that if we were to use the full suite of vertebrate assemblages, including amphibians and fishes, the distinction between this habitat and surrounding ones would be extremely obvious. The great strength of our system of using bird assemblages to refine habitat delineation also shows its weakness, compared to what could be, and we think should be, done with the use of other vertebrate and invertebrate groups. If readers have readily identifiable animals that we can use to make our system better, please contact us, and let's see how we can incorporate them into the algorithms we are building.

HOW DOES *HABITATS OF THE WORLD* COMPLEMENT OTHER GLOBAL HABITAT CLASSIFICATION SYSTEMS?

The understanding and correct classification of habitats is crucial to the development of useful and viable nature-reserve systems, as is knowing what wildlife occurs in threatened habitats within them. The problem is that, as of now, there is no system to classify all the world's habitats at a level that is appreciable to most casual naturalists, birders, conservationists, and ecologists. There are reasons for this, such as, but not limited to, systems and typologies being overly hierarchical by design, and the challenges of trying to syncretize different national mapping systems. The Global Ecosystem Typology (GET) system developed by the International Union for Conservation of Nature (IUCN) and the International Vegetation Classification (IVC), mainly developed through NatureServe, both have excellent ecosystem classifications that aim to define and protect ecological communities. These systems are incredibly useful in principle, but neither works globally at a scale that conservation groups, birders, or ecologists can easily use, because they do not yet have all habitats described at a level that is convenient to use and understand (see fig. 1). However, as explained earlier, we do use the IVC/NatureServe Group levels to build our system, with the IVC Macrogroups as a starting point. Our Habitats of the World (HotW) system works as a "Rosetta Stone" for applying the GET and IVC habitat classification systems at a global scale. A complete walk-through from the HotW system to the IVC and GET systems is available online at www. habitatsoftheworld.org/intotheweedstypology/NorthAmerica.

The GET system jumps from 108 global (described) units at the "Group" level to between 3500 and 3700 (undescribed) units at the "Regional Ecotype" level. Similarly, the IVC system jumps from 76 (described) units at the "Division" level to 1196, often undescribed, units at the "Macrogroup" level. Neither system describes the animals living in the habitats. It will be many years before either system has the coverage required for global use at the most detailed scale.

The HotW system has global coverage and includes 650 global (84 North American), mainly terrestrial habitats, covering those home to almost all the world's birds and much of the other wildlife. At this level, it becomes much easier for the non-botanist to discern one habitat from another, understand how they differ, and develop the understanding and criteria to be able to comprehend how the ecologies of these systems differ. The HotW system should make it easier to incorporate habitats into conservation planning, mapping, and ecological work.

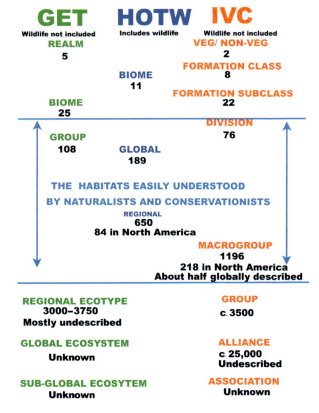

Fig. 1. Global habitat classification systems

Habitats (sometimes called "vegetation types") are amalgamations of various species of plants and animals under specific environmental conditions with artificially human-imposed boundaries delineating them from adjacent similar habitats in what is almost always a gradual boundary at some scale. They are not taxonomic entities the way animals and plants are. Organisms have a distinct genetic code and evolutionary history that infers relatedness, which can be detailed in a strict dendrogram form (fig. 2). However, all the habitat classification systems use a hierarchical typology that just doesn't fit this rigid structure. As you will see in the breakdowns of different biomes in the Biomes of North America section below, the dendrograms are helpful in showing relationships, but many habitats are crossovers or can easily be classified in multiple biomes. The relationships are not hierarchical but often more weblike. Examples include Bald Cypress–Tupelo Gum Swamp, which fits in both forest and wetland biomes, and Tamaulipan Mezquital (not a liquor), which may be described as both a desert thornscrub and a savanna; these are not either/ors but both/ands.

One reason there are so many more birders than bat, rat, or beetle enthusiasts is that birds are readily identifiable animals of a limited number, around 10,000 species. It is possible to learn most of the world's bird species, to identify them, and to catalog them (i.e., to keep lists), as so many birders are prone to doing. This then becomes a meaningful contribution to citizen-science projects like Cornell's eBird, which can be used to analyze global trends in species distribution and occurrence. To compare, beetles have roughly 400,000 known species, a number that defies easy identification or the ability to discern relationships between what has been identified. Bats and rats suffer the problem of being usually nocturnal, often cryptic, and extremely difficult to identify, which results in a dearth of bat and rat enthusiasts and, consequently, much less knowledge on these groups and their use in habitat delineation. The Habitats of the World system employs the "Goldilocks complex," which makes it "just right": detailed enough to be valuable but easy enough for anyone to understand. When trying to develop a system of understanding habitats that allows conservationists, ecologists, and planners to communicate across continents, we are left with similar problems, where the systems are either so broad as to be of little use at the birder and conservationist scale, or so detailed and difficult to separate that most users, including conservationists, don't understand them.

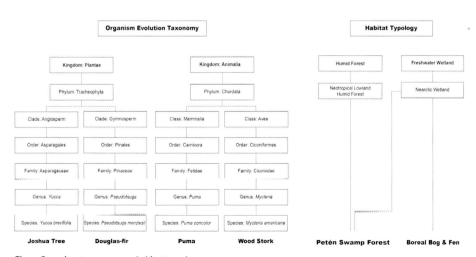

Fig. 2. Organism taxonomy vs. habitat typology

TYPES OF HABITAT BOUNDARIES AND ECOTONES

An ecotone is a place where two or more biomes meet, usually possessing traits of both. For example, mangrove is an ecotone between marine systems and terrestrial systems; savannas are ecotones between tropical rainforests and deserts; and monsoon forests are ecotones between savannas and rainforests. So most locales are ecotones at some scale. We try to avoid use of this confusing term in the book and prefer to treat zones between defined habitats as boundaries, where the ends of the transitions are different habitats with different bird assemblages. Sometimes the transitions are extremely **sharp**, especially where natural forests abut anthropogenic farmlands or wetland systems in arid terrains (fig. 3). **Mosaics** have distinct patches of different habitats in one area. This type of transition is very common in coastal forests and savanna edges. In a **mélange**, distinct systems intertwine in a complex manner across a broad zone. This pattern is very common in mountainous areas with complex geomorphology and geology and complex microclimates. The fourth kind of transition is **nebulous**, where the changes are so gradual that it is difficult to determine which habitat you are in. The bird and animal assemblages mix in this type of ecotone, and it can be difficult to determine the habitat based on either plant or animal assemblages; in a finer-scale habitat typology, these nebulous transition zones might be split out as a different habitat.

There are also regions where habitats **intrude** into one another, such as moist forests that extend far into arid terrains along waterways. The opposite exists where dry and heath-type habitats can extend as **outliers** in very humid environments along ridgelines with nutrient-deficient rocks such as granites. To confuse everything further, another system exists on mountains that are high enough to become cold and/or attract orographic rainfall. Here the system flips, and wetter forests can occur on mountains, such Mount Lemmon, Arizona, surrounded by the Sonoran Desert.

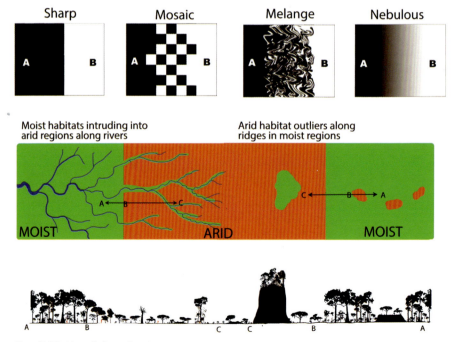

Fig. 3. Habitat boundaries and ecotones

AREA COVERED BY THIS BOOK

This book covers all of continental North America, from Alaska to Mexico's border with Guatemala/ Belize. It includes Greenland, the Aleutian Islands and other islands of the Bering Sea such as the Pribilofs. It includes the Hawaiian Islands and the Caribbean islands, except those just off the coast of South America such as Trinidad and Tobago.

CLIMATE DESCRIPTIONS AND GRAPHS

Throughout the book, each habitat description includes a brief overview of the climate (often with the Köppen climate code, discussed below) and a heavily adapted version of the Walter-Lieth climate graph, which create a powerful tool when combined. Looking at habitat distributions and their relationships to not only temperature and rainfall but also distribution of rainfall through the year, it became apparent that this annual rainfall distribution is often a more important factor in vegetation type than average precipitation alone. To help illustrate these variations through the year, we have created climate graphs for each habitat, based on the original work of Walter and Lieth, though we have heavily modified them to make them easier to read and interpret.

Reading these graphs may seem intimidating at first, but when their relevance is explained, they become more scrutable (see fig. 4). When temperature and precipitation are plotted together, and where each 20 mm (0.8 in.) of precipitation is compared to each 10°C (50°F), some really interesting patterns emerge. When the precipitation plot drops below the temperature plot, the area is in a period of water stress (drought) because transpiration rates (the rate at which plants lose water) are higher than the precipitation level. We have colored these drought periods in orange. When the precipitation plot lifts above the temperature line, the area has a surplus of water, and plant growth is strong; these periods are colored light blue. However, once the precipitation exceeds 100 mm (4 in.) a month, there is an extreme surplus of water, and regardless of the temperature, most water runs off and is not used by plants; we have colored these periods in dark blue. Because the whole method makes sense only when used with the metric system, we have included temperature only in Celsius and rainfall in millimeters on the graphs.

MONSOON FOREST: Awa

> Temperature hot much of the year
> Dry conditions for some months in winter
> Very intense monsoonal summer rains
> Significant overlap with savanna climate

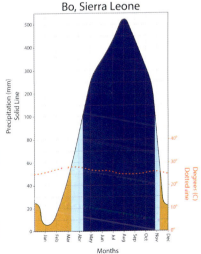

Fig. 4. Sample climate graphs (above and overleaf)

SAVANNA: Awa, Awb

> Temperature hot throughout the year
> Drought conditions in winter
> Very intense monsoonal summer rains

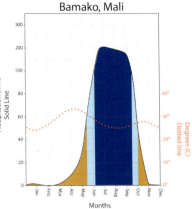

Bamako, Mali

Exposed ridges are far more fire prone

LOWLAND RAINFOREST: Afa, Afb

> Temperature hot throughout the year
> Abundant precipitation throughout the year

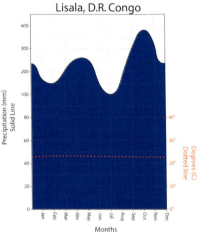

Lisala, D.R. Congo

MEDITERRANEAN SCRUB: Csa, Csb

> Cold winters, warm summers
> Wet winters
> Moderately dry summers

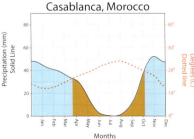

Casablanca, Morocco

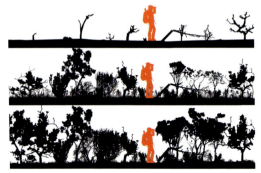

WARM DESERT: Bwh
> Dry and hot throughout the year

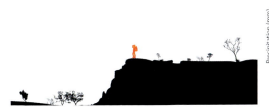

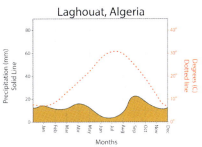

THE KÖPPEN CLIMATE CLASSIFICATION

The Köppen climate classification system is the most widely used global method to classify and categorize different climatic regions. Each climate is assigned a simple two- or three-letter code.
    The first letter denotes the average temperature (B is an exception).

A: Tropical climate, with year-round average temperatures above 18°C (64°F).
B: Arid climate with low precipitation.
C: Mid-latitude climate with mild to cool temperatures.
D: Mid-latitude climate with cold winters and mild to cool summers.
E: Polar or alpine climates with extremely cold temperatures.

The second letter denotes when most precipitation occurs:

f: Year-round rainfall pattern, with precipitation evenly distributed throughout the year.
m: Monsoonal, with a pronounced wet season and a dry season.
w: Dominant dry winter season.
s: Dominant dry summer season.
T: Lacks a true summer.

The third letter denotes maximum and minimum temperatures, or wet/hot desert:

a: Hot summers, with the warmest month having an average temperature above 22°C (71.6°F).
b: Mild summers, with the warmest month averaging below 22°C (71.6°F) but above 10°C (50°F).
c: Cool summers, with the warmest month averaging below 10°C (50°F) but above 0°C (32°F).
d: Very cold winters, with the coldest month averaging below 0°C (32°F).
e: Cold summers, with the warmest month averaging below 10°C (50°F).
h: Hot desert.
k: Cold desert.

North America encompasses a wide range of temperature zones from the polar regions of Baffin Island, Canada, through the tropical zones of s. Mexico. Simultaneously, there are also varying rainfall regimes, resulting in everything from polar deserts and hot deserts to steamy rainforests, and pretty much everything in between. Using the Köppen system, we have assigned the environments the following codes. When used in conjunction with the climate graphs explained earlier, these Köppen codes can explain why most habitats occur where they do.

1. Tropical humid climate (**Afa**, **Afb**): Areas with this climate type receive high amounts of rainfall and have high temperatures all year. Habitats are moist forests, mainly MESOAMERICAN LOWLAND RAINFORESTS of Chiapas, Mexico, and some islands of the Caribbean.
2. Tropical monsoonal climate (**Awa**, **Awb**): These regions have distinct wet summer and dry winter seasons. Some locations would have sufficient precipitation to support rainforest if the rain were distributed more evenly throughout the year. The main habitats are moist savannas, tropical grasslands, and monsoon forests. They are prevalent in the Yucatán Peninsula.
3. Mediterranean climate (**Csa**, **Csb**): These climates occur in the temperate zone of the west coast of California and nw. Mexico. They are categorized by hot, dry summers and mild, wet winters. The main habitat is PACIFIC CHAPARRAL.
4. Desert (**Bwh**, **Bwk**): These regions are characterized by extremely low annual precipitation, high temperatures, and little vegetation. They include the NEARCTIC DESOLATE DESERT, MOJAVE DESERT, and CHIHUAHUAN DESERT.
5. Semiarid climate (**Bsh**, **Bsk**): These areas receive more rain than deserts but not enough rain in the wet season to allow the development of lush savanna. The main habitats are EASTERN MESQUITE and TAMAULIPAN MEZQUITAL.
6. Temperate climate (**Cfa**, **Csa**): These areas have mild winters that get cold but not freezing for long periods, and mild summers that are not hot for too long. The main habitats are NEARCTIC TEMPERATE DECIDUOUS FOREST and NEARCTIC TEMPERATE MIXED FOREST.

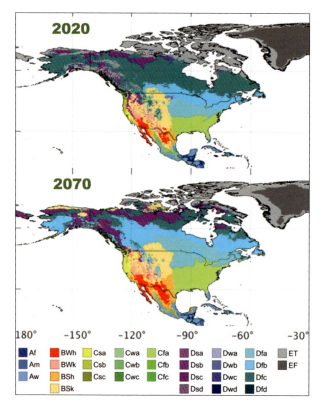

Fig. 5. Köppen climate maps for North America, 2020 and 2070. H. E. Beck, N. E. Zimmermann, T. R. McVicar, N. Vergopolan, A. Berg, and E. F. Wood (2018), Present and future Köppen-Geiger climate classification maps at 1-km resolution, *Scientific Data* 5: **180214.** LICENSED UNDER CC BY 4.0 DEED

In figure 5, the Köppen climate for the recent past is presented against the projected Köppen climate for North America in the late 21st century. Although climate change is of great concern, it is beyond the scope of this book to predict future habitats related to these changes in North America. What this prediction does show is that northern latitudes of North America are going to go through a profound change, with the climate of Alaska becoming unsuitable for tundra (e.g., NEARCTIC ROCKY TUNDRA and NEARCTIC BOGGY TUNDRA) and the BOREAL CONIFER FOREST greatly reduced.

BIOMES OF NORTH AMERICA

Multiple biomes, or ecological communities, are described in this book. Those in most of mainland North America and Greenland fall within the Nearctic biogeographical realm, while those in much of Mexico and the Caribbean are in the Neotropical biogeographical realm. The Nearctic has much in common with the Palearctic of Europe, n. Africa, and most of Asia. The Neotropics extend through all of South America. The boundary between the two weaves though Mexico and, arguably, southernmost Florida, but for ease of use, we have incorporated all of Mexico in this book. Where the habitats extend from Mexico into Central America, they are often referred to as Mesoamerican, which generally refers to Mexico and Central America. The Hawaiian habitats are within the Oceanian realm.

The broad habitat categories and subcategories used in this book are briefly explained in this section; the example habitats listed can be located in the table of contents. Refer to Useful Habitat Jargon for further explanations of most of the terms used here. Note that the color-coding used here corresponds with that used in the maps throughout the book. These descriptions broadly correspond to the major ecological community types known as "biomes."

CONIFER FORESTS: Forests made up of coniferous trees (which generally don't seasonally lose their leaves, with the exception of larches and few others).
- **Temperate Conifer Forest:**
  Example: **Nearctic Boreal Conifer Forest**
- **Dry Conifer Forest:** Forests and woodlands in dry temperate and tropical areas.
  Example: **Pinyon-Juniper Woodland**

DESERTS AND ARID SCRUBS: Arid areas with little plant growth.
- **Barren Desolate Desert:** Harshest of deserts, where little grows, with areas of rock and sand dunes.
  Example: **Nearctic Desolate Desert**
- **Desert and Semi-desert Shrubland:** Open arid areas with small shrubs with generally small leaves; cacti or euphorbias can be present and may be large.
  Example: **Sonoran Desert**
- **Desert and Semi-desert Thornscrub:** Arid areas with thickets of tall thornbushes and little grass growth.
  Example: **Tamaulipan Mezquital**
- **Arctic Polar Desert:** Extremely cold and dry areas where almost nothing grows.

TEMPERATE DECIDUOUS FORESTS: Broadleaf forests that lose their leaves in winter.
Example: **Nearctic Temperate Deciduous Forest**

TROPICAL HUMID FORESTS: Quintessential warm and wet rainforest-type environments.
- **Lowland Rainforest:** Wet, evergreen tall forest with thick full canopy cover and open undergrowth.
  Example: **Mesoamerican Lowland Rainforest**

- **Semi-Evergreen Forest:** Generally humid forests with near-complete canopy cover in which a minority of the trees lose their leaves.
  Example: **Mesoamerican Semi-Evergreen Forest**
- **Montane/Subtropical Evergreen Forest:** Warm, wet forests with almost closed canopy of evergreen or partially deciduous trees.
  Example: **Mesoamerican Cloudforest**

DRY DECIDUOUS FORESTS: Warm forests that lose most of their leaves in dry periods.

- **Closed Deciduous Forest:** Closed-canopy, dry deciduous forests that in summer appear lush, but many trees lose their leaves in winter. Fire-intolerant.
  Example: **Yucatán Dry Deciduous Forest**

SAVANNAS AND SEASONALLY MOIST SHRUBLANDS: Habitats with an open canopy, lots of grass or shrubbery, and a strongly seasonal (usually wet-summer/dry-winter) climate. Most habitats in this category are heavily influenced by fire.

- **Thorn Savanna:** Open (tall or short) woodlands with lots of grass cover. Trees are often dominated by acacias (of various genera), many of them with spines.
  Example: **Caribbean Thornscrub (covered in Deserts and Arid Scrubs)**

GRASSLANDS AND STEPPES: Habitats dominated by grasses, with or without shrubs and flowers, and few or no trees. Fire-dependent.

- **Temperate Grassland:** Grasslands that have cold winters and warm summers. Grasses can grow throughout the year but are dependent on rain. Fire-tolerant.
  Example: **Tallgrass Prairie**
- **Montane Grassland:** Grasslands in highlands, often receiving orographic rainfall. Fire-tolerant.
  Example: **Mexican Bunchgrass and Zacatonal**
- **Flooded Grassland:** Grasslands that spend most of the year as lush grasslands but turn into huge wetlands during the wet season.
  Example: **Mesoamerican Savanna and Grassland**

MEDITERRANEAN FORESTS, WOODLANDS, AND SHRUBLANDS: Thick scrub in areas with climates defined by cold, wet winters and dry, hot summers.

- **Maquis, Chaparral, and Matorral:** Low shrubland that can be either closed or open. Dominated by fire and grazing. Plants are often similar to those of nearby forests.
  Example: **Pacific Chaparral**

TUNDRAS: Very low vegetation dominated by mosses and many lichens. Found at extreme latitudes or elevations, where temperatures, snow cover, or exposure to wind prohibit the growth of trees.
Example: **Nearctic Rocky Tundra**

FRESHWATER HABITATS: Habitats whose most important aspect is their inundation with fresh water.

- **Swamp Forest:** Forested habitats that are seasonally or permanently inundated.
  Example: **Bald Cypress–Tupelo Gum Swamp (covered in Temperate Deciduous Forest)**
- **Freshwater Wetland:** Nonforested habitats whose most important aspect is that they are seasonally or permanently flooded.
  Example: **Nearctic Reedbed Marshes**

■ **Freshwater Aquatic Habitats:** Nonforested habitats whose most important aspect is that they are seasonally or permanently flooded.
Example: **Nearctic Upland Rivers**

SALT-DOMINATED HABITATS: Habitats where the dominant force is the presence of high levels of salt in the water or soil.

■ **Salt Pan:** Areas in which evaporation or volcanic activity has produced extremely high salt concentrations in the soil. Mostly unvegetated, though algae grows quickly when floods occur.
Example: **North American Playas**

■ **Mangrove:** A specialized forest that grows in tidally flooded coastal areas.
Example: **Mesoamerican Mangroves**

■ **Salt Marsh:** Habitat of salt-tolerant marsh vegetation that grows in sheltered coastal areas periodically flooded with seawater.
Example: **Nearctic Salt Marsh**

■ **Tidal Mudflat:** Nutrient-rich areas of mud that are frequently flooded with seawater, usually in estuaries.
Example: **Nearctic Tidal Mudflat**

■ **Rocky Coastline and Sandy Beach:** Nutrient-poor sandy and rocky beaches, cliffs, and other coastline types.
Example: **Nearctic Sandy Beach and Dunes**

■ **Pelagic Waters:** Marine environments with deep water.
Example: **Nearctic Pelagic Waters**

■ **Offshore Islands:** Small islands that are well offshore and support a low growth of grass and/or shrubs.
Example: **Nearctic Seacliffs and Offshore Islands**

ANTHROPOGENIC HABITATS: The primary force in shaping these habitats is the presence of humans.

■ **Grazing Lands:** Areas that are heavily grazed by domestic animals.
■ **Cultivated Lands:** Areas cultivated by humans for the production of crops.
■ **Human Habitation:** Areas directly inhabited by humans.

SOIL GROUPS AND HABITATS

There are numerous soil classification systems, all with different names for the various soil types. The global soil reference is the World Reference Base for Soil Resources (WRB). The American system is the USDA's Soil Taxonomy, which might be better described as "Soil Typology," because although it is hierarchical, it does not have an evolutionary direction, and soils can change from one type to another. In this book, we usually use the USDA system and clarify it with more specific names such as "laterite" (a type of ferralsol) when needed. Although a direct walk-through between the two soil systems is difficult because the WRB system has 32 types and the USDA 12 types, we can do a rough comparison with biomes, USDA order, and their WRB equivalents where they exist (fig. 8).

The soils in the "order" level of the USDA classification are as follows:

— **Alfisols** are moderately leached soils that have a subsurface horizon of clay accumulation. They are fertile and mainly found in temperate forests such as NEARCTIC TEMPERATE DECIDUOUS FOREST.

- **Andisols** are formed in volcanic ash and other volcanic materials. They chemically weather very quickly in tropical humid terrains so are very fertile and generally retain water well; for these reasons, they tend to promote growth of rainforests such as MESOAMERICAN CLOUDFOREST.
- **Aridisols** are dry soils typical of both hot deserts such as the SONORAN DESERT and cold deserts such as SAGEBRUSH SHRUBLAND. They often show evidence of soil horizon development but have limited organic matter due to limited vegetation cover.
- **Entisols** are young soils with little or no horizon development. They are commonly found in areas of recent sediment deposition, colluvial slopes, and alluvial plains after massive flooding. In waterlogged areas, when mid-gray in color through leaching and anaerobic conditions, they can be called "gleysols," though this is not part of the USDA soil taxonomy. They will form into one of the other soil groups and generally do not determine vegetation type.
- **Gelisols** are the soils that develop over permafrost that is close to the surface in polar regions. Because leaching is impeded by the ice, and decomposition is so slow, they usually develop organic-rich surface horizons. Because chemical weathering of the underlying rock is so limited, they are minimally affected by the chemistry of the inorganic matter. They are typical of NEARCTIC ROCKY TUNDRA.
- **Histosols** are soils found in areas of impeded drainage and seasonal or permanent flooding. They have little soil development and are usually composed of organic materials and can form peat. They are found mainly in marshes or flooded forests such as PETÉN SWAMP FOREST.
- **Inceptisols** are a slightly more developed version of entisols, with minimal horizon development. They are widespread, can be found in a variety of environments, and don't really have a strong relationship with any vegetation type.
- **Mollisols** are soils rich in organic matter that have a thick, dark surface horizon. They are mainly associated with temperate grasslands such as TALLGRASS PRAIRIE.
- **Oxisols** are the highly weathered tropical soils found in tropical humid environments with fairly uniform rainfall. They are characterized by low fertility due to intense leaching over time but can be fertile if formed on mafic (iron and magnesium) igneous rocks such as basalt. Typical habitats are TROPICAL LOWLAND RAINFOREST.

Biome	USDA Soil Group	WORLD (WRB)
Conifer Forests	Spodosol	Podzol
Deserts and Arid Scrubs	Aridisol	Durisol Regosol
Temperate Deciduous Forests	Alfisol Spodosol (weak)	Luvisol Podzol (weak)
Tropical Humid Forests	Oxisol Andisol	Ferralsol Andosol
Dry Deciduous Forests	Oxisol Inceptisol	Ferralsol Cambisols
Savanna Habitats	Ultisol Entisol	Acrisols Leptosols
Grasslands and Steppes	Mollisol Vertisol	Chernozem Vertisol
Mediterranean Habitats	Mollisol Aridisol	Chernozem Calisol
Tundras	Gelisol	Cryosol
Freshwater Wetlands	Histosol	Histosol Gleysol
Salt-Dominated Habitats	Histosol	Solonchak

Fig. 6. Soil types

- **Spodosols** (called podzols in most parts of the world) are acidic soils under coniferous forests in cool, moist environments, such as NEARCTIC BOREAL CONIFER FOREST. The intense leaching of nutrients caused by the highly acidic waters removes organic material and most minerals from the surface, leaving it white-colored, and deposits them in a dark iron- and organic-rich horizon within 6 ft. (2 m) of the surface.
- **Ultisols**, though not widespread in North America, are the dominant soil type in older, stable landscapes such as in sub-Saharan Africa, Australia, non-Amazonian Brazil, and India. They are highly weathered, with a subsurface horizon of clay accumulation, and usually have a very high iron and aluminum-oxide concentration at the soil surface. Because they form in environments with strong seasonal rainfall (monsoonal regions) and fluctuating water tables, they promote the development of MESOAMERICAN SAVANNA.
- **Vertisols** are clayey soils that swell when wet and shrink when dry, causing deep cracks during dry periods and sometimes making it difficult for large trees to grow. In Texas they are associated with coastal TALLGRASS PRAIRIE and in Mexico with TAMAULIPAN MEZQUITAL, but they can underlie a variety of other grasslands or low scrub habitats.

It is a general understanding that soil is determined by underlying geology and hydrology, and that it greatly influences vegetation type. Changes in hydrology affect the soil type; typical examples would be the impeding of drainage over a mollisol in the grasslands and the resulting formation of a histosol, or the drying of a humid region and the underlying soil becoming more desiccated and changing from an oxisol (where the iron minerals are usually oxyhydroxides like goethite) to a type of ultisol called ferralsol or laterite (where the iron minerals are oxides such as hematite).

Vegetation can also influence soil type, such as when desertification occurs or, as is well documented in Europe, when TEMPERATE DECIDUOUS FOREST is replaced by plantations of spruce or pine, and the increase in acidity of the waters percolating from the decomposing conifer needles changes the soils from alfisols to spodosols (aka podzols).

TAXONOMY

For birds, we follow the eBird-Clements taxonomy. It is up to date and carefully maintained, and is the most popular global taxonomy for birders. For mammals, reptiles, amphibians, insects, and plants, we mainly follow Wikipedia and/or iNaturalist. This is sure to shock some scientists and purists, but in writing this book, we found these sources to be accurate and up to date for the groups that we know intimately well, giving us confidence that other groups are covered similarly. In an effort to keep the text flowing, we use only common names for most species mentioned, adding scientific names only for a few herps (reptiles and amphibians) and for plants, since this is how plants are normally discussed even by amateur naturalists.

ENDEMIC BIRD AREAS

The publication *Endemic Bird Areas of the World* (Stattersfield et al. 1998) is a favorite bird book of one of our authors and for over 20 years has always been in his various living rooms over four continents; it is just that good—a must-have for people interested in bird biogeography.

Endemic Bird Areas (EBAs), first identified in 1987 by Birdlife International, are defined as areas that contain two or more bird species with restricted ranges. A Secondary EBA is one that contains the range of a single species. Range-restricted species are defined as those with a breeding range of less than 19,300 sq. mi. (50,000 km²), as recorded historically, since 1800. If at some point after 1800, the species had a breeding range larger than this, it is not considered a range-restricted species. The size of each EBA is flexible and is dictated by the ranges of the species contained therein. While the identification of an EBA is a valuable tool in pinpointing areas of endemism, it doesn't show the whole picture, especially for the habitat-based approach used in this book. In the EBA designation, there is a natural bias toward island species, the ranges of which are intrinsically restricted, though they tend to be generalists and catholic with habitat requirements. The same holds true for continental species restricted to montane environments; however, montane species tend to be more habitat exclusive. Despite the fact that a bird species is restricted to a single continental lowland habitat, it can have a large distribution that is more extensive than the measurable threshold of a range-restricted species, and the area in which it lives may not count as an EBA, even though it is a major area of endemism. Examples of such broad habitats include NEARCTIC BOREAL CONIFER FOREST, TALLGRASS PRAIRIE, and ROCKY TUNDRA. In addition, although this book focuses primarily on bird distribution, it does incorporate other vertebrates, an approach obviously different from that of the purely bird-driven EBA concept. For this reason the EBA regions are dealt with only when of major significance to the habitats.

USEFUL HABITAT JARGON

The following definitions will help the reader to understand some of the most important terms used in naming and defining habitats. These terms appear over and over in the book.

— **Desert.** Very dry and either unvegetated or sparsely vegetated habitat.
— **Endemic.** Limited to a specific geographic area.
— **Forest.** A stand of trees over 15 ft. (5 m) tall with a closed canopy of interlocking trees or an open canopy with over 70% cover.
— **Grassland.** Habitat dominated by grasses, with few shrubs or trees.
— **Halophytic.** Refers to a plant or organism that can grow in highly saline environments.
— **Heath/Heathland.** Shrubland dominated by fine-leaved evergreen members of the erica family (Ericaceae).
— **Indicator species (IS).** A species whose presence or relative abundance is closely tied to the presence of specific habitat factors.
— **Mesic.** Refers to a wet environment with plentiful moisture.
— **Obligate.** Refers to species that are found or breed only within a specific habitat.
— **Rainforest.** Lush forest that receives abundant moisture.
— **Savanna.** A lightly wooded or treeless tropical grassland with prominent wet and dry seasons.
— **Sclerophyll.** Plant with hard, desiccation-resistant leaves; the leaves are often, but not exclusively, small.
— **Semi-evergreen forest.** Forest that has rainforest structure but in which some trees lose at least some of their leaves at some point during the year.
— **Wetland.** Habitat that is frequently or permanently flooded.
— **Woodland.** Habitat with abundant trees, forming a nearly interlocking canopy, but in which sun still reaches the ground, allowing the growth of an understory such as shrubs, grasses, or forbs.
— **Xeric.** Refers to a dry environment with little moisture.

COMMON CANOPY LEAF TYPES AND THE FORESTS WHERE YOU MAY FIND THEM

Figure 7 presents the most common leaf types used in describing different types of forest canopy and some of the habitats where they are prominent. This does not take into account the many types of leaves of understory plants such as grasses, sedges, ferns, and euphorbias.

ABOUT THIS BOOK

The bulk of this book consists of habitat accounts; these are organized by biomes. While some habitats could reasonably be classified under multiple biomes, each is described only once. The introduction to each of the biomes includes a dendrogram illustrating how the North American habitat relates to similar habitats within the global *Habitats of the World* book. For much more detailed explanations and dendrograms, readers are referred to the Habitats of the World website (www.habitatsoftheworld.org).

LEAF SHAPE		LEAF NAME	HABITATS
G Y M N O S P E R M S		Conifer Lobe Flat, lobed, evergreen	Temperate forests, mixed conifer/broadleaf forests
		Conifer Needle Thin linear leaves. Usually evergreen.	Boreal conifer forests, dry conifer forests
A N G I O S P E R M S		Deciduous Broadleaf Broad, thin leaves that grow quickly and last one season.	Temperate deciduous forests, wet/dry deciduous forests
		Evergreen Broadleaf Broad, thin, often with drip tips. They last a long time.	Rainforests, cloud forests
		Sclerophyllous Evergreen Thick, leathery leaves resist transpiration and fires.	Eucalypt forests, sclerophyll forests, heathlands, maquis, fynbos, mallee, Mulga, matorral, cerrado
		Microphyllous Small Leaves that resist transpiration.	Acacia savanna, thornscrub, Chaco seco, desert scrubs

Fig. 7. Leaf types

Each of the habitat accounts includes the following sections and elements.

In a Nutshell: A succinct explanation of what makes the habitat distinctive and worthy of separation from other habitats.

Global Habitat Affinities: Habitats from other continents that are structurally similar, providing a cross-reference to habitats that may be familiar to you, helping you to understand the unfamiliar habitat covered.

Continental Habitat Affinities: Habitats from elsewhere in North America that are structurally similar. For these cross-references to other habitats within this book, we drop the broad regional designation and name just the habitat; for example, we list BOREAL CONIFER FOREST rather than NEARCTIC BOREAL CONIFER FOREST.

Species Overlap: The habitats that have the most similar assemblages of birds (predominantly) and mammals. These are ranked from the most similar habitat to the least. The vast majority of these are habitats within the same zoogeographic region as the habitat covered. As with Continental Habitat Affinities, for habitats within North America, we do not include the regional designation in the name.

Habitat Silhouette: These silhouettes are designed to give a quick visual snapshot of a habitat, showing some of its distinctive plant shapes and its overall height and structure. They include a human silhouette for scale.

Range Map: These are visual representations of a habitat's occurrence within a given zoogeographic region. Dark shading is used for areas where the habitat is the predominant habitat, or one of the predominant habitats. In some maps, pale shading is used to indicate areas where the habitat is found only locally.

Description: This section explains what makes a habitat distinctive and how it works. Some of the information commonly included is the height and composition of the various layers of vegetation, the overall "feel" and accessibility, local temperature, and rainfall. The accompanying climate graphs are discussed in "Climate Descriptions and Graphs," on p. 13. In these descriptions, we have purposefully chosen not to always include exactly the same information, or to present it in the same order. This allows us to both stress what is most important about a given habitat and simply vary these sections to keep them interesting for readers.

Wildlife: This section may be the most interesting for a typical reader. Beyond the nuts and bolts of what makes a habitat distinctive, and what makes it work, most visitors are keen to learn about and to find its wildlife. Throughout this book, when considering wildlife, larger mammals and birds are our primary focus, but in many accounts we go well beyond this to feature a broad array of vertebrates. Species that are restricted to a certain habitat (endemics) are given special weight, as finding these will be the priority for many visitors. A species that is an indicator species for that habitat has "(IS)" beside its name.

Conservation: This section provides a quick summary of the conservation status of the habitat and major issues it is facing.

Distribution: This section and the accompanying range map indicate where the habitat occurs within a given zoogeographic region. The elevations at which it is found are sometimes mentioned, though this information may also be in the Description.

Where to See: These are places that you can visit to experience a given habitat. In general, these are the most readily or frequently visited places, in the most accessible country or countries.

Photos: Photos are included that illustrate both the habitat itself and some of its charismatic wildlife. Some photos are chosen because they effectively show both the habitat and some of its wildlife.

Sidebars: Throughout the book there are boxes or sidebars that discuss aspects of a habitat, biome, or region—in some cases these discussions are somewhat tangential, in others more in-depth. Many of these are about geology, ecology, or climate. We have chosen to place this sort of information in side boxes to make it more accessible and relevant (rather than in long, dry introductory sections that are likely to be ignored by most readers).

AMERICAN BIRD CONSERVANCY

American Bird Conservancy (ABC) is dedicated to conserving wild birds and their habitats throughout the Americas. This mission has guided the organization throughout its 30-year history. With an emphasis on achieving results and working in partnership, ABC takes on the greatest problems facing birds today, innovating and building on rapid advancements in science to halt extinctions, conserve and protect habitats, eliminate threats, and build capacity for bird conservation. www.abcbirds.org.

NATURESERVE

For 50 years, NatureServe has been the authoritative source for biodiversity data and the central coordinating organization for a Network of over 60 member programs throughout North America. Together, NatureServe and its Network are dedicated to developing, collecting, and analyzing biodiversity information to support informed decisions about managing, protecting, restoring, and conserving natural resources. NatureServe and the Network develop and manage data for over 100,000 species and ecosystems, answering fundamental questions about what exists, where it is found, and how it is doing. NatureServe's mission is to leverage the power of science, data, and technology to guide biodiversity conservation and stewardship.

ACKNOWLEDGMENTS

The authors would like to sincerely thank Dan Chaon, Ethan Gyllenhaal, Jen Brumfield, Jessie Williamson, Erik Enbody, Keith Barnes, and Owen Hilchey for general advice and guidance throughout the project. Kurt Ongman, Alex Harper, Jessie Reese, Ken Behrens, Andy Jones, Michael Retter, Regan Smyth, Mike Parr, Christopher Tracey, David Wiedenfield, and Tom Johnson all provided valuable information about specific habitats and regions. The authors would also like to express their appreciation to Dave Spangenburg, Jared Mizanin, Alex Wang, and Graham Talaber for help with photos.

ABBREVIATIONS

Directions (north, south, east, west, central) are abbreviated only when they directly precede a geographical place name.

aka	also known as	kg	kilogram	s.	south/southern
c.	central	km	kilometer	sc.	south-central
cm	centimeter	km²	square kilometer	se.	southeastern
e.	east/eastern	lb.	pound	sp.	species (singular)
EBA	Endemic Bird Area	m	meter	spp.	species (plural)
ec.	east-central	MYA	million years ago	sq. mi.	square mile
ft.	foot/feet	mi.	mile	sw.	southwestern
ha	hectare	mm	millimeter	w.	west/western
HoTW	Habitats of the World book series	n.	north/northern	wc.	west-central
		nc.	north-central	YBP	years before present
in.	inch/inches	ne.	northeastern		
IS	indicator species	nw.	northwestern		

BIBLIOGRAPHY

"Acadian-Appalachian Montane Spruce-Fir Forest." 2007. NatureServe Explorer. https://explorer.natureserve. org/Taxon/ELEMENT_GLOBAL.2.723038.

Anderson, R. C., J. S. Fralish, and J. M. Baskin. 1999. *Savannas, Barrens, and Rock Outcrop Plant Communities of North America*. Cambridge: Cambridge University Press.

Atlantic Coastal Plain Blackwater/Brownwater Stream Floodplain Forest. n.d. The Nature Conservancy. https://www.conservationgateway.org/ConservationByGeography/NorthAmerica/UnitedStates/edc/ Documents/HabitatGuides/15.pdf.

Ayala Téllez, H. L., L. I. Iñiguez-Dávalos, M. Olvera-Vargas, and J. A. Vargas Contreras. 2018. "Bats Associated to Caves in Jalisco, Mexico." *Therya* 9 (1): 29–40.

Banko, P. C., J. M. Black, and W. E. Banko. 2020. "Hawaiian Goose (*Branta sandvicensis*), v. 1.0." In A. F. Poole and F. B. Gill (eds.), *Birds of the World*. Ithaca, NY: Cornell Lab of Ornithology. https://birdsoftheworld. org/bow/species/hawgoo/cur/habitat.

Barker, J. R. 1983. "Habitat Differences between Basin and Wyoming Big Sagebrush in Contiguous Populations." *Journal of Range Management* 36: 450–54.

Bergan, J. "Western Gulf Coastal Grasslands." In T. Ricketts, E. Dinerstein, and D. Olson (eds.), *Terrestrial Ecoregions of North America: A Conservation Assessment*, 307–10. Washington, DC.: Island Press.

The Biology of Caves. n.d. National Park Service, Ozark National Scenic Riverways, Missouri. https://www.nps.gov/ozar/learn/education/cave-biology.htm.

Bocetti, C. I., D. M. Donner, and H. F. Mayfield. 2020. "Kirtland's Warbler (*Setophaga kirtlandii*)." In A. F. Poole and F. B. Gill (eds.), *Birds of the World*. Ithaca, NY: Cornell Lab of Ornithology.

Briggs, M. K., E. A. Lozano-Cavazos, H. Mills Poulos, and J. Ochoa-Espinoza. 2019. "The Chihuahuan Desert: A Binational Conservation Response to Protect a Global Treasure." In M. I. Goldstein and D. A. DellaSala (eds.), *Encyclopedia of the World's Biomes*, 126–38. Amsterdam: Elsevier.

Brown, D. E., and E. Markings. 2014. "A Guide to North American Grasslands." *Desert Plants* 29 (2): 1–160.

California Natural Diversity Database (CNDDB). 2023. *State and Federally Listed Endangered and Threatened Animals of California*. Sacramento: California Department of Fish and Wildlife.

"Caribbean Rockland Hammock." 2013. NatureServe Explorer. https://explorer.natureserve.org/Taxon/ ELEMENT_GLOBAL.2.889966.

Cave or Cavern? Background for Teachers. n.d. Texas Parks and Wildlife. https://tpwd.texas.gov/education/ resources/keep-texas-wild/cave-creatures/background-for-teachers-cave-or-cavern.

"Central Atlantic Coastal Plain Wet Longleaf Pine Savanna and Flatwoods." 2014. NatureServe Explorer. https://explorer.natureserve.org/Taxon/ELEMENT_GLOBAL.2.723221.

"Chihuahuan Desert Scrub." 2015. NatureServe Explorer. https://explorer.natureserve.org/Taxon/ELEMENT_ GLOBAL.2.860504.

Clements, J. F., P. C. Rasmussen, T. S. Schulenberg, M. J. Iliff, T. A. Fredericks, J. A. Gerbracht, D. Lepage et al. 2023. *The eBird/Clements Checklist of Birds of the World*, v2023b. https://www.birds.cornell.edu/ clementschecklist/download/.

Comer, P. J., D. Faber-Langendoen, R. Evans, S. C. Gawler, C. Josse, G. Kittel, S. Menard et al. 2003. *Ecological Systems of the United States: A Working Classification of U.S. Terrestrial Systems*. NatureServe, Arlington, Virginia. https://www.natureserve.org/publications/ecological-systems-united-states.

Cushing, C. E., and J. D. Allan. 2001. *Streams: Their Ecology and Life*. San Diego and London: Academic Press.

Dennis, J. V. 1958. "Some Aspects of the Breeding Ecology of the Yellow-breasted Chat (*Icteria virens*)." *Bird-Banding* 29: 169–83.

Dick-Peddie, W. A. 1993. *New Mexico Vegetation: Past, Present, and Future*. Albuquerque: University of New Mexico Press.

"East Gulf Coastal Plain Interior Shortleaf Pine-Oak Forest." 2015. NatureServe Explorer. https://explorer. natureserve.org/Taxon/ELEMENT_GLOBAL.2.723082.

"Ecosystems: Hardwood Hammock." 2015. National Park Service, Everglades National Park, Florida. https://www.nps.gov/ever/learn/nature/hardwoodhammock.htm.

"Effects of Experimental Removal of Barred Owls on Population Demography of Northern Spotted Owls in the Pacific Northwest." 2018. US Geological Survey, Forest and Rangeland Ecosystem Science Center. https://www.usgs.gov/centers/forest-and-rangeland-ecosystem-science-center/science/effects-experimental-removal-barred.

"Emerald Ash Borer." 2024. US Department of Agriculture, APHIS. https://www.aphis.usda.gov/plant-pests-diseases/eab.

Endangered and Threatened Species of the Sonoran Desert Region. 2000. Arizona-Sonora Desert Museum. https://www.desertmuseum.org/center/edu/docs/4-6_Endangered_handout.pdf.

Epstein, E. E. 2017. "Natural Communities, Aquatic Features, and Selected Habitats of Wisconsin." In *The Ecological Landscapes of Wisconsin: An Assessment of Ecological Resources and a Guide to Planning Sustainable Management*, ch. 7. PUB-SS-1131H. Madison: Wisconsin Department of Natural Resources.

"Florida Dry Prairie." 2014. NatureServe Explorer. https://explorer.natureserve.org/Taxon/ELEMENT_GLOBAL. 2.723136.

Forest Types of Michigan: Jack Pine. 2014. Michigan State University, MSU Forestry Extension Team. https://www.canr.msu.edu/uploads/resources/pdfs/forest_types_of_michigan-jack_pine_(e3202-11).pdf.

Forman, Richard. 1998. *Pine Barrens: Ecosystem and Landscape.* New Brunswick, NJ: Rutgers University Press.

Frelich, Lee E. 2020. "Boreal and Taiga Biome." In M. I. Goldstein and D. A. DellaSala (eds.), *Encyclopedia of the World's Biomes*, 103–15. Amsterdam: Elsevier.

Giller, P. S., and B. Malmqvist. 1998. *The Biology of Streams and Rivers.* Oxford: Oxford University Press.

Gillespie, T., A. Grijalva, and C. Farris. 2000. "Diversity, Composition, and Structure of Tropical Dry Forests in Central America." *Plant Ecology* 147: 37–47.

Gómez-Pompa, A. 1987. "On Maya Silviculture." *Mexican Studies/Estudios Mexicanos* 3 (1): 1–17.

Hargrove, L., and J. T. Rotenberry. 2011. "Breeding Success at the Range Margin of a Desert Species: Implications for a Climate-Induced Elevational Shift." *Oikos* 120 (10): 1568–76.

"Hawaiian High Islands Ecoregion." 2007. Nature Conservancy, Hawai'i. http://www.hawaiiecoregionplan.info/MHT.html.

"Hawaiian Montane-Subalpine Dry Shrubland and Grassland." 2016. NatureServe Explorer. https://explorer. natureserve.org/Taxon/ELEMENT_GLOBAL.2.860804.

"Hawai'i Lowland Dry Grassland." 2015. NatureServe Explorer. https://explorer.natureserve.org/Taxon/ELEMENT_GLOBAL.2.821129.

"Hawai'i Montane Cloud Forest." 2009. NatureServe Explorer. https://explorer.natureserve.org/Taxon/ELEMENT_GLOBAL.2.770635.

Hottman, R. M., and M. J. Mossman. 1993. "Birds of Wisconsin's Northern Swamps and Bogs." *Passenger Pigeon* 55 (2): 113–37.

Iknayan, K. J., and S. R. Beissinger. 2018. "Collapse of a Desert Bird Community over the Past Century Driven by Climate Change." *Proceedings of the National Academy of Sciences USA* 115 (34).

"Intermountain Basins Cliff, Scree and Badland Sparse Vegetation." 2014. NatureServe Explorer. https://explorer.natureserve.org/Taxon/ELEMENT_GLOBAL.2.860416.

"Inter-Mountain Basins Subalpine Limber–Bristlecone Pine Woodland." 2014. NatureServe Explorer. https://explorer.natureserve.org/Taxon/ELEMENT_GLOBAL.2.722882.

Jahrsdoerfer, S. E., and D. M. Leslie. 1988. *Tamaulipan Brushland of the Lower Rio Grande Valley of South Texas: Description, Human Impacts, and Management Options.* Biological Report 88 (36). Washington, DC: US Department of the Interior, US Fish and Wildlife Service.

Johnson, K. 2021. "The Impact of Emerald Ash Borer." *Good Growing* (blog), University of Illinois, College of Agriculture, Consumer, and Environmental Sciences. https://extension.illinois.edu/blogs/good-growing/2021-05-04-impact-emerald-ash-borer.

Kaufmann, M. R., D. W. Huisjen, S. Kitchen, M. Babler, S. R. Abella, T. S. Gardiner, D. McAvoy, J. Howie, and D. H. Page Jr. 2016. *Gambel Oak Ecology and Management in the Southern Rockies: The Status of Our Knowledge.* SRFSN Publication 2016-1. Fort Collins: Colorado State University, Southern Rockies Fire Sciences Network.

Keddy, Paul A. 2010. *Wetland Ecology: Principles and Conservation.* 2nd ed. Cambridge: Cambridge University Press.

Last Stand: The Vanishing Hawaiian Forest. 2003. Honolulu: Nature Conservancy of Hawai'i. https://www.nature.org/media/hawaii/the-last-stand-hawaiian-forest.pdf.

Leopold, A. S., and R. A. McCabe. 1957. "Natural History of the Montezuma Quail in Mexico." *Condor* 59: 3–26.

Lindström, Å., M. Green, G. Paulson, H. G. Smith, and V. Devictor. 2013. "Rapid Changes in Bird Community Composition at Multiple Temporal and Spatial Scales in Response to Recent Climate Change." *Ecography* 36 (3): 313–22.

"Lodgepole Pine." 2024. Colorado State Forest Service, Colorado State University. https://csfs.colostate.edu/colorado-forests/forest-types/lodgepole-pine/.

Logan, J. A., and J. A. Powell. 2001. "Ghost Forests, Global Warming, and the Mountain Pine Beetle." *American Entomologist* 47: 160–73.

McCann, J. M. 1999. "Before 1492: The Making of the Pre-Columbian Landscape. Part II: The Vegetation, and Implications for Restoration for 2000 and Beyond." *Ecological Restoration, North America* 17 (3): 107–19.

McGlashen, A. 2019. "The Kirtland's Warbler Has Recovered, but the Hard Work of Saving It Will Never Stop." *Audubon*, July.

"Mexican Burrowing Toad." n.d. Edge of Existence. https://web.archive.org/web/20090803172408/http://www.edgeofexistence.org/amphibians/species_info.php?id=1355.

Milman, O. 2017. "US Glacier National Park Is Losing Its Glaciers, with Just 26 of 150 Left." *Guardian*, May 11. https://www.theguardian.com/environment/2017/may/11/us-glacier-national-park-is-losing-its-glaciers-with-just-26-of-150-left.

"Mojave Mid-Elevation Mixed Desert Scrub." 2016. NatureServe Explorer. https://explorer.natureserve.org/Taxon/ELEMENT_GLOBAL.2.722930.

Moore, M., and S. Rider. 2022. "Paddlefish: *Polyodon spathula*." *IUCN Red List of Threatened Species*: e.T17938A81763841. https://dx.doi.org/10.2305/IUCN.UK.2022-1.RLTS.T17938A81763841.en.

Muldavin, E., and F. J. Triepke. 2020. "North American Pinyon–Juniper Woodlands: Ecological Composition, Dynamics, and Future Trends." In M. I. Goldstein and D. A. DellaSala (eds.), *Encyclopedia of the World's Biomes*, 516–31. Amsterdam: Elsevier.

Nelson, J. T., M. K. Reeves, F. Amidon, and S. Miller. 2019. "Hawai'i Wet Grassland and Shrubland." In M. I. Goldstein and D. A. DellaSala (eds.), *Encyclopedia of the World's Biomes*, 900–922. Amsterdam: Elsevier.

Nogueira-Filho, S.L.G., S.S.C. Nogueira, and J.M.V. Fragoso. 2009. "Ecological Impacts of Feral Pigs in the Hawaiian Islands." *Biodiversity Conservation* 18: 3677–83.

"North American Desert Shrubland." 2024. Wrangle, University of Arizona, College of Agriculture and Life Sciences. https://wrangle.org/ecotype/north-american-desert-shrubland.

"North American Ponderosa Pine Woodlands." 2024. Wrangle, University of Arizona, College of Agriculture and Life Sciences. https://wrangle.org/ecotype/north-american-ponderosa-pine-woodlands.

"North American Warm Desert Riparian Mesquite Bosque." 2014. NatureServe Explorer. https://explorer.natureserve.org/Taxon/ELEMENT_GLOBAL.2.722920.

"North American Warm Semi-Desert Cliff, Scree and Rock Vegetation." 2014. NatureServe Explorer. https://explorer.natureserve.org/Taxon/ELEMENT_GLOBAL.2.860641.

"North American Warm Semi-Desert Dune and Sand Flats." 2015. NatureServe Explorer. https://explorer.natureserve.org/Taxon/ELEMENT_GLOBAL.2.879239.

"Northeastern Great Plains Aspen Woodland." 2016. NatureServe Explorer. https://explorer.natureserve.org/Taxon/ELEMENT_GLOBAL.2.849192.

"Northern Dry Jack Pine–Red Pine–Hardwood Woodland." 2012. NatureServe Explorer. https://explorer.natureserve.org/Taxon/ELEMENT_GLOBAL.2.878439.

Nussear, K. E., and T. C. Esque. 2020. "Desert Biogeography: Mojave." In M. I. Goldstein and D. A. DellaSala (eds.), *Encyclopedia of the World's Biomes*, 99–109. Amsterdam: Elsevier.

"Otter Mound Preserve." Collier County (FL) Public Services. https://www.colliercountyfl.gov/government/public-services/divisions/conservation-collier/preserve-information/otter-mound-preserve.

"Pacific Mesoamerican Seasonal Dry Forest." 2015. NatureServe Explorer. https://explorer.natureserve.org/Taxon/ELEMENT_GLOBAL.2.884630.

Parker, V. T. 2020. "Chaparral of California." In M. I. Goldstein and D. A. DellaSala (eds.), *Encyclopedia of the World's Biomes*, 457–72. Amsterdam: Elsevier.

Persons, T. B., and E. M. Nowak. 2007. *Inventory of Amphibians and Reptiles at Mojave National Preserve: Final Report*. MOJA-00129. Reston, VA: US Geological Survey.

Pojar, R. A. 1995. *Breeding Bird Communities in Aspen Forests of the Sub-boreal Spruce (dk Subzone) in the Prince Rupert Forest Region*. Victoria: Province of British Columbia, Ministry of Forests.

Polidoro, B. A., K. E. Carpenter, L. Collins, N. C. Duke, A. M. Ellison, J. C. Ellison, E. J. Farnsworth et al. 2010. "The Loss of Species: Mangrove Extinction Risk and Geographic Areas of Global Concern." *PLoS One* 5: e10095.

Portillo-Quintero, C. A., and G. A. Sánchez-Azofeifa. 2010. "Extent and Conservation of Tropical Dry Forests in the Americas." *Biological Conservation* 143 (1): 144–55.

Pranty, B., and J. W. Tucker Jr. 2006. "Ecology and Management of the Florida Grasshopper Sparrow." In R. F. Noss (ed.), *Land of Fire and Water: The Florida Dry Prairie Ecosystem*, 188–200. DeLeon Springs, FL: Painter.

Rentch, J. S., and T. M. Schuler. 2009. *Conference on the Ecology and Management of High-Elevation Forests in the Central and Southern Appalachian Mountains: Proceedings of a Conference Held at Snowshoe Mountain Resort, Slatyfork, WV, May 14–15, 2009*. Newtown Square, PA: US Forest Service. https://www.nrs.fs.usda.gov/pubs/gtr/gtr_nrs-p-64.pdf.

"Rocky Mountain Montane-Subalpine Limber Pine Woodland." 2021. NatureServe Explorer. https://explorer.natureserve.org/Taxon/ELEMENT_GLOBAL.2.1225592.

Rosenstock, S. S. "Influence of Gambel Oak on Breeding Birds in Ponderosa Pine Forests of Northern Arizona." *Condor* 100: 485–92.

Rzedowski, J. 2005. *Vegetación de México*. 1st digital ed. Tlalpan, Mexico: Comisión Nacional para el Conocimiento y Uso de la Biodiversidad. https://www.academia.edu/9142430/VEGETACION_DE_MEXICO_Jerzy_Rzedowski.

Sioli, H. 1975. "Tropical Rivers as Expressions of Their Terrestrial Environments." In F. B. Golley and E. Medina (eds.), *Tropical Ecological Systems: Trends in Terrestrial and Aquatic Research*. Heidelberg and New York: Springer-Verlag.

"South Valley Park, Jefferson County: Rocky Mountain Gambel Oak Mixed Mountain Shrublands." Colorado Native Plant Society. https://conps.org/project/foothills-gambel-oak-shrublands/.

Stattersfield, A. J., M. J. Crosby, A. J. Long, and D.C. Wege. 1998. *Endemic Bird Areas of the World*. BirdLife International; First Edition.

Stone, C. P., and L. W. Pratt. 1994. *Hawai'i's Plants and Animals*. Honolulu: University of Hawai'i Press.

"Tamaulipan Dry Mesquite and Thornscrub." 2015. NatureServe Explorer. https://explorer.natureserve.org/Taxon/ELEMENT_GLOBAL.2.837258.

"Tamaulipan Mixed Deciduous Thornscrub." 2014. NatureServe Explorer. https://explorer.natureserve.org/Taxon/ELEMENT_GLOBAL.2.722722.

"Texas-Louisiana Coastal Prairie." 2014. NatureServe Explorer. https://explorer.natureserve.org/Taxon/ELEMENT_GLOBAL.2.723052.

Toledo V. M., B. Ortiz-Espejel, L. Cortés, P. Moguel, and M. J. Ordoñez. 2003. "The Multiple Use of Tropical Forests by Indigenous Peoples in Mexico: A Case of Adaptive Management." *Conservation Ecology* 7 (3): 9.

"Viscaino-Baja California Desert Scrub." 2014. NatureServe Explorer. https://explorer.natureserve.org/Taxon/ELEMENT_GLOBAL.2.860516.

Wakabayashi, J., and T. L. Sawyer. 2001. "Stream Incision, Tectonics, Uplift, and Evolution of Topography of the Sierra Nevada, California." *Journal of Geology* 109 (5): 539.

Ward, R., D. Friess, R. Day, and R. MacKenzie. 2016. "Impacts of Climate Change on Mangrove Ecosystems: A Region by Region Overview." *Ecosystem Health and Sustainability* 2 (4): 1–25.

Waters, H. 2019. "Grazing Like It's 1799: How Ranchers Can Bring Back Grassland Birds." *Audubon*, Summer.

Webb, R. H., and R. M. Turner. 2020. "Biodiversity of Perennial Vegetation in the Desert Regions of Baja California and Baja California Sur, Mexico." In M. I. Goldstein and D. A. DellaSala (eds.), *Encyclopedia of the World's Biomes*, 139–51. Amsterdam: Elsevier.

"Where Are Glaciers Found in Continental North America?" 2024. US Geological Survey. https://www.usgs.gov/faqs/where-are-glaciers-found-continental-north-america.

"White-Nose Syndrome Killed over 90% of Three North American Bat Species." US Geological Survey. https://www.usgs.gov/news/national-news-release/white-nose-syndrome-killed-over-90-three-north-american-bat-species.

White-Nose Syndrome Response Team. 2024. https://www.whitenosesyndrome.org/.

Wilkens, H., D. C. Culver, and W. Humphreys. 2000. *Subterranean Ecosystems*. Ecosystems of the World 30. Amsterdam: Elsevier Science.

Youngberg, E., and A. Panjabi. 2016. *Bird Conservancy of the Rockies: Best Management Practices for Grassland Birds*. Brighton, CO: Bird Conservancy of the Rockies. https://www.birdconservancy.org/wp-content/uploads/2017/03/Bird-Conservancy-BMP-for-Grassland-Birds-CSLB.pdf.

North American Conifer Forests Dendrogram

Global Conifer Forest Associations

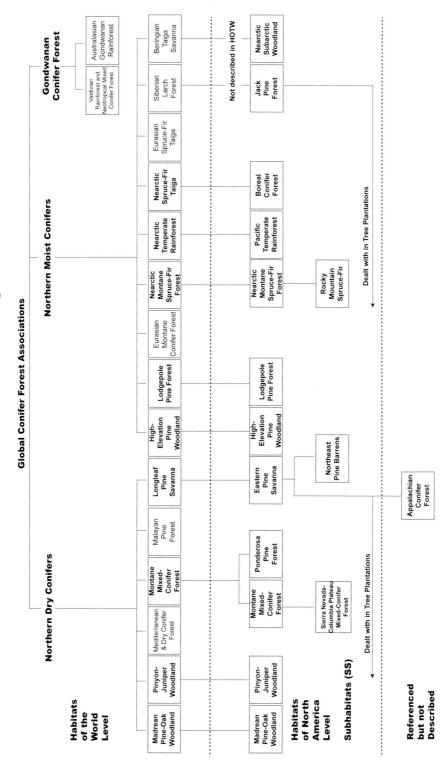

CONIFER FORESTS

Ne1A NEARCTIC SUBARCTIC WOODLAND

IN A NUTSHELL: This habitat is a hybrid of ROCKY or SHRUB TUNDRA and BOREAL CONIFER FOREST with low spongy ground and a few small conifers.
Global Habitat Affinities: EURASIAN TUNDRA TAIGA.
Continental Habitat Affinities: None. **Species Overlap:** BOREAL CONIFER FOREST; ROCKY TUNDRA.

DESCRIPTION: In this habitat south of the tundra, average midsummer temperatures rise above the 50°F (10°C) limit for tundra, though the climate is still harsh (Köppen **Ef**), with average temperature of 23°F (−5°C), very short summers with temperatures between 46°F and 54°F (8–12°C), and very cold winters, from −12°F to −7°F (−24.5 to −21.5°C). With annual precipitation ranging from 8 in. (200 mm) to 16 in. (400 mm), some of these areas could be classified as arid terrain, but because evapotranspiration is so low, the landscape remains humid through much of the year.

In the southern zone of the SHRUB TUNDRA, and where the birch and aspen groves of the SUBARCTIC RIPARIAN WOODLAND become widespread, the tundra starts to become dotted with stunted spruces, pines, and larches. This is the Subarctic Woodland, a habitat in the zone (ecotone) between the more typical tundra and the forest proper. In some areas, such as east of Nome, Alaska, on the Seward Peninsula, the transition from ROCKY TUNDRA to BOREAL CONIFER FOREST is rapid, but in other areas, such as around Hudson Bay, the transition is nebulous, and this woodland is widespread. Subarctic Woodland has a mosaic of individual trees between boggy mires; Black Spruce (*Picea mariana*), often associated with Red-stemmed Feather Moss (*Pleurozium schreberi*), grows in the wetter areas, White Spruce (*Picea glauca*) in better-drained areas. These trees also occur in groves along with other conifers such as Balsam Fir (*Abies balsamea*) and the deciduous Tamarack Larch (*Larix laricina*), along with small patches of SUBARCTIC RIPARIAN WOODLAND dominated by Dwarf Birch (*Betula nana*), Quaking Aspen (*Populus tremuloides*), and Balsam Poplar (*Populus balsamifera*). Permafrost is usually present in these woodlands, but the habitat can form in regions without permafrost.

Covered in glaciers throughout the ice ages, this region was only recently exposed and is still rising from isostatic rebound (the earth buckling because of a release of pressure from the

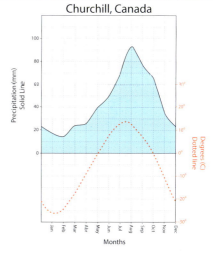

Churchill, Canada

thick sheets of ice). The landscape is dotted with lakes, eskers, tills, and terminal moraines—evidence of the glacial scouring—combined with permafrost features such as pingos (mounds of earth formed through expanding ice over frozen permafrost). The drainage in these areas is often impeded and rarely dendritic (the normal branching drainage pattern typical of temperate regions). This creates the conditions for many bogs, where large hummocks of sphagnum mosses grow with marsh grasses in the channels between them.

Bonaparte's Gull is the only tree-nesting gull species.
© GLENN BARTLEY PHOTOGRAPHY

WILDLIFE: Subarctic Woodland is critical habitat for nesting shorebirds. The majority of the New World shorebirds that winter to the south (in areas as remote from the subarctic as Argentina and Chile), as well as some Old World shorebirds from Asia and Australia, come to this habitat to

Hudsonian Godwit migrates from Chile and Argentina to nest in the Nearctic Subarctic Woodland.
© BEN KNOOT, TROPICAL BIRDING TOURS

Subarctic Woodland exists as a savanna-like transition zone between Boreal Conifer Forest and various tundra habitats. © IAIN CAMPBELL, TROPICAL BIRDING TOURS

nest, arriving in late May as the snow first begins to melt, uncovering the marshy areas beneath it. Typical breeding shorebirds here include the Hudsonian Godwit, Whimbrel, Greater Yellowlegs, Solitary Sandpiper, and Lesser Yellowlegs. Larids (members of the family Laridae) include Sabine's, Bonaparte's, and Little Gulls. Species shared with the BOREAL CONIFER FOREST to the south include ground birds such as Willow Ptarmigan and passerines such as Olive-sided Flycatcher, Canada Jay, Boreal Chickadee, and Wilson's Warbler.

The few mammals include some very intriguing ones, like Wolverine, Moose, and Caribou. In the Hudson Bay area, Polar Bears den and give birth in this habitat. In Alaska, Brown Bear is the dominant bear species.

CONSERVATION: There are few protection efforts directed specifically at Nearctic Subarctic Woodland. With increasing world temperatures, this habitat is migrating north into tundra habitats and, in its core range, is being replaced by thicker woodlands of the same tree species to its south, turning this very open woodland into BOREAL CONIFER FOREST.

DISTRIBUTION: This forest is very widespread from Seward Peninsula in westernmost continental Alaska to Labrador in e. Canada. In the west, it generally forms a narrow band on the southern edge of ROCKY TUNDRA or as a mosaic with SHRUB TUNDRA. In Canada it becomes a broad swath hundreds of miles wide that surrounds much of Hudson Bay. It is likely that this habitat will become more widespread with global warming, as conifers colonize areas that were dominated by Rocky and Shrub Tundras.

WHERE TO SEE: Council Road, south of Nome, Alaska, US; Katmai National Park, Alaska, US; Churchill, Manitoba, Canada; Yellowknife, NW Territories, Canada.

Ne1B BOREAL CONIFER FOREST

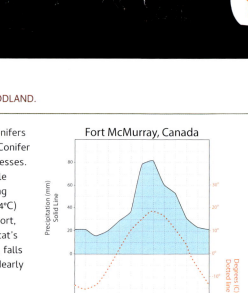

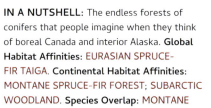

IN A NUTSHELL: The endless forests of conifers that people imagine when they think of boreal Canada and interior Alaska. **Global Habitat Affinities:** EURASIAN SPRUCE-FIR TAIGA. **Continental Habitat Affinities:** MONTANE SPRUCE-FIR FOREST; SUBARCTIC WOODLAND. **Species Overlap:** MONTANE SPRUCE-FIR FOREST; TEMPERATE MIXED FOREST; ASPEN FOREST AND PARKLAND; SUBARCTIC WOODLAND.

DESCRIPTION: A massive belt of unending conifers stretching from Quebec to Alaska, the Boreal Conifer Forest is one of the planet's last great wildernesses. The winters here are incredibly harsh, with little daylight and temperatures rarely above freezing (32°F/0°C) and plummeting as low as −65°F (−54°C) at nighttime. The summers, by contrast, are short, moist, and extremely buggy. Most of this habitat's precipitation, 15–20 in. (400–500 mm) annually, falls between the months of May and September. Nearly all plant growth also happens during this time period.

When you visit this kind of forest, it feels very monotonous, certainly much more so than grassland or desert. The forest seems endless, with heavy canopy cover between 60 and 160 ft. (20–50 m) tall, though usually lower than 90 ft. (30 m), and little undergrowth. Areas of forest are typically even-aged, adding to the uniformity of the landscape. The tree diversity is low, as is typical at high latitudes. The dominant tree species are narrow, conical spruces as well as a smattering of firs and pines. Black Spruce (*Picea mariana*) tends to predominate in wet, boggy areas, while White Spruce (*Picea glauca*), Jack Pine (*Pinus banksiana*), and Balsam Fir (*Abies balsamea*) prefer more well-drained soils. There are areas of scattered deciduous trees as well, though these are generally treated as separate habitats in this

Fort McMurray, Canada

Precipitation (mm) Solid Line

Degrees (C) Dotted line

Months

book. Paper Birch (*Betula papyrifera*), Resin Birch (*Betula neoalaskana*), Mountain Maple (*Acer spicatum*), and Quaking Aspen (*Populus tremuloides*) are the most notable deciduous species.

The forest floor is covered in a litter of conifer needles, decaying trunks, and lichens. You can easily walk through the drier parts of this forest without a trail, as the understory is generally sparse. Deadfall can be heavy, but there are few shrubs to impede walking. The shrubs that are found here are often similar to those found in the EURASIAN SPRUCE-FIR TAIGA and include Canada Buffaloberry (*Shepherdia canadensis*), Prickly Wild Rose (*Rosa acicularis*), Bearberry (*Arctostaphylos uva-ursi*), Lingonberry (*Vaccinium vitis-idaea*), and Mooseberry (*Viburnum edule*). Boggy areas are dominated by many sphagnum and feather mosses and shrubs like blueberry and cranberry (*Vaccinium* spp.). Even though precipitation is not high, the low temperatures mean that precipitation exceeds evaporation, producing an abundance of water. Glacial deposits block drainage, generating many potholes and depressions, and this, in combination with the positive water balance, means the whole region is dotted by OPEN WATER, BOREAL BOG AND FEN, and SEDGE AND GRASSLAND MARSHES.

The **Ne1B-1 Northern Spruce-Fir** subhabitat is a southern form of the Boreal Conifer Forest found at higher elevations in the n. Appalachian Mountains. This forest is dominated by Balsam Fir, with lesser numbers of Red Spruce (*Picea rubens*), Mountain White Birch (*Betula cordifolia*), and mountain-ash (*Sorbus* spp.) present. The steep slopes characteristic of this subhabitat result in more well-drained soils and fewer mosses and other bryophytes or bog-associated plants. Additionally, high winds and heavy winter ice accumulation cause widespread tree-fall and other disturbance. As a result, this subhabitat is much denser, with many small or stunted trees and impassable piles of debris.

Farther south, the **Ne1B-2 Appalachian Conifer Forest** subhabitat largely resembles the Boreal Conifer Forest in structure and wildlife. The tree composition varies somewhat, with the endemic Fraser Fir (*Abies fraseri*) and Red Spruce dominating. Black Spruce and Balsam Fir are absent.

WILDLIFE: The Boreal Conifer Forest is home to a tough and well-adapted set of resident mammals. Although the mammals are generally sparse in this wild country, there are some exciting possibilities. Iconic predators like Wolverine, Fisher, American Marten, Canada Lynx, Gray Wolf, Brown Bear (aka Grizzly Bear), and American Black Bear are all found here. Moose and Caribou both make the boreal forest their home, and Snowshoe Hare and American Red Squirrel are common throughout.

The mammals found here have many special adaptations for dealing with this harsh and variable climate. Canada Lynx, Wolverine, and Snowshoe Hare have enormous feet that help them walk more easily on top of the snow. Snowshoe Hares also develop a stark white winter pelage that serves to camouflage them during the snowy winters. The winters come with a scarcity of food. American Black Bear and Brown Bear will hibernate to avoid this scarcity, while Gray Wolves, Wolverines, American

Boreal Conifer Forest is one of the largest and most intact habitat types on the planet.
© BEN KNOOT, TROPICAL BIRDING TOURS

Left: **Gray Wolf is a keystone predator throughout the Boreal Conifer Forest. The loss of wolves has major, cascading ecological effects.** © JARI PELTOMAKI, FINNATURE

Below: **Black-backed Woodpecker is most common in burned areas, where it is well camouflaged against the scorched trunks.** © BEN KNOOT, TROPICAL BIRDING TOURS

Red Squirrels, and others will cache food to retrieve later. These food caches often end up buried in snow, and a deep tunnel surrounded by gore is a good sign a Gray Wolf has recently retrieved prey.

The birdlife here consists of a small set of year-round residents and a large number of breeding birds that visit for a short time during summer. Residents include Spruce Grouse (IS), Great Gray Owl, Northern Hawk Owl, Boreal Owl, Golden Eagle, Black-backed Woodpecker, Common Raven, Canada Jay (IS), Boreal Chickadee (IS), Pine Grosbeak, and White-winged Crossbill. In the summer, the forest is alive with insects that fuel a new generation of Neotropical migrants. Olive-sided Flycatcher, Yellow-bellied Flycatcher (IS), Gray-cheeked Thrush (IS), Swainson's Thrush, Cape May Warbler, Connecticut Warbler, Blackpoll Warbler (IS), and Canada Warbler all add to the astonishing spectacle that is the boreal summer.

The Northern Spruce-Fir Forest subhabitat has most of the same species but is also home to Bicknell's Thrush (IS), which is an endemic breeding bird in this habitat.

Few reptiles and amphibians are found in the Boreal Conifer Forest and Northern Spruce-Fir subhabitats, though Mink Frog and Wood Frog both make their homes in the many wetlands that dot this habitat. Wood Frogs occur farther north than any other amphibian, and their tissue can survive freezing solid for months at a time.

Due to limited area and heavy isolation, Appalachian Conifer Forest lacks the large boreal mammals and resident birds (Canada Jay, Boreal Chickadee, etc.) found in the extensive forests farther north. Many more migratory boreal birds, such as Red Crossbill, Mourning Warbler, and Olive-sided Flycatcher, can be found here in the summer months. The unobtrusive Pygmy Salamander (IS) is a near-endemic to this habitat.

The Spruce Grouse, sometimes known as the Fool Hen for its remarkably tame demeanor, is one of the most arboreal grouse species. © PHIL CHAON

CONSERVATION: The Boreal Conifer Forest still covers vast areas of the far north and, due to the lack of human habitation, is largely intact. Major threats include logging, exploitation for tar sands or other mineral deposits, and flooding for hydropower developments. Probably the largest landscape-level threat not attributable to resource exploitation is climate change. Drying caused by higher temperatures increases the likelihood of wildfire, and the habitat is slow to recover. Fires are increasing in frequency and severity at a visible rate. The summer of 2023 saw more than 30 million acres (12 million ha) burn in Canada alone. Heat and drought stress and kill large swaths of boreal forest along the prairie-forest border, allowing grassland or more southerly forest types to encroach and replace this northern forest type. Milder winters fail to control populations of Spruce Coneworm, Mountain Pine Beetle, and Spruce Bark Beetle, resulting in widespread tree death and increased fire risk. Increasingly, the recognition of Boreal Conifer Forests as the world's largest terrestrial source of carbon storage has led to new conservation measures. In 2010 the Canadian government protected two areas of Boreal Conifer Forest totaling 5000 sq. mi. (13,000 km²) and set a goal to protect at least 20% of the country's forested land. Across Canada, many Indigenous nations are also proposing, creating, and managing protected areas throughout the Boreal Conifer Forest.

In comparison to the vast areas of Boreal Conifer Forest, the Appalachian Conifer Forest is severely endangered. Limited to a few mountain ridges, the forest has been decimated by logging and disease over the past century. In particular, the Balsam Woolly Adelgid is responsible for killing most mature Fraser Firs during the second half of the 20th century, and no effective control methods are currently known. For this forest, like many species and habitats found on isolated mountaintops, climate change is a dire and immediate threat, as there is nowhere for it to escape to as the planet warms. At the moment, 95% of the remaining Appalachian Conifer Forest is found on protected state and federal lands. Despite this, the future of this subhabitat looks grim.

DISTRIBUTION: The Boreal Conifer Forest is one of the most expansive habitats in the Nearctic, covering a giant swath of Canada and Alaska and dipping southward into the contiguous United States. Reaching its eastern extent at the Atlantic Ocean in Newfoundland, the Boreal Conifer Forest spans westward to w. Alaska, though it doesn't reach coastal areas there. At the southern limits of the range, the boreal forest reaches n. Minnesota and Michigan, where it transitions to TEMPERATE MIXED FOREST. In the north, throughout Arctic Canada and Alaska, as the stature and density of the forest decrease, and tundra (ROCKY TUNDRA and BOGGY TUNDRA) appears between conifer stands, this habitat looks more like European Tundra Taiga of the Palearctic. At high elevations in the west, Boreal Conifer Forest is replaced by ALPINE TUNDRA. The Northern Spruce-Fir Forest subhabitat is distributed on mountain slopes in New England, n. New York, and e. Canada. It occurs as low as 1500 ft. (450 m) in the northern part of the range, though it is found significantly higher in the south, appearing around 3800 ft. (1150 m) at its southernmost extent on Slide Mountain in New York.

In addition to the Boreal Conifer Forest of the far north, there are small, isolated pockets of the similar Appalachian Conifer Forest in the s. Appalachian Mountains of the e. United States. This habitat is a relic of recent ice ages and occupies an area of less than 100 sq. mi. (160 km²) in Tennessee, North Carolina, and Virginia.

WHERE TO SEE: BOREAL CONIFER FOREST—Sax-Zim Bog, Minnesota, US; Algonquin Provincial Park, Ontario, Canada; Yukon-Charley Rivers National Preserve, Alaska, US. NORTHERN SPRUCE-FIR FOREST—White Mountain National Forest, New Hampshire, US. APPALACHIAN CONIFER FOREST—Great Smoky Mountains National Park, North Carolina, US.

Ne1C NEARCTIC MONTANE SPRUCE-FIR FOREST

IN A NUTSHELL: A dense, uniform forest of spruce and fir trees that grows at high elevations. **Global Habitat Affinities:** EUROPEAN MONTANE SPRUCE-FIR FOREST; ASIAN MONTANE SPRUCE-FIR FOREST; HIMALAYAN SPRUCE-FIR FOREST. **Continental Habitat Affinities:** BOREAL CONIFER FOREST. **Species Overlap:** BOREAL CONIFER FOREST; NEARCTIC MONTANE MIXED-CONIFER FOREST; HIGH-ELEVATION PINE WOODLAND.

DESCRIPTION: This high-elevation habitat is in many ways a southern equivalent of the northern BOREAL CONIFER FOREST. While the steep slopes and rocky soil preclude the development of the muskegs and bogs found in the boreal forest, the structure and fauna are quite similar. Expansive and uniform, these forests form the seemingly endless, dark-green vistas that are typical of the high-elevation mountain west. This is a forest of the subalpine zone, and often this is the last forested habitat encountered before reaching tree line. This habitat is cold year-round and has snow cover beginning as early as September and often persisting until midsummer. The vast majority of the precipitation falls as snow, and annual precipitation generally totals 19–30 in. (500–750 mm) in the Rocky Mountains. Snowfall is generally heavier in the Cascades and Sierra Nevada, reaching upward of 50 in. (1250 mm).

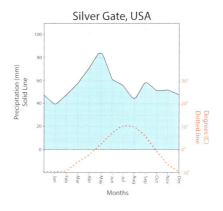

Silver Gate, USA

These are relatively simple forests that we classify into two basic subhabitats. The first, **Ne1C-1 Rocky Mountain Spruce-Fir Forest**, is dominated by two species of narrow, slow-growing conifers: Engelmann Spruce (*Picea engelmannii*) and Subalpine Fir (*Abies lasiocarpa*). These two species form co-dominant or monotypic stands that rarely include other trees. Douglas-fir (*Pseudotsuga menziesii*), Lodgepole Pine (*Pinus contorta*), and Quaking Aspen (*Populus tremuloides*) do occur in small numbers, especially near areas of recent disturbance. These trees grow with even spacing and are typically 30–80 ft. (9–24 m) tall, though individual trees can reach heights of 130 ft. (40 m). The canopy is dense, its coverage ranging from 60 to 90%, and often precludes the development of shrub and herbaceous layers.

The second subhabitat, **Ne1C-2 Sierra Nevada–Columbia Plateau Spruce-Fir Forest**, is similar in structure and fauna to the Rocky Mountain subhabitat but differs in the types of trees present and overall diversity. Dominant trees in this subhabitat are Red Fir (*Abies magnifica*), Noble Fir (*Abies*

Montane Spruce-Fir Forest in Glacier National Park, Montana, US. © DAVE SPANGENBURG

procera), Pacific Silver Fir (*Abies amabilis*),
Lodgepole Pine, and Mountain Hemlock (*Tsuga mertensia*). In the Cascades, Engelmann Spruce
and Subalpine Fir appear but are not dominant
trees. The forest here is slightly but appreciably
taller than the Rocky Mountain type, with canopy
trees reaching 50–100 ft. (15–30 m) in height.

In Montane Spruce-Fir Forest, shrub and
herbaceous layers are typically sparse or
absent due to late-lingering snow and the
dense canopy. Shrubs that occur include White
Rhododendron (*Rhododendron albiflorum*),
serviceberries (*Amelanchier* spp.), Five-leafed
Bramble (*Rubus pedatus*), gooseberries
(*Ribes* spp.), buckbrushes (*Ceanothus* spp.),
and willows (*Salix* spp.). In areas that have
experienced avalanches, blowdowns, or other
major disturbance, grassy meadows can be
found.

WILDLIFE: The wildlife is a blend of species
from the BOREAL CONIFER FOREST and species
of adjacent montane conifer habitats. The
mammals include most of the classic boreal
species such as Moose, Snowshoe Hare,
American Red Squirrel, Southern Red-backed
Vole, American Ermine, American Marten,
Fisher, and the elusive Canada Lynx. The
lynx ranges as far south as Colorado, where
populations were reestablished in the 1990s.
Both Moose and Canada Lynx are absent from
the Sierra Nevada–Columbia Plateau subhabitat.

Many species of boreal birds are found in
this habitat, including Spruce Grouse, Boreal
Owl (IS), Great Gray Owl (Sierra subhabitat,
IS), American Three-toed and Black-backed
Woodpeckers, Canada Jay, Black-capped
Chickadee, Golden-crowned Kinglet, Pine
Grosbeak (IS), Evening Grosbeak, and White-
winged and Red Crossbills. These occur
alongside more typical Rocky Mountain

Top: **Listening for the alarm calls of squirrels and
songbirds is a good way to locate the cute but
ferocious American Marten.** © MISSY MANDEL PHOTOGRAPHY

Right: **Pine Grosbeak brightens the Montane
Spruce-Fir Forest with a flash of color and a cheery
song.** © BEN KNOOT, TROPICAL BIRDING TOURS

Boreal Owl is most vocal in March and April, when deep snows make this mountain habitat extremely difficult to access. © PHIL CHAON

species like Northern Pygmy-Owl, Steller's Jay, Clark's Nutcracker, Mountain Chickadee, and Cassin's Finch. In winter, Gray-crowned, Black, and Brown-capped Rosy-Finches come down to this habitat from higher elevations, especially during inclement weather. Flocks of hundreds can sometimes appear at bird feeders after a winter storm.

This forest can have snow on the ground during any month of the year, and many locations experience frosts throughout the summer. Additionally, the steep mountain slopes leave little room for pooled groundwater and wetlands. For that reason, amphibians and reptiles are almost completely absent.

CONSERVATION: Nearctic Montane Spruce-Fir Forest is slow-growing, and unlike most western conifer habitats, it typically experiences low-frequency, high-intensity fires. With warmer temperatures due to climate change, stands of this forest have suffered massive die-offs due to Mountain Pine Beetles, a pest that would historically have died off in winter. These dead trees create large swaths of forest that are highly susceptible to sweeping wildfires, from which the forests need centuries to recover. In general, this habitat is not valuable for timber and is relatively free of human habitation and development. Most current threats come from disease and fire exacerbated by climate change.

DISTRIBUTION: This is a high-elevation habitat. The Rocky Mountain Spruce-Fir Forest subhabitat is found throughout the Rocky Mountains and n. Cascades from British Columbia and Alberta south to n. New Mexico. It occurs as far east as c. Montana in montane islands, and as far west as the Olympic Mountains in w. Washington. The Sierra Nevada–Columbia Plateau Spruce-Fir Forest subhabitat occurs in the Sierra Nevada of California as far south as Sequoia National Park, and extends north through the Cascades and slowly transitions to the Rocky Mountain subhabitat in n. Oregon, where trees from both forest subhabitats can be found. As is typical of montane ecosystems, the elevation at which Montane Spruce-Fir Forest occurs increases closer to the equator. At the northern end of the range in British Columbia, these forests occur as low as 3300 ft. (1000 m), while at the southern limit in New Mexico, this habitat occurs as high as 11,000 ft. (3350 m). Upslope, this habitat is replaced by HIGH-ELEVATION PINE WOODLAND or ALPINE TUNDRA, and downslope, it is usually replaced by MONTANE MIXED-CONIFER FOREST. In the Olympic Mountains, this habitat occurs only on drier east-facing slopes; on west-facing slopes it is replaced by TEMPERATE RAINFOREST.

WHERE TO SEE: Yellowstone National Park, Wyoming, US; Waterton Lakes National Park, Alberta, Canada; Cameron Pass, Colorado, US.

Ne1D NEARCTIC MONTANE MIXED-CONIFER FOREST

IN A NUTSHELL: A mid-elevation temperate conifer forest with many co-dominant tree species. **Global Habitat Affinities:** HIMALAYAN PINE FOREST. **Continental Habitat Affinities:** PONDEROSA PINE FOREST; MADREAN PINE-OAK WOODLAND. **Species Overlap:** MONTANE SPRUCE-FIR FOREST; PINYON-JUNIPER WOODLAND; LODGEPOLE PINE FOREST; ASPEN FOREST AND PARKLAND.

DESCRIPTION: A widely distributed and highly variable habitat of w. North America, Montane Mixed-Conifer Forest is the quintessential western forest of towering conifers, with the smell of vanilla coming off sun-warmed Ponderosa Pine and the distant drumming of woodpeckers. Anyone who has spent time hiking in the mountains of the w. Nearctic region has enjoyed these vast and inviting forests.

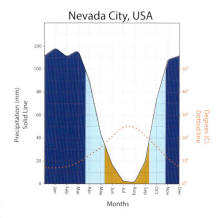

The canopy is fairly open at the lowest elevations, where this habitat grades into PONDEROSA PINE FOREST, and becomes more closed farther upslope. While the height of the canopy is generally 65–120 ft. (20–35 m), some of the larger trees can surpass heights of 200 ft. (60 m). The **Ne1D-1 Rocky Mountain Mixed-Conifer Forest** subhabitat tends to be shorter overall and lacks the gargantuan trees found in the **Ne1D-2 Sierra Nevada–Columbia Plateau Mixed-Conifer Forest** subhabitat. With a sparse midstory and a variable shrub layer, these forests are quite open and easily traversed, making them a pleasant place for hiking and wildlife observation.

One of the hallmarks of the Montane Mixed-Conifer Forest is the diversity of conifer species present. Douglas-fir (*Pseudotsuga menziesii*) and Ponderosa Pine (*Pinus ponderosa*) are the two most widespread components of the canopy, found at all but the lowest elevations. In the Rocky Mountain Mixed-Conifer Forest subhabitat, other important co-dominant trees are Lodgepole Pine (*Pinus contorta*), Grand Fir (*Abies grandis*), White Fir (*Abies concolor*), Blue Spruce (*Picea pungens*), and Western Redcedar (*Thuja plicata*). The Sierra Nevada–Columbia Plateau Mixed-Conifer Forest subhabitat has a different set of co-dominant trees, with Sugar Pine (*Pinus lambertiana*), Jeffrey Pine (*Pinus jeffreyi*), Western White Pine (*Pinus monticola*), Incense Cedar (*Calocedrus decurrens*), and White Fir all occurring widely. The Giant Sequoia (*Sequoiadendron giganteum*) is found in the Montane Mixed-Conifer Forest of the c. Sierra Nevada. This most massive of trees changes the structure of the forests, as little understory and large canopy gaps surround these living giants.

In Montane Mixed-Conifer Forest, the midstory is typically very sparse and comprises smaller individuals of the dominant tree types. Depending on frequency of fire and canopy density, the shrub layer can be absent to dense. The shrub layer is highly diverse over this habitat's range, with well over 100 species represented. Shrubs typically found throughout the range include Big Sagebrush (*Artemisia tridentata*), manzanitas (*Arctostaphylos* spp.), buckbrushes (*Ceanothus* spp.), ninebarks (*Physocarpus* spp.), dogwoods (*Cornus* spp.), Huckleberry Oak (*Quercus vacciniifolia*), and Gambel Oak (*Quercus gambelii*). Stands with a more closed canopy can completely lack herbaceous or shrubby ground cover, with little but fallen conifer needles covering the forest floor.

The high variability in species composition and structure means the fire regime is also highly variable. Historically, frequent low-intensity fires were more common in the Sierra Nevada, while the Rocky Mountains experienced a full spectrum of fire regimes. Fire suppression has led to denser forests and more shade-tolerant species like White Fir. This also tends to result in high-intensity fires when they do occur.

Nearctic Montane Mixed-Conifer Forest includes a wide array of tree species. © BEN KNOOT, TROPICAL BIRDING TOURS

Above: **Steller's Jay is a raucous and obvious resident in many montane habitats.**
© BEN KNOOT, TROPICAL BIRDING TOURS

Right: **White-headed Woodpecker is a specialty bird in the Sierra Nevada–Columbia Plateau Mixed-Conifer Forest subhabitat.** © BEN KNOOT, TROPICAL BIRDING TOURS

WILDLIFE: Bordering a variety of habitats that all share aspects of vertebrate communities, Montane Mixed-Conifer Forest is home to the majority of forest-dwelling mammal species of the west. Widespread large mammals include Elk, White-tailed and Mule Deer, American Black Bear, Puma (aka Mountain Lion, Cougar, or Panther), and Gray Wolf. Other small predators such as Fisher, Gray Fox, Long-tailed Weasel, and Bobcat are all found locally. While mice and rats are present, the most noticeable rodents in this habitat are squirrels and chipmunks, which feed heavily on the variety of cones readily found here. Abert's, Western Gray, American Red, Douglas's, and Northern Flying (IS) Squirrels, and Least and Yellow-pine Chipmunks are all common.

The bird communities are similarly diverse. Game birds like Mountain Quail, Dusky Grouse (IS), and Sooty Grouse are readily found. The American Goshawk is the top avian predator in this habitat. Northern Saw-whet Owl, Northern Pygmy-Owl, Long-eared Owl, Cooper's Hawk, and Red-tailed Hawk are also regularly found here. In the Sierra Nevada, this forest is the principal habitat of the California Spotted Owl (IS). Common resident birds like Brown Creeper, Pygmy and Red-breasted Nuthatches, Mountain Chickadee, and Steller's Jay are readily seen around campgrounds and picnic areas. This forest has a high diversity of woodpeckers: White-headed (IS), Hairy, Downy, Pileated, and Black-backed Woodpeckers, along with Red-breasted, Red-naped, and Williamson's Sapsuckers, can be found exploiting mixed-aged and burned forests. In the summer, inundated with breeding migrant birds, Montane Mixed-Conifer Forests come alive with song. Olive-sided (IS), Hammond's (IS), and Western Flycatchers; Golden-crowned Kinglet; Cassin's Vireo; Yellow-rumped, Townsend's, and Hermit Warblers; Western Tanager; and Black-headed Grosbeak all bring an extra splash of life and color.

Reptiles and amphibians are generally sparse, as is typical of montane environments in the west. However, rubber boas, California Mountain Kingsnake, Sharp-tailed Snake, Western Fence Lizard, and western alligator lizards (*Elgaria* spp.) all occur in the Sierra Nevada–Columbia Plateau subhabitat.

CONSERVATION: Both historically and currently, these forests have been among the most heavily logged habitats in North America. This, combined with changing fire regimes and fire suppression, has led to widespread destruction of one of the most common habitats in w. North America.

The Giant Sequoia (*Sequoiadendron giganteum*) is among the most iconic and endangered tree species of this habitat. Many of the most massive Giant Sequoias were logged during the 19th century, and many more have been lost as a result of fire suppression. The conservation damages have been twofold. First, "ladder fuels," including brush, leaf litter, branches, and dead trees, which would regularly burn under natural regimes, have accumulated, resulting in massive, high-intensity fires in the early 21st century. These fires kill mature trees that would otherwise survive, and they frequently destroy the topsoil also. The 2020 Castle Fire in c. California was responsible for the loss of nearly 20% of remaining sequoias. Second, fire suppression has also eliminated the gentle, understory-clearing fires needed for Giant Sequoias to reproduce. Thick-barked mature Giant Sequoias easily survive low-intensity fires, and their serotinous cones open only after fire and germinate only in open, sunny environments. Recruitment (successful regeneration) of Giant Sequoias has been low for the past century. Drought is also a major concern.

Giant Sequoias are the largest trees on the planet.
NOAA/WIKIMEDIA COMMONS

The threatened California Spotted Owl has also declined due to the pressures of logging and fire. Additionally, this subspecies is facing increasing competitive pressure from invasive Barred Owls (see sidebar 1).

Thankfully, this is a widespread habitat with relatively few specialized species and little endemism—as such, it is generally of lower conservation concern. Much of this habitat is found in large national parks and other public lands. The best time to conserve a habitat is when it is still intact and abundant, and conservation of this habitat, hopefully, will be a priority before the situation becomes dire.

DISTRIBUTION: Montane Mixed-Conifer Forests are distributed widely throughout the temperate regions of the w. Nearctic. Ranging as far north as s. British Columbia, Canada, and south through the w. United States to n. Baja California, n. Sonora, and Chihuahua, Mexico, these forests can be found in all but the driest mountains and wettest coastal ranges. They reach their eastern extent in isolated patches in c. Montana and are bounded to the west by the Pacific Ocean. Montane Mixed-Conifer Forest typically grows at elevations between 2000 and 6000 ft. (600–1800 m), though it can be found significantly higher or lower at the extreme ends of its range. At the upper limits, it transitions to MONTANE SPRUCE-FIR FOREST, LODGEPOLE PINE FOREST, or HIGH-ELEVATION PINE WOODLAND. At its lower elevational limit, it is most commonly bordered by PONDEROSA PINE FOREST but also by PINYON-JUNIPER WOODLAND, CALIFORNIA OAK SAVANNA, PACIFIC CHAPARRAL, and TEMPERATE RAINFOREST. There are often broad ecotones at these elevational boundaries.

WHERE TO SEE: Yosemite National Park, California, US; Rocky Mountain National Park, Colorado, US.

Ne1E PONDEROSA PINE FOREST

IN A NUTSHELL: An open, grassy woodland dominated by Ponderosa Pine found at lower elevations in the mountain west. **Global Habitat Affinities:** MEDITERRANEAN DRY PINE FOREST; MIDDLE EASTERN DRY CONIFER FOREST. **Continental Habitat Affinities:** MONTANE MIXED-CONIFER FOREST; MADREAN PINE-OAK WOODLAND; PINYON-JUNIPER WOODLAND. **Species Overlap:** MONTANE MIXED-CONIFER FOREST; MADREAN PINE-OAK WOODLAND; LODGEPOLE PINE FOREST.

DESCRIPTION: Another archetypal forest of the west, Ponderosa Pine Forest is possibly the most abundant forest habitat in w. North America. Found in foothills and lower montane zones, this habitat is generally pleasant, mild, and fairly dry. Annual precipitation is around 15–20 in. (400–500 mm), though it can be slightly higher along the Pacific coast and Sierra Nevada. In the western part of the range, most of the precipitation falls as snow during the winter months, but in the Rocky Mountains, most of the precipitation comes as late summer monsoon thunderstorms.

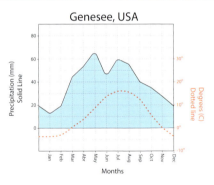

Structurally, Ponderosa Pine Forest can range from a closed-canopy forest with little to no understory to an open, grassy savanna woodland. Historically, the open, grassy Ponderosa Pine woodland was the most common form this habitat took, but frequent, low-intensity fires are required to maintain this form, and many examples have become overgrown over the past century. Even the densest of Ponderosa Pine Forests should still feel quite open and provide a long line of sight. Ponderosa Pine Forests vary significantly in height; warmer, drier forests reach only 30–45 ft. (9–14 m), while those in the northern and especially western parts of the habitat's range can be towering, reaching heights of 70–120 ft. (20–35 m) with occasional trees over 200 ft. (60 m) tall.

The canopy is not particularly diverse and is always heavily dominated by Ponderosa Pine (*Pinus ponderosa*). Douglas-fir (*Pseudotsuga menziesii*), Limber Pine (*Pinus flexilis*), Two-needle Pinyon (*Pinus edulis*), Single-leaf Pinyon (*Pinus monophylla*), White Fir (*Abies concolor*), and various junipers (*Juniperus* spp.) can occasionally be found in the canopy but rarely as a major component.

Ponderosa Pine Forest is usually quite open, making it a pleasant habitat in which to camp and hike.

© BEN KNOOT, TROPICAL BIRDING TOURS

The understory in this habitat also tends to be negligible. Sapling Ponderosa Pines are often the most noticeable component. Small oaks can be an obvious part of the understory—particularly Gambel Oak (*Quercus gambelii*) in the east and California Black Oak (*Quercus kelloggii*) in the west. Other common shrubs include Antelope Bitterbrush (*Purshia tridentata*), ninebarks (*Physocarpus* spp.), snowberries (*Symphoricarpos* spp.), Bearberry (*Arctostaphylos uva-ursi*), Big Sagebrush (*Artemisia tridentata*), and buckbrushes (*Ceanothus* spp.). Historically, shrubs were almost completely absent, as the fire-return interval in this habitat was two to five years. A dense understory is a clear sign of an unhealthy Ponderosa Pine Forest.

In all but the densest Ponderosa Pine Forests, the ground layer is full of grasses and grasslike sedges. The grassy understory is the most diverse vegetative component of this habitat and varies widely throughout the range. Bluejoint (*Calamagrostis canadensis*), sedges (*Carex* spp.), fescues (*Festuca* spp.), Bluebunch Wheatgrass (*Pseudoroegneria spicata*), and gramas (*Bouteloua* spp.) are all major components of Ponderosa Pine Forest ground cover.

WILDLIFE: As largely transitional habitat, Ponderosa Pine Forests have a high abundance of wildlife from both higher montane forests and lower shrub habitats. Puma (Mountain Lion), American Black Bear, Gray Wolf, and Coyote are all present in this habitat. Smaller mammals like North American Porcupine, Bushy-tailed Woodrat, Rock Squirrel, various chipmunks, and Mountain Cottontail are also common. Abert's Squirrel is a Ponderosa Pine specialist, and the Kaibab Squirrel (IS) subspecies is endemic to this habitat. The open, grassy aspect of this forest makes it especially valuable as grazing habitat for Elk and Mule Deer, which are abundant here. Historically, Indigenous peoples used controlled burns to improve Ponderosa Pine Forests for grazing species.

Above: **Despite its name, American Black Bear comes in a wide variety of color morphs including white, blond, cinnamon, and silver.**
© DAVE SPANGENBURG

Right: **Male (pictured) and female Williamson's Sapsuckers look so different from each other they were thought to be separate species for decades.**
© BEN KNOOT, TROPICAL BIRDING TOURS

This traditional habitat management was adopted by cattle ranchers in the 19th and early 20th centuries before widespread fire suppression began. The large, loose sheets of bark found on Ponderosa Pines are great roosting habitat for bats, and Long-legged Myotis, Long-eared Myotis, Arizona Myotis, Big Brown Bat, Hoary Bat, and others are particularly abundant.

Ponderosa Pine Forest has few true obligates but sees a variety of birds from adjacent habitats. These forests also have a mix of forest and open-country species due to their savanna-like structure. Steller's Jay, Mountain Chickadee, Pygmy Nuthatch, Violet-green Swallow, Western Bluebird, Mountain Bluebird, Brown-headed Cowbird, Chipping Sparrow,

Grace's Warbler is strongly tied to Ponderosa Pine Forests in the s. Rockies. © PHIL CHAON

Red Crossbill, and Pine Siskin are all abundant. A wide array of woodpeckers—Downy, Hairy, Lewis's, and White-headed Woodpeckers as well as Northern Flicker and Williamson's Sapsucker (IS)—are frequently encountered. Among the Neotropical migrants utilizing this habitat are Broad-tailed Hummingbird (IS), Western Flycatcher, Western Wood-Pewee, House Wren, Plumbeous Vireo, Western Tanager, and Yellow-rumped Warbler. Grace's Warbler (IS) is an abundant breeding bird in southern Ponderosa Pine Forests. Flammulated Owl (IS) breeds almost exclusively in Ponderosa Pine Forest. This small owl feeds heavily on insects and migrates to Mexico and Guatemala during the winter. Thanks to its propensity for tall trees and a soft low hoot that is difficult to pinpoint, Flammulated Owl can be devilishly hard to see, even in areas where it is abundant.

CONSERVATION: Ponderosa Pine Forest is widespread and supports few true specialist or endemic species. It faces many of the same problems confronting most western coniferous habitats—a long history of logging and a future with increased risks for fire, drought, and disease. Overgrown forests face elevated risks of fire and insect outbreaks and would benefit from a frequent low-intensity fire regime. Unlike most conifer forests in the west, Ponderosa Pine Forest suffers from overgrazing, which can be damaging for native grasses, allowing invasive species to intrude.

Flammulated Owl breeds primarily in this habitat and is a species of special concern. This owl requires large, mature trees with cavities for nesting. Areas with heavy logging rotations do not have trees of adequate size to support Flammulated Owls, American Goshawks, woodpeckers, and a variety of other species. Maintaining mixed-age stands with large trees, cavities, and snags should be a management priority for this habitat.

DISTRIBUTION: Generally found in foothill and lower montane environments, Ponderosa Pine Forest is arguably the most common forest type in the w. United States, stretching from Canada's Rocky Mountains in s. British Columbia to n. Mexico's Sierra Madre. Ponderosa Pine Forests are distributed in bands along the western regions of the Sierra Nevada and Cascade Mountains, as well as in multiple locations throughout the Rocky Mountains, including the Laramie and Bighorn Mountains of Wyoming, and in the Black Hills of South Dakota. The Ponderosa Pine woodlands within these areas occur in belts of varying widths, ranging from 5 to 25 mi. (8–40 km) wide, at elevations spanning from 500 to 9500 ft. (1500–2900 m). Ponderosa Pine Forest is replaced by MONTANE MIXED-CONIFER FOREST at higher elevations. At lower elevations, it grades into several habitats, including PINYON-JUNIPER WOODLAND, SAGEBRUSH SHRUBLAND, FOOTHILL OAK SHRUBLAND, and CALIFORNIA OAK SAVANNA.

WHERE TO SEE: Kings Canyon National Park, California, US; Kaibab National Forest, Arizona, US.

Ne1F EASTERN PINE SAVANNA

Longleaf Pine Savanna has large, widely spaced trees and an open understory.

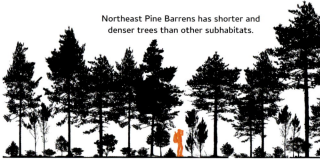

Northeast Pine Barrens has shorter and denser trees than other subhabitats.

IN A NUTSHELL: An open, grassy pine woodland or savanna with poorly drained soils occurring on flat coastal plains and sc. US mountain ranges.
Global Habitat Affinities: INDO-MALAYAN PINE FOREST. **Continental Habitat Affinities:** PONDEROSA PINE FOREST. **Species Overlap:** TALLGRASS PRAIRIE; TEMPERATE DECIDUOUS FOREST; TEMPERATE MIXED FOREST (especially Appalachian Pine-Oak Forest); FLORIDA SCRUB.

DESCRIPTION: The Eastern Pine Savanna is a broad umbrella habitat that encompasses four major subhabitats with overlapping features. Throughout most of the range of Eastern Pine Savanna, winters are mild, and the temperature rarely drops below freezing. Summers are hot and humid, with daily highs around 90°F (32°C). Most of the rain falls in the spring and summer months, with 43–68 in. (1100–1750 mm) accumulating annually. In the Longleaf Pine zone, especially, precipitation from tropical storms and hurricanes in the warm months is an important seasonal feature. In the Northeast Pine Barrens, the winters are colder, and there is often long-lasting snow accumulation. Summers are somewhat milder but still hot and humid, especially in New Jersey, Delaware, and Maryland.

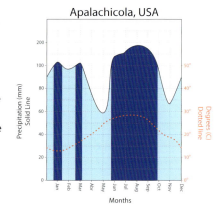

Apalachicola, USA

Throughout much of their range, Eastern Pine Savannas are open-canopied woodlands or savannas occurring on the low-lying coastal plains and in the Mississippi River valley of the se. United States. The tall, narrow-trunked pines that dominate the **Ne1F-1 Longleaf Pine Savanna** and **Ne1F-2 Shortleaf Pine Savanna** subhabitats generally grow to a height of 70 ft. (22 m), though occasionally as tall as 130 ft. (40 m). Under historical fire regimes, trees are widely spaced (100 ft./30 m apart) and do not form a solid canopy, allowing high light conditions that support an open understory of grasses and small shrubs. However, with fire-suppression practices, dense shrubby undergrowth encroaches, and it can make moving through unmanaged

Pygmy Rattlesnake is a gorgeous but unobtrusive resident of the Longleaf Pine Savanna subhabitat.
PUBLIC HEALTH IMAGE LIBRARY, CDC

Regular fires are needed to maintain the open understory of Longleaf Pine Savanna.
© SAM WOODS, TROPICAL BIRDING TOURS

Northeast Pine Barren is the most restricted of the Eastern Pine Savanna subhabitats.
© F. A. MARTIN/WIKIMEDIA COMMONS

savannas difficult. The **Ne1F-3 Northeast Pine Barrens** subhabitat has a shorter and denser canopy and features a dense understory even under natural fire regimes. Because the soil is often poorly drained, all three subhabitats are dotted with wet grasslands, pitcher-plant bogs, and cedar swamplands. Swamplands dominated by Atlantic White Cedar (*Chamaecyparis thyoides*) are an especially important feature of the Northeast Pine Barrens.

The primary canopy tree is a major defining feature of each of these three major subhabitats. In Longleaf Pine Savanna the dominant canopy tree is Longleaf Pine (*Pinus palustris*), a fire-tolerant and slow-growing species. Shortleaf Pine Savanna is characterized by abundant Shortleaf Pine (*Pinus echinata*), and Northeast Pine Barrens mostly by Pitch Pine (*Pinus rigida*). Throughout Eastern Pine Savanna habitat, Slash Pine (*Pinus elliottii*), Sand Pine (*Pinus clausa*), Pond Pine (*Pinus serotina*), and Virginia Pine (*Pinus virginiana*) are all also present, though rarely co-dominant. Loblolly Pine (*Pinus taeda*) is a fast-growing but fire-susceptible species that often outcompetes and displaces Longleaf Pine in woodlands where fire is suppressed. Loblolly is also common around the wetter, boggier sections of Longleaf Pine Savanna and often replaces both Shortleaf and Longleaf Pine in managed TREE PLANTATIONS.

The midstory of Eastern Pine Savanna is generally sparse and includes Sweetbay Magnolia (*Magnolia virginiana*), Southern Wax Myrtle (*Myrica cerifera*), Sweetgum (*Liquidambar styraciflua*), and Red Maple (*Acer rubrum*). Shortleaf Pine Savanna and Northeast Pine Barren subhabitats often have a diverse array of oaks (*Quercus* spp.) and hickories (*Carya* spp.), which create a significant midstory and occasionally join the canopy, especially in the Ouachita and Ozark Mountains.

The shrub layer is variable, and density is largely dependent on the frequency of fire. Saw Palmetto (*Serenoa repens*) or Dwarf Palmetto (*Sabal minor*) is present in all but the northernmost Eastern Pine Savannas. The shrub composition varies widely across the range, but Shining Fetterbush (*Lyonia lucida*), Gallberry (*Ilex glabra*), tupelo or gum trees (*Nyssa* spp.), and various blueberries (*Vaccinium* spp.) are usually common.

The herbaceous layer of the Eastern Pine Savanna is by far the most diverse vegetative component. In frequently burned areas, the ground cover is dominated by three-awns (*Aristida* spp.), Little Bluestem (*Schizachyrium scoparium*), muhly grasses (*Muhlenbergia* spp.), and a variety of sedges (*Carex* spp.). Eastern Pine Savannas have a wide variety of orchids, including many rare and endangered species like Giant Orchid (*Pteroglossaspis ecristata*), Yellow Fringeless Orchid (*Platanthera integra*), and Eaton's Ladies-tresses (*Spiranthes eatonii*).

The poorly drained, acidic soils of the Eastern Pine Savanna are perfect conditions for the formation of **Pocosins**, or evergreen shrub bogs. These peat-forming wetlands (see BOREAL BOG AND FEN) are an important component of Eastern Pine Savannas and support the vast majority of Nearctic carnivorous plant species, including a diverse array of pitcher plants (*Sarracenia* spp.), sundews (*Drosera* spp.), and bladderworts (*Utricularia* spp.). The famous Venus Flytrap (*Dionaea muscipula*) is found nowhere else.

Ne1F-4 Caribbean Pine Forest is a subhabitat that includes the s. Florida rocklands, Bahamian pineyards, and w. Cuban pine forests. This subhabitat is dominated by Slash Pine (*Pinus elliottii*) or Caribbean Pine (*Pinus caribaea*). Secondary canopy and understory components are frequently similar to those of Caribbean Hardwood Hammock (see COASTAL HAMMOCK, CHENIER, AND WOODLOT), and Gumbo-limbo (*Bursera simaruba*) and Poisonwood (*Metopium toxiferum*) are common here.

WILDLIFE: In much of the e. Nearctic, the mammal communities, especially of large and conspicuous mammals, are similar. Virginia Opossum, White-tailed Deer, Bobcat, American Black Bear, Striped Skunk, and Common Raccoon are all abundant and noticeable in Eastern Pine Savanna. The less widespread Nine-banded Armadillo favors this habitat, especially areas with well-drained, sandy soils. Invasive feral hogs are a common feature and cause great damage to sensitive understory plants and terrestrial fauna.

The bird community is more distinctive. Red-cockaded Woodpecker (IS), Brown-headed Nuthatch (IS), and Bachman's Sparrow (IS) are three pinewoods specialists that are rare to absent in other habitats. (All three birds are absent from the Northeast Pine Barrens subhabitat.) The endangered Red-cockaded Woodpecker nests in mature Longleaf and Loblolly Pine stands, where it excavates a nest cavity in a living tree. Under these nest cavities, the woodpecker drills a number

The otherworldly Venus Flytrap is found only in wet areas of Longleaf Pine Savanna.

The endangered Red-cockaded Woodpecker is one of the only woodpeckers to nest in trunks of living trees.
© SAM WOODS, TROPICAL BIRDING TOURS

Brown-headed Nuthatch is often detected by its squeaky rubber ducky–like call.
© SAM WOODS, TROPICAL BIRDING TOURS

of sap wells, the sticky pitch from which helps deter snakes and other nest predators. Among the common e. Nearctic birds, Wild Turkey, Mourning Dove, Barred Owl, Red-bellied and Pileated Woodpeckers, White-breasted Nuthatch, Eastern Bluebird, Eastern Towhee, and Eastern Meadowlark are particularly abundant. This habitat is one of the few areas still containing stable populations of Northern Bobwhite. In summer, returning migrants make up a significant percentage of the avifauna. The abundant insect life provides food for Swallow-tailed and Mississippi Kites, Common Nighthawk, Chuck-will's-widow, Eastern Wood-Pewee, Great Crested Flycatcher, White-eyed Vireo, Blue-gray Gnatcatcher, Common Yellowthroat, Northern Parula, Prairie Warbler, Pine Warbler (IS), Indigo Bunting, Blue Grosbeak, and Summer Tanager. The Caribbean Pine Forest subhabitat is home to several regional endemics including the Olive-capped Warbler, Bahama Warbler, and West Indian Woodpecker. The critically endangered (potentially extinct) Bahama Nuthatch is found exclusively in this subhabitat. Kirtland's Warblers frequently winter in Caribbean Pine Forest in the Bahamas.

Reptiles and amphibians are perhaps the most exciting vertebrates found in Eastern Pine Savanna habitat. The endangered Gopher Tortoise remains mostly in Longleaf Pine Savanna, where it excavates large burrows, which are utilized by more than 300 other species of reptiles, mammals, invertebrates, and even birds: Bachman's Sparrows have been observed disappearing into Gopher Tortoise burrows when escaping predators. Among the more than 30 species of snakes in this habitat, the spectacular Scarlet Snake, imposing Eastern Diamondback Rattlesnake, dainty Pygmy Rattlesnake, comical Eastern and Southern Hognose Snakes, and endemic Pine Woods Snake (IS) are all regularly seen. Eastern Indigo Snake, the largest snake in the Nearctic, is also found here, though it is endangered. Eastern and Slender Glass Lizards, a pair of bizarre, legless, snakelike lizards, can be seen hunting for insects among the dry pine needles. There are dozens of amphibian species, with Reticulated and Frosted Flatwoods Salamanders, Striped Newt, Ornate Chorus Frog,

Pine Barrens Tree Frog (IS), and Carpenter Frog among the specialists. In 2018, a new species of aquatic salamander was described that lives in boggy flatwoods of sw. Alabama and nw. Florida; at over 24 in. (60 cm) in length, the Reticulated Siren is one of the largest salamanders in the world.

CONSERVATION: Eastern Pine Savanna is a habitat of high conservation concern and one of the most endangered habitats in North America. The combination of widespread habitat destruction, poor forest management, high diversity, and high levels of endemism create a system with many immediate threats. Across the habitat's range, less than 10% of each of the subhabitats remains intact. Major threats include urbanization, logging, insect and disease outbreaks, and fire suppression. Pine savannas are currently home to several hundred threatened or endangered plant species and dozens of rare insects. They are also the principal habitat for endangered birds like Bachman's Sparrow and Red-cockaded Woodpecker, as well as rare herps like Pine Woods Snake, Eastern Indigo Snake, Pine Barrens Tree Frog, and Reticulated and Frosted Flatwoods Salamanders.

Shortleaf Pine Savanna is the most widespread of the three major subhabitats but has also received the least ecological attention in terms of management and preservation. While it is still found in abundance, many remaining blocks of this subhabitat are highly degraded and largely interspersed with low-diversity tree plantations. High-quality Longleaf Pine Savanna is very rare, with less than 5% remaining. However, this habitat has received significant conservation attention, as management for Red-cockaded Woodpecker has focused on restoring Longleaf Pine Savanna. The management practices benefiting the woodpecker, especially frequent burns, tend to benefit other rare and declining pine savanna specialists as well. The Northeast Pine Barrens are the most heavily modified of the main subhabitats, absent throughout most of their former range, with very little remaining in any condition. However, nearly all the remnant Northeast Pine Barrens are found in well-protected areas with active management, and the future prospects for this habitat are good.

Caribbean Pine Forest is severely threatened by development and climate change. Most of the habitat in the s. Florida rocklands has been destroyed for commercial development. The largest remaining tracts in the Bahamas were severely damaged by Hurricanes Matthew (2016) and Dorian (2019). During these large storms, the last few Bahama Nuthatches were likely killed.

DISTRIBUTION: The Longleaf Pine Savanna subhabitat is found in low-lying areas of the se. US coastal plain, from Virginia south into much of peninsular Florida, west along the Gulf of Mexico to e. Texas, and north along the Mississippi River valley through Arkansas to far s. Illinois. The Shortleaf Pine Savanna subhabitat has extensive overlap with the Longleaf Pine Savanna. It tends to predominate farther inland and on sandier, more well-drained soils. This is a major habitat in the Ouachita and Ozark Mountains in Arkansas, Oklahoma, and Missouri. Shortleaf Pine also extends north into New Jersey on sandy soils relatively close to the coast. There is a long ecotone along the Atlantic coast where Shortleaf Pine Savanna blends into the Pitch Pine–dominated Northeast Pine Barrens. Extending up the Atlantic coast, the Northeast Pine Barrens subhabitat remains only in isolated pockets found in New Jersey, New York's Long Island, and Cape Cod, Massachusetts. The Eastern Pine Savannas are broadly bounded to the north by TEMPERATE DECIDUOUS FOREST and to the west by TALLGRASS PRAIRIE. The Northeast Pine Barrens are bordered to the west by Temperate Deciduous Forest and TEMPERATE MIXED FOREST. Caribbean Pine Forest is found in southern peninsular Florida, the Florida Keys, the Bahamas, and c. and w. Cuba. The montane pine forests found in e. Cuba and on Hispaniola are not included in this habitat.

WHERE TO SEE: LONGLEAF PINE SAVANNA—Apalachicola National Forest, Florida, US; Croatan National Forest, North Carolina, US. SHORTLEAF PINE SAVANNA—Poison Springs State Forest, Arkansas, US. NORTHEAST PINE BARRENS—New Jersey Pinelands National Reserve, New Jersey, US.

Ne1G HIGH-ELEVATION PINE WOODLAND

IN A NUTSHELL: Open, high-elevation coniferous forests growing on dry, rocky soils in the w. Nearctic. **Global Habitat Affinities:** EUROPEAN SUBALPINE TIMBERLINE WOODLAND. **Continental Habitat Affinities:** MONTANE SPRUCE-FIR FOREST. **Species Overlap:** MONTANE SPRUCE-FIR FOREST; LODGEPOLE PINE FOREST; ALPINE TUNDRA; GLACIER AND SCREE.

DESCRIPTION: These sparse woodlands are found near timberline on dry, rocky ridges and slopes in the mountains of the w. Nearctic and are populated by only the hardiest of trees. The trees are short in stature, rarely exceeding 35 ft. (11 m) in height, and in persistent and intense winds are often reduced to the stunted form known as krummholz. In the zone where these woodlands are found, winters are long, and temperatures regularly go as low as −10°F (−23°C). In the hot, dry summer, daytime temperatures reach 90°F (32°C), though nighttime temperatures can still dip below freezing. Precipitation is generally scarce, with average rainfall ranging from 10 in. (250 mm) in Great Basin Bristlecone Pine woodland in Nevada to 35 in.

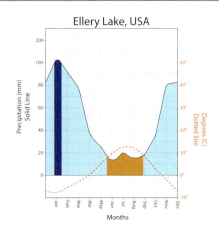

(900 mm) in Foxtail Pine woodland in California. This habitat is a stark and emblematic feature of the high-mountain west, and spending time here usually requires a hike through some stunning mountain scenery. While the vegetation presents no obstacles, the steep slopes and loose, rocky soil can make exploration difficult.

High-Elevation Pine Woodlands are open stands composed of five species in the white (five-needled) pine group that are often referred to as the "high five": Great Basin Bristlecone Pine (*Pinus longaeva*), Rocky Mountain Bristlecone Pine (*Pinus aristata*), Foxtail Pine (*Pinus balfouriana*), Whitebark Pine (*Pinus albicaulis*), and Limber Pine (*Pinus flexilis*). With increasing elevation, tree size diminishes and distance between trees increases. Often these trees can grow only where they are sheltered from the wind by rocks or snow. Slow growth occurs at the base of the tree, which is often large and thick, and the vegetation is often shrublike and dense. The upper parts of these trees are gnarled and frequently devoid of bark, often appearing dead. These woodlands are generally monotypic, as each species has a disjunct range, though Limber Pine is occasionally mixed with the more restricted species. In parts of the n. Rocky Mountains and the Cascades, Alpine Larch (*Larix lyallii*) will also form open monotypic stands at the edge of timberline. However,

Certain Great Basin Bristlecone Pines are the longest-lived individual organisms known, reaching ages of 4,800 years or more. © RICK GOLDWASSER/WIKIMEDIA COMMONS (CC BY 2.0 DEED)

these larch woodlands lack the large-seeded cones of the high five and also lack most of the animals found in High-Elevation Pine Woodland.

There is no notable midstory, and the ground cover is mostly bare rock, with only 5–25% vegetative ground cover on average. The sparse ground cover comprises small woody shrubs such as manzanitas (*Arctostaphylos* spp.), mountain mahoganies (*Cercocarpus* spp.), junipers (*Juniperus* spp.), gooseberries and currants (*Ribes* spp.), and bitterbrush (*Purshia* spp.). Herbaceous ground cover is diverse, due to the wide elevational and geographic ranges covered by this habitat, but usually includes a few grasses, especially fescues (*Festuca* spp.). The high five are all considered keystone and foundational species that heavily influence the structure, diversity, and stability of high-montane communities and are major sources of food for alpine animals.

Some of these pines are impressively ancient—all high five species have specimens known to be over 1000 years old. Foxtail and Rocky Mountain Bristlecone can reach over 3000 years of age, and an individual Great Basin Bristlecone Pine, at a staggering 4900 years old, is considered the oldest single organism on the planet.

High-Elevation Pine Woodlands are extremely susceptible to fire, and even low-intensity fires cause widespread tree death. The wood of these trees is incredibly dense and resinous, which is an effective defense against most insects, but ignites quite easily.

WILDLIFE: A sparse and rocky habitat, High-Elevation Pine Woodland is home to relatively few animals. American Pikas live among the boulder-piled slopes, as do Yellow-bellied Marmots. American Ermine and Wolverine will utilize this habitat. Golden-mantled Ground Squirrel, American Red Squirrel, and Least Chipmunk all feed on the sizable seeds of Whitebark and Limber Pines.

Above: **Clark's Nutcracker plays an important role in the propagation of High-Elevation Pine Woodland.** © BEN KNOOT, TROPICAL BIRDING TOURS

Left: **Abundant cones with large seeds are a key food source for Golden-mantled Ground Squirrel in this harsh environment.** © BEN KNOOT, TROPICAL BIRDING TOURS

Throughout the year, squirrels create large middens of pine nuts as a winter food source. In the fall, these stockpiles are often raided by American Black Bear and Brown (Grizzly) Bear, both of which reap a large caloric windfall at the squirrels' expense.

The bird communities at these elevations are made almost entirely of granivorous (seed-eating) species that survive on the ample pine nuts. Pine Grosbeak, Cassin's Finch, Red Crossbill, Gray-crowned Rosy-Finch, and Dark-eyed Junco are all regularly found in this habitat. Clark's Nutcracker is a major seed disperser in High-Elevation Pine Woodlands, and the survival of Whitebark Pine is especially dependent on it. An individual nutcracker will fervently cache upward of 90,000 seeds in a single year, often in far-flung locations. While the birds remember the location of most seeds, forgotten pine nuts germinate to form woodlands on isolated peaks and after fires.

CONSERVATION: Many of the stands of ancient trees lie within protected federal lands, and because most of this habitat is found in remote and hostile environments, it is almost completely free from development. Yet, these slow-growing, long-lived woodlands are heavily threatened, despite their perceived toughness. Non-native White Pine Blister Rust has been decimating this habitat throughout the w. Nearctic, as have large outbreaks of Mountain Pine Beetle. These outbreaks have been especially damaging to Whitebark Pines, with many populations experiencing greater than 50% mortality. As a result, Whitebark Pine was listed as endangered in Canada in 2010 and the United States in 2022. Climate change and the continued march of lower-elevation habitats upslope also threaten to displace or consume these ridgetop species. High-Elevation Pine Woodlands are extremely dry and susceptible to increasing drought.

DISTRIBUTION: High-Elevation Pine Woodlands are scattered across the w. Nearctic, largely in the United States. The ranges of the individual tree species vary; the highly restricted Foxtail Pine is found in a few disjunct sites in California, while the widespread Whitebark Pine occurs in the Rocky Mountains, Cascade Range, Sierra Nevada, and the Great Basin ranges, from British Columbia south to Arizona and New Mexico. These forests grow only at higher elevations, occurring as low as 6000 ft. (1800 m) and as high as 12,000 ft. (3650 m). At their lower elevational limit, they are replaced by MONTANE SPRUCE-FIR FOREST, MONTANE MIXED-CONIFER FOREST, or PINYON-JUNIPER WOODLAND. At their upper elevational limit, they transition to GLACIER AND SCREE, areas of permanent snowpack, or ALPINE TUNDRA.

WHERE TO SEE: Ancient Bristlecone Pine Forest, California, US; Crater Lake National Park, Oregon, US; Lincoln National Forest, New Mexico, US.

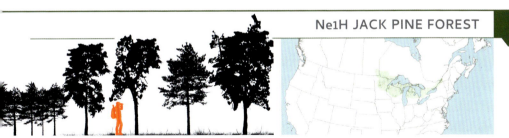

Ne1H JACK PINE FOREST

IN A NUTSHELL: A woodland found on sandy soils in the upper Great Lakes states and Canada, dominated by Jack Pine and shaped by frequent fire. **Global Habitat Affinities:** MAGHREB PINE FOREST. **Continental Habitat Affinities:** EASTERN PINE SAVANNA; LODGEPOLE PINE FOREST. **Species Overlap:** BOREAL CONIFER FOREST; TEMPERATE MIXED FOREST; TALLGRASS PRAIRIE.

DESCRIPTION. Jack Pine Forest is a relatively restricted habitat found almost entirely on sandy soils in the upper Great Lakes region. While Jack Pine (*Pinus banksiana*) has a broad range and is an important component in BOREAL CONIFER FOREST and many northern TREE PLANTATIONS, this specific habitat is an early successional one, closely tied to fire.

The canopy of this forest is almost entirely Jack Pine. Commonly acknowledged as a pioneer species in forest succession, Jack Pine is a small, short-lived species intolerant of shade. Jack Pines typically live less than 100 years and are rarely more than 50 ft. (17 m) tall. Large mature trees of this size are usually fully integrated into TEMPERATE MIXED FOREST. Jack Pine Forest habitat is short, even-aged, and with low to moderate (20–65%) canopy cover. Trees are often patchily distributed, with small grassy openings between them. Other sandy-soil-loving trees may join the mix, especially Red Pine (*Pinus resinosa*) and Northern Pin Oak (*Quercus ellipsoidalis*).

The shrub layer here is sparse, and walking through these forests is generally quite easy. Serviceberries (*Amelanchier* spp.), Lowbush Blueberry (*Vaccinium angustifolium*), Common Juniper (*Juniperus communis*), and Sand Cherry (*Prunus pumila*) are all co-dominant shrubs in this habitat.

The ground here is usually open and sandy, covered with many lichens, low forbs, creeping shrubs, and grasses. The silvery, cloudlike forms of Reindeer Lichen (*Cladonia rangiferina*)

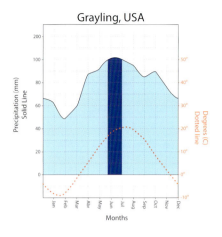

Regular disturbance is needed to maintain healthy Jack Pine Forest. © BEN KNOOT, TROPICAL BIRDING TOURS

Abundant in Jack Pine Forest during the summer, Common Nighthawks will congregate around ponds to drink and bathe. © PHIL CHAON

are an especially common sight. Typical ground-cover plants include Wintergreen (*Gaultheria procumbens*), Bearberry (*Arctostaphylos uva-ursi*), Grove Bluegrass (*Poa alsodes*), False Melic Grass (*Schizachne purpurascens*), sedges (*Carex* spp.), Sweetfern (*Comptonia peregrina*), and Bracken Fern (*Pteridium aquilinum*).

WILDLIFE: The mammals found in Jack Pine Forest broadly overlap with those found in TEMPERATE MIXED FOREST. White-tailed Deer, Eastern Cottontail, North American Porcupine, Bobcat, Gray Fox, and American Black Bear are all present.

The birdlife is significantly more divergent from surrounding areas. The open nature of this habitat is favorable for grassland and savanna species like Sharp-tailed Grouse, Short-eared Owl, Upland Sandpiper, Common Nighthawk, and Grasshopper, Vesper, and Clay-colored (IS) Sparrows. Other common birds include Northern Harrier, American Kestrel, Brown Thrasher, Nashville Warbler, Pine Warbler, Eastern Towhee, Brown-headed Cowbird, and Indigo Bunting. Brewer's Blackbird is also found here, well east of its principal range. Most importantly, Jack Pine Forest is the sole breeding habitat for the threatened Kirtland's Warbler. This bird prefers young stands of Jack Pine between 5 and 15 years old and no older than 20. These pine stands are usually 5–15 ft. (2–5 m) tall and have live branches near ground level. Kirtland's Warbler is a ground-nesting species, and these low branches provide important cover for nests and recently fledged birds. Due to the isolated and fleeting nature of Jack Pine Forest, Kirtland's Warblers breed colonially in high densities. Anecdotally, there have been a notable number of records of vagrant male Kirtland's Warblers in Jack Pine habitats in New York, Quebec, and Maine, far east of their normal breeding range.

Jack Pine Forest holds populations of reptiles associated with more southerly habitats, particularly Eastern Hognose Snake and Common Five-lined Skink.

CONSERVATION: Jack Pine Forest is rare and, due to the suppression of natural fires in its range, needs frequent management action to maintain it. By the mid-20th century, this habitat had nearly vanished. The passage of the US Endangered Species Act of 1973 and the strong link between Jack Pine Forest and Kirtland's Warbler eventually turned the tide for both bird and habitat.

There were as few as 167 male Kirtland's Warblers in 1974 when the species became one of the first listed under the Endangered Species Act. Early restoration efforts focused on the bird's breeding habitat, by clear-cutting, burning, and planting Jack Pines in order to create young, even-aged stands. Controlling Brown-headed Cowbird parasitism and Blue Jay predation were also important management techniques. There are currently 188,000 acres (76,000 ha) reserved for Kirtland's Warbler habitat management in the Lower Peninsula of Michigan. Of this land, roughly 38,000 acres (15,000 ha) are maintained as young Jack Pine breeding habitat for the bird, with patches cyclically cleared and subsequently aging into mature timber. In 2018, the global population of Kirtland's Warbler was estimated at 2300 pairs, and the species was removed from the US endangered species list. However, Kirtland's Warblers still rely entirely on active management to create appropriate habitat, and without human intervention the species will quickly decline.

Modern management rarely uses prescribed burns due to difficulties controlling these fires and the relatively high levels of human habitation nearby. Jack Pine Forest is extremely rare as a naturally occurring habitat and mostly occurs as managed stands that blur the lines between natural habitats and TREE PLANTATIONS.

DISTRIBUTION: Jack Pine Forest habitat has largely disappeared over the past century due to fire suppression and today is found mostly in managed areas. Always patchily distributed, this habitat occurs in areas with regularly occurring fires at early seral stages. Currently, the habitat is largely restricted to the n. Lower Peninsula of Michigan; it also occurs in parts of Michigan's Upper Peninsula, Wisconsin, Minnesota, and adjacent Ontario. There are some sandy Jack Pine Forests found around e. Lake Ontario in New York and Quebec, though these are not regularly maintained. There are also small patches of analogous habitat in parts of Maine and New Brunswick, though they tend to lack the diagnostic faunal assemblage.

Interestingly, this habitat largely existed on the se. US coastal plain during the last ice age. It is likely that Kirtland's Warbler evolved during this period, wintering in the Bahamas and breeding in nearby coastal mainland sites. As the glaciers retreated, this habitat has migrated northward in patches of suitable sandy soils. Kirtland's Warblers have followed in turn.

WHERE TO SEE: Huron National Forest, Michigan, US.

IN A NUTSHELL: A successional forest composed of uniformly aged Lodgepole Pines found at middle elevations in the mountainous west. **Global Habitat Affinities:** None. **Continental Habitat Affinities:** MONTANE MIXED-CONIFER FOREST; MONTANE SPRUCE-FIR FOREST. **Species Overlap:** ASPEN FOREST AND PARKLAND; MONTANE MIXED-CONIFER FOREST; MONTANE SPRUCE-FIR FOREST; HIGH-ELEVATION PINE WOODLAND.

DESCRIPTION: Lodgepole Pine Forest is a common habitat in mountainous areas of the w. Nearctic. It generally occurs at 8500–10,000 ft. (2600–3000 m) in areas where the climate is wet and cool with a very brief frost-free period in summer.

Lodgepole Pine Forest is a near monoculture that colonizes after major fires or other large-scale disturbances. Characterized by dense stands of even-age Lodgepole Pines (*Pinus contorta*), this forest has few other canopy trees. The postfire forests, often called "dog-hair stands," can reach incredible densities of 20,000 trees per acre (50,000/ha). If soil conditions are favorable, small pockets of other early successional trees like Quaking Aspen (*Populus tremuloides*) may be found.

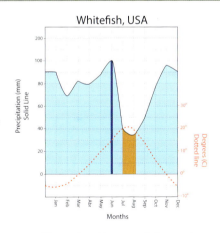

The shrub and forb layers are also sparse and depauperate. Manzanitas (*Arctostaphylos* spp.), blueberries (*Vaccinium* spp.), buckbrushes (*Ceanothus* spp.), and Meadowsweet (*Filipendula ulmaria*) are the most common shrubs and can be abundant in early successional stages of this forest. Despite the relatively sparse understory, this habitat can be surprisingly difficult to move through. Exposed to frequent fire and high winds, the forest floor is often a maze of fallen trunks. Younger generations of Lodgepole Pines grow on top of old burns. Short forests with the burned trunks of previous generations still intact and standing are a common landscape feature.

Lodgepole Pine has fire-adapted serotinous cones, which open and release seeds only after exposure to fire or other heat. If left undisturbed, Lodgepole Pine Forest is replaced by MONTANE

In Lodgepole Pine Forest, the vast majority of trees are the same age and size. © BEN KNOOT, TROPICAL BIRDING TOURS

SPRUCE-FIR FOREST or MONTANE MIXED-CONIFER FOREST. But with the increased frequency and scale of fires in the w. Nearctic, the extent of Lodgepole Pine Forest has increased.

WILDLIFE: The high elevation, lack of floristic diversity, sparse understory, and intense fire associated with this habitat mean it is relatively wildlife-poor. There is enough food to support a variety of small mammals, especially during years with significant cone production. Conspicuous small mammals include American Red and Douglas's Squirrels, Least Chipmunk, Golden-mantled Ground Squirrel, and Snowshoe Hare. Elk, Mule Deer, and Bighorn Sheep will use Lodgepole Pine Forest for cover but spend significant periods of time here only in areas with developed understory. The same is true of American Black Bear, while smaller predators like American Marten and Long-tailed Weasel make use of this habitat throughout the year, and Wolverine uses it for hunting and denning in winter.

The bird communities of Lodgepole Pine Forest are similar to those of surrounding habitats but lack species that need dense understory or larger trees. Widespread species like American Robin, Hermit Thrush, Western Wood-Pewee, Canada Jay, Ruby-crowned Kinglet, Yellow-rumped Warbler, Dark-eyed Junco, Red Crossbill, and Pine Siskin are found here, as are high-elevation species like Clark's Nutcracker and Pine Grosbeak. In older stands, American Goshawk and Boreal Owl sometimes occur.

One notable feature of Lodgepole Pine Forest is the abundance of standing dead trees, which provide excellent habitat for cavity-nesting birds. With frequent fire and large die-offs caused by Mountain Pine Beetle, this habitat is heavily used by American Three-toed (IS) and Black-backed Woodpeckers. Other woodpecker species are also common, and secondary cavity nesters like Mountain Bluebird, Black-capped Chickadee, Merlin, and even Northern Hawk Owl take advantage of available cavities, normally a scarce resource.

Reptiles and amphibians are almost entirely absent from this habitat.

CONSERVATION: This is a habitat of low conservation concern for birds. The avian diversity is quite low, and all species are generalists or shared with adjacent habitats in some configuration.

Above: **Red Crossbill has a bill specially adapted to remove pine seeds. The bill varies in size depending on the type of cone the local population is consuming.**
© BEN KNOOT, TROPICAL BIRDING TOURS

Left: **American Three-toed Woodpecker is common in large stands of dead or burned Lodgepole Pine.**
© BEN KNOOT, TROPICAL BIRDING TOURS

Lodgepole Pine Forest aggressively colonizes areas after fire, and as mega-fires have increased in w. North America, this habitat has expanded in turn. Assessments predict this habitat to be quite resilient to climate change.

Historically, this forest was an important source of timber, as Lodgepole Pines tend to be very straight and uniform. The trees were heavily used for fence posts, railroad ties, utility poles, and as the name implies, the construction of houses.

DISTRIBUTION: This habitat occurs at middle elevations in the Rocky Mountains of Canada and the United States, from Alberta and British Columbia south through Colorado, and in the e. Cascades south through Oregon, along the Sierra Nevada, and on isolated mountaintops to s. California and Nevada.

WHERE TO SEE: Glacier National Park, Montana, US; Yellowstone National Park, Wyoming, US.

Ne1J NEARCTIC TEMPERATE RAINFOREST

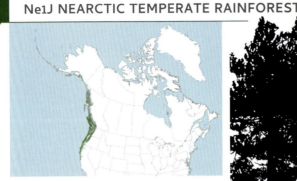

IN A NUTSHELL: An extremely wet and mossy Pacific coastal coniferous forest with towering trees. **Global Habitat Affinities:** NEOTROPICAL MAGELLANIC RAINFOREST; NEOTROPICAL VALDIVIAN RAINFOREST. **Continental Habitat Affinities:** None. **Species Overlap:** MONTANE MIXED-CONIFER FOREST; MONTANE SPRUCE-FIR FOREST.

DESCRIPTION: Nearctic Temperate Rainforest, a towering forest laden with epiphytes, hugs a narrow strip along the Pacific coast of North America from c. California to Alaska. It is dominated by a few massive conifer species and has little midstory and a thick understory layer of ferns, mosses, and evergreen shrubs. Temperate Rainforest grows in a wet, stable climate, rarely colder than 32°F (0°C) and only occasionally warmer than 75°F (25°C) in a given year. Average precipitation is around 80 in. (2000 mm) per year, but some areas, such as the Olympic Peninsula of Washington, receive upward of 170 in. (4300 mm) annually. This habitat has two distinct seasons—a long, wet rainy season from October to May, and a short, dry, foggy summer from June to September. During the dry season, this forest receives 7–12 in. (180–300 mm) of precipitation from fog alone. Despite the heavy fog, this habitat is best visited from April to September, outside the worst of the winter rains.

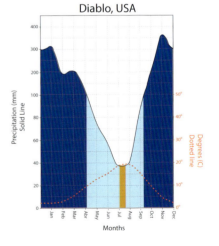

Diablo, USA

The Temperate Rainforest is perhaps the most dramatic of the Nearctic habitats. The multilayered canopy, regularly soaring upward of 300 ft. (90 m), is dominated by Douglas-fir (*Pseudotsuga menziesii*), Sitka Spruce (*Picea sitchensis*), Western Hemlock (*Tsuga heterophylla*), Alaska Cedar (*Callitropsis nootkatensis*), and Western Redcedar (*Thuja plicata*). From the Oregon-California border south, Coast Redwood (*Sequoia sempervirens*) is co-dominant with Douglas-fir. The massive Coast Redwood can reach 380 ft. (115.8 m) in height and 29.2 ft. (8.9 m) in diameter, placing it among the largest trees on earth. The towering canopy trees are often laden with epiphytic mosses, lichens, and ferns. Infrequently, small trees will sprout from the soils harbored on massive limbs high in the canopy.

Underneath is a sparse midstory layer made up of conifer saplings and smaller shade-tolerant deciduous trees like Bigleaf Maple (*Acer macrophyllum*), Vine Maple (*Acer circinatum*), and dogwoods (*Cornus* spp.). The forest floor, replete with fallen logs, usually supports a dense assemblage of Western Sword Fern (*Polystichum munitum*), Lady Fern (*Athyrium filix-femina*), rhododendrons (*Rhododendron* spp.), Salmonberry (*Rubus spectabilis*), Evergreen Huckleberry (*Vaccinium ovatum*), Devil's Club (*Oplopanax horridus*), Salal (*Gaultheria shallon*), and mosses. This thick, often saturated understory is mostly 3–6 ft. (1–2 m) tall and can be difficult to walk through.

These forests very rarely burn. In the drier, Coast Redwood–dominated forests, low-intensity fires would periodically clear out the understory. Redwood germination is associated with these fires, but the species is not a fire obligate.

WILDLIFE: The Temperate Rainforest is home to a large array of the Nearctic's charismatic megafauna. The diminutive Columbian Black-tailed Deer is common throughout the range, and Roosevelt Elk is found in large herds in the habitat's southern extent. Puma (Mountain Lion), Bobcat, and American Black Bear are common throughout, and Gray Wolf and Brown (Grizzly) Bear are still common in the British Columbia and Alaska stretch of the Temperate Rainforest. This stretch is also home to the Kermode Bear, a large subspecies of American Black Bear famous for having a spectacular white color morph, and the massive Kodiak subspecies of Brown Bear,

Coast Redwoods, the tallest trees on earth, dominate the southern Nearctic Temperate Rainforests.

which can reach 10 ft. (3 m) in length and upward of 1500 lb. (680 kg). Watching these bears fatten themselves on salmon along the Frazer Lake on Kodiak Island, Alaska, is one of the great North American wildlife spectacles. Apart from the megafauna, the Temperate Rainforest is also home to smaller predators like Fisher, American Marten, Gray Fox, and American Ermine. Other common mammals include Humboldt's Flying Squirrel (IS), American Red and Douglas's Squirrels, Townsend's Chipmunk, Common Raccoon, and numerous vole species, including the Red Tree Vole (IS), which spends its entire life in the canopy eating Douglas-fir needles.

The Temperate Rainforest's relatively limited set of birds includes a few specialties and some widespread but uncommon species. Many of the smaller songbirds utilize the upper stratum of the canopy and are best detected by ear. Band-tailed Pigeon, Brown Creeper, Golden-crowned Kinglet, Townsend's and Hermit Warblers, Red Crossbill, and Pine Siskin can all be found feeding hundreds of feet up in the massive canopy and are best looked for along the forest edge, where they will often venture to lower levels. Lower down within the forest is a nice variety of raptors, woodpeckers, corvids, and songbirds, including American Goshawk, Merlin, Red-breasted Sapsucker, Pileated and Hairy Woodpeckers, Northern Flicker, Western Flycatcher, Canada and Steller's Jays, Common Raven, American Crow, and Chestnut-backed Chickadee. Ruffed Grouse, Dusky Grouse, Pacific Wren, and Hermit, Swainson's, and Varied (IS) Thrushes are all common in the understory and perhaps more than any other set of birds contribute to the unique and haunting soundscape of this habitat. The two most famous avian residents are the endangered Northern Spotted Owl (IS) and Marbled Murrelet (IS), which are icons of the early 1990s campaign to protect this habitat. The Marbled Murrelet, the last species of bird in the United States to have its nest discovered, was found nesting on broad limbs high in the redwood canopy during the 1970s. These diminutive and fascinating seabirds nest exclusively in old-growth Temperate Rainforest but are most easily observed out on the open ocean.

The Temperate Rainforest region is also notable for the high diversity of endemic salamanders, including 19 species that are found almost exclusively in this habitat. This hub of amphibian diversity includes three endemic families—Dicamptodontidae (Pacific giant salamanders), Rhyacotritonidae (torrent salamanders), and Ascaphidae (tailed frogs). The Wandering Salamander is commonly found on the forest floor but may also live its entire life high up in the trees. One individual was spotted 200 ft. (60 m) up in a Coast Redwood, walking alongside a Marbled Murrelet nest.

The Olympic Peninsula forest is a small center of endemism, home to Olympic Marmot, Olympic Torrent Salamander, Olympic Mudminnow, and a dozen or so endemic insects.

The ethereal whistles of Varied Thrush are a common sound in Nearctic Temperate Rainforest.
© BEN KNOOT, TROPICAL BIRDING TOURS

Marbled Murrelet nests on large limbs high in old-growth Nearctic Temperate Rainforest— the first nests were discovered in 1974!
© BEN KNOOT, TROPICAL BIRDING TOURS

The Northern Spotted Owl was closely tied to the fight to save old-growth Nearctic Temperate Rainforest.
© PHIL CHAON

CONSERVATION: The massive timber of the Nearctic Temperate Rainforest made it a valuable commodity during the 19th century and most of the 20th, when huge tracts (especially of Coast Redwood forests) were lost to logging. Less than 10% of the historic Temperate Rainforest remains in California, Oregon, and Washington. Since the latter half of the 20th century, there has been a concerted public effort to conserve old-growth Temperate Rainforest, and most of the remaining old-growth tracts are found on protected public lands. Some of these massive tracts, including the Tongass National Forest of se. Alaska and the Great Bear Rainforest of British Columbia, cover millions of acres. These areas are still open to logging, and major timber sales do occur.

Apart from logging, these forests are particularly susceptible to drought. Climate-change-driven variations in average rainfall and maximum average temperature pose a major threat. Irregularities in the fog belt are of particular concern for Coast Redwoods.

Marbled Murrelet and Northern Spotted Owl are two endangered flagship birds associated with the movement to conserve this habitat. While their habitat is now largely protected, these populations continue to decline, probably because of other factors. Marbled Murrelet declines are

---

SIDEBAR 1 ▶ **INVASIVE SPECIES: BARRED OWL**

The term "invasive" is generally applied to species of organisms translocated by humans from their natural range of distribution to another. However, invasive species can also be native organisms that become harmful to the environment following anthropogenic changes to habitats. Removal of predators, changes to fire regimes, and introduction of foreign species can lead to major changes in the role of native species. One surprising example from the late 20th century comes from the westward expansion of the Barred Owl, a large and adaptable species of forested areas of e. North America. Barred Owls were not found west of the Great Plains until the early 20th century. It is theorized that a combination of fire suppression and planting of large trees in prairie environments allowed Barred Owls to spread across the plains and through the Canadian BOREAL CONIFER FOREST. Upon reaching forested environments in the west, Barred Owls have rapidly moved down the Pacific coast from British Columbia as far south as c. California. The arrival of Barred Owl has been one of two major sources of decline of its smaller congener the Northern Spotted Owl. Larger, more aggressive, and more generalist, Barred Owls have negatively impacted Spotted Owls through competition for territories and resources as well as occasional hybridization and direct mortality. The effects of the Barred Owl's expansion on small mammals, amphibians, and other prey species remains poorly understood. In areas where lethal Barred Owl removal has taken place, there has been a corresponding increase in the survival rates of Northern Spotted Owls.

associated with rising ocean temperatures and declines in prey species. Increased human presence is also associated with larger corvid populations and increased nest predation. Northern Spotted Owl declines are largely associated with displacement by invasive Barred Owls (see sidebar 1). Efforts to remove Barred Owls are underway in some areas, with promising results.

DISTRIBUTION: The Temperate Rainforest stretches for nearly 2000 mi. (3200 km) along the Pacific coast of North America, from c. California through coastal Oregon, Washington, and British Columbia to the eastern end of Alaska's Kodiak Archipelago. Found in a series of Pacific coastal mountain ranges, it is bounded to the west by the Pacific Ocean and to the east by MONTANE MIXED-CONIFER FOREST. Water is the key limiting factor in this habitat, and Temperate Rainforest does not occur in any areas without sufficient rain and fog or with unfavorably high average temperatures. Temperate Rainforest is a fairly contiguous habitat where it occurs, only occasionally interrupted by intertidal SALT MARSH, WESTERN RIPARIAN WOODLAND, ROCKY COASTLINE, or SANDY BEACH AND DUNE habitats.

WHERE TO SEE: Humboldt Redwoods State Park/Redwoods National Park, California, US; Olympic National Park, Washington, US; Great Bear Rainforest, British Columbia, Canada; Tongass National Forest, Alaska, US.

Ne1K PINYON-JUNIPER WOODLAND

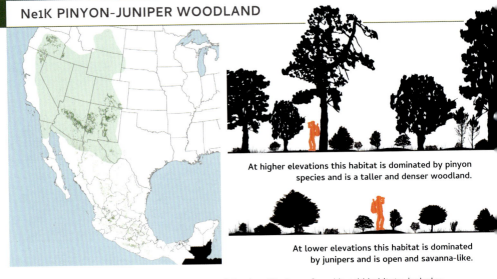

At higher elevations this habitat is dominated by pinyon species and is a taller and denser woodland.

At lower elevations this habitat is dominated by junipers and is open and savanna-like.

IN A NUTSHELL: An open woodland of pinyons (pines) and junipers found in arid habitats; includes elements of grassland and xeric shrub communities. **Global Habitat Affinities:** MAGHREB JUNIPER OPEN WOODLAND; MIDDLE EASTERN JUNIPER FOREST. **Continental Habitat Affinities:** PONDEROSA PINE FOREST; OAK-JUNIPER WOODLAND. **Species Overlap:** SAGEBRUSH SHRUBLAND; PONDEROSA PINE FOREST; CHIHUAHUAN DESERT GRASSLAND; CHIHUAHUAN DESERT; OAK-JUNIPER WOODLAND.

DESCRIPTION: Pinyon-Juniper Woodland is one of the major habitats of the Great Basin and broader intermountain west of the United States (and into Mexico). Occurring in a narrow elevational band, at 5000–8000 ft. (1500–2400 m), in dry mountains and foothills, this habitat experiences an extreme range of temperatures and receives little rainfall, just 12–16 in. (300–400 mm) annually. This a short, shrublike woodland, with trees rarely taller than 25 ft. (7.5 m). Tree density is variable, and canopy cover ranges from about 50% in the northwest to a savanna-like 15% in the southeast. Regardless, this habitat is open enough to move through easily and is readily explored.

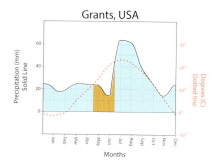

The tree component of Pinyon-Juniper Woodland consists almost entirely of pinyon pines and junipers. The species composition and structure vary throughout the range (mostly on a northwest–southeast gradient), but key tree species include Western (*Juniperus occidentalis*), Utah (*Juniperus osteosperma*), Single-seed (*Juniperus monosperma*), Alligator (*Juniperus deppeana*), and Rocky Mountain Junipers (*Juniperus scopulorum*) in association with Single-leaf Pinyon (*Pinus monophylla*) or Two-needle Pinyon (*Pinus edulis*). In general, juniper species are dominant at lower elevations, while pinyons are the majority of the trees at the upper end of the elevational range.

The understory component of Pinyon-Juniper Woodland also varies along a northwest-southeast gradient and is strongly influenced by adjacent habitats. In the northwest, Pinyon-Juniper Woodland takes on characteristics of SAGEBRUSH SHRUBLAND, with a dense understory of sagebrushes (*Artemisia* spp.), bitterbrushes (*Purshia* spp.), rabbitbrushes (*Chrysothamnus* spp.), and mountain mahoganies

Above: **Pinyon-Juniper Woodland is a prevalent habitat on the Colorado Plateau.**
© BEN KNOOT, TROPICAL BIRDING TOURS

Left: **At lower elevations, Pinyon-Juniper Woodland is open and dominated by junipers.**
© BEN KNOOT, TROPICAL BIRDING TOURS

(*Cercocarpus* spp.), with scattered perennial tussock grasses. In the southeast, the understory is composed of warm-season grasses characteristic of SHORTGRASS PRAIRIE and CHIHUAHUAN DESERT GRASSLAND, such as Blue, Black, Hairy, and Side-oats Gramas (*Bouteloua* spp.). In the s. Rockies and on the Colorado Plateau, montane shrubs like Gambel Oak (*Quercus gambelii*) constitute a significant portion of the ground cover.

As a result of overgrazing and the suppression of high-frequency, low-intensity fires, Pinyon-Juniper Woodland has expanded rapidly over the past 150 years. It often invades the more open habitats at its lower elevation limit. This expansion is a threat to more restricted habitats and the species that depend on them; in particular, it is detrimental to Greater Sage-Grouse, and pinyon-juniper removal is actively taking place in many protected areas.

WILDLIFE: The wildlife of Pinyon-Juniper Woodlands is heavily influenced by adjacent habitats and holds many of the mammal species characteristic of the dry intermountain west. Mountain and Desert Cottontails, Black-tailed Jackrabbit, Mule Deer, Desert Bighorn Sheep, and Elk all feed on the understory vegetation. Pinyon species produce large and nutritious seeds (pine nuts), feeding a wide array of squirrels, chipmunks, mice, and woodrats. Pinyon Mouse is a specialist of this habitat. Dense junipers provide good cover not available in adjacent areas, and large herbivores of grassland and SAGEBRUSH SHRUBLAND habitats frequently seek shelter among them.

An interesting set of bird species, from high-mountain to desert specialists, occurs in this habitat depending on time of year. Pinyons and junipers are both important food sources, and in winter, large flocks of frugivorous birds can be found gorging on juniper berries. American Robin; Eastern, Western, and Mountain Bluebirds; Townsend's Solitaire; and Cedar and Bohemian Waxwings are all species that take advantage of this berry bonanza. The large and nutritious pinyon seeds are animal-dispersed, unlike the winged, wind-dispersed seeds of many pine species. Pinyon pine nuts are important food for Woodhouse's Scrub-Jay, Steller's Jay, and Clark's Nutcracker, but it is the Pinyon Jay (IS) that truly specializes in this food source. Arriving in flocks that sometimes number in the hundreds, Pinyon Jays gorge on pine nuts and cache the rest for later. Forgotten pine nuts later germinate, and the movement of Pinyon Jay flocks has been shown to directly influence landscape-level genetics of pinyon forests. While the bird communities of Pinyon-Juniper Woodland vary in close association with adjacent habitats, there are several other species closely tied to this habitat. Mountain Quail, Black-chinned Hummingbird, Ash-throated Flycatcher, Black-throated Gray Warbler, and Scott's Oriole use Pinyon-Juniper Woodland preferentially over other habitats. Virginia's Warbler and Gray Flycatcher (IS) are near specialists, and Gray Vireo (IS) and Juniper Titmouse (IS) are true specialists, breeding only in Pinyon-Juniper Woodlands.

Opposite: **The gregarious Pinyon Jay is nomadic within Pinyon-Juniper Woodlands.** © BEN KNOOT, TROPICAL BIRDING TOURS

Right: **Gray Vireo prefers the lower, juniper-heavy areas of this habitat.** © PHIL CHAON

Greater Short-horned Lizard eats mostly ants. © DENNIS ANDRE BOYD

As Pinyon-Juniper Woodland occurs in a very dry climate with exceedingly cold winters, very few amphibians are found here. The reptile communities vary widely throughout the range, but common and conspicuous reptiles include Western Whiptail, Gilbert's Skink, Sagebrush Lizard, Common Side-blotched Lizard, Greater Short-horned Lizard, Gopher Snake, Regal Ring-necked Snake, and Prairie Rattlesnake.

CONSERVATION: Pinyon-Juniper Woodland is a habitat of lower conservation priority than other similar habitats, especially the juniper component. The extent of these woodlands has increased significantly over the past century. In many areas, juniper savannas are cleared en masse for grazing lands, but these areas were likely grassland or sagebrush in the recent past. Pinyon pines by contrast are more susceptible to climate-related stressors, particularly drought. Extended drought leads to poor cone crops and increased mortality from insect pests.

Pinyon Jay is a vulnerable and declining species endemic to this habitat. Despite increases in Pinyon-Juniper Woodland, the jay has continued to decline. This may be tied to human population increase and oil and gas development in the northern parts of the habitat's range. Increasing droughts have also resulted in many years with poor pinyon cone crops and a lack of food for jays.

DISTRIBUTION: Pinyon-Juniper Woodland occupies areas of the Great Basin, the Colorado Plateau, the Rocky Mountains, and the Sonoran and Chihuahuan Deserts of the United States and Mexico, where it extends southward to 18°N in the states of Jalisco and Puebla. The habitat is bounded by coniferous forest (usually PONDEROSA PINE FOREST) at its upper elevational limit, and at its lower elevational limit it transitions to SAGEBRUSH SHRUBLAND, CHIHUAHUAN DESERT GRASSLAND, SHORTGRASS PRAIRIE, or CHIHUAHUAN DESERT shrubland. An extension of Pinyon-Juniper Woodland is found outside of mountainous areas on limestone breaks in the Great Plains.

WHERE TO SEE: Lava Beds National Monument, California, US; Grand Canyon National Park, Arizona, US; Colorado National Monument, Colorado, US.

Ne1L MADREAN PINE-OAK WOODLAND

IN A NUTSHELL: A montane pine- and oak-dominated woodland with a variable canopy found from the far sw. United States through Mexico and Guatemala. **Global Habitat Affinities:** NEOTROPICAL PINE-OAK WOODLAND; INDO-MALAYAN PINE FOREST. **Continental Habitat Affinities:** MONTANE MIXED-CONIFER FOREST; PONDEROSA PINE FOREST. **Species Overlap:** MONTANE MIXED-CONIFER FOREST; PONDEROSA PINE FOREST; MESOAMERICAN CLOUDFOREST; MESOAMERICAN PACIFIC DRY DECIDUOUS FOREST.

DESCRIPTION: Madrean Pine-Oak Woodland is the dominant habitat in the mountains of the far sw. United States, w. Mexico, and Guatemala. It consists of pines and evergreen broadleaf trees. This habitat generally occurs at 5000–9000 ft. (1500–2750 m). The climate is temperate to subtropical, with winter lows near 40°F (5°C) and summer highs close to 90°F (32°C). The amount of precipitation is highly dependent on elevation and slope aspect and varies from 16 in. (400 mm) to 100 in. (2500 mm) per year.

Ciudad Madera, Mexico

Structurally, Madrean Pine-Oak Woodland varies from open to moderately dense, with canopy coverage in the range of 10–40%. The height of the canopy is highly variable and dependent on dominant species, reaching 50–100 ft. (15–30 m). The mid-canopy and tall shrub layers are fairly dense, but the understory is usually open, and this is a pleasant habitat for hiking, especially in shady canyons.

Botanically, this habitat is incredibly diverse, containing over 5000 species, more than a quarter of the plant species of Mexico. There is high diversity not only in herbaceous plants but among canopy trees as well—over 20 conifer species and nearly 50 oak species are present. No single canopy species is found throughout the entire range, but several of the most widespread and common canopy trees are Apache Pine (*Pinus engelmannii*), Chihuahuan Pine (*Pinus leiophylla*), Montezuma Pine (*Pinus montezumae*), Hartweg's Pine (*Pinus hartwegii*), Engelmann Oak (*Quercus engelmannii*), and Uricua Oak (*Quercus laurina*). At higher elevations, the canopy is pine-dominated, and occasionally fir trees are present. The midstory is open to moderately dense and usually comprises smaller oaks and madrones (*Arbutus* spp.). The understory varies significantly with rainfall and canopy density. Woodlands with a more open canopy have understories dominated by perennial grasses like muhly grasses (*Muhlenbergia* spp.), lovegrasses (*Eragrostis* spp.),

Above: **Madrean Pine-Oak Woodland reaches its northern limit in Arizona and New Mexico.** © BEN KNOOT, TROPICAL BIRDING TOURS

Left: **Madrean Pine-Oak Woodland in Chiapas, Mexico.** © PHIL CHAON

and Mexican Feathergrass (*Nassella tenuissima*). Small shrubby oaks are also a common feature of the understory, along with manzanitas (*Arctostaphylos* spp.) and silktassels (*Garrya* spp.). In parts of s. Mexico, this habitat can be quite wet and cloudforest-like, with a dense broadleaf and herbaceous understory and pines draped in hanging mosses and bromeliads.

The **Ne1L-1 Oyamel Forest** subhabitat (sidebar 2) is found from 10,000–11,500 ft. (3000–3500 m) and is dominated by the Oyamel (or Sacred) Fir (*Abies religiosa*).

WILDLIFE: The mammalian fauna of Madrean Pine-Oak Woodland has a strong Nearctic influence, though some Neotropical species are found here as well. Carnivores include Puma (Mountain Lion), American Black Bear, Jaguarundi, Bobcat, and even Jaguar—and some Jaguars still occasionally

Above: **The ornate Tufted Jay is endemic to pine-oak woodlands in w. Mexico.** © PHIL CHAON

Right: **Small tufts of long wispy feathers on the side of the head give the Eared Quetzal its name.**
© BEN KNOOT, TROPICAL BIRDING TOURS

cross into the United States. White-nosed Coati is an abundant and conspicuous omnivore, along with Ringtail and several species of skunks. Endemic small mammals restricted to this habitat include Zacatecan Deer Mouse and Peters's Squirrel.

Over 600 species of birds are found in this mountain habitat, and there are many pockets of endemism scattered throughout. The Madrean Pine-Oak Woodland avian fauna has a strong Neotropical influence, and many tropical families and subfamilies, including trogons, woodcreepers, euphonias, and motmots, reach their northern extent here, as does Gray Silky-flycatcher. The spectacular Tufted, White-throated, and Dwarf Jays are endemic to isolated areas of pine-oak forest in w. Mexico. White-eared Hummingbird (IS), Mexican Jay, Elegant Trogon, Eared Quetzal (IS), Collared

Despite its arboreal habit, Red-faced Warbler is a ground-nesting species.
© BEN KNOOT, TROPICAL BIRDING TOURS

Towhee, Mexican Chickadee (IS), Band-tailed Pigeon, and Long-tailed Wood-Partridge are other species regularly encountered in this habitat. In winter, large flocks of migrant warblers contain Red (IS), Red-faced (IS), Hermit, Townsend's, Grace's, and Golden-cheeked Warblers, among others. Thick-billed and Maroon-fronted Parrots, the sole members of the genus *Rhynchopsitta*, both thrive in this habitat on a specialized diet of pine nuts. Olive Warbler (IS), the sole member of its family, is another taxonomic oddity of the Madrean Pine-Oak Woodland. The bird's Spanish common name, Ocotero, refers to its association with Ocote, or Montezuma Pine, one of the habitat's key species.

Reptile diversity is high in this habitat, and nearly 400 species are present. The spiny lizards (*Sceloporus* spp.), anoles (*Anolis* spp.), and constrictors (Colubridae) are particularly well represented, comprising more than half of the species found here. Amphibian diversity is also high, comprising over 200 species found especially in the moister forests at high elevations. The most notable feature of the amphibian communities is the remarkable degree of endemism among salamanders. More than 15% of the world's salamander species are found in Madrean Pine-Oak Woodland, and 40 species are found nowhere else. Isolated moist refugia scattered throughout the mountains have contributed to the level of endemism, and new species are still regularly discovered.

SIDEBAR 2   MICROHABITAT: OYAMEL FOREST

A relic forest of the glacial past, Oyamel is found high (10,000–11,500 ft./3000–3500 m) on the slopes of volcanoes in the Sierra Madre Occidental, immediately above the MADREAN PINE-OAK WOODLAND. These cool, wet coniferous forests are dominated by Hartweg's Pine (*Pinus hartwegii*) and Oyamel (or Sacred) Fir (*Abies religiosa*), which are adapted to the regular winter snowfall in the region. Structurally, Oyamel has a tall (100 ft./30 m) and fairly closed canopy, a sparse shrub layer, and a thick carpet of forbs and mosses on the ground.

Oyamel is most famous as the primary wintering habitat for Monarch butterflies, which reach staggering concentrations of 20–50 million individuals per hectare (2.5 acres)! Much of the vertebrate fauna is shared with the adjacent Madrean Pine-Oak Woodland, though Oyamel does have quite a few unique amphibians, including several recently described species.

Within its limited range in Michoacán, Guerrero, and Oaxaca, Mexico, and Guatemala, less than 2% of the original Oyamel remains. The area has been extensively logged for valuable timber, and even within reserves, illegal logging is a persistent source of conflict. Oyamel is also severely threatened by climate change, in terms of both rapid drying and increasingly frequent and severe fires. The area suitable for Oyamel is likely to diminish by a further 96% by 2090 and disappear completely within the Monarch Butterfly Biosphere Reserve.

Patches of Madrean Pine-Oak Woodland are geographically disjunct on several major mountain ranges and have been further separated during recent ice ages. There are multiple EBAs (see "Endemic Bird Areas" in the Introduction), including the woodlands of Oaxaca, the Trans-Mexican Volcanic Belt, Sierra Madre del Sur, and the Chiapas-Guatemalan Highlands.

CONSERVATION: This habitat is widespread and relatively common, but loss of old-growth stands and high levels of endemism make it a habitat of high conservation concern. Less than 2% of old-growth Madrean Pine-Oak Woodland remains, and logging is still an issue. Increased drought and a century of fire suppression mean this habitat is at high risk of unnaturally intense and destructive fires. Unsustainable grazing practice is also of considerable concern.

Rare or threatened species found in Madrean Pine-Oak Woodland include Short-crested Coquette, Thick-billed Parrot, Maroon-fronted Parrot, Tufted Jay, Dwarf Jay, and White-throated Jay. The largest woodpecker in the world, the Imperial Woodpecker, was endemic to this habitat but went extinct around 1960. Many of the largest and best-protected areas that remain are managed by *ejidos* (communally owned landholdings; see TAMAULIPAN MEZQUITAL).

DISTRIBUTION: Madrean Pine-Oak Woodland is a montane ecosystem common through the mountains of the Sierra Madre Occidental, Oriental, del Sur, and del Guatemala, as far south as El Salvador. It is found in isolated pockets called "sky islands" as far north as se. Arizona and w. Texas in the United States. Below 5000 ft. (1500 m), these woodlands are replaced by MADREAN ENCINAL, CHIHUAHUAN DESERT GRASSLAND, MESOAMERICAN CLOUDFOREST, and SONORAN DESERT, among other habitats. At higher elevations this habitat is replaced by MONTANE MIXED-CONIFER FOREST or MEXICAN BUNCHGRASS AND ZACATONAL.

WHERE TO SEE: Chiricahua Mountains, Arizona, US; La Cumbre Ixtepeji, Oaxaca, Mexico; Durango Highway, Durango, Mexico.

Madrean Pine-Oak Woodland is home to several rattlesnake species, including the handsome Ridge-nosed Rattlesnake. © NOLAN WALKER

North American Desert Dendrogram

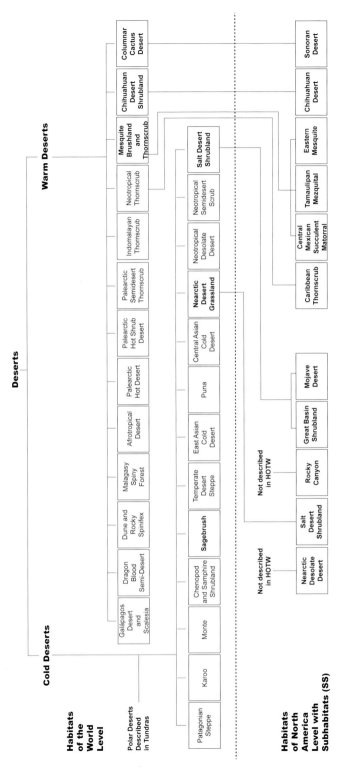

Deserts

Cold Deserts

Warm Deserts

Habitats of the World Level

Polar Deserts Described in Tundras

Patagonian Steppe

Karoo

Monte

Chenopod and Samphire Shrubland

Galápagos Desert and Scalesia

Dragon Blood Semi-Desert

Dune and Rocky Spinifex

Sagebrush

Malagasy Spiny Forest

Afrotropical Desert

Palearctic Hot Desert

Palearctic Hot Shrub Desert

Palearctic Semidesert Thornscrub

Indomalayan Thornscrub

Neotropical Thornscrub

Mesquite Brushland and Thornscrub

Chihuahuan Desert Shrubland

Columnar Cactus Desert

Temperate Desert Steppe

East Asian Cold Desert

Puna

Central Asian Cold Desert

Nearctic Desert Grassland

Neotropical Desolate Desert

Neotropical Semidesert Scrub

Salt Desert Shrubland

Habitats of North America Level with Subhabitats (SS)

Not described in HOTW

Nearctic Desolate Desert

Salt Desert Shrubland

Rocky Canyon

Great Basin Shrubland

Mojave Desert

Not described in HOTW

Caribbean Thornscrub

Central Mexican Succulent Matorral

Tamaulipan Mezquital

Eastern Mesquite

Chihuahuan Desert

Sonoran Desert

DESERTS AND ARID SCRUBS

IN A NUTSHELL: A Creosote- and mesquite-dominated desert shrubland with summer monsoon rains and cold, dry winters. **Global Habitat Affinities:** CAUCASIAN SHRUB DESERT; NEOTROPICAL DESERT GRASSLAND PUNA. **Continental Habitat Affinities:** CHIHUAHUAN DESERT GRASSLAND; SONORAN DESERT; EASTERN MESQUITE. **Species Overlap:** CHIHUAHUAN DESERT GRASSLAND; SONORAN DESERT; DESOLATE DESERT; SHORTGRASS PRAIRIE.

DESCRIPTION: Along with CHIHUAHUAN DESERT GRASSLAND, this is one of the two main habitats of the vast Chihuahuan Desert of the sw. United States and n. Mexico. The abundance of desert grasses and lack of large cacti produce a landscape vastly different from that of the neighboring SONORAN DESERT. In this short and open shrubland, with only tall spikes of flowering agaves breaking the uniform expanse of Creosote bushes, you can often see for miles.

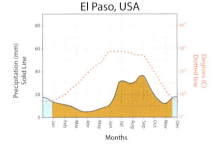

El Paso, USA

Precipitation (mm) Solid Line / Degrees (C) Dotted line / Months

Climatically, the combination of cold, dry winters and intense summer monsoons separates the Chihuahuan Desert from other Nearctic deserts. While it occurs at the same latitudes as the Sonoran Desert, the higher elevation and distance from the ocean mean the Chihuahuan Desert shrublands have comparatively frigid winters. The region experiences temperatures below freezing nearly one-third of the year, and winter lows regularly reach 20°F (−7°C). In summer, temperatures are normally around 95–104°F (35–40°C). The most vibrant time of year is July to September, when monsoons deposit 90% of the region's annual precipitation. Cooler daytime temperatures, rapid plant growth, and renewed animal activity make this the best time to visit the region.

As in many of the s. Nearctic desert shrublands, the dominant feature on the landscape is the omnipresent Creosote (*Larrea tridentata*). Covering huge swaths of land, this resinous, odoriferous shrub is incredibly efficient at securing water, often to the point of precluding the growth of nearby plants. Its ability to dominate the floristic landscape has earned it the common name *gobernadora*, or "governess," in Mexico. Other members of the moderately dense shrub layer of Chihuahuan Desert shrubland are Honey Mesquite (*Prosopis glandulosa*), Velvet Mesquite (*Prosopis velutina*), Whitethorn Acacia (*Vachellia constricta*), and American Tarbush (*Flourensia cernua*). In the foothills and upper elevational limits, this habitat can form dense brushy patches that are structurally like PACIFIC CHAPARRAL and are prone to fire. Despite the structural difference, the floral and faunal composition of Chihuahuan Desert shrubland remains nearly identical at all elevations.

Spiky forbs like Soaptree Yucca (*Yucca elata*), sotols (*Dasylirion* spp.), and Lechuguilla (*Agave lechuguilla*) are prominent in the landscape, especially when they bloom, producing flowering stalks as tall as 12 ft. (3.7 m). While cacti are not as large and prominent here as in the Sonoran Desert to the west, the Chihuahuan Desert shrublands are nevertheless home to over 25% of the world's cactus species. Botanists theorize that cacti originated in this region and radiated throughout the Americas from this epicenter of diversity. Plant endemism is generally high in this habitat, with 67 families, 263 genera, and 671 species found nowhere else.

Above: **An Antelope Jackrabbit's large ears help it to shed excess heat.**
© BEN KNOOT, TROPICAL BIRDING TOURS

Right: **The Chihuahuan is the most extensive desert in North America.**
© BEN KNOOT, TROPICAL BIRDING TOURS

The understory is frequently bare, covered with pebbly desert pavement. When the understory is grassy, it shares many species with the adjacent Chihuahuan Desert Grassland, including Black Grama (*Bouteloua eriopoda*), Blue Grama (*Bouteloua gracilis*), Bush Muhly (*Muhlenbergia porteri*), dropseeds (*Sporobolus* spp.), and three-awns (*Aristida* spp.).

WILDLIFE: As in many desert habitats, large mammals are scarce, and Pronghorn and Collared Peccary are the only two found regularly. The bulk of the mammalian fauna comprises small seed-eating mammals like Antelope Jackrabbit, Desert Cottontail, White-throated Woodrat, Yellow-nosed Cotton Rat, Southern Grasshopper Mouse, Ord's Kangaroo Rat, and Spotted Ground Squirrel. The primary mammalian predators of these rabbits and rodents are Gray Fox, Kit Fox, and Coyote.

The bird communities here have relatively low diversity that changes little throughout the year. Terrestrial birds like Gambel's Quail, Scaled Quail, Mourning Dove, and Greater Roadrunner are common. The shrubs often hold Pyrrhuloxia, Black-tailed Gnatcatcher, Black-throated Sparrow,

Verdin, Cactus Wren, and Curve-billed Thrasher (IS). The tall flowering stalks of Lechuguilla and other agaves are a great place to look for perching flycatchers and birds of prey. Swainson's and Red-tailed Hawks, American Kestrel, Loggerhead Shrike, Chihuahuan Raven (IS), Say's Phoebe, and Cassin's and Western Kingbirds all regularly hunt from these high perches. In the early morning, Lechuguilla stalks are also a preferred display perch for many songbirds. At dusk, Lesser Nighthawks are often seen cruising low over the desert, giving their odd bleating calls.

Reptiles are abundant in this habitat, especially small lizards. Greater Earless Lizard, Marbled Whiptail, Common Side-blotched Lizard, Texas Banded Gecko (IS), and various spiny lizards (*Sceloporus* spp.) are common. While the majority of reptiles endemic to this habitat are found in its southern reaches in Durango and Coahuila, Mexico, the diminutive Round-tailed Horned Lizard (IS) is present throughout the Chihuahuan Desert shrublands. Common snakes include Black-necked Garter Snake, Chihuahuan Hook-nosed Snake, Eastern Patch-nosed Snake, Desert Night Snake, Coachwhip, Trans-Pecos Rat Snake, Glossy Snake, and Western Diamondback Rattlesnake, among many others. On cool summer nights after rain, snakes drawn to warm pavement are readily encountered by anyone cruising along slowly and carefully searching the roads.

Many isolated springs in this habitat have rare endemic freshwater fish. A wide variety of pupfish, shiner, and splitfin species are extremely range-restricted, with each species' entire range limited to a single basin. Pupfishes in particular are well adapted to desert environments and can survive water temperatures reaching 108°F (42°C).

CONSERVATION: This is a resilient habitat with few threats to its conservation. In fact, overgrazing, fire suppression, and other human disturbances favor the spread of Creosote and mesquite. In many cases, Chihuahuan Desert shrubland has inundated and replaced CHIHUAHUAN DESERT GRASSLAND. A 2017 assessment found that 13,863 sq. mi. (35,905 km²), or 7%, of the ecoregion is in protected areas. While the habitat and the fauna within it are generally of low conservation concern, there are many rare cacti in this habitat, which is home to over 100 endangered species. Primary conservation concerns for cacti are overgrazing and overcollecting.

DISTRIBUTION: The Chihuahuan Desert shrubland is found over a broad area of the sw. United States and n. Mexico, covering an

Above: **The raucous calls of Cactus Wren are a familiar sound, frequently used in Western movies.**
© BEN KNOOT, TROPICAL BIRDING TOURS

Below: **Western Diamondback Rattlesnake is an ambush predator and will wait near areas where small mammals and birds congregate.**
© BEN KNOOT, TROPICAL BIRDING TOURS

expanse exceeding 54,000 sq. mi. (140,000 km²). Spanning approximately 900 mi. (1500 km) from north to south, the Chihuahuan Desert ecoregion stretches from just south of Albuquerque, New Mexico, to the Trans-Mexican Volcanic Belt, situated around 155 mi. (250 km) north of Mexico City. This habitat extends from c. Texas westward to se. Arizona and south over large portions of Chihuahua, Coahuila, and Durango to as far south as Zacatecas, Mexico. Chihuahuan Desert shrubland lies in the rain shadows of the Sierra Madre Occidental and the Sierra Madre Oriental and is largely bounded by these two ranges. Throughout its range, Chihuahuan Desert shrubland is dotted with CHIHUAHUAN DESERT GRASSLAND, ribbons of WESTERN RIPARIAN WOODLAND, and in the smaller mountain ranges, islands of MADREAN ENCINAL and MADREAN PINE-OAK WOODLAND. The northern extent of the Chihuahuan Desert shrubland is a wide transitional zone with SHORTGRASS PRAIRIE, where elements of both habitats may be present.

WHERE TO SEE: Big Bend National Park, Texas, US; Sevilleta National Wildlife Refuge, New Mexico, US.

The Vizcaíno–Baja California Desert is known for strange plants like the Boojum and Elephant-tree.

Ne2B SONORAN DESERT

The plants of the Sonoran Desert have root systems well adapted to utilizing the sparse and sporadic precipitation.

IN A NUTSHELL: A warm semi-desert shrubland characterized by giant columnar cacti and late-summer monsoon rains. **Global Habitat Affinities:** DRAGON'S BLOOD TREE SEMI-DESERT; GALÁPAGOS LOWLAND DESERT; ATACAMA DESOLATE DESERT (Peruvian Coastal Desert subhabitat). **Continental Habitat Affinities:** CHIHUAHUAN DESERT; MOJAVE DESERT; CENTRAL MEXICAN SUCCULENT MATORRAL. **Species Overlap:** CHIHUAHUAN DESERT; MOJAVE DESERT; DESOLATE DESERT; CENTRAL MEXICAN SUCCULENT MATORRAL; PACIFIC CHAPARRAL; CHIHUAHUAN DESERT GRASSLAND.

DESCRIPTION: The Sonoran Desert is the lushest and most iconic of Nearctic desert landscapes. This botanically diverse desert is home to some of the strangest flora on the continent, including the emblematic Saguaro (*Carnegiea gigantea*) and colossal Mexican Giant Cardón (*Pachycereus pringlei*) cacti and the otherworldly Boojum Tree (*Fouquieria columnaris*). The spectacular flora and fauna here are best seen in April–May or in the monsoon period of late summer, when animals are active and the landscape is green. This habitat is open enough that it is easily walked through, though spiny plants and midday heat should be avoided.

The Sonoran Desert is the hottest of the Nearctic desert regions, with mild winters and scorching summers, when temperatures approach 120°F (49°C), especially along the lower Colorado River. There is some relief from the summer heat when monsoon rains cool things off by roughly 10°F (5°C) in July and August. The monsoons drop about half of the region's annual rain in intense and unpredictable late-

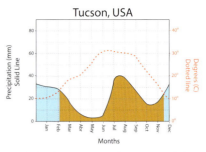

Tucson, USA

afternoon thunderstorms. The intense burst of plant growth following monsoons is accompanied by widespread herp movements and the second nesting of many bird species. This period is often called the "second spring" and is the best time for wildlife observation. The rest of the region's rain falls more consistently in December and January, for an annual total of 3–20 in. (75–500 mm).

The most notable botanical feature here is the array of giant cacti, which are often the tallest plants. Saguaro grows to heights of 50 ft. (15 m), and Organ Pipe Cactus (*Stenocereus thurberi*) reaches 20 ft. (6 m). These widely spaced cacti live for centuries and serve the same function as

trees for cavity-nesting birds. Along with these giants, there is a large variety of common, smaller succulents, including agaves (*Agave* spp.), yuccas (*Yucca* spp.), barrel cacti (*Echinocactus* spp.), pricklypears (*Opuntia* spp.), and chollas (*Cylindropuntia* spp.). Apart from succulents, the other common plants are thorny shrubs and small trees, which are the dominant vegetation by area if not by mass. The most prominent of these shrubs is Creosote

Above: **Endemic to the Sonoran Desert, Saguaro is one of the most iconic plants in North America.**
© BEN KNOOT, TROPICAL BIRDING TOURS

Right: **Boojum Tree (center) and Elephant-tree (right) are distinctive features of the Baja California sections of the Sonoran Desert.** © PHIL CHAON

(*Larrea tridentata*), the most common plant in this and many other Nearctic desert shrublands. Paloverdes (*Parkinsonia* spp.), mesquites (*Prosopis* spp.), Catclaw Acacia (*Senegalia greggii*), Ocotillo (*Fouquieria splendens*), and Desert Ironwood (*Olneya tesota*) are also abundant. In areas with higher amounts of available water, mesquites can form impenetrable thickets. In the foothills and upper elevational limits, this habitat can form dense brushy patches that are structurally like PACIFIC CHAPARRAL and are prone to fire. Despite the structural difference, floral and faunal composition remains nearly identical at all elevations.

The **Ne2B-1 Vizcaíno–Baja California Desert** subhabitat of the Sonoran Desert habitat covers most of the Baja Peninsula and is notably different in appearance from the habitat elsewhere. Coastal areas are dominated by the massive Mexican Giant Cardón. This is the largest cactus on the planet, reaching 60 ft. (18 m) in height. Other prominent features on the landscape include numerous Boojum Trees and small stands of squat, gnarled Elephant-tree (*Bursera microphylla*) and other *Bursera* species. This subhabitat is found in the driest sections of the Sonoran Desert and typically lacks many of the low thorny shrubs found in the n. Sonoran Desert. However, this subhabitat has the most diverse array of small succulent plants and cacti in North America and is arguably the most spectacular and alien desert landscape on the continent.

Near springs and areas of abundant water in the lower Colorado River and Baja sectors, palm oases occur. These tall, isolated forests have a canopy strongly to completely dominated by California Fan Palm (*Washingtonia filifera*), with an understory of Alkali Sacaton (*Sporobolus airoides*) and three-awns (*Aristida* spp.).

WILDLIFE: The Sonoran Desert is the lushest and most diverse of the Nearctic desert habitats; however, like many desert environments, it is relatively poor in big mammals. Collared Peccary (aka Javelina) is the most common large mammal and can often be found feeding on pricklypear fruits in season. Desert Bighorn Sheep, Coyote, Bobcat, and Puma (Mountain Lion) are among the other large mammals. The Vizcaíno–Baja California subhabitat of the Sonoran Desert is home to a critically endangered subspecies of Pronghorn. Medium-size and small mammals are more abundant than large ones throughout the desert. Driving through at night, one is likely to see Antelope Jackrabbit, Desert Cottontail, several species of kangaroo rats, and occasionally Kit Fox. During the summer months, especially around monsoons, swarms of nectivorous Lesser Long-nosed and Mexican Long-tongued Bats move through the area. While taking advantage of the sugary feast provided by blooming cacti, they often visit hummingbird feeders as well and in the late summer will drain them dry overnight.

Common Sonoran Desert birds include Gambel's Quail, White-winged Dove, Harris's Hawk, Greater Roadrunner, Black Vulture, Turkey Vulture, Pyrrhuloxia, Curve-billed Thrasher, Cactus Wren, Verdin, Black-tailed Gnatcatcher, Black-throated Sparrow, and Abert's Towhee. Gila Woodpecker and the

While largely terrestrial, Greater Roadrunner does occasionally fly.
© BEN KNOOT, TROPICAL BIRDING TOURS

Gilded Flicker creates cavities in Saguaros that are used by many other animals.
© BEN KNOOT, TROPICAL BIRDING TOURS

endemic Gilded Flicker (IS) act as ecosystem engineers by constructing nesting cavities in the trunks of large cacti. These cavities allow birds that normally require trees for nesting to live in this environment; beneficiaries include Elf Owl, Ferruginous Pygmy-Owl, Purple Martin, and Brown-crested Flycatcher. In late summer, flowering Ocotillo and agave are visited by many birds, including Costa's Hummingbird, Broad-billed Hummingbird, Black-chinned Hummingbird, Hooded Oriole, and Scott's Oriole. Hooded Orioles are especially fond of palm oases. Gray Thrasher (IS), Xantus's Hummingbird (IS), and the Vizcaíno subspecies of LeConte's Thrasher (IS) are all endemic to the Vizcaíno–Baja California Desert subhabitat.

The herpetofauna of the Sonoran Desert landscape is highly diverse and is dominated by snakes and lizards. Whiptails (*Aspidoscelis* spp.), spiny lizards (*Sceloporus*), Regal Horned Lizard, Coast Horned Lizard, and Zebra-tailed Lizard are all commonly encountered during the day. The large Common Chuckwalla is often seen basking in the early morning but disappears into rocky crevices in the day's heat. Gila Monster, a slow-moving, rotund, black and orange or pink lizard, is the habitat's most famous reptilian resident and one of only two venomous lizards in North America. Several species of spiny-tailed iguanas (*Ctenosaura* spp.) are found on the s. Baja Peninsula and coastal Sonora. The Flat-tailed Horned Lizard is endemic to especially low-lying hot regions along the Colorado River. There are more than 10 species of rattlesnakes, including Western Diamondback, Mojave, Speckled, Baja California, and Tiger Rattlesnakes. Most of the

other snakes here are rarely seen, being small, fossorial, and/or nocturnal. Amphibians are almost absent, though large numbers of Sonoran Desert Toads and Couch's Spadefoots emerge to breed after summer monsoons.

The small islands found around the Baja Peninsula have many endemic herp species and a few true oddities. San Esteban Chuckwallas are a classic example of island gigantism. Weighing up to 3 lb. (1.4 kg), these chunky lizards are three to four times the size of their mainland counterparts! On its namesake island, the Santa Catalina Island Rattlesnake is an endemic species that has lost its rattle. With a lack of predators and large herbivores, there was nothing to warn with a rattle, and the vestigial segment of rattle is lost with each shedding of the snake's skin. This is also one of the only semi-arboreal rattlesnakes, having evolved to eat birds in response to the scarcity of mammals on the island.

The Gila Monster is one of two species of venomous lizards in North America. © BEN KNOOT, TROPICAL BIRDING TOURS

CONSERVATION: The main threat to the n. Sonoran Desert has been an explosion in the human population. One of the fastest growing areas of the United States, the Sonoran Desert is under new pressures from major population centers like Phoenix and Tucson, Arizona, and Hermosillo and Mexicali, Mexico. These fragile and resource-limited habitats have experienced increased fragmentation, agricultural development, and water extraction. Managing demand for water is of exceptional importance for conservation in the region.

The Vizcaíno–Baja California Desert subhabitat is incredibly sparsely populated, and nearly 60%—a huge portion—of the habitat is protected. The largest tract of protected land is El Vizcaíno Biosphere Reserve, which covers 10,000 sq. mi (24,500 km²). However, the area has a large number of fragile, endemic plants, and overgrazing and depletion of groundwater are still major concerns. The Mexican Giant Cardón and many of the other largest cacti grow in areas found within the coastal fog belt. Climate change may result in the disappearance of the fog belt, and with it, these massive cacti.

Most of the region's endangered animals are found in Baja California, particularly on outlying islands. Peninsular Pronghorn, Santa Catalina Island Rattlesnake, Slevin's Mouse, and San José Brush Rabbit are all critically endangered, as is a subspecies of Elf Owl. Most of the island endemics are threatened by invasive species like feral cats, feral goats, and Black Rats. Some of the islands have implemented extensive eradication programs for these invasive species, but most have not.

DISTRIBUTION: The Sonoran Desert is found at low elevations, below 3600 ft. (1100 m), from sw. Arizona and se. California in the United States to ne. and c. Baja California and w. Sonora, Mexico. The northern extent of this habitat is limited by the Rocky Mountains and PINYON-JUNIPER WOODLAND. The western limit is formed by the San Gabriel Mountains and the Peninsular Ranges. Most of the eastern boundary is formed by the Sierra Madre Occidental, where the habitat transitions to MADREAN ENCINAL and MADREAN PINE-OAK WOODLAND. South of Sonora, the habitat transitions to MESOAMERICAN PACIFIC DRY DECIDUOUS FOREST.

The Vizcaíno–Baja California Desert subhabitat extends from s. and c. Baja California northeast along the Gulf of California to the Colorado River valley and south along the west coast of Sonora as far as Guaymas. It is also the major habitat type on most of the large islands found around the Baja peninsula. In the northeast corner of the peninsula, this habitat is replaced by PACIFIC CHAPARRAL.

WHERE TO SEE: Saguaro National Park, Arizona, US; Anza-Borrego Desert State Park, California, US; El Vizcaíno Biosphere Reserve, Baja California, Mexico.

Ne2C MOJAVE DESERT

IN A NUTSHELL: A small and very arid transitional desert with cold winters found at high elevations between the Sonoran Desert and the Great Basin. **Global Habitat Affinities:** CAUCASIAN SHRUB DESERT; AFROTROPICAL HOT SHRUB DESERT. **Continental Habitat Affinities:** SONORAN DESERT; SAGEBRUSH SHRUBLAND (Great Basin Shrubland). **Species Overlap:** SONORAN DESERT; NEARCTIC DESOLATE DESERT; PINYON-JUNIPER WOODLAND; SAGEBRUSH SHRUBLAND (Great Basin Shrubland).

DESCRIPTION: The Mojave Desert is a limited habitat found in the transitional zone between the Sonoran Desert and the Great Basin. It is often considered a high desert—the majority of this habitat is found between 2000 and 6000 ft. (600–1800 m) elevation—though it also encompasses Death Valley, the lowest elevation on the planet (−282 ft./−86 m). The Mojave is also the driest of the deserts, receiving only 2–6 in. (50–150 mm) of precipitation, mostly in the form of winter rain and snow. It experiences an extreme range of temperatures, with summer highs upward of 110°F (43°C) and winter lows as cold as 10°F (−12°C). Winter and spring in this area are famously windy, with strong dusty gales persisting much of the time.

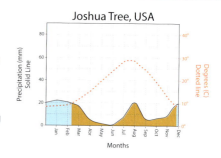

Joshua Tree, USA

The Mojave Desert is almost entirely devoid of trees. The most iconic and prominent plants on the landscape are Western and Eastern Joshua Trees (*Yucca brevifolia* and *Yucca jaegeriana*,

Joshua trees are found in the higher elevations of the Mojave Desert. © BEN KNOOT, TROPICAL BIRDING TOURS

Lower elevations in the Mojave Desert have a wide array of cacti and shrubs. © BEN KNOOT, TROPICAL BIRDING TOURS

respectively), which are not typical woody trees but tall branching yuccas. Joshua trees can reach heights of 50 ft. (15 m) and are immediately recognizable. Commonly seen in movies and on television, Joshua trees are a sure indicator that the scene was filmed in the Mojave Desert.

Aside from Joshua trees, the Mojave Desert has a low and sparse shrub layer that is open enough to move through easily. At lower elevations, this layer is dominated by Creosote (*Larrea tridentata*) and White Bursage (*Ambrosia dumosa*) along with Hop-sage (*Grayia spinosa*), Winterfat (*Krascheninnikovia lanata*), and saltbushes (*Atriplex* spp.). Most of these species will continue into higher elevations where Cheesebush (*Hymenoclea salsola*), rabbitbrushes (*Ericameria* spp.), Mormon-teas (*Ephedra* spp.), and especially Blackbrush (*Coleogyne ramosissima*) are co-dominant or dominant. The cacti in this desert do not have the diversity of form and species seen in warmer deserts, but Teddy-bear Cholla (*Cylindropuntia bigelovii*) and pricklypears (*Opuntia* spp.) are common near rocky outcroppings. In the foothills and upper elevational limits, this habitat can form dense brushy patches that are structurally like PACIFIC CHAPARRAL and are prone to fire. Despite the structural difference, floral and faunal composition remains nearly identical at all elevations of this desert habitat.

The Mojave Desert has the most climatic variability of the North American deserts, with long periods of extreme drought interspersed with rare wet years when precipitation can be up to five times that of a typical year. These wet years create intense pulses of vegetation and corresponding booms in wildlife populations. The explosive years are highly asynchronous and cannot be described as cyclical in any meaningful way. Wet years stimulate spectacular "superblooms" of flowering plants that can coat entire valleys in an ever-shifting patchwork of yellow, purple, orange, and white. These blooms are typically dominated by species such as Brittlebush (*Encelia farinosa*), California Poppy (*Eschscholzia californica*), Desertbell (*Phacelia campanularia*), Desert Sunflower (*Geraea canescens*), Popcorn Flower (*Plagiobothrys nothofulvus*), and Desert Lily (*Hesperocallis undulata*). Many other rare and endemic annuals can also be found during these events.

WILDLIFE: The Mojave has a relatively high diversity of mammals when compared to similar environments worldwide. One can find a diverse array of small mammals; among them are White-tailed Antelope Squirrel, Black-tailed Jackrabbit, Desert Cottontail, and several species of kangaroo rats, pocket mice, and pocket gophers. The Mojave Ground Squirrel (IS) is one of the only true endemics. Desert Bighorn Sheep is the only large ungulate found here, though Mule Deer and Pronghorn are occasionally present. The predators in the region are mostly smaller meso-carnivores like Western Spotted Skunk, Kit Fox, Coyote, and American Badger.

Desert Bighorn Sheep is one of the few large mammals found in the Mojave Desert.
© BEN KNOOT, TROPICAL BIRDING TOURS

Verdin is the only member of the penduline-tit family in the Western Hemisphere. © PHIL CHAON

The birdlife here lacks any true endemics and has characteristic species from surrounding arid habitats. Common species in the Mojave include Gambel's Quail, Mourning Dove, Costa's Hummingbird, Greater Roadrunner, Ladder-backed Woodpecker, Say's Phoebe, Loggerhead Shrike, Common Raven, Horned Lark, Verdin, Rock Wren, Cactus Wren, and Black-throated Sparrow. Great Horned Owl and other large raptors will nest in Joshua trees and use them as hunting perches. LeConte's Thrasher is one of the few Mojave specialists, and the vast majority of individuals occur here. These birds hide amazingly well in the stunted shrubs and are often glimpsed only when running short distances between clumps of brush.

The reptile assemblage is the most distinctive of the Mojave Desert vertebrate communities. There are few amphibians here, and Red-spotted Toad is the only common species in this habitat. Snakes regularly found include Desert Rosy Boa, Mojave Glossy Snake (IS), Mojave Shovel-nosed Snake (IS), Coachwhip, Spotted Leaf-nosed Snake, Long-nosed Snake, Speckled Rattlesnake, Panamint Rattlesnake (IS), Sidewinder, and Mojave Rattlesnake. Long-nosed Leopard Lizard, Desert Iguana, Common Chuckwalla, Desert Horned Lizard, and Common Side-blotched Lizard are all regularly encountered. The Desert Night Lizard (IS) is an abundant but cryptic resident that is commonly associated with Joshua trees and other yuccas. The endangered Desert Tortoise is iconic of the region. Protections afforded this species have had an umbrella effect, restricting development to the benefit of many other species.

CONSERVATION: The Mojave Desert is more threatened by development than other North American desert habitats. While human population within the desert remains relatively low, most of the desert is sandwiched between the major urban centers of Los Angeles and

Desert Tortoise has a large bladder that can store nearly 40% of the tortoise's weight, a useful adaptation for long periods without rainfall.
© BEN KNOOT, TROPICAL BIRDING TOURS

Las Vegas. The land is often seen as being of little value and is frequently used for off-road vehicle recreation, large military installations, extensive solar- and wind-energy centers, and landfill sites. The land has also seen heavy mining activity over the past century. Most pressingly, water is at a premium out here, and cities and croplands always get the first sip. Waterways are more and more frequently dry, riparian zones and small wetlands are disappearing, and basin lakes and playas like the Owens Valley are mostly dust. A 2020 study resurveyed Mojave sites for birds, a century after they were originally surveyed, and found that sites averaged a 43% reduction in species present. Most of these losses were posited to be connected to declines in surface water.

In spite of these challenges, large areas of the desert are still intact, and there are several large protected areas in the region. The 1994 California Desert Protection Act designated 69 wilderness areas and established Death Valley National Park, Joshua Tree National Park, and Mojave National Preserve. The 2013 Desert Renewable Energy Conservation Plan (DRECP) protected another huge chunk of land, with the Bureau of Land Management designating 4.2 million acres (1.7 million ha) as protected wilderness. Despite these strides, protecting the habitat can have only so much effect in the face of a changing climate and dwindling water.

DISTRIBUTION: The Mojave Desert is the smallest of the North American deserts, encompassing an area of approximately 50,000 sq. mi. (130,000 km²). It is distributed across the interior of s. California, s. Nevada, sw. Utah, and nw. Arizona, largely at elevations between 2000 and 6000 ft. (700–1800 m). The habitat is bounded by the SONORAN DESERT to the south and SAGEBRUSH SHRUBLAND of the Great Basin to the north. At higher elevations to the east and west, this habitat often transitions to PINYON-JUNIPER WOODLAND, while DESOLATE DESERT and PLAYAS are often found in low basins in the area.

WHERE TO SEE: Joshua Tree National Park, California, US; Mojave National Reserve, California, US.

Ne2D NEARCTIC DESOLATE DESERT

IN A NUTSHELL: A desert environment completely or mostly lacking in vegetation and dominated by sand flats, dunes, scree, and desert pavement. **Global Habitat Affinities:** NAMIB ROCK DESERT; NAMIB SAND DESERT; SAHARAN ERG DESERT; ATACAMA DESOLATE DESERT. **Continental Habitat Affinities:** SONORAN DESERT; CHIHUAHUAN DESERT; MOJAVE DESERT; ROCKY CANYON. **Species Overlap:** SONORAN DESERT; CHIHUAHUAN DESERT; MOJAVE DESERT; ROCKY CANYON.

DESCRIPTION: Nearctic Desolate Desert is a broad assemblage of landforms scattered throughout the desert habitats of North America. These areas are united by a lack of permanent vegetation and a corresponding dearth of wildlife. Desolate Desert includes areas of bare plateau, stabilized dune systems, ergs (moving sand dunes that support little vegetation), desert pavements or regs, and clay or salt pans. Desolate Desert habitat occurs in a wide variety of arid

The Imperial Dunes of California are the second-largest expanse of Desolate Desert in North America. © BEN KNOOT, TROPICAL BIRDING TOURS

environments, and temperatures can range from 125°F (52°C) in the Mojave and lower Sonoran Deserts to 5°F (−15°C) in n. Nevada.

This habitat typically has woody shrub cover on less than 2% of the surface. The few tiny shrubs growing here are usually Creosote (*Larrea tridentata*) or saltbushes (*Atriplex* spp.). Desert pavements, pans, and scree slopes will occasionally experience large blooms of herbaceous plants following rare rain events. Common plants in these blooms include Devil's Spineflower (*Chorizanthe rigida*), Desert Trumpet (*Eriogonum inflatum*), and Desert Sunflower (*Geraea canescens*). Ergs, dune fields, and sand flats can develop sparse vegetation if properly protected from wind and stabilized. Most of the plants here are stoloniferous grasses (especially *Swallenia* spp.) that grow clonally from runners under the sand before sprouting. Other herbaceous plants found on dunes include Desert Sand Verbena (*Abronia villosa*), Basket Evening Primrose (*Oenothera deltoides*), and crotons (*Croton* spp.). An odd fuzzy tuber dotted in purple flowers can be found in the dunes as well. Called Sandfood (*Pholisma sonorae*), it is a parasite that takes nutrients (but not water) from various sparse desert shrubs. The plant was an important food source for Indigenous peoples during difficult desert crossings.

Vegetation does not usually grow in these environments for several reasons. A few of them are too dry, with extremely low rainfall and extremely high temperatures. This is especially true in parts of the Mojave Desert and the Vizcaíno peninsula off the west-central coast of Baja California, where annual rainfall is often less than 4 in. (100 mm). Many of the low valley pans are too saline or too alkaline for plant growth. In ergs and dune fields, the substrate is too unstable and constantly shifting for plants to become established.

The most common form of Nearctic Desolate Desert is reg or desert pavement. Reg is formed when fine soils erode between small pebbles. Over time, wind and occasionally water will winnow down these small rocks and create pavements of interlocking stones. As regs age further, they develop "desert varnish," a shiny, thin patina of clays, iron, and manganese baked onto the surface.

LeConte's Thrashers are well camouflaged in the pale sands of the Desolate Desert. © PHIL CHAON

WILDLIFE: Nearctic Desolate Desert is virtually devoid of vertebrate life. Unlike desolate deserts found in South America, Africa, and the Palearctic, these deserts in North America are a minor habitat with lots of variation and a widely disjunct distribution. As a result, noticeably few species have evolved the special traits needed to survive here.

The only mammalian residents in this habitat are a smattering of antelope squirrel, kangaroo rat, and pocket mice species. Even these are generally marginal. Desert pavement environments are extremely durable and preclude the presence of small burrowing rodents. Other mammals will occasionally visit these desert areas after rain events and the large blooms that follow. Desert Bighorn Sheep are seen on scree slopes in desert foothills.

Birds are equally sparse, though a few species scavenge or hunt insects in Desolate Desert. Common Ravens will visit, and LeConte's Thrashers frequently hunt on open flats, sprinting across the dunes at lightning pace.

The primary residents are reptiles, especially lizards, with the fringe-toed lizard (IS) group representing one of the habitat's most diverse species radiations. Specializing in sandy areas, the Colorado Desert, Coachella Valley, Mohawk Dunes, and Yuma Desert Fringe-toed Lizards are found in the Sonoran Desert; Mojave Fringe-toed Lizard in the Mojave Desert; and Chihuahuan Fringe-toed Lizard and Fringe-toed Sand Lizard in the Chihuahuan Desert. These lizards spend much of their time buried in the sand. Elongated scales on the hind foot create the eponymous "fringe-toe" that allows the lizards to sprint quickly over the sand's surface without sinking. Other reptiles regularly encountered in this habitat include Zebra-tailed Lizard, Flat-tailed Horned Lizard,

Common Side-blotched Lizard, Western Shovel-nosed Snake, Mojave Glossy Snake, Western Ground Snake, and Sidewinder. Bleached Earless Lizard and Little White Whiptail are endemic to the gypsum dunes of White Sands National Park, New Mexico.

CONSERVATION: Desolate Desert habitat is largely devoid of both plants and animals and is generally of low conservation concern. Due to the hostility of the environment, there is also little to no pressure from development or invasive species. The exception is within the Colorado Desert section of the Sonoran Desert, where development and recreation (particularly off-road vehicle use) threaten dune-loving species like Coachella Valley Fringe-toed Lizard.

DISTRIBUTION: Desolate Desert is found in isolated pockets throughout the major desert environments of North America. There are especially large expanses of this habitat in the Black Rock Desert of Nevada, in other low, alkaline valleys in the Great Basin, and in low-lying areas of the Mojave. Large areas of the lower Colorado River valley and the Vizcaíno peninsula (wc. Baja California), along with the Gran Desierto de Altar in Sonora and Imperial and Algodones Dunes in California are predominantly Desolate Desert.

The erg formations in the Desolate Desert are perhaps the only feature in the habitat that is also found on Saturn's moon Titan.

WHERE TO SEE: Gran Desierto de Altar, Sonora, Mexico; Vizcaíno Biosphere Reserve, Baja California Sur, Mexico; White Sands National Park, New Mexico, US; Black Rock Desert, Nevada, US.

Coachella Valley Fringe-toed Lizard has specialized scales on its hind toes that allow it to move quickly across soft, sandy dunes. © ZACHARY A CAVA

Ne2E SAGEBRUSH SHRUBLAND

IN A NUTSHELL: An arid steppe or short-statured shrubland dominated by sagebrush. **Global Habitat Affinities:** TEMPERATE DESERT STEPPE; CASPIAN WORMWOOD DESERT; CHENOPOD SHRUBLAND. **Continental Habitat Affinities:** MOJAVE DESERT. **Species Overlap:** PINYON-JUNIPER WOODLAND; PONDEROSA PINE FOREST; SHORTGRASS PRAIRIE; MOJAVE DESERT.

DESCRIPTION: An arid to semiarid mosaic of shrubs and grasses, this habitat occurs in the flat basins and plateaus of the intermountain region of w. North America. Mostly present in cold semi-deserts, sagebrush country experiences hot, dry summers with persistent wind and bitterly cold winters. The majority of the scant (10 in./250 mm) annual precipitation falls as snow during the boreal winter. Growth of grasses and forbs is dependent on spring snowmelt. Based on elevation and seasonal timing of precipitation, the structure of Sagebrush Shrubland and its subhabitats varies between steppe dominated by grasses and dense shrublands.

Ne2E-1 Interior Sagebrush Shrubland communities are typically dominated by a single sagebrush species, often Big Sagebrush (*Artemisia tridentata*). Rubber Rabbitbrush (*Ericameria nauseosa*), Antelope Bitterbrush (*Purshia tridentata*), and Winterfat (*Krascheninnikovia*

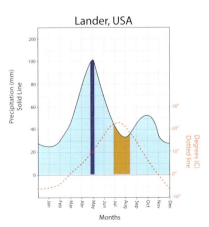

Lander, USA

lanata) are also commonly present but never dominant. This Sagebrush Shrubland subhabitat is typically grassier than the Great Basin Shrubland (see the following paragraph), with large clearings blanketed in Thick-stem Wheatgrass (*Elymus lanceolatus*), Blue Grama (*Bouteloua gracilis*), and Idaho Fescue (*Festuca idahoensis*). The understory also supports a diverse array of forbs that are important forage for herbivores incapable of digesting sagebrush. The associated faunal assemblage depends more on habitat structure than on the species of sagebrush present. While this is typically a short and stunted shrub community (3 ft./1 m in height), Big Sagebrush is historically capable of reaching heights over 10 ft. (3 m), particularly in the eastern part of its range.

In the more arid **Ne2E-2 Great Basin Shrubland**, the prevalence of perennial grasses is greatly diminished, and the density of shrub species decreases as well. Big Sagebrush is still a major feature on the landscape, but other woody shrubs play an important role as well. Shadscale Saltbush (*Atriplex confertifolia*), Yellow Rabbitbrush (*Chrysothamnus viscidiflorus*), Blackbrush (*Coleogyne ramosissima*), and greasewoods (*Sarcobatus* spp.) can all be co-dominant. In these areas, cryptobiotic crust composed of blue-green algae, fungi, mosses, and lichens is an important part of the biological community; it stabilizes barren soil, retains moisture, and aids in seed establishment.

Fire is an important driver in the mosaic structure of Sagebrush Shrubland, and healthy sagebrush communities have small, infrequent, stand-replacing fires resulting in a patchwork of plant ages and density. Human activities including grazing, fire suppression, and introduction of non-native grasses have changed this regime, resulting in larger, more frequent, and higher-intensity fires.

Sagebrush Shrubland commonly occurs in low-lying valleys in the Rocky Mountains.
© BEN KNOOT, TROPICAL BIRDING TOURS

Pronghorns evolved to outrun the now extinct North American Cheetah and are capable of reaching speeds of 60 mi. (100 km) per hour. © BEN KNOOT, TROPICAL BIRDING TOURS

WILDLIFE: Sagebrush Shrubland is home to an abundance of native mammals, including several endemic species. Pronghorn is widespread and common in the region. Along with the endangered Pygmy Rabbit (IS), Pronghorn is among the few species capable of digesting sagebrush. Great Basin Pocket Mouse and Sagebrush Vole are less conspicuous but widespread sagebrush obligates. The habitat is important as a winter grazing area for Mule Deer and holds the continent's largest wintering herds of Elk, which spend summers at higher elevations. Other widespread mammals include White-tailed Deer, Black-tailed Jackrabbit, Desert and Mountain Cottontails, White-tailed Prairie Dog, Coyote, Bobcat, and American Badger. Widely extirpated, large predators like Brown Bear and Gray Wolf frequently feed and forage in this habitat, though they are not resident.

Sagebrush Shrubland has relatively limited bird diversity and few species that are resident through the harsh winters. Greater (IS) and Gunnison (IS) Sage-Grouse are iconic residents, present year-round and able to eat sagebrush. Denser stands of sagebrush support most of the true sagebrush specialists, including Sagebrush Sparrow (IS), Brewer's Sparrow, and Sage Thrasher (IS), as well as Blue-gray Gnatcatcher, Black-throated Sparrow, Gray Flycatcher, and Green-tailed Towhee. More open areas of sagebrush support a mixture of more widespread grassland and shrubland species, including Sharp-tailed Grouse, Long-billed Curlew, Mourning Dove, Swainson's Hawk, Burrowing Owl, Common Nighthawk, Loggerhead Shrike, American Kestrel, Western Meadowlark, Say's Phoebe, Western Kingbird, and Vesper Sparrow. In winter, the abundant

Male Greater Sage-Grouse performs their annual displays in March and April.
© BEN KNOOT, TROPICAL BIRDING TOURS

small-mammal populations provide food for large numbers of raptors, including Red-tailed Hawk, Ferruginous Hawk, Golden Eagle, Northern Harrier, Prairie Falcon, and Short-eared Owl.

Sagebrush Lizard, Greater Short-horned Lizard, Prairie Rattlesnake, and Gopher Snake are all common and conspicuous residents throughout the habitat.

CONSERVATION: Historically, there has been little value placed on the conservation of Sagebrush Shrubland habitat. Sagebrush was often burned or plowed to clear land for grazing. The area has been heavily invaded by Cheatgrass (*Bromus tectorum*), and conversion to agriculture is becoming more common with modern irrigation techniques. In areas where fire has been suppressed, there is considerable encroachment of conifers and a lack of variation in age and structure of sagebrush. The area is also a hotbed for oil and gas development, with associated infrastructure leading to severe fragmentation.

Greater Sage-Grouse and Gunnison Sage-Grouse are the two most emblematic species of this habitat. Unfortunately, both have declined massively over the past 50 years. Greater Sage-Grouse is vulnerable but unprotected, while Gunnison Sage-Grouse is endangered, and its numbers have continued to decline sharply, from an estimated 4000 in 2014 to 1800 in 2019. Sage-grouse are easily impacted by land-use changes and development, and most of their remaining habitat is on private lands. The Sage Grouse Initiative (a conservation easement program developed by the US Department of Agriculture) has partnered with 2600 ranchers across 11 states since 2010, conserving 9 million acres (3.6 million ha) of sage grouse habitat.

DISTRIBUTION: The entire Sagebrush Shrubland region covers approximately 155.5 million acres (63 million ha) of the interior w. United States. Almost entirely contained within the rain shadows of the Sierra Nevada, Cascade Range, and Rocky Mountains, Sagebrush Shrubland is prevalent in much of the Great Basin and the Wyoming Basin, and reaches into the Snake River plain, Columbia Basin, sw. Montana, Colorado Plateau, sw. Colorado, and n. New Mexico, with incursions into sw. Canada and nw. Mexico. The northern part of this habitat is Interior Sagebrush Shrubland, where shrubs and perennial grasses are co-dominant. This subhabitat is often intermixed with SHORTGRASS PRAIRIE and PONDEROSA PINE FOREST. From the Great Basin southward, in the much drier Great Basin Sagebrush vegetation type, the habitat blends with MOJAVE DESERT, DESOLATE DESERT, and PINYON-JUNIPER WOODLAND. The entire Sagebrush Shrubland region is dotted with small mountain ranges, and it experiences influence from coniferous forests throughout its range. Along the eastern slopes of the Sierra Nevada in ne. California and Nevada and the Cascades in c. Oregon, the habitat most commonly transitions to PINYON-JUNIPER WOODLAND or MOJAVE DESERT.

WHERE TO SEE: Yellowstone and Grand Teton National Parks, Wyoming, US; Arapaho National Wildlife Refuge, Colorado, US; Malheur National Wildlife Refuge, Oregon, US.

Black-billed Magpie and American Bison are both found in the Sagebrush Shrublands of Yellowstone National Park. © BEN KNOOT, TROPICAL BIRDING TOURS

Ne2F TAMAULIPAN MEZQUITAL

IN A NUTSHELL: A low, scrubby habitat made up of thorny bushes with small leaves, small spiny trees, and abundant cacti. **Global Habitat Affinities:** WEST ASIAN THORNSCRUB; INTERANDEAN THORNSCRUB; TUMBESIAN THORNSCRUB; AFRICAN NORTHERN DRY THORN SAVANNA; KALAHARI DRY THORN SAVANNA. **Continental Habitat Affinities:** EASTERN MESQUITE; CARIBBEAN THORNSCRUB. **Species Overlap:** CARIBBEAN THORNSCRUB; EASTERN MESQUITE; PACIFIC DRY DECIDUOUS FOREST; WESTERN RIPARIAN WOODLAND (Lower Rio Grande and Tamaulipan Riparian Woodland); CHIHUAHUAN DESERT.

DESCRIPTION: Tamaulipan Mezquital is a semiarid, subtropical shrubland dominated by mesquite groves, small thorny trees, and dense brush. This habitat can vary widely in structure. Typically, it is characterized by a short and relatively open canopy and a dense, brushy thicket in the midstory and understory, often with many vines. In drier areas with more frequent fire and less heavy grazing, the habitat can also appear quite open and grassy. Tamaulipan Mezquital is a dynamic habitat that is subjected to frequent droughts, tropical storms, and fire. As a result, a single area can vary dramatically in appearance from year to year.

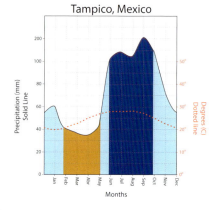

Tampico, Mexico

Also known as mesquite shrubland, thornscrub, or *pastizal*, this habitat has a mesquite-dominated canopy that reaches heights up to 20 ft. (6 m). Mesquites (*Prosopis* spp.) are joined by Round-flowered Catclaw (*Senegalia roemeriana*), Guajillo (*Senegalia berlandieri*), Huisache (*Vachellia farnesiana*), Texas Ebony (*Ebenopsis ebano*), torchwoods (*Amyris* spp.), Sugar Hackberry (*Celtis laevigata*), and Desert Hackberry or Granjeno (*Celtis ehrenbergiana*). This is the most diverse of the arid shrublands, and the shrub layer can contain dozens of species. In more pristine areas, the understory is composed of species such as Texas Sage (*Leucophyllum frutescens*), Blackbrush (*Coleogyne ramosissima*), amargosas (*Castela* spp.), Lindheimer Pricklypear (*Opuntia lindheimeri*), Berlandier Wolfberry (*Lycium berlandieri*), Coyotillo (*Karwinskia humboldtiana*), Lotebush (*Ziziphus obtusifolia*), and Texas Persimmon (*Diospyros texana*), among others. This botanically rich shrub layer increases in both density and diversity with increasing rainfall from west to east. Degraded areas are heavily dominated by Honey Mesquite (*Prosopis glandulosa*) and pricklypears (*Opuntia* spp.).

In more open areas, the understory is grassy and was historically dominated by Curly Mesquite Grass (*Hilaria belangeri*), Hooded Finger Grass (*Trichloris pluriflora*), and various grama grasses (*Bouteloua* spp.). Open, grassy mezquital has become rare with the alteration of fire and grazing

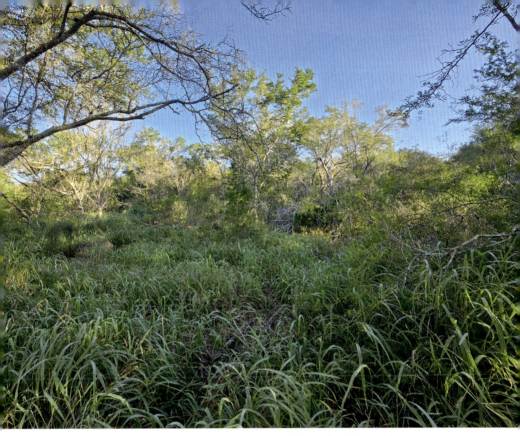

Invasive grasses have drastically changed the understory of the Tamaulipan Mezquital in s. Texas. © PHIL CHAON

regimes. In areas like the King Ranch of s. Texas, intensive and conscientious management has preserved some prime examples of mezquital grasslands that are preferred by many game species of birds and mammals.

Lower Rio Grande and Tamaulipan Riparian Woodland is a subhabitat closely allied with Tamaulipan Mezquital in terms of both floral and faunal species assemblages. However, as it is distinctly not arid shrubland, we chose to cover this subhabitat within the WESTERN RIPARIAN WOODLAND habitat account.

WILDLIFE: There are few endemic mammals in this habitat, though widespread species like White-nosed Coati, Bobcat, Collared Peccary, Nine-banded Armadillo, and White-tailed Deer all occur commonly. Small rodents are also common. Within the United States, Tamaulipan Mezquital habitat is critical to the survival of the Ocelot. Margay and Jaguar are found in this habitat in ne. Mexico but are extremely rare.

Bird communities vary slightly over the range of this habitat but tend to include skulking species that favor dense undergrowth. Thicket Tinamou, Northern Bobwhite, White-tipped Dove, Ferruginous Pygmy-Owl, Brown-crested Flycatcher, Couch's Kingbird, Golden-crowned Warbler, Scrub Euphonia (IS), Audubon's Oriole, Northern Cardinal, and Painted Bunting are typical birds. Long-billed Thrasher (IS), Tamaulipas Crow (IS), and Crimson-collared Grosbeak (IS) are endemic to this habitat. In the lower Rio Grande valley, the northern reaches of this habitat provide refuge for a variety of typically tropical birds. These impenetrable thickets are essentially the only habitat

home within the United States to Buff-bellied Hummingbird, Olive Sparrow, Green Jay, Plain Chachalaca, Altamira Oriole, Common Pauraque, and many other species, making the region they occupy one of the premier birding destinations in the country. Dense shrubland communities often have particularly loud and spectacular bouts of dawn chorus. The raucous songs of tropical birds give the s. Texas Tamaulipan Mezquital a soundscape unlike anywhere else in the United States.

This semiarid area holds few amphibian species, but several toad species can be abundant, including North American Green Toad, Texas Toad, Gulf Coast Toad, and Cane Toad. The bizarre Mexican Burrowing Toad emerges in this habitat after heavy rains. Part of a lineage nearly 200 million years old, it is the sole living species in the family Rhinophrynidae. Reptiles are significantly more prominent. The large Texas Tortoise can be found slowly making its way through the Tamaulipan region of s. Texas and ne. Mexico. The gorgeous Texas Indigo Snake is another gem of the northern reaches of the mezquital. In s. Texas, indigo snakes are well known for their fondness for rattlesnakes as prey items and are considered an ally by many ranchers and farmers. Endemic lizards include Laredo Striped Whiptail and the endangered Reticulate Collared Lizard. Other more common reptiles include Texas Coral Snake, Central American Boa, Neotropical Whipsnake, Mexican Spiny-tailed Iguana, Eastern Spiny Lizard, and Brown Anole.

Above: **Green Jay is a flashy and conspicuous resident of the Tamaulipan Mezquital.**
© BEN KNOOT, TROPICAL BIRDING TOURS

Left: **Ocelot is found in a wide variety of habitats but in the United States occurs only in Tamaulipan Mezquital.**
© SANTIAGO SALAZAR

CONSERVATION: Tamaulipan Mezquital habitat has been heavily cleared and disturbed for agriculture, particularly cattle grazing. Intact stands are now quite rare, and what is left is often degraded in ways similar to other overgrazed habitats (EASTERN MESQUITE, CHIHUAHUAN DESERT GRASSLAND). Climate-change modeling predicts increased temperatures and decreased rainfall that could eventually lead to widespread desertification. The area, while well adapted to periodic drought, has already seen persistent droughts lasting upward of a decade that have severely stressed the environment.

Speckled Racer is a tropical species that reaches its northern limit in s. Texas. © MIDWEST HERPING

Protected areas in this habitat are generally small and scattered. The largest and best-preserved examples are administered by *ejidos* in Mexico. *Ejidos* are communally owned landholdings that are administered by a municipal council. While sections are allotted for agriculture and development, conservation is heavily weighed, and large-scale commercial exploitation generally does not occur. Many well-protected areas in Mexico are under control of an *ejido*, including famous sites for Thick-billed Parrot and Tufted Jay in the MADREAN PINE-OAK WOODLAND of w. Mexico. Most of the remaining wintering areas for Monarch butterflies in the Oyamel Forest (sidebar 2) are also managed this way.

In the lower Rio Grande valley of Texas, Tamaulipan Mezquital is critical to the survival of the US Ocelot population. Despite the presence of high-quality habitat, only 50 or so individuals remain here. Strong conservation measures are underway to save not only the Ocelot but also the Jaguarundi, absent from Texas for decades. Plans to reintroduce this shy tropical feline are currently being developed, with a goal of 500-plus individuals by 2050.

DISTRIBUTION: Found largely in dry coastal environments and adjacent uplands in s. Texas and ne. Mexico, Tamaulipan Mezquital is the dominant habitat in the region. Reaching its northern extent in the sw. United States, it extends as far north as Corpus Christi, Texas, where it transitions to EASTERN MESQUITE and OAK-JUNIPER WOODLAND. In Mexico, most of Tamaulipas and areas of n. Veracruz, San Luis Potosí, and Nuevo Leon have large swaths of this habitat. In the south, this habitat transitions to MESOAMERICAN SAVANNA AND GRASSLAND and MESOAMERICAN SEMI-EVERGREEN FOREST. At higher elevations to the east, this habitat transitions to MESOAMERICAN CLOUDFOREST, MADREAN ENCINAL, and MADREAN PINE-OAK WOODLAND.

WHERE TO SEE: Santa Ana National Wildlife Refuge, Texas, US; King Ranch, Texas, US; Naranjo, Tamaulipas, Mexico.

Ne2G EASTERN MESQUITE

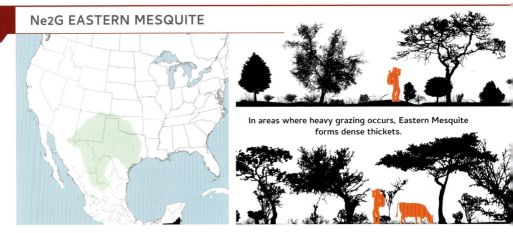

In areas where heavy grazing occurs, Eastern Mesquite forms dense thickets.

IN A NUTSHELL: A low, scrubby habitat dominated by mesquite with a significant grassland component. **Global Habitat Affinities:** None. **Continental Habitat Affinities:** TAMAULIPAN MEZQUITAL; CHIHUAHUAN DESERT. **Species Overlap:** CHIHUAHUAN DESERT GRASSLAND; MIXED-GRASS PRAIRIE; SHORTGRASS PRAIRIE; TAMAULIPAN MEZQUITAL; OAK-JUNIPER WOODLAND.

DESCRIPTION: Eastern Mesquite is a moderately open to dense shrubland occurring in arid areas of the s. Great Plains. This habitat is humid relative to other arid shrublands, and summers can be brutally hot, with temperatures regularly breaking 100°F (38°C). Most of the region's precipitation (16–25 in./400–650 mm) falls during the summer months, though winter snows are an annual occurrence.

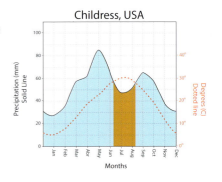

Eastern Mesquite is strongly dominated by a single plant—Honey Mesquite (*Prosopis glandulosa*). This thorny member of the acacia family can form open shrub savannas or impenetrable thickets and is typically 2–10 ft. (0.5–3.0 m) in height. In wetter areas, small trees like Netleaf Hackberry (*Celtis reticulata*) and Western Soapberry (*Sapindus saponaria*) are present. The shrub layer is typically species-poor, and Lotebush (*Ziziphus obtusifolia*), Chickasaw Plum (*Prunus angustifolia*), and baccharises (*Baccharis* spp.) usually occur only as a minor component.

In all but the densest of mesquite stands, this habitat is quite grassy and has a wide assemblage of graminoids typical of SHORTGRASS PRAIRIE and MIXED-GRASS PRAIRIE. Switchgrass (*Panicum virgatum*), Little Bluestem (*Schizachyrium scoparium*), Texas Wintergrass (*Nassella leucotricha*), Blue Grama (*Bouteloua gracilis*), and Ring Muhly (*Muhlenbergia torreyi*) are all important native grasses. Invasive grasses like Bermudagrass (*Cynodon dactylon*) and Field Brome (*Bromus arvensis*) are prevalent and can be dominant.

Honey Mesquite, the dominant and diagnostic plant in this system, is also present as an invader in many adjacent habitats. Because of this, it becomes challenging to differentiate this system from regions where the species has spread due to human land-use activities. It could be argued that this is a largely anthropogenic habitat.

Eastern Mesquite in se. New Mexico. © PHIL CHAON

WILDLIFE: The fauna in this habitat ranges from prairie species to animals more typical of the southwest. Common mammals include Black-tailed Jackrabbit, Mule Deer, White-tailed Deer, Coyote, Striped Skunk, and Bobcat. Pronghorn, Black-tailed Prairie-dog, and American Badger occur regularly in more open areas.

The birdlife here varies strongly depending on the density of mesquite stands. More open and grassy sections have Scaled Quail, American Kestrel, Western Kingbird, Scissor-tailed Flycatcher, Loggerhead Shrike, Chihuahuan Raven, Cassin's Sparrow, Field Sparrow, and Western Meadowlark. Birds like Northern Bobwhite, Mississippi Kite, Golden-fronted Woodpecker, Ladder-backed Woodpecker, Ash-throated Flycatcher, Bell's Vireo, Black-crested Titmouse, Blue Grosbeak,

Northern Bobwhite will avoid Eastern Mesquite when it becomes too overgrown and dense.
© BEN KNOOT, TROPICAL BIRDING TOURS

Above: **Scissor-tailed Flycatcher is a common summer visitor in the Eastern Mesquite.**
© BEN KNOOT, TROPICAL BIRDING TOURS

Below: **Painted Bunting is incredibly colorful— whether it is beautiful or gaudy is a matter of debate.**
© BEN KNOOT, TROPICAL BIRDING TOURS

and Northern Cardinal are typical of dense mesquite scrub. Painted Bunting is especially common here.

The presence of reptiles and amphibians is largely influenced by surrounding habitats and varies across the range of this ecosystem. Prairie Rattlesnake, Gopher Snake, Coachwhip, Eastern Hognose Snake, Texas Horned Lizard, Great Plains Skink, Ornate Box Turtle, Woodhouse's Toad, and Couch's Spadefoot are all widespread in Eastern Mesquite.

CONSERVATION: Eastern Mesquite habitat is of very low conservation concern. Historically, its extent was likely much more restricted. Overgrazing and fire suppression have resulted in rapid expansion of this habitat throughout its range. Even in areas where it existed naturally, the mesquite shrub component has grown significantly denser.

Efforts to control mesquite and restore grassland components are widespread on public lands in this habitat.

DISTRIBUTION: This lowland habitat, found in flat areas of the sw. Great Plains, is widespread in e. New Mexico, Oklahoma, and most of Texas in the United States, and parts of n. Chihuahua and n. Coahuila in Mexico.

WHERE TO SEE: Matador Wildlife Management Area, Texas, US.

Ne2H ROCKY CANYON

IN A NUTSHELL: A largely abiotic habitat of sheer rock faces widely distributed in mountainous areas and arid zones. **Global Habitat Affinities:** INSELBERGS AND KOPPIES. **Continental Habitat Affinities:** GLACIER AND SCREE; SEACLIFFS AND OFFSHORE ISLANDS. **Species Overlap:** Overlaps broadly with adjacent habitats.

DESCRIPTION: Rocky Canyon habitat generally exists in small pockets within other habitat matrices. Largely devoid of vegetation, it consists of expansive slabs of exposed rock, often with boulder-strewn hillsides below. These cliffs and canyons typically form from sandstone, limestone, chalk, dolomite, granite, or basalt.

A wide variety of geological processes can result in the formation of cliffs and canyons. Most canyons are the result of downcutting by flowing water slowly eroding through its bed, creating steep embankments on either side. This phenomenon is especially prevalent in areas with soft bedrock. The Colorado River, cutting through the red sandstone of the Colorado Plateau, has produced one of the most extensive canyonlands in the world and certainly the largest and most impressive example of this habitat in North America. Canyons are also formed when rivers downcut gaps between mountain peaks, and occasionally are formed through tectonic activity. Especially narrow canyons with smooth walls are termed "slot canyons." Canyons that have only one entrance are called "box canyons"; during wetter times of year, the closed wall of a box canyon often features a waterfall. Cliffs are generally more widespread than canyons and are formed by weathering, erosion, and occasionally geological uplift.

The structure and composition of cliffs and canyons depends largely on the surrounding bedrock. Different substrates produce specific microfeatures to varying degrees. Important microfeatures for wildlife include narrow fissures, ledges, overhangs, potholes, and caves. The defensibility and lack of predators make many cliffs important nesting sites for birds. For the large colonies of cliff-nesting seabirds, see SEACLIFFS AND OFFSHORE ISLANDS.

WILDLIFE: Rocky Canyons tend to share much of the mammal fauna with surrounding environments. Bighorn Sheep and Mountain Goats are both well adapted to walking along narrow ledges and steep rock faces and spend much of their time in this habitat. A variety of rodents are found in this environment, and Rock Squirrel, Cliff Chipmunk (IS), and Hopi Chipmunk (IS) are especially prevalent. Ringtails are generalists but show strong preference for this habitat when it is

available. Puma (Mountain Lion) and Jaguar frequently hunt in canyons and use ledges as vantage points but can't navigate the steepest sections or cliff faces.

In much of w. North America, a visit to any rocky cliff or canyon is accompanied by the raspy screeching of White-throated Swifts (IS) and the cascading whistles of Canyon Wrens (IS). The latter has an extremely long bill specifically for reaching into narrow, insect-filled refugia in the rocks. These two species, as well as Cliff Swallow, Cave Swallow, Great Swallow-tailed Swift, and Chestnut-collared Swift (the latter two in Mexico), take advantage of protected fissures and crevices high in the rock for nesting and foraging. Buff-collared Nightjar, Rufous-crowned Sparrow, and Rock Wren are also common but less strongly associated with the habitat than the previous species. Steep rock faces also provide important nesting habitat for many raptor species. Peregrine Falcon (IS) is especially fond of nesting on narrow shelves high up on expanses of vertical rock. Prairie Falcon, Orange-breasted Falcon, Gyrfalcon, Golden Eagle, California Condor, and Great Horned Owl all nest preferentially on cliff ledges. Mexican Spotted Owl prefers forest

Top: **The rims of Rocky Canyons provide a great vantage point for eye-level views of White-throated Swift.** © BEN KNOOT, TROPICAL BIRDING TOURS

Above: **Canyon Wren uses its long bill to extract insects from fissures in the walls of Rocky Canyons.** © BEN KNOOT, TROPICAL BIRDING TOURS

Left: **Running water has cut numerous Rocky Canyons into the soft sandstone of the Colorado Plateau.** © BEN KNOOT, TROPICAL BIRDING TOURS

in narrow slot canyons and frequently nests directly on cliffs. Common Raven is also an abundant nesting bird in this habitat. The advent of large skyscrapers and bridges provides an urban analogue for many birds adapted to utilizing Rocky Canyons.

A wide variety of reptiles and amphibians will use this habitat, though true specialists are more limited. The two species of lyre snakes (IS) are real obligates, spending most of the day deep in rock crevices and emerging at night to hunt along the canyon wall. In wetter, unvegetated cliff and canyon environments, salamanders will come out at night to prowl the cliff face, especially after rains. Green Salamander (IS) and Spotted-tail Salamander are especially adept climbers. The Desert Slender Salamander, a canyon specialist, may be extinct. Canyon Tree Frog (IS) is another canyon specialist, breeding in pools at canyon bottoms and retreating into deep crevices during dry periods.

CONSERVATION: Rocky Canyons suffer few threats from a conservation standpoint. They are not heavily impacted by development, invasive species, or climate change. The main threat to wildlife in

Sonoran Lyre Snake spends the day deep inside rocky crevices, emerging at night to hunt lizards, rodents, and bats. © PHIL CHAON

this habitat is disturbance due to recreational activities. Many cliff-nesting birds, especially raptors, are quite sensitive to human presence and will abandon nests in areas that are popular for rock climbing. Appropriately timed seasonal closures related to nesting birds can prevent this problem and are a standard practice in many areas.

DISTRIBUTION: Rocky Canyons are scattered widely across the continent in a variety of habitats. They occur more often in arid zones, where dense vegetation is less likely to cover the walls. Areas with particularly high concentrations of Rocky Canyon include the Colorado Plateau, the Rocky Mountains, the Sierra Nevada, and the Sierra Madre Occidental. To a lesser extent, this habitat also occurs in the Appalachian, Ozark, Ouachita, Cascade, and Sierra Madre Oriental ranges.

WHERE TO SEE: Grand Canyon National Park, Arizona, US; Zion National Park, Utah, US; Sumidero Canyon National Park, Chiapas, Mexico.

Ne2l CENTRAL MEXICAN SUCCULENT MATORRAL

IN A NUTSHELL: A subtropical semiarid thornscrub in c. and s. Mexico with an abundance of prominent columnar cacti and other succulents. **Global Habitat Affinities:** BAGAN THORNSCRUB; INTERANDEAN THORNSCRUB; SPINY FOREST. **Continental Habitat Affinities:** CHIHUAHUAN DESERT; SONORAN DESERT; TAMAULIPAN MEZQUITAL. **Species Overlap:** TAMAULIPAN MEZQUITAL; PACIFIC DRY DECIDUOUS FOREST; CHIHUAHUAN DESERT; SONORAN DESERT; MADREAN ENCINAL.

DESCRIPTION: Central Mexican Succulent Matorral is a diverse and often stunning array of thornscrub environments spread throughout the interior of Mexico. This habitat is characterized by dense spiny undergrowth broken by towering cacti, yuccas, and agaves. Mostly found at elevations of 4000–6000 ft. (1200–1800 m), the region is cooler than most arid shrublands on the continent. Summer high temperatures rarely break 85°F (29°C), and winter lows are well above freezing (48°F/9°C). The matorral (scrub) receives scant precipitation during the summer monsoon season (June–September), which typically totals 7–18 in. (180–460 mm), depending on the year. Occasionally, hurricanes on the Pacific coast can lead to exceptional rain events that result in massive flourishes of growth.

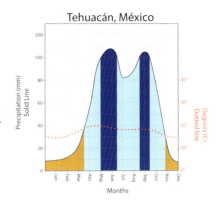

While there is no canopy layer here, several plants still reach impressive heights. The most evident botanical features on the landscapes are the massive cacti. The Cardón Blanco (*Cephalocereus columna-trajani*) grows in dense stands of single unbranched columns reaching 25–30 ft. (8–10 m) tall and blanketing hillsides with an unnervingly simplistic coat of giant green toothpicks. Many branched species like Candelabro (*Pachycereus weberi*), Royen's Tree Cactus (*Pilosocereus royenii*), and Bilberry Cactus (*Myrtillocactus geometrizans*) can also reach considerable heights (up to 40 ft./12 m). Mature individuals can be as broad as they are tall, with dozens of widely branching arms. The yuccas in this environment are equally impressive. The unbranched Tree Yucca

Central Mexican Succulent Matorral in the Tehuacán valley, Puebla, Mexico. © PHIL CHAON

This Mexican Ponytail Palm (a relative of the yuccas) is estimated to be around 800 years old. © PHIL CHAON

(*Yucca filifera*) and the many-armed Izote (*Yucca periculosa*) both reach upward of 33 ft. (10 m) and contribute to the bizarre nature of this landscape. Perhaps the most impressive member of the otherworldly flora here is the Mexican Ponytail Palm or Sotolín (*Beaucarnea gracilis*). With a massive bulbous trunk and spindly arms topped in pom-pom-like clusters of leaves, the Sotolín can live for over 500 years and is truly one of the most whimsical and breathtaking plants on the continent.

The principal shrub layer of Central Mexican Succulent Matorral is dense and spiny, usually reaching 5–10 ft. (1.5–3.0 m) in height. This scrub is extremely difficult to move through and can be reminiscent of Tamaulipan Mezquital, though generally shorter and drier. Dominant shrub-layer plants include Smooth Mesquite (*Prosopis laevigata*), Camachile (*Pithecellobium dulce*), Boat-spine Acacia (*Vachellia campechiana*), Huisache (*Vachellia farnesiana*), American Tarbush (*Flourensia cernua*), and Creosote (*Larrea tridentata*). There is typically very little grassy or herbaceous undergrowth, except after monsoon rain events when impressive blooms of salvia (*Salvia* spp.) and other bright flowering plants emerge. Large shrubs often serve as nurse plants—well-established plants that help small seedlings survive early in their development. Checking the bases of nurse plants will often reveal a plethora of small, cryptic cactus species.

Individual patches of Central Mexican Succulent Matorral are separated from each other by complex mountain ranges cloaked in MADREAN PINE-OAK WOODLAND. The extreme isolation has led to high levels of endemism, especially among cacti, yuccas, agaves, bromeliads (*Hechtia* spp.), and salvias. This habitat is considered a global center for biodiversity among these groups. The matorral of the Tehuacán valley alone is home to more than 2700 species of plants—30% of which are endemic!

WILDLIFE: Central Mexican Succulent Matorral habitat has several endemic small mammals but is largely dominated by widespread generalists that are found in a variety of North American habitats. Frequently encountered species include White-tailed Deer, Collared Peccary, Gray Fox, Coyote, White-nosed Coati, Ringtail, Hooded Skunk, and American Hog-nosed Skunk. Readily apparent small mammals include Rock Squirrel, Mexican Cottontail, and several species of kangaroo rats.

Central Mexican Succulent Matorral largely shares its bird community with surrounding arid environments. West Mexican Chachalaca, Inca Dove, White-winged Dove, Lesser Roadrunner, Greater Roadrunner, Black Vulture, Harris's Hawk, Crested Caracara, Ladder-backed Woodpecker, Northern Beardless-Tyrannulet, Cassin's Kingbird, Curve-billed Thrasher, Phainopepla, Black-throated Sparrow, Scott's Oriole, and Streak-backed Oriole are all widespread species frequently encountered here. The isolated nature of matorral habitat has also led to high levels of endemism, especially in the southern extents of its range in Puebla and Oaxaca. Large cacti provide nest sites for Gray-breasted Woodpecker (IS) and secondarily for Ash-throated and Nutting's Flycatchers.

Like many birds in the matorral, Bridled Sparrow
is quite retiring and takes some effort to see well.
© PHIL CHAON

The striking Slaty Vireo is a localized endemic
in s. Mexico. © PHIL CHAON

The dense, spiny undergrowth is home to several range-restricted species including Dusky
Hummingbird, Beautiful Hummingbird (IS), Boucard's Wren (IS), Ocellated Thrasher (IS), Slaty
Vireo, Dwarf Vireo, White-throated Towhee, and Bridled Sparrow (IS). The birding in this habitat
is most productive in early spring (February–April) while much of the vegetation is denuded and
stealthy species are more vocal.

Over 100 species of reptiles and amphibians are found in Central Mexican Succulent Matorral,
many endemic. Lizards are the most abundant and diverse of the habitat's herpetofauna.

Boucard's Wren is found among large, mature stands of cacti in Central Mexican Succulent Matorral. © PHIL CHAON

Several species of large spiny-tailed iguanas (*Ctenosaura* spp.) occur along with many whiptails (*Aspidoscelis* spp.) and spiny lizards (*Sceloporus* spp.). This habitat has several species of bizarre horned lizards including Mexican Plateau Horned Lizard (*Phrynosoma orbiculare*), Mexican Horned Lizard (*Phrynosoma taurus*), Short-tailed Horned Lizard, and Giant Horned Lizard. The reptiles and amphibians here are most commonly seen in spring and summer, especially after monsoon rains.

CONSERVATION: Central Mexican Succulent Matorral is a highly imperiled habitat with only about 6% remaining intact. Historically, it occurred in large intermountain valleys, many of which are now home to major cities including Mexico City, Puebla, and Oaxaca. Of the remaining matorral in Mexico, 85% is found within protected areas, while the remaining 15% continues to be at risk, mostly from intensive agricultural development, livestock grazing, and urban expansion. A diverse array of rare and spectacular cacti are endemic to this habitat and are an increasingly popular target for poachers. The habitat is protected by several large biosphere reserves, notably the Tehuacán-Cuicatlán Biosphere Reserve.

DISTRIBUTION: Widespread in dry intermontane valleys throughout the interior of c. and s. Mexico, Central Mexican Succulent Matorral largely occurs south of the Chihuahuan Plateau, on the Mexican Plateau, and at lower elevations in the Sierra Madre Occidental and Sierra Madre del Sur. It reaches its northern limit in s. Durango, Zacatecas, San Luis Potosí, and Tamaulipas. Near its southern limit, it is found in large arid valleys in Puebla, Guerrero, and Oaxaca. The habitat is bounded to the east by the Sierra Madre Oriental and the west by the Sierra Madre Occidental. This habitat occupies the lowest elevations within its range; at higher elevations (above 5000–6000 ft./1500–1800 m) it is replaced by MADREAN ENCINAL or MADREAN PINE-OAK WOODLAND.

WHERE TO SEE: Tehuacán-Cuicatlán Biosphere Reserve, Puebla, Mexico; Yagul, Oaxaca, Mexico.

Ne2J CARIBBEAN THORNSCRUB

IN A NUTSHELL: A low, scrubby habitat made up of thorny small-leaved bushes and abundant cacti, found along much of the Caribbean coastline and extending into Central and South America. **Global Habitat Affinities:** TUMBESIAN THORNSCRUB; WEST ASIAN THORNSCRUB; NORTHERN DRY THORN SAVANNA. **Continental Habitat Affinities:**

TAMAULIPAN MEZQUITAL; EASTERN MESQUITE. **Species Overlap:** TAMAULIPAN MEZQUITAL; YUCATÁN DRY DECIDUOUS FOREST.

DESCRIPTION: Caribbean Thornscrub can be quite varied in luxuriance and structure within a small area, yet over vast regions remains fairly constant. Thornscrub habitats may be divided into thorn savanna, thornscrub, thorn brush, and thorn thicket in regions like Africa, the Middle East, and India, where all these forms have their own plant species assemblages. But in North America, the plants remain fairly uniform, and the bird assemblages of both thornscrub and thorn thickets are usually the same, so they are treated as a single habitat.

Caribbean Thornscrub habitat includes deciduous, sclerophyllous, and microphyllous canopy trees, 10–27 ft. (3–9 m) in height, including Mexican Logwood (*Haematoxylon brasiletto*), which also grows in deciduous forests, Trupillo (*Prosopis juliflora*), an invasive plant over much of the world, and Huisache (*Vachellia farnesiana*). In particularly dry or nutrient-deficient conditions, the canopy also contains cacti such as Caribbean Cholla (*Cylindropuntia caribaea*). Beneath it, the midstory is dominated by

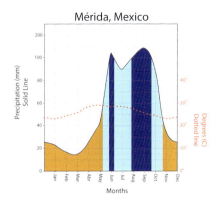

microphyllous plants and more widespread species such as Twisted Acacia (*Vachellia tortuosa*) and Cascalote (*Libidibia coriaria*). The ground cover has a seemingly incongruous combination of plants such as Pyramid Bush (*Melochia tomentosa*), Red Spinach (*Amaranthus dubius*), and Bellyache Bush (*Jatropha gossypiifolia*), all of which are introduced pests around the world, as well as cacti, bromeliads and orchids. The abundance of Spanish Moss (*Tillandsia usneoides*) also seems out of place in this environment. Many of the deciduous shrubs bloom during the dry season, when they don't have leaves, creating a profusion of flowers in an otherwise Spartan scene.

Caribbean Thornscrub on the island of Curaçao. © BEN KNOOT, TROPICAL BIRDING TOURS

Absolute rainfall can be high in these areas, but it is periodic, leaving prolonged spells of drought. It is the erratic and intense nature of the wet and dry seasons that promotes thornscrub over other types of arid vegetation; the dry, sandy soils are the determining factor, and would promote a heathland in more temperate climates. Neotropical thornscrub forms over a wide variety of tropical conditions that are unfavorable for more lush forest growth. Cyclical extreme droughts discourage semi-evergreen forests from colonizing these areas. Aridity and locally harsh growing conditions are caused by a variety of factors. In some coastal locations, localized aridity is caused by easily drained sandy soils derived from the widespread limestones that were deposited in the late Cretaceous (80–65 MYA) and even more so by the very chemically inert Miocene (23–5 MYA) sand deposits.

Combined, these attributes of arid and wet environments give the Caribbean Thornscrub a distinctive feel within North America. Walking through this habitat is very difficult, as the midstory brush layer is 3–9 ft. (1–3 m) tall and very thick.

WILDLIFE: Endemic mammals are not well represented in Caribbean Thornscrub, which mostly hosts more widespread species with catholic habitat requirements like Ocelot, Margay, and White-nosed Coati. Some may have fairly restricted ranges but are still habitat generalists, such as Gaumer's Spiny Pocket Mouse and Yucatán Brown Brocket. As in many dry forests and thornscrubs, reptiles are prominent in this habitat, with species such as Yucatán Spiny-tailed

Venezuelan Troupial is found in thornscrub areas of n. Venezuela as well as adjacent islands in the **Caribbean.** © BEN KNOOT, TROPICAL BIRDING TOURS

Juvenile Yucatán Jay has a bright orange bill and eye-ring, which become black as it matures. © PHIL CHAON

A variety of different iguana species occur in Caribbean Thornscrub.
© BEN KNOOT, TROPICAL BIRDING TOURS

Iguana, Central American Banded Gecko, and Cope's Vine Snake sharing the habitat with species found in a variety of other forests, such as Yucatán Banded Gecko and Yucatecan Cantil.

The thornscrub has far fewer species of birds than surrounding MESOAMERICAN SEMI-EVERGREEN FORESTS. However, because the environment is more open, and the birds that are here are much easier to see, the general impression is of an environment with many bird species. Another interesting trait of this environment is that bird waves (flocks of different species moving together) can happen throughout the day, so when bird activity in primary MESOAMERICAN LOWLAND RAINFOREST seems to have died down, it may be intense in the thornscrub, with alarm calls ringing as birds chase down the odd Ferruginous Pygmy-Owl that made the mistake of calling during the day. Typical widespread birds that are regular in this habitat include Plain Chachalaca, Lesser Roadrunner, Lesser Nighthawk, Turquoise-browed Motmot, Golden-fronted Woodpecker, White-fronted Parrot, and Olive-throated Parakeet. Smaller widespread but typical birds include Canivet's Emerald, Cinnamon Hummingbird, Northern Beardless-Tyrannulet, Scrub Euphonia, Orange Oriole, Altamira Oriole, and Morelet's Seedeater. Yucatán Flycatcher, Mangrove Vireo, and Yucatán Jay are all fairly restricted-range species but are also found in forest habitats and/or MESOAMERICAN MANGROVES. Birds that are strong indicators of this habitat, though they also occur in others, are the Black-throated Bobwhite and Yucatán Woodpecker. Caribbean Thornscrub has few obligate species, but Mexican Sheartail (IS), Yucatán Gnatcatcher (IS), and Yucatán Wren (IS) occur only in this habitat.

CONSERVATION: Much of the Caribbean Thornscrub has been cleared for cattle ranching and farming, but because it generally develops on soil poor for agriculture, widespread monoculture is fairly limited to agave. Much of the protection of this habitat is incidental, centered on archaeological sites on the Yucatán Peninsula, but overall this is not a particularly "charismatic" or evocative landscape, so there is little appetite for serious protection. Furthermore, the Yucatán Cactus (*Lophophora williamsii*), an endangered species indigenous to the region, is experiencing heightened rarity owing to the escalating illicit harvest of these plants from their native habitats for domestic and international trade. Harvesting of this plant results in immense disturbance for the surrounding vegetation. It is somewhat ironic that this vegetation that is a result of disturbance of the YUCATÁN DRY DECIDUOUS FOREST is also undergoing serious degradation.

DISTRIBUTION: This habitat is a northward continuation of the Central American thornscrub that occurs as a mosaic with semi-evergreen forest from Guatemala to Venezuela. In North America it is found primarily on the northern and eastern side of the Yucatán Peninsula.

WHERE TO SEE: Río Lagartos, Yucatán, Mexico.

North American Deciduous Forests Dendrogram

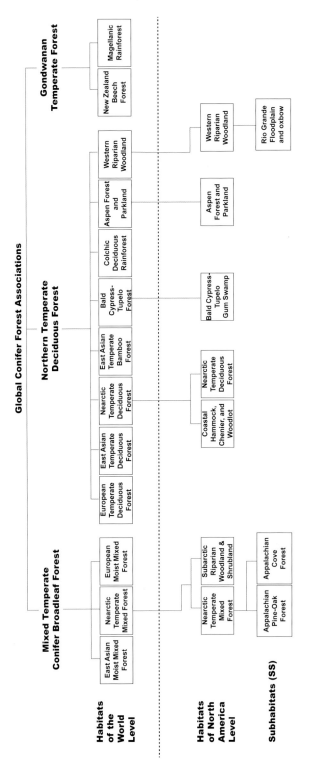

Global Conifer Forest Associations

Habitats of the World Level

Mixed Temperate Conifer Broadleaf Forest
- East Asian Moist Mixed Forest
- Nearctic Temperate Mixed Forest
- European Moist Mixed Forest

Northern Temperate Deciduous Forest
- European Temperate Deciduous Forest
- East Asian Temperate Deciduous Forest
- Nearctic Temperate Deciduous Forest
- East Asian Temperate Bamboo Forest
- Bald Cypress-Tupelo Forest
- Colchic Deciduous Rainforest
- Aspen Forest and Parkland
- Western Riparian Woodland

Gondwanan Temperate Forest
- New Zealand Beech Forest
- Magellanic Rainforest

Habitats of North America Level

- Nearctic Temperate Mixed Forest
- Subarctic Riparian Woodland & Shrubland
- Coastal Hammock, Chenier, and Woodlot
- Nearctic Temperate Deciduous Forest
- Bald Cypress-Tupelo Gum Swamp
- Aspen Forest and Parkland
- Western Riparian Woodland

Subhabitats (SS)

- Appalachian Pine-Oak Forest
- Appalachian Cove Forest
- Rio Grande Floodplain and oxbow

TEMPERATE DECIDUOUS FORESTS

Ne3A BALD CYPRESS–TUPELO GUM SWAMP

IN A NUTSHELL: Tall, flooded riverine forests of Bald Cypress and several species of broadleaf trees. **Global Habitat Affinities:** None. **Continental Habitat Affinities:** WESTERN RIPARIAN WOODLAND. **Species Overlap:** TEMPERATE DECIDUOUS FOREST; EASTERN PINE SAVANNA; NEARCTIC LOWLAND RIVERS.

DESCRIPTION: One of the most visually distinctive habitats in the Nearctic, Bald Cypress–Tupelo Gum Swamp is often the first image that comes to mind when one pictures the se. United States. Dominated by tall, broad-based, epiphyte-laden trees, the canopy is typically dense and reaches heights of 60–100 ft. (18–30 m), though Bald Cypress (*Taxodium distichum*) can be as tall as 145 ft. (44 m). Bald Cypress–Tupelo Gum Swamps form in hot, humid environments that typically receive 35–65 in. (900–1650 mm) of rainfall per year. This habitat occurs along the floodplains of blackwater streams originating on the coastal plain or appears as cypress domes in the middle of open wetlands. The ground is permanently or seasonally flooded, and the maze of back channels is best explored by canoe or boardwalk.

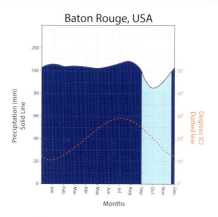

Baton Rouge, USA

This is an entirely deciduous forest, where even the conifers lose their needles in winter. The majority of the canopy is composed of Bald Cypress and either Water Tupelo (*Nyssa aquatica*) or Swamp Tupelo (*Nyssa biflora*), though Water Hickory (*Carya aquatica*) is occasionally co-dominant. Bald Cypress and Water Tupelo are both extremely broad-based trees with tapered trunks, and Bald Cypress can be as stout as 17 ft. (5 m) in diameter. The midstory of these forests is generally sparse and consists of young tupelos and smaller, shade-tolerant trees like Red Maple (*Acer rubrum*), Pop Ash (*Fraxinus caroliniana*), and Green Ash (*Fraxinus pennsylvanica*). Vines are a common feature of the midstory and may be abundant. Epiphytes, including large bromeliads, orchids, and especially Spanish Moss (*Tillandsia usneoides*) are prevalent in the canopy and midstory.

Water levels in Bald Cypress–Tupelo Gum Swamps fluctuate throughout the year. © MICHAEL JEFFORDS AND SUE POST

The understory is the most variable element and is dependent mostly on depth and variability of water levels. Frequently, the understory is entirely flooded seasonally, and apart from some aquatic vegetation, the only noticeable feature is the protruding "cypress knees," woody root projections whose purpose is not well understood. In seasonally dry forests, the understory can be extremely lush, dominated by rapidly growing plants tolerant of wet soil. Sedges (*Carex* spp.), False Nettle (*Boehmeria cylindrica*), Lizard's Tail (*Saururus cernuus*), and Greater Marsh St.-John's-wort (*Hypericum virginicum*) grow in areas that are flooded for much of the year, while relatively drier areas have Swamp Fern (*Acrostichum aureum*), Yellowseed False Pimpernel (*Lindernia dubia*), and Camphorweed (*Heterotheca subaxillaris*), and woody shrubs like Buttonbush (*Cephalanthus occidentalis*), willows (*Salix* spp.), rhododendrons (*Rhododendron* spp.), Coastal Sweet Pepperbush (*Clethra alnifolia*), Northern Arrowwood (*Viburnum recognitum*), and Virginia Sweetspire (*Itea virginica*). Cinnamon Fern (*Osmundastrum cinnamomeum*) can also be abundant.

These swamps naturally exist as a diverse multi-age system with major disturbance events coming in the form of violent storms, windthrow, and exceptional flooding. Fire is a rare but important part of this habitat. Drought events expose dry land, and fires clear old forest, allowing for the germination of new trees.

WILDLIFE: Bald Cypress–Tupelo Gum Swamps have a complex matrix of flooded lands and upland areas that are home to a mixture of both forest and wetland animal species. Swamp Rabbit, White-tailed Deer, American Black Bear, Common Raccoon, Bobcat, and the endangered Florida Panther, a subspecies of Puma, all utilize better-drained areas. The flooded channels are home to North American River Otter, Common Muskrat, and the introduced Nutria.

This habitat is a critical nesting area for many large wetland birds; large rookeries of egrets, herons, cormorants, and Wood Storks are a notable feature. Barred Owls and Red-shouldered

Above: **North American River Otters utilize Bald Cypress–Tupelo Gum Swamps when water levels are high.** © JARED MIZANIN

Right: **Wood Stork is the largest bird found in Bald Cypress–Tupelo Gum Swamp.**
© BEN KNOOT, TROPICAL BIRDING TOURS

Hawks are abundant, readily adapting to a diet of frogs, salamanders, and other aquatic vertebrates. Red-headed and Pileated Woodpeckers are also more common here than in many adjacent habitats. Many species of dabbling duck spend the winter in large numbers, and Wood Duck is a ubiquitous resident. In spring and summer, many breeding Neotropical migrants arrive. Yellow-billed Cuckoo, Acadian Flycatcher, Great Crested Flycatcher, Red-eyed and Yellow-throated Vireos, Yellow-throated Warbler, and Northern Parula are all abundant breeding species. In early to mid-spring, watch for Northern Parulas and Yellow-throated Warblers constructing nests in clumps of Spanish Moss. Prothonotary Warbler (IS), formerly known as Golden Swamp Warbler, is the quintessential summer resident of Bald Cypress–Tupelo Gum Swamp, frequently nesting inside rotting cypress knees. Chimney Swift seems to be very common in this habitat, which likely represents a vestige of its former preferred habitat, before it shifted to man-made structures (that's anecdotal, though!).

Reptiles and amphibians are both common and diverse in Bald Cypress–Tupelo Gum Swamp habitat. American Alligator is perhaps the most famous resident—an apex predator capable of reaching 15 ft. (4.5 m) in length. Alligators can be seen cruising the forested channels with their eyes barely breaking the water's surface. This swamp habitat is also home to nearly 30 species

Left: **The Cottonmouth displays its pale mouth lining when it feels threatened.** © JARED MIZANIN

Below: **Prothonotary Warbler nests in cavities in the swamp forest.** © KEN BEHRENS, TROPICAL BIRDING TOURS

of turtles, from the 180 lb. (80 kg) Alligator Snapping Turtle to the diminutive Loggerhead Musk Turtle. At night, the swamp comes alive with the sound of frogs—Southern Leopard, Pig, and River Frogs; American Bullfrog; American Green and Barking Tree Frogs; and Southern Cricket Frog are among the common species. Fully aquatic salamanders including Greater Siren and Three-toed Amphiuma lurk in the murky waters. Cottonmouth, Banded and Brown Water Snakes, Rough Green Snake, and Eastern Rat Snake are common. The spectacular black-and-crimson Mud Snake (IS) is a habitat specialist.

Much of the endemism and diversity within this habitat lies under the water in taxa that include fishes, crayfishes, and freshwater mussels; this aspect of the swamp forest is treated in the LOWLAND RIVERS habitat.

CONSERVATION: There are few surviving tracts of old-growth Bald Cypress–Tupelo Gum Swamp forest in the e. Nearctic. The inaccessible nature of these forests protected them longer than many adjacent forests, but heavy logging in the early 20th century eliminated much of the remaining ancient forest. Agriculture and flood-control-related changes to hydrology, saltwater intrusion due to rising sea levels, and increased pollution have damaged and diminished existing tracts. Bald Cypresses are capable of reaching staggering ages, and several known specimens are over 2000 years old. A 3500-year-old Bald Cypress in Florida was, sadly, destroyed by arson in 2012.

At the beginning of the 20th century, American Alligators, egrets, herons, and Wood Storks were hunted to dangerously low levels for skins and feathers. Thanks to concerted conservation efforts, these species have made a strong comeback, though Wood Storks are still listed as threatened in the United States.

DISTRIBUTION: Bald Cypress–Tupelo Gum Swamp forest is primarily associated with low-lying wet areas of the Atlantic and Gulf of Mexico coastal plains of the se. United States. It occurs from Delaware to s. Florida, west to e. Texas and se. Oklahoma, and north along the Mississippi and Ohio River drainages to s. Illinois and extreme se. Indiana. Upland areas generally transition into TEMPERATE DECIDUOUS FOREST.

WHERE TO SEE: Corkscrew Swamp Sanctuary, Florida, US; Francis Beidler Forest, South Carolina, US; Cache River State Natural Area, Illinois, US.

Ne3B NEARCTIC TEMPERATE DECIDUOUS FOREST

IN A NUTSHELL: A diverse, closed-canopy deciduous forest of the e. Nearctic dominated by beech, maple, oak, and hickory. **Global Habitat Affinities:** EUROPEAN DECIDUOUS RAINFOREST; EUROPEAN BEECH FOREST; HIMALAYAN SUBTROPICAL BROADLEAF FOREST; MAGHREB BROADLEAF WOODLAND. **Continental Habitat Affinities:** TEMPERATE MIXED FOREST. **Species Overlap:** TEMPERATE MIXED FOREST; BALD CYPRESS–TUPELO GUM SWAMP; EASTERN PINE SAVANNA.

Top left: **Temperate Deciduous Forest looks starkly different in the leafless winter (purple) and verdant summer (red).**

Left: **Eastern Riparian Woodland occurs along waterways and floodplains.**

DESCRIPTION: South of the taiga (or boreal) zone, this is the most widespread habitat in the e. Nearctic, familiar to almost everyone who has spent time outdoors east of the Mississippi River. Vast broadleaf forests have historically blanketed the e. Nearctic, and many large swaths of forest are still intact. Nearctic Temperate Deciduous Forest experiences distinct seasons with cold winters, hot and humid summers, and significant rainfall. Winter lows vary from 30°F to –15°F (–1 to –26°C), while summer highs are in the range of 80–95°F (27–35°C). Precipitation falls consistently year-round as either rain or snow and totals 30–60 in. (750–1500 mm).

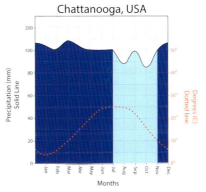

Chattanooga, USA

Precipitation (mm) Solid Line

Degrees (C) Dotted line

Months

Temperate Deciduous Forest typically has a closed canopy and well developed midstory, shrub layer, and understory. The canopy height is typically 50–80 ft. (15–25 m), the trees closely spaced. The understory and shrub layer can be quite thick and difficult to navigate off trails, except in rare old-growth stands. Several understory plants flower in early spring before the canopy leafs out, including trilliums (*Trillium* spp.), Yellow Trout Lily (*Erythronium americanum*), and Eastern Skunk Cabbage (*Symplocarpus foetidus*). During much of spring and early summer, the ground can

be flooded or dotted with ephemeral pools. Thankfully, nature reserves in this habitat are well developed and plentiful, and extensive trail networks make exploring the habitat quite easy.

This forest has a high diversity of canopy trees compared to other Nearctic habitats, and species composition varies throughout the range. In general, this forest is dominated by a wide range of oak (*Quercus*) and hickory (*Carya*) species, especially in drier, more westerly forests and south-facing slopes. Wetter forests and those on cooler north-facing slopes predominantly consist of maples (*Acer* spp.), American Beech (*Fagus grandifolia*), American Basswood (*Tilia americana*), and ashes (*Fraxinus* spp.). Tuliptree (*Liriodendron tulipifera*) is common throughout. American Chestnut (*Castanea dentata*) was a major part of this habitat but is functionally extinct. Historically, there were regular, low-intensity fires in this habitat, a regime that favors oaks and hickories. Fire suppression over the past century has resulted in a shift toward more mesic, shade-loving species.

Ne3B-1 Early Successional Temperate Deciduous Forest is a distinct subhabitat with its own set of flora and fauna. This subhabitat occurs in areas that have been recently cleared, including regenerating pastures, powerline cuts, windfalls, and forest edges. This subhabitat generally includes saplings from the surrounding forest as well as a wide variety of low dense shrubs. Common shrubs include dogwoods (*Cornus* spp.), persimmons (*Diospyros* spp.), blackberries (*Rubus* spp.), Black Locust (*Robinia pseudoacacia*), sumac (*Rhus* spp.), and Sassafras (*Sassafras albidum*) along with the highly invasive Japanese Honeysuckle (*Lonicera japonica*). Often, many of the small eastern subhabitats of TALLGRASS PRAIRIE will progress to this habitat before turning into mature Temperate Deciduous Forest.

Ne3B-2 Eastern Riparian Woodland, another distinct subhabitat, is found along waterways and in floodplains within Temperate Deciduous Forest and extending into TEMPERATE MIXED FOREST.

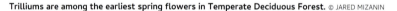

Trilliums are among the earliest spring flowers in Temperate Deciduous Forest. © JARED MIZANIN

This forest is occasionally flooded though generally not for extended periods of time. American Sycamore (*Platanus occidentalis*), Silver Maple (*Acer saccharinum*), Sugar Hackberry (*Celtis laevigata*), Green Ash (*Fraxinus pennsylvanica*), and Sweetgum (*Liquidambar styraciflua*) are typical trees—especially the sycamore. The forest is often very tall, with many snags and stands of dead trees after extensive flooding. The understory is quite shrubby, especially in heavily disturbed areas of the floodplain, and often dominated by willows (*Salix* spp.). An herbaceous understory consisting mostly of Spotted Jewelweed (*Impatiens capensis*) is also a regular feature of this subhabitat.

WILDLIFE: Most large mammals in Temperate Deciduous Forest were eliminated by the beginning of the 20th century through overhunting and persecution. The most notable large mammal is White-tailed Deer, which is abundant to the point of being destructive. In many forests, there is a clear browse line, beneath which all understory vegetation has been eliminated by deer. American Black Bear is common in many areas and increasing in much of its range. Other common mammals include Southern Flying Squirrel, Eastern Fox and Eastern Gray Squirrels, Eastern Chipmunk, Eastern Cottontail, Common Raccoon, Virginia Opossum, Striped Skunk, Red Fox, Coyote, and Bobcat.

The bird communities include many Neotropical migrants. In larger, unbroken forest tracts, the diversity of resident species is relatively low; Wild Turkey, Cooper's and Red-tailed Hawks, Barred Owl, Eastern Screech-Owl, Red-bellied and Downy Woodpeckers, Blue Jay, American Crow, Carolina Chickadee, Tufted Titmouse, White-breasted Nuthatch, and Carolina Wren are common year-round. In spring and summer, the bird diversity in these forests more than doubles, as dozens of species of songbirds return to breed. Eastern Wood-Pewee; Great Crested and Acadian (IS) Flycatchers; Red-eyed and Yellow-throated Vireos; Blue-gray Gnatcatcher; Wood Thrush; Worm-eating, Kentucky (IS), Hooded (IS), and Cerulean (IS) Warblers; and Summer Tanager fill the

Above: **Barred Owl is a year-round resident of Nearctic Temperate Deciduous Forest.** © JARED MIZANIN

Right: **Kentucky Warbler spends most of its time in the forest understory.** © BEN KNOOT, TROPICAL BIRDING TOURS

Cerulean Warbler can be difficult to see as it spends much of its time high in the canopy.
© BEN KNOOT, TROPICAL BIRDING TOURS

Wood Ducks nest in tree cavities in the Eastern Riparian Woodland subhabitat.
© JARED MIZANIN

forest with song. The months of May and June are fantastic for observing birds in this habitat. Early Successional Temperate Deciduous Forest has a unique subset of birds, depending on the successional stage. Birds found in this subhabitat that are absent from more mature forests include Brown Thrasher, Orchard Oriole, White-eyed Vireo, Prairie Warbler, Yellow-breasted Chat, and Blue Grosbeak. Eastern Riparian Woodlands have an interesting mix of species that includes early successional birds like Indigo Bunting and Blue-winged Warbler as well as wetland species like Wood Duck, Green Heron, Prothonotary Warbler, and Red-headed Woodpecker. This habitat extends north into areas of TEMPERATE MIXED FOREST and provides a foothold for more southerly species. In the northern parts of their ranges, Cerulean Warbler and Yellow-throated Warbler (IS) are found almost exclusively in this subhabitat.

Temperate Deciduous Forest also holds large numbers of endemic reptiles and amphibians. Gray Tree Frog, Spring Peeper, Wood Frog, American Toad, Southern Two-lined Salamander, Red Salamander, Eastern Rat Snake, Smooth Earth Snake, Eastern Garter Snake, Copperhead, Broad-headed Skink, and Eastern Box Turtle are common. The salamander diversity is particularly high; Temperate Deciduous Forest and Temperate Mixed Forest of the Appalachian Mountains are the global center for salamander diversity, with more than 20% of the world's species. The Great Smoky Mountains have exceedingly high amphibian diversity and levels of endemism.

CONSERVATION: Temperate Deciduous Forest is the best-preserved example of temperate broadleaf forests in the world. However, all but a tiny fraction of this habitat was logged before 1930, and what remains is principally second growth. Additionally, American Chestnut, a keystone tree species that once comprised 25% of the individual trees of this habitat, was virtually eliminated by the fungus-caused chestnut blight by about 1940. Other tree species of this habitat that have succumbed to pathogens include American Elm (Ulmus americana) and its congeners and many ash species, which have been decimated by Dutch elm disease and Emerald Ash Borer (see sidebar 3), respectively. Despite these losses, forest cover in the e. United States has been steadily increasing since 1920, and Temperate Deciduous Forest now occupies 70% of its original range.

DISTRIBUTION: Temperate Deciduous Forest is found over most of the e. United States and small sections of s. Ontario, Canada. At its far northern boundaries in c. Wisconsin and

A wide variety of salamanders occur here, including the Red Salamander. © JARED MIZANIN

Massachusetts, it transitions to TEMPERATE MIXED FOREST. Temperate Deciduous Forest is replaced by Temperate Mixed Forest at higher elevations in the Appalachian Mountains. Along its western boundary, from Texas north to Minnesota, this forest was historically bordered by TALLGRASS PRAIRIE, but these areas have largely been converted to agriculture. In the south, from s. Georgia to coastal Texas and along the coastal plain north to Virginia, Temperate Deciduous Forest is supplanted by EASTERN PINE SAVANNA and BALD CYPRESS–TUPELO GUM SWAMP.

WHERE TO SEE: Shawnee State Forest, Ohio, US; Mammoth Cave National Park, Kentucky, US; George Washington and Jefferson National Forests, Virginia, US.

| SIDEBAR 3 | INVASIVE SPECIES: EMERALD ASH BORER |

Over the past century, the composition of Nearctic TEMPERATE DECIDUOUS FORESTS and TEMPERATE MIXED FORESTS has been irrevocably changed by introduced pests and pathogens. The most recent of these landscape-altering invaders is the Emerald Ash Borer (*Agrilus planipennis*). First detected in Michigan in 2002, Emerald Ash Borers have since spread to 30 US states and Ontario. This small, bright green beetle has affected tens of millions of trees in the genus *Fraxinus*, often killing all ash trees in a given area within 10 years of first detection. As with earlier losses of American Chestnut (*Castanea dentata*) and American Elm (*Ulmus americana*), the massive die-offs of ashes have led to drastic changes in landscapes and forest communities. The loss of trees leads to major forest gaps that allow for the intrusion of invasive species like Japanese Honeysuckle (*Lonicera japonica*) and Russian Olive (*Elaeagnus angustifolia*). Ashes are also the host plant for over 300 species of arthropods, which in turn are important food sources for many birds and mammals. Like many invasive insect pests, the Emerald Ash Borer has benefited from a lack of natural resistance in host plants and a dearth of predators or parasites. Most Emerald Ash Borer control efforts have focused on limiting the spread of ash products like firewood. Introduction of parasitoid wasps from the beetle's native range have been somewhat successful. In some of the examined areas, up to 80% of Emerald Ash Borer larvae had been parasitized. Hopefully, biological control measures can slow the spread of Emerald Ash Borer and allow North American ash species to remain an important component of deciduous forests.

Ne3C NEARCTIC TEMPERATE MIXED FOREST

IN A NUTSHELL: A closed-canopy forest dominated by deciduous maples, beeches, and birches, along with coniferous Eastern Hemlock and Eastern White Pine. **Global Habitat Affinities:** (SARMATIC) TEMPERATE OAK FOREST; EAST ASIAN TEMPERATE MIXED FOREST; JAPANESE MIXED FOREST; MANCHURIAN MIXED FOREST. **Continental Habitat Affinities:** TEMPERATE DECIDUOUS FOREST; BOREAL CONIFER FOREST. **Species Overlap:** TEMPERATE DECIDUOUS FOREST; BOREAL CONIFER FOREST.

DESCRIPTION: Found in the e. United States and se. Canada, Temperate Mixed Forest is a shady, moist, mossy forest crisscrossed by hemlock-lined ravines. This habitat walks the line between TEMPERATE DECIDUOUS FOREST and BOREAL CONIFER FOREST while remaining distinct from both. The climate is characterized by long, cold winters and warm summers. Snow is often on the ground for five months of the year and contributes a significant portion of the 30–50 in. (750–1250 mm) of precipitation received annually.

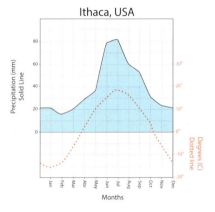

Ithaca, USA

Precipitation (mm) Solid Line

Degrees (C) Dotted line

Months

Temperate Mixed Forest has a very dense canopy that is typically 50–65 ft. (15–20 m) tall. The poorly lit area under the canopy is home to only the most shade-tolerant plants and is often very open. Primary canopy species include American Beech (*Fagus grandifolia*), Sugar Maple (*Acer saccharum*), Red Maple (*Acer rubrum*), Black Cherry (*Prunus serotina*), and Eastern White Pine (*Pinus strobus*). The midstory is dominated by Eastern Hemlock (*Tsuga canadensis*), which adds a distinctly northern feel. Smaller maples as well as Sweet Birch (*Betula lenta*), Yellow Birch (*Betula alleghaniensis*), and dogwoods (*Cornus* spp.) make up most of the remaining midstory. The shrub layer is often quite open. One major exception to this is encountered in the impenetrable thickets of rhododendrons (*Rhododendron* spp.) and Mountain Laurel (*Kalmia latifolia*) that grow along streams and ravines. The understory is sparse and typically includes mosses, ferns, and a few herbaceous plants like violets (*Viola* spp.) and May-apple (*Podophyllum peltatum*).

Ne3c-1 Appalachian Cove Forest in many ways is a southern elevational range extension of Temperate Mixed Forest, though it has a subset of canopy trees that are more typical of southern Temperate Deciduous Forest. Yellow Buckeye (*Aesculus flava*), American Basswood

A shrubby, early successional Temperate Mixed Forest, Fort Drum, New York, US. © KURT ONGMAN

The coming of fall reveals the dark green foliage of Eastern Hemlocks in the understory. © JARED MIZANIN

(*Tilia americana*), Tuliptree (*Liriodendron tulipifera*), and Fraser Magnolia (*Magnolia fraseri*) are prominent here and rare or absent throughout the rest of the habitat.

Ne3C-2 Appalachian Pine-Oak Forest is a subhabitat found on dry south-facing slopes and rocky soils throughout the Appalachian, Ozark, and Ouachita Mountains. The canopy trees vary significantly, and the forest floor is often dry and bare apart from dense leaf litter. White Oak (*Quercus alba*), Chestnut Oak (*Quercus montana*), Southern Red Oak (*Quercus falcata*), Scarlet Oak (*Quercus coccinea*), Shagbark Hickory (*Carya ovata*), Red Hickory (*Carya ovalis*), Pignut Hickory (*Carya glabra*), Virginia Pine (*Pinus virginiana*), and Shortleaf Pine (*Pinus echinata*) are important trees in this subhabitat. While this forest subhabitat is a mixed deciduous-conifer forest, the wildlife life here more or less overlaps with Temperate Deciduous Forest and is covered there.

Early in its succession, Temperate Mixed Forest is a dense thicket of shrubs and small trees with an entirely different feel. Lacking in the shade-loving Eastern Hemlock, this seral stage is characterized by a canopy of small Quaking Aspen (*Populus tremuloides*) and alders (*Alnus* spp.).

The understory and shrub layer of Temperate Mixed Forest are dense and typically contain fescues (*Festuca* spp.), dogwoods (*Cornus* spp.), willows (*Salix* spp.), goldenrods (*Solidago* spp.), blackberries (*Rubus* spp.), viburnums (*Viburnum* spp.), White Meadowsweet (*Spiraea alba*), and small maples (*Acer* spp.).

WILDLIFE: The wildlife here shares features with both the TEMPERATE DECIDUOUS FOREST and BOREAL CONIFER FOREST. Widespread species like White-tailed Deer, American Black Bear, Common Raccoon, Red Fox, Eastern Cottontail, Eastern Gray Squirrel, American Red Squirrel, and Eastern Chipmunk are apparent. The Appalachian Cottontail (IS) and Allegheny Woodrat are endemic to the Appalachian Cove Forest subhabitat of this habitat. Classic boreal mammals like North American Porcupine, Least Weasel, Southern Bog Lemming, and Snowshoe Hare reach the southern extent of the easterly portion of their range in Temperate Mixed Forest. One of the most fascinating and unique mammals in all of North America is found in this habitat, though it is almost never seen. The Star-nosed Mole spends almost its entire life underground where it uses an alien-looking, fleshy, multi-tendril appendage (called an Eimer's organ) to sense prey moving in the soil. Equipped with more than 25,000 tiny sensory receptors, Star-nosed Mole detects, identifies, and consumes prey in less than 120 milliseconds, making it the fastest-eating mammal on the planet!

Many birds also reach the southern extent of their breeding range in Temperate Mixed Forest. Migratory species like Alder Flycatcher; Blue-headed (IS) and Red-eyed Vireos; Brown Creeper; Winter Wren; Hermit Thrush; Black-throated Blue (IS), Black-throated Green, and Blackburnian (IS) Warblers; Scarlet Tanager; and Dark-eyed Junco breed here during the summer months. The delineation between the more southerly Carolina Chickadee and the more northerly Black-capped Chickadee tends to follow the borders between Temperate Deciduous Forest

Left: **Scarlet Tanager glows in the dark understory.** © BEN KNOOT, TROPICAL BIRDING TOURS

Opposite: **North American Porcupine is a common resident of this habitat.**
© BEN KNOOT, TROPICAL BIRDING TOURS

Golden-winged Warbler nests in dense brush in young Temperate Mixed Forest. © PHIL CHAON

and Temperate Mixed Forest in the east and can be a good indicator of the transition. Like Black-capped Chickadee, Common Raven is broadly present in this habitat and absent in Temperate Deciduous Forest. Black-throated Blue Warbler and Blue-headed Vireo both have subspecies endemic to the Appalachian Cove Forest subhabitat. Open secondary growth associated with Temperate Mixed Forest is the primary breeding area for Golden-winged Warbler (IS). Dense rhododendron thickets in Appalachian Cove Forest are an important breeding microhabitat for Swainson's Warbler within the region.

Wood Turtle is one of the few reptiles regularly seen in Temperate Mixed Forest, usually encountered slowly making its way through the forest, often far from water. In contrast, amphibian diversity is high, especially among salamanders. Mossy stream edges are home to nearly a dozen species of dusky salamanders (*Desmognathus*), and the surrounding forests hold many more. In spring, snowmelt produces temporary pools (see VERNAL POOLS AND EPHEMERAL WETLANDS), free of predatory fish, which serve as critical breeding habitat for Blue-spotted and Jefferson Salamanders, Wood Frog, and Spring Peeper.

CONSERVATION: Temperate Mixed Forest habitat is largely intact and has increased since the mid-20th century. Even though bird numbers have declined across the board in recent decades, there has been a general trend of forest regeneration in the east over the past century, and this has relatively benefited forest species while early-successional species have declined. Golden-winged Warbler is one species that has undergone massive declines. It is largely found in this habitat, especially in regenerative stands of shrubs and young trees. Lack of natural disturbance leading to growth of early successional microhabitats has caused widespread declines. Hybridization with Blue-winged Warblers may become a serious conservation issue with this species. Another major conservation

---

SIDEBAR 4   **MOUNTAINS CAN BE TWO-FACED**

In the Northern Hemisphere between 30° and 50° latitude, north-facing slopes receive significantly less direct sunlight throughout the year. This results in a cooler and generally wetter microclimate on these slopes, which affects plant communities and their associated fauna. In the dry mountainous west, many localized and endemic salamanders, like the Jemez Mountains Salamander of New Mexico, are restricted to moist refugia on north-facing slopes. In the TEMPERATE DECIDUOUS FOREST of the e. Nearctic, north-facing slopes often have trees more characteristic of TEMPERATE MIXED FOREST, especially Eastern Hemlock. These cool microclimates also host more northerly breeding birds like Dark-eyed Junco, Black-throated Green Warbler, and Winter Wren, which might be absent from the southern slope of the same hillside.

concern is the rapid loss of Eastern Hemlock throughout this habitat. This defining tree is of great importance to breeding birds. Major die-offs caused by the Hemlock Woolly Adelgid, an introduced insect, have decimated hemlock populations, especially in the southern part of the tree's range.

DISTRIBUTION: This habitat of the e. United States and se. Canada is generally found to the north of TEMPERATE DECIDUOUS FOREST but reaches as far south as n. Georgia at higher elevations in the Appalachian Mountains. It transitions to TALLGRASS PRAIRIE at its western limit in Minnesota and stretches east as far as s. Newfoundland. In se. Canada, Temperate Mixed Forest is replaced by BOREAL CONIFER FOREST.

WHERE TO SEE: Great Smoky Mountains National Park, Tennessee–North Carolina, US; Allegheny National Forest, Pennsylvania, US.

Ne3D WESTERN RIPARIAN WOODLAND

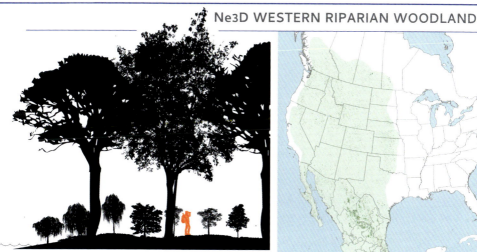

Top: **Western Riparian Woodland is typically dominated by cottonwoods with an understory of willows and other small tree/shrubs.**

Above: **Lower Rio Grande and Tamaulipan Riparian Woodland is shorter and more tropical than other Western Riparian subhabitats.**

IN A NUTSHELL: Disjunct areas of taller trees, particularly cottonwoods and willows, growing along permanent and semipermanent waterways and usually surrounded by more arid habitat types. **Global Habitat Affinities:** MEDITERRANEAN RIPARIAN FOREST. **Continental Habitat Affinities:** TEMPERATE DECIDUOUS FOREST. **Species Overlap:** TEMPERATE DECIDUOUS FOREST; SUBARCTIC RIPARIAN WOODLAND AND BOREAL SHRUBLAND MOSAIC; BALD CYPRESS-TUPELO GUM SWAMP; LOWLAND RIVERS.

DESCRIPTION: In the open expanses of the Great Plains and the western shrublands and deserts, Western Riparian Woodland often appears as an oasis in the distance: isolated ribbons of impressively tall trees growing along the banks of rivers and streams as they traverse the landscape. This habitat spans a huge area of the United States, from the cold prairies of Montana to the sunbaked landscapes of New Mexico and California, and extends into s. Canada and n. Mexico. Despite this large range, the structure and nature of Western Riparian Woodland remain consistent throughout—islands of dense, distinctly layered, deciduous broadleaf woodlands in a sea of other habitats. Taller forests occur in flatter areas with a wider floodplain. Steep, narrow, or largely dry waterways may have few or no large trees and include only the shrub layer.

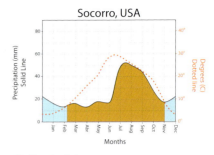

Although there are few unifying climatic characteristics, the plant composition is relatively consistent throughout the habitat's range. The largest and most dominant species in the canopy are either Fremont (*Populus fremontii*) or Eastern Cottonwood (*Populus deltoides*), which are separated by the Rocky Mountains. These trees form a dense canopy, usually greater than 60% coverage, and grow to a height of 65–80 ft. (20–25 m). Under the dense canopy, the woodland can be open and parklike, with little understory. Along with these primary trees, Arizona Walnut (*Juglans major*), Goodding's Willow (*Salix gooddingii*), and California (*Platanus racemosa*) and Arizona Sycamores (*Platanus wrightii*) are present and sometimes co-dominant in the southern half of the range. In the northern parts of the range, alders (*Alnus* spp.), Black Cottonwood (*Populus trichocarpa*), Box Elder (*Acer negundo*), and Quaking Aspen (*Populus tremuloides*) contribute to the canopy.

The shrub layer is diverse, dense, and variable. Generally, it forms a dense thicket at the water's edge, which thins as it is shaded out by canopy trees. In areas where there are no large cottonwoods,

Western Riparian Woodlands are often a lush oasis in an otherwise arid environment. © PHIL CHAON

these thickets can form a dense woodland and grow up to 30 ft. (10 m) tall, though heights of 5–15 ft. (1.5–4.5 m) are more typical. Willow (*Salix* spp.) is almost always the primary component or at least co-dominant. A large array of other shrubs includes elderberries (*Sambucus* spp.), serviceberries (*Amelanchier* spp.), dogwoods (*Cornus* spp.), poison oaks and ivies (*Toxicodendron* spp.), mesquites (*Prosopis* spp.), and various cherries (*Prunus* spp.). In arid areas, the invasive Athel Tamarisk (*Tamarix aphylla*) is a common component and can completely supplant native riparian vegetation. The herbaceous layer is strongly dependent on distance from water, successional stage, and geographic range. Some grass is almost always present, especially close to the water's edge or on most recently exposed banks. In particularly wet areas, there are REEDBED and SEDGE AND GRASSLAND MARSHES.

The **Ne3D-1 Western Mesquite Bosque** subhabitat occurs in the sw. United States and nw. Mexico within the Sonoran Desert. This subhabitat is notably shorter than most Western Riparian Woodlands, with a canopy entirely dominated by Velvet (*Prosopis velutina*) and Honey Mesquites (*Prosopis glandulosa*) and a relatively sparse understory. The waterways in this subhabitat frequently lack surface water and can remain as sandy channels for years at a time.

The **Ne3D-2 Lower Rio Grande and Tamaulipan Riparian Woodland** subhabitat is also quite distinctive. This habitat has little vegetative overlap with other Western Riparian Woodlands, and instead its canopy is composed largely of Texas Ebony (*Ebenopsis ebano*), Anacua (*Ehretia anacua*), Mexican Ash (*Fraxinus berlandieriana*), Great Leadtree (*Leucaena pulverulenta*), Montezuma Cypress (*Taxodium mucronatum*), and Cedar Elm (*Ulmus crassifolia*). Dense, swampy stands of Mexican Sabal Palm (*Sabal mexicana*) are another important but endangered feature of this habitat in the Rio Grande delta. Small oxbow wetlands and resacas (dry channels) are also common along the floodplain of this habitat. Farther south in forested parts of Mexico, riparian corridors often have extensions of habitats found in wetter climates.

The structure and continued survival of Western Riparian Woodland depends on the waterways themselves. Changes in peak and minimum flows, the duration for which surface water is present, and the period between floods drastically affect the species composition and health of this habitat. Regular floods are important for creating successional zones, depositing fresh nutrients, and germinating dormant seeds. If floods are too intense, the entire area can be scoured clean and in the process robbed of nutrient-rich soils that would normally allow for regeneration.

WILDLIFE: Western Riparian Woodlands generally lack unique fauna, but they do have a much higher diversity and abundance of wildlife than surrounding habitats. Riparian zones serve as both magnets and corridors for nearby animals, especially those not comfortable in open environments. Common mammals include White-tailed Deer, Common Raccoon, Virginia Opossum, various squirrels, North American River Otter, North American Porcupine, woodrats, Gray Fox, and Bobcat. North American Beaver is abundant and is a very important ecosystem engineer. Dams built by beavers create wetlands and increase shrub diversity in the area. Beaver-created wetlands also protect riparian zones during periods of heavy flooding.

The bird communities of riparian zones are distinct from those of surrounding habitats, though they also include species from these adjacent habitats. The structure provided by large trees is important for nesting birds, especially raptors. Bald Eagle and Great Horned Owl are common in riparian zones throughout the range. In the southwest, Gray Hawk and Common Black Hawk prefer to nest in riparian woodlands. Woodpeckers are common, Red-headed and Lewis's Woodpeckers, Red-naped Sapsucker, and Northern Flicker especially so. Secondary cavity nesters, including Eastern Bluebird and smaller owls like Western Screech-Owl and Elf Owl, take advantage of the many available woodpecker cavities. The dense willow thickets are full of birds. Yellow Warbler is omnipresent and perhaps defines this habitat more than any other species. Song Sparrow, Blue Grosbeak, Indigo and Lazuli Buntings, Bullock's Oriole, Summer Tanager, and Yellow-breasted Chat (IS) are also common.

SIDEBAR 5   WETLAND OF THE DAMMED

Apart from humans, few mammals are capable of altering the landscape and creating habitat quite like the North American Beaver. When people think of these large, paddle-tailed rodents, their iconic dams are often the first thing that come to mind. Beavers create dams across small streams and waterways, downing trees with their powerful jaws and chisel-like teeth and carrying timber, mud, and stones to create a barrier. American Beavers can fell trees up to 150 ft. (45 m) tall and 45 in. (114 cm) in diameter, though moving such massive trees is obviously impossible for a 50 lb. (23 kg) animal. The dams can reach massive scales over time; one dam in Montana was found to be 2130 ft. (650 m) long and 14 ft. (4.3 m) high.

Beaver dams create a variety of freshwater wetlands that benefit innumerable species. Beaver ponds are important rearing and foraging grounds for small fish including young trout and salmon. The dams can create barriers that impede the dispersal of non-native fish species up smaller waterways. The small wetlands are great habitat for amphibians, turtles, and all manner of aquatic insects. One species of dragonfly even bears the name Beaverpond Basket-tail. An abundance of rich aquatic vegetation means beaver ponds are often preferred foraging areas for Moose. The large numbers of amphibians and small fish also make beaver ponds important hunting grounds for American Mink, North American River Otter, Common Raccoon, Belted Kingfisher, and herons.

Beaver dams perform flood control after heavy rains, as water is slowly released over the tops of dams instead of rushing down in a torrent. The slowed passage of water through dams allows for excess sediment to settle in the ponds, resulting in clearer water. The creation of small wetlands also removes pollutants (metabolized by wetland-loving bacteria) and excess nitrogen (which leaves the water as gaseous bubbles). Abandoned dams will often become REEDBED MARSHES or SEDGE AND GRASSLAND MARSHES as sedimentation progresses. While North American Beavers have been hunted for fur and persecuted as pests for centuries, the benefits of beaver dams are now more widely recognized, and efforts to protect and even reintroduce beavers are increasing.

North American Beavers are amazing habitat engineers that creates a variety of different habitat features.
© PAUL VAN DER WERF/CREATIVE COMMONS (CC BY 2.0)

As the name suggests, Summer Tanager is an abundant summer resident in this habitat.
© BEN KNOOT, TROPICAL BIRDING TOURS

The boisterous and varied song of Yellow-breasted Chat is a common summer feature in riparian areas.
© BEN KNOOT, TROPICAL BIRDING TOURS

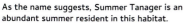

In the desert southwest, endangered subspecies of Willow Flycatcher (IS) and Yellow-billed Cuckoo (IS) are found exclusively in dense riparian habitat. Lucy's Warbler (IS) is strongly associated with the Western Mesquite Bosque subhabitat. The bird communities in the Lower Rio Grande and Tamaulipan Riparian Woodland subhabitat are closely related to the birds in TAMAULIPAN MEZQUITAL. Tropical freshwater wetland species like Least Grebe, Boat-billed Heron, Bare-throated Tiger-Heron, and Amazon Kingfisher are found in this habitat but not in the mezquital. The endangered Red-crowned Parrot strongly favors this subhabitat as well.

Riparian zones have fairly simple reptile communities that are often a subset of generalist species from surrounding areas. A wide variety of turtles and water snakes are common here. The importance of Western Riparian Woodlands to amphibians, on the other hand, cannot be overstated. Throughout much of the west, this habitat and associated wetlands provide the sole breeding grounds for frogs and toads in drier climates. Great Basin and Couch's Spadefoots; Western and Red-spotted Toads; Plains, Northern, and Relict Leopard Frogs; Canyon Tree Frog; and Northern Cricket Frog are just a few of the species that rely on this habitat for survival.

CONSERVATION: This is one of the most threatened habitats in w. North America due to complex issues related to water and overgrazing of the riparian vegetation. Flood controls have strongly altered spring flooding regimes. Water diversion for agriculture has reduced flow and killed vast swaths of woodland. Climate change has altered the length of droughts and the intensity of flooding, damaging riparian zones on both extremes of the precipitation spectrum. Additionally, non-native woody species such as Athel Tamarisk (*Tamarix aphylla*) and Russian Olive (*Elaeagnus angustifolia*) are replacing willow and cottonwood stands and depleting valuable water, especially in desert ecosystems.

Large swaths of Western Riparian Woodland have been cut for timber or cleared for agriculture along their associated rich and fertile floodplains. The situation is especially dire for the Lower Rio Grande and Tamaulipan Riparian Woodland subhabitat, of which less than 10% remains.

DISTRIBUTION: Western Riparian Woodland is found along permanent and semipermanent waterways, springs, and seeps throughout the w. United States. Tall, cottonwood-dominated woodlands are most common at low elevations, in flat areas, and along rivers with wide beds. As defined here, this habitat is found from the Great Plains west to the Central Valley of California. It occurs as far north as s. Saskatchewan and Alberta, Canada, and as far south as n. Chihuahua and Sonora, Mexico. The Western Mesquite Bosque subhabitat occurs along smaller waterways in the Sonoran Desert. The Lower Rio Grande and Tamaulipan Riparian Woodland subhabitat occurs along major rivers in far s. Texas and ne. Mexico, especially the Rio Grande, Nueces, and Tampaón.

WHERE TO SEE: Bosque del Apache National Wildlife Refuge, New Mexico, US; Cosumnes River Preserve, California, US; Missouri Headwaters State Park, Montana, US. LOWER RIO GRANDE AND TAMAULIPAN RIPARIAN WOODLAND—Santa Ana National Wildlife Refuge, Texas, US. WESTERN MESQUITE BOSQUE—Juan Bautista de Anza National Historic Trail, Arizona, US.

Ne3E ASPEN FOREST AND PARKLAND

IN A NUTSHELL: Stands of Quaking Aspen, often interspersed with meadows, typically occurring within patches of coniferous forest or at the transition between grassland and coniferous forest. **Global Habitat Affinities:** EUROPEAN MONTANE BIRCH-ASPEN FOREST; RIPARIAN WOODLAND. **Continental Habitat Affinities:** SUBARCTIC RIPARIAN WOODLAND AND BOREAL SHRUBLAND MOSAIC. **Species Overlap:** BOREAL CONIFER FOREST; MONTANE SPRUCE-FIR FOREST; SUBARCTIC RIPARIAN WOODLAND AND BOREAL SHRUBLAND MOSAIC; LODGEPOLE PINE FOREST; TEMPERATE MIXED FOREST.

DESCRIPTION: Occurring in the mountainous west and throughout the boreal zone, Aspen Forest and Parkland provides a welcome bit of variety within vast conifer-dominated areas. Aspen habitat has high biological productivity compared to surrounding areas and in summer is teeming with life. In the fall, Aspen Forest and Parkland is clearly visible as a golden blaze amid a sea of dark green. As the name suggests, this habitat comprises both stands of forest with an open or semi-open canopy, and parklands, or open meadows with a few scattered young trees. Quaking Aspen (*Populus tremuloides*) dominates, and few other tree species are present. Dense, often uniform-age stands of aspen grow to heights of 30–70 ft. (10–22 m). In the mountainous west, firs (*Abies* spp.), spruces (*Picea* spp.), and Douglas-fir (*Pseudotsuga menziesii*) co-occur and if undisturbed will eventually replace the short-lived and shade-averse aspen. In the Aspen Forest and Parkland of the n. Great Plains and the subboreal zone, Bur Oak (*Quercus macrocarpa*), Paper Birch (*Betula papyrifera*), Balsam Poplar (*Populus balsamifera*), and Red Maple (*Acer rubrum*) are notable co-occurring canopy trees.

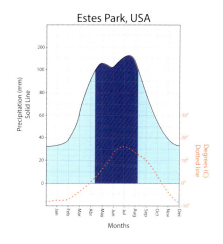

Estes Park, USA

Aspen Forest and Parkland has an open canopy that allows for a diverse and lush understory of shrubs, grasses, and forbs. This habitat's association with high disturbance and grassland

Aspen Forests turn a brilliant yellow in fall. © BEN KNOOT, TROPICAL BIRDING TOURS transitional zones means that small meadows and glades are an important component. Standing patiently along the edge of these glades can be an excellent strategy for wildlife-watching.

This habitat forms most commonly in areas of major disturbance—fire, landslide, avalanche, windthrows, and insect kills—or in transitional zones between grassland and forest. In areas with frequent disturbance, Quaking Aspen is destroyed aboveground but quickly regenerates clonal colonies spread through its roots. Individual sprouts from these colonies are called ramets or suckers. One such colony in Utah, known as Pando, weighs 13 million lb. (6 million kg) and is an estimated 80,000 years old—making it a contender for the planet's heaviest and oldest organism.

WILDLIFE: Aspen Forest and Parkland is prime mammalian grazing and browsing habitat, especially compared with the surrounding coniferous forest. This results in a high concentration of ungulates, such as White-tailed Deer, Elk, Bighorn Sheep, and Moose, along with small herbivores like ground squirrels, pocket gophers, and Snowshoe Hare. With the presence of so many prey animals, these areas are attractive to Gray Wolf, Coyote, Red Fox, and American Mink. The abundant forbs include many species with edible bulbs and tubers—a favorite food for both American Black Bear and Brown (aka Grizzly) Bear. Young Quaking Aspen is a preferred food tree for North American Beaver, and older trees are often utilized in dam building. While the disturbance is helpful in maintaining Aspen Forest and Parkland communities, flooding from dams can create conditions too wet for Quaking Aspen to grow. On the n. Great Plains, Richardson's Ground Squirrel, Thirteen-lined Ground Squirrel, and pocket gophers significantly contribute to maintaining the balance between aspen groves and grasslands. These burrowing rodents create mounds of fresh soil, providing excellent conditions for aspen seed germination. As the trees take root, they expand by suckering, leading to the formation of new aspen groves.

The bird communities here have similarities with those of both WESTERN RIPARIAN WOODLAND and the surrounding coniferous habitats, though with higher diversity. Aspen trees are easily excavated and host an abundance of cavity-nesting birds, including Mountain and Eastern Bluebirds, Yellow-bellied (IS) and Red-naped (IS) Sapsuckers, Merlin, House Wren, Northern Pygmy-Owl, and even Boreal Owl. Least Flycatcher, Dusky Flycatcher, Warbling Vireo, MacGillivray's and Wilson's Warblers, Lincoln's Sparrow, and Western Tanager are more common in aspen forests than in surrounding habitats in the west. In the east, American Woodcock likes

the wet soil and clearings associated with this habitat, and the lush understory is critical breeding habitat for Ruffed Grouse. Veery, Mourning and Connecticut Warblers, Ovenbird, and Dark-eyed Junco are other ground-nesters that take advantage of the increased leaf litter and ground cover for nesting.

Aspens are soft trees that are easy to make cavities in, leading to an abundance of Red-naped Sapsuckers.
© BEN KNOOT, TROPICAL BIRDING TOURS

If you think you are hearing a Humpback Whale singing in the mountains, it is most likely a bugling Elk. © BEN KNOOT, TROPICAL BIRDING TOURS

The aspen groves in Chihuahua are an important nesting habitat for the endangered Thick-billed Parrot. As in many montane and boreal habitats, the reptile and amphibian diversity is negligible.

CONSERVATION: Aspen Forest and Parkland has undergone massive declines in the past century, especially in the n. Great Plains. Primary causes are land clearance for agriculture or cattle grazing, and fire suppression. Overgrazing by cattle and wildlife alike can hinder regeneration in aspen forests. A famous study in Yellowstone National Park found that the loss of Gray Wolves and the subsequent increase in Mule Deer and Elk led to declines of Aspen Forest and associated birds.

Warbling Vireo is quite plain but has a lovely song. © BEN KNOOT, TROPICAL BIRDING TOURS

DISTRIBUTION: Aspen Forest and Parkland occurs in mid- to upper elevations (generally 5000–10,000 ft./1500–3000 m) in the mountainous west, from British Columbia, Canada, south into the United States through the Cascades and Sierra Nevada to c. California, and south through the Rocky Mountains to c. Arizona and New Mexico. It is a common habitat feature within MONTANE MIXED-CONIFER FOREST, LODGEPOLE PINE FOREST, and MONTANE SPRUCE-FIR FOREST and an occasional feature in SAGEBRUSH SHRUBLAND. Aspen Forest and Parkland is common at high latitudes from North Dakota west through the Canadian prairie provinces to c. Alberta and occurs at the transition zone between TALLGRASS PRAIRIE or MIXED-GRASS PRAIRIE and BOREAL CONIFER FOREST. The habitat is also patchily distributed throughout the boreal and subarctic zones in well-drained soils from Maine and the Canadian Maritimes west to c. Alaska. Pockets of aspen woodland also occur at high elevations in the Sierra Madre, as far south as Durango, Mexico, usually in the upper limits of MADREAN PINE-OAK WOODLAND.

WHERE TO SEE: Yellowstone National Park, Wyoming, US; Rocky Mountain National Park, Colorado, US; Sax-Zim Bog, Minnesota, US.

Ne3F COASTAL HAMMOCK, CHENIER, AND WOODLOT

IN A NUTSHELL: Patchy, broadleaf-dominated woodlands found on raised sections of coastal plain along the Gulf of Mexico and Atlantic and in the Caribbean. **Global Habitat Affinities:** None. **Continental Habitat Affinities:** TEMPERATE DECIDUOUS FOREST. **Species Overlaps:** TEMPERATE DECIDUOUS FOREST (Early Successional subhabitat), MESOAMERICAN SEMI-EVERGREEN FOREST.

DESCRIPTION: Coastal Hammock, Chenier, and Woodlot is a rather limited habitat occurring in slightly elevated coastal areas. The terms woodlot, hammock, and chenier are all used regionally to describe small, isolated patches of closed-canopy broadleaf woodlands. This habitat is divided into two principal subhabitats separated by geography, fauna, and flora: **Ne3F-1 Live Oak Hammock and Chenier**—live-oak dominated forests found on the southeastern coastal plains of the United States; and **Ne3F-2 Caribbean Hardwood Hammock**—tropical hardwood hammocks found mainly on Caribbean islands. Both subhabitats tend to form on slightly

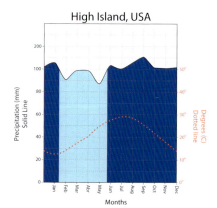

High Island, USA

elevated, well-drained soils, typically on storm-created berms, stabilized dunes, limestone flats, salt domes, and shell mounds. The most significant of these woodlands form on salt domes along the n. Gulf of Mexico. These domes are formed when large salt deposits beneath the sediment rise in response to differential loading. The largest salt dome on the Gulf coast is High Island, Texas, which at 38 ft. (11.6 m) above sea level is the highest point along the Gulf for hundreds of miles in either direction. Among the Caribbean Hardwood Hammocks, small shell-mound hammocks are anthropogenic in origin, formed from middens used as disposal sites for mollusk shells by Indigenous peoples and reaching heights well above the regular flood line. Both Live Oak Hammock and Chenier and Caribbean Hardwood Hammock occur in regions that are generally humid year-round, with pleasant, frost-free winters and hot summers. Large storms are prevalent in the summer months, and roughly 80% of the annual precipitation occurs during this period.

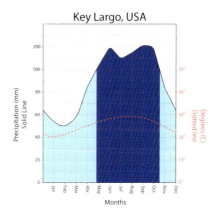

Key Largo, USA

   The Live Oak Hammock and Chenier subhabitat is a dense, closed-canopy forest, typically quite short (12–35 ft./4–10 m tall), and often gnarled and bent by persistent winds. This woodland can be shrubby and dwarfed in areas exposed to salt spray. The canopy of Live Oak Hammock and Chenier is heavily dominated by Southern Live Oak (*Quercus virginiana*), with smaller numbers of Sand Laurel Oak (*Quercus hemisphaerica*), Sand Live Oak (*Quercus geminata*), Pignut Hickory (*Carya*

Dense palmettos and Spanish Moss are common features of Live Oak Cheniers. © PETER MAY

glabra), Cabbage Palm (*Sabal palmetto*), and Sugar Hackberry (*Celtis laevigata*). The understory also tends to be quite dense, with a diverse array of fruiting shrubs that are an important food source for wildlife. American Beautyberry (*Callicarpa americana*), Gallberry (*Ilex glabra*), Southern Wax Myrtle (*Myrica cerifera*), Swamp Bay (*Persea palustris*), and Saw Palmetto (*Serenoa repens*) are all common in this subhabitat. The forest floor is usually devoid of herbaceous plants and grasses.

The Caribbean Hardwood Hammock subhabitat tends to be taller and more diverse than the chenier subhabitat and generally occurs in larger stands. This subtropical forest contains nearly 200 species of canopy trees across its range and nearly a dozen co-dominants; Gumbo-limbo (*Bursera simaruba*), Pigeon-plum (*Coccoloba diversifolia*), West Indian Mahogany (*Swietenia mahagoni*), and White Stopper (*Eugenia axillaris*) are almost always present. Poisonwood trees (*Metopium* spp.) growing in this environment can cause severe skin irritation and should be avoided if moving off trail—look for a tree with drooping clusters of five leaflets and flaky bark with oily black patches of dried sap. The dense canopy creates a more humid environment than the surroundings and promotes growth of shade-tolerant plants including many epiphytic orchids and bromeliads. There is a moderately dense midstory of vines and smaller canopy trees. The forest floor in this habitat is often bare, apart from leaf litter.

Coastal Hammock, Chenier, and Woodlot does not experience frequent fire, but disturbance is an important part of this habitat. The low-lying coastal nature of this forest means it is regularly exposed to intense storms and hurricanes. Entire hammocks and cheniers may disappear after a strong storm, but hurricanes also create high beach ridges upon which new hammocks and cheniers can grow.

WILDLIFE: Mammals are relatively sparse in this habitat and tend to include generalists from surrounding areas. In cheniers, Swamp Rabbit, Eastern Cottontail, Nine-banded Armadillo, Virginia Opossum, White-tailed Deer, and Bobcat are all common. Even fewer mammals are found in Caribbean Hardwood Hammock as the Caribbean itself is nearly devoid of mammalian fauna. In the Florida Keys, endangered mammals like Key Deer, Key Largo Woodrat, and Florida Bonneted Bat are found in this subhabitat. In the Caribbean, rare small mammals including the shrewlike Hispaniolan Selenodon and several species of hutia (rodents similar to the agoutis of the Neotropics) occupy this habitat. The endemic Pygmy Raccoon is found in hammocks on Cozumel, Mexico.

The bird communities are widely divergent between the two subhabitats. Live Oak Hammock and Chenier is relatively bird-free for much of the year, especially during the summer months, when Northern Cardinal, Northern Mockingbird, Carolina Wren, White-eyed Vireo, and Painted Bunting are just about the only birds to be found. For

White-eyed Vireo is one of the few birds breeding in Live Oak Chenier during the summer. © BEN KNOOT, TROPICAL BIRDING TOURS

SIDEBAR 6   MIGRANT TRAPS AND FALLOUT

The annual migration of birds from the Neotropics to their temperate breeding grounds is one of the great wildlife spectacles in the Western Hemisphere. While fall migration is more prolonged and leisurely, spring migration is a desperate race to reach nesting territories as quickly as possible. When searching out migrant birds, birders often visit areas that are known as "migrant traps." A migrant trap is simply any site that is visited by unusually high concentrations of migrating birds. Birds may find themselves concentrated in these areas for many reasons, though concentrations are principally the result of geography or habitat.

Frequently, migrant traps are found at the end of peninsulas or on islands, where the natural shape of the coastline concentrates birds in a location where they will pause before crossing over open water. Conversely, these peninsulas may be the first piece of land a bird sees after a long water crossing. Famous examples of peninsular migrant traps include Point Pelee, Ontario, and Cape May, New Jersey. Migrant traps may also occur at strategic points along long mountain ridges where mountains present a barrier to migration, or at the end of mountain chains that birds follow as important migratory corridors.

Habitat-driven traps usually occur in areas where most of the surrounding area lacks cover or food needed by migratory birds. Small oases of trees and water on the open plains or in the desert are great for attracting large concentrations of birds, as they are generally the only source of good resources for many miles. Melrose Woods on the eastern plains of New Mexico or Furnace Creek in California's Death Valley are both good examples of this sort of trap. The migrant trap at Magee Marsh in Ohio is a forested beach ridge that is mostly surrounded by open freshwater wetlands. At times, the limitations are driven not by natural habitat but by urban development. Central Park in New York City and Montrose Point in Chicago will be teeming with both birds and birders on any given day in migration.

The famous migrant traps along the Gulf of Mexico are bolstered by both factors. In spring, many birds will take a shortcut from the Yucatán Peninsula directly over the Gulf. This time-saving route is often perilous, with nowhere to rest during the 500+ mi. (800 km) flight over the water. The tall live oaks of COASTAL HAMMOCK, CHENIER, AND WOODLOT habitat are often the only trees immediately on the coastline and the only suitable habitat for tired migratory birds. If birds encounter major adverse weather events during these crossings, the result is called a "fallout." In these cases, storms or unfavorable shifts in wind direction have expended nearly all of a bird's energy, and the migrants barely make it to land, dropping en masse along the coastline. These events can be jaw-dropping, with thousands of buntings, orioles, warblers, and thrushes arriving in a single location at once. It should be noted that while amazing for birding, these events are extremely stressful for birds, and exhaustion should not be mistaken for tameness. Like all birds in migrant traps, these birds need to rest and feed to continue their incredible journey.

a few weeks in spring, this habitat has arguably the best birding in North America. In April and early May, cheniers on the Gulf coast experience the full force of billions of Neotropical migrant songbirds pouring northward. Birds making exhausting trans-Gulf flights drop into the first forests they encounter. In most cases, these are cheniers. Dozens of species of warblers, lawns covered in Indigo Buntings, and fruiting trees dripping with Baltimore Orioles, Orchard Orioles, Rose-breasted Grosbeaks, and Scarlet Tanagers are common phenomena following a fallout (see sidebar 6).

Caribbean Hardwood Hammocks by contrast are relatively poor sites for migration and have a broader suite of resident, wintering, and breeding bird species. In Florida, this is the primary

For a few weeks in spring, Live Oak Cheniers are full of migrating songbirds like American Redstart.
© BEN KNOOT, TROPICAL BIRDING TOURS

habitat for White-crowned Pigeon, Black-whiskered Vireo (IS), and Gray Kingbird. Additionally, many vagrant Caribbean birds, including Western Spindalis, Thick-billed Vireo, Key West Quail-Dove (IS), and La Sagra's Flycatcher will show up solely in this habitat. Historically, several of these species may have been permanent residents. In the Caribbean, most species are habitat generalists, present in Caribbean Hardwood Hammocks as well as other lowland forest types. Species composition is more strongly based on the island and the elevation than any habitat. Doves and pigeons are especially common

Western Spindalis occurs in Caribbean Hardwood Hammocks throughout the Caribbean. © PHIL CHAON

in hammocks due to the prevalence of fruiting trees. In the Bahamas, the endangered Kirtland's Warbler winters in the scrubbier portions of this habitat.

Virtually all reptiles and amphibians found in Coastal Live Oak and Hammock are generalists and are representative of those found in adjacent habitats. The critically endangered Rim Rock Crown Snake is found in this habitat in se. Florida and the Florida Keys. Less than 2% of its range remains undeveloped.

CONSERVATION: Live Oak Hammock and Chenier is a rare and threatened habitat. Most of it has already been lost to rampant coastal development, which continues to be a problem. Increasingly, fierce hurricanes and saltwater incursion threaten the future of these coastal forests. In Florida, the small percentage of Caribbean Hardwood Hammocks that remain have been acquired as conservation sites and are no longer threatened by development. Many of the important Live Oak Hammocks and Cheniers along the Gulf Coast have been protected by local conservation organizations, largely due to their popularity with birdwatchers.

DISTRIBUTION: This habitat is distributed in scattered patches along the coastal plain in the se. United States and in low-lying areas of the Bahamas and Greater Antilles. These areas must be elevated enough to avoid major saltwater intrusion and generally occur in small pockets of only a few acres. The Live Oak Hammock and Chenier subhabitat is found from North Carolina south through Florida and along the Gulf of Mexico to s. Texas. The Caribbean Hardwood Hammock subhabitat is located in extreme s. Florida, especially the Florida Keys, the Bahamas, Cuba, Puerto Rico, and Hispaniola. It is also present in Jamaica but is more limited. Cozumel holds the only examples of Caribbean Hardwood Hammock in Mexico. Low-lying areas of Coastal Hammock, Chenier, and Woodlot are generally surrounded by SALT MARSH, MESOAMERICAN MANGROVES, the Gulf Coast Prairie subhabitat of TALLGRASS PRAIRIE, CARIBBEAN THORNSCRUB, or SANDY BEACH AND DUNES.

WHERE TO SEE: High Island, Texas, US; Key Largo, Florida, US.

Ne3G SUBARCTIC RIPARIAN WOODLAND AND BOREAL SHRUBLAND MOSAIC

IN A NUTSHELL: Deciduous shrubs and trees that grow along rivers and protected areas of tundra. **Global Habitat Affinities:** BOREAL MIXED WOODLAND; EURASIAN SUBARCTIC RIPERIAN WOODLAND; EURASIAN SHRUBBY TUNDRA. **Continental Habitat Affinities:** None. **Species Overlap:** SHRUB TUNDRA; TEMPERATE MIXED FOREST; BOREAL CONIFER FOREST.

DESCRIPTION: A common misconception is that conifers are the northernmost trees. But on the southern edge of the tundra, where there is an extremely short growing season (Köppen **ET**), permafrost below, abundant snow, and high exposure to wind, an Arctic scrub of birch and aspen groves, not evergreen conifers, grows in the most protected areas. These shrublands of Dwarf

Birch (*Betula nana*), Alaska Willow (*Salix alaxensis*),
Balsam Poplar (*Populus balsamifera*), and Paper
Birch (*Betula papyrifera*) comprise the same general
assemblage as in WESTERN RIPARIAN WOODLAND.
Where these groves exist between the conifers and
tundra, they expand in favorable years and contract
in more severe years. In the toughest conditions of
the subarctic, conifers such as spruce and fir are
unable to survive through the winter due to the fact
that they are evergreen—any tree that carries leaves
at all, and that thus needs to eke out water from the
permafrost during the winter months, finds it difficult
to survive. When these evergreens succumb, they
are replaced by colonist deciduous angiosperms and
deciduous conifers, such as Tamarack Larch (*Larix

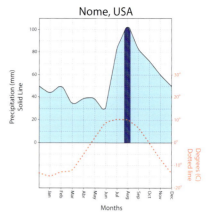

laricina*). These groves are generally very open, with a krummholz canopy (wind-blown in one
direction), usually around 4 ft. (1.2 m) tall on exposed areas and 20 ft. (6 m) tall in more protected
areas, especially where there are snowbanks. The lowest shrubs are dominated by European

Subarctic Riparian Woodlands and Boreal Shrublands are usually surrounded by tundra or coniferous forest.
© BEN KNOOT, TROPICAL BIRDING TOURS

Blueberry (*Vaccinium myrtillus*) and Bog Bilberry (*Vaccinium uliginosum*). In contrast to the soils of the tundra, these shrublands cause a strong spodosol (podzol) soil (heavily leached at surface in an acidic environment) to develop underneath, which is typical of the conifer forests to the south.

In the boreal areas to the south with a more moderate climate (Köppen **Dsd**), along riverine areas and in recently disturbed environments (perhaps after severe storms), those same Balsam Poplars and Paper Birches are joined by Black Spruce (*Picea mariana*) and closed stands of Quaking Aspen (*Populus tremuloides*), forming a mixed woodland with a canopy 60–90 ft. (20–30 m) high that is generally erect, without a krummholz form. The understory of these woodlands is dominated by dwarf shrubs, many of which are circumpolar and familiar to people from n. Europe, such as Alpine Bearberry (*Arctous alpina*), Black Crowberry (*Empetrum nigrum*), and Blue Mountainheath (*Phyllodoce caerulea*), as well as subshrubs such as Twinflower (*Linnaea borealis*). The ground is covered with lichens and mosses such as Glittering Woodmoss (*Hylocomium splendens*) and Red-stemmed Feather Moss (*Pleurozium schreberi*).

There are many small glades in this habitat with fields of the mixed small shrubs mentioned above, joined with grasses and forbs such as Edlund's Fescue (*Festuca edlundiae*), Wavy Hair-grass (*Deschampsia flexuosa*), Lapland Reedgrass (*Calamagrostis lapponica*), Bigelow's Sedge (*Carex bigelowii*), and Lapland Lousewort (*Pedicularis lapponica*). In marshy areas, Highland Rush (*Oreojuncus trifidus*) can become dominant. At first pass, the nature of these fields may suggest

Moose favor Subarctic Riparian Woodland and Boreal Shrubland Mosaic for the abundance of deciduous vegetation. © PHIL CHAON

that they be classified as TALLGRASS PRAIRIE, but they lack the bird or animal assemblages of those grasslands to the south and are better regarded as light gaps within the broader riparian and shrubland habitat.

WILDLIFE: The mammal assemblage in these shrublands, in contrast with birds, is the same as that of the surrounding conifer forests, though the mammals use them at different times. At their northern extent in Alaska, Brown Bears, rare in the SUBARCTIC WOODLAND, concentrate and hibernate in these shrublands, venturing into the southern tundra to forage in summer. Many bird species find their northern limits where these shrublands extend along protected areas into tundra, such as Arctic Warbler, Gray-cheeked Thrush, Bluethroat (in Alaska), Rusty Blackbird, Yellow Warbler, and Blackpoll Warbler. The bird assemblage departs from that of the surrounding BOREAL CONIFER FOREST farther south, and Subarctic Riparian Woodland and Boreal Shrubland Mosaic lack species such as Ruffed Grouse, Spruce Grouse, American Three-toed Woodpecker, Canada Jay, Boreal Chickadee, Red-breasted Nuthatch, and Red Crossbill.

CONSERVATION: This habitat is fascinating in that as a colonizer, and sometimes successional habitat, it is quick to take advantage of changing conditions. It has recently become common around Nome as a shrubland, with small groves replacing the ROCKY TUNDRA and SHRUB TUNDRA. As global warming continues (see fig. 9, the Köppen climate map for Alaska), vast regions of n. Alaska and n. Canada will change to a climate much more conducive to growth of conifer forest and these woodlands and shrublands. Conifers are much slower at advancing than poplar, birch, and willow, so the potentially massive void will be first exploited by this habitat.

DISTRIBUTION: This habitat is found from the northern limits of the BOREAL CONIFER FOREST near Nome to a broad swath around Hudson Bay in Canada. There are small patches as outliers well within tundra zones, such as in Utqiagvik (Barrow), Alaska.

WHERE TO SEE: Churchill, Manitoba, Canada; Council Road, Nome, Alaska, US.

Right: **The Bluethroat breeds mostly in the Palearctic but is also found in riparian areas in w. Alaska.**
© BEN KNOOT, TROPICAL BIRDING TOURS

Below: **Despite their large size, Brown (aka Grizzly) Bears (pictured with Elk prey) can hide quite well in Subarctic Riparian Woodland. Caution should be exercised when entering this habitat.**
© BEN KNOOT, TROPICAL BIRDING TOURS

North American Humid Forests Dendrogram

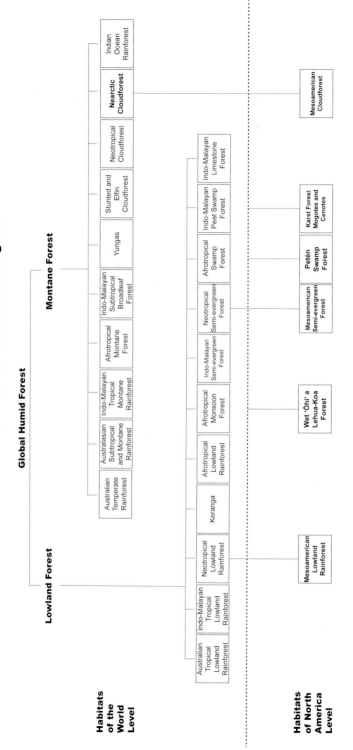

TROPICAL HUMID FORESTS

Ne4A MESOAMERICAN CLOUDFOREST

IN A NUTSHELL: Cloudforests, their large trees laden with mosses and bromeliads and constant water dripping off the leaves, are the quintessential forests of the mountains of s. Mexico through Central America. **Global Habitat Affinities:** ANDEAN CLOUDFOREST; AFROTROPICAL MOIST MONTANE FOREST; AUSTRALASIAN TROPICAL MONTANE RAINFOREST; SUNDA MONTANE RAINFOREST. **Continental Habitat Affinities:** WET 'ŌHI'A LEHUA–KOA FOREST. **Species Overlap:** MADREAN PINE-OAK WOODLAND; MESOAMERICAN SEMI-EVERGREEN FOREST; MESOAMERICAN LOWLAND RAINFOREST; KARST FOREST MOGOTES AND CENOTES.

DESCRIPTION: The mountain ranges of tropical Mexico, with elevations between 3300 ft. and 11,500 ft. (1000–3500 m), receive precipitation not only as rainfall but also as a perpetual billow of cloud and fog cover that emanates humidity resulting in a Köppen climate of (**Cwb**). The high humidity, amounting to 47–160 in. (1200–4000 mm) of precipitation annually, combined with the very steep nature of the slopes on which this habitat grows, produces frequent landslides and a constant recolonization by cloudforest. In regions of higher rainfall, the cloudforests have a pretty obvious and logical boundary, the MESOAMERICAN LOWLAND RAINFOREST, governed by elevation. In drier regions, the boundaries become a much more complex mosaic of isolated patches of cloudforest surrounded by drier forests, in a mélange, with the cloudforests occupying protected ravines and steep slopes, and the drier habitats such as PACIFIC DRY DECIDUOUS FOREST or MADREAN

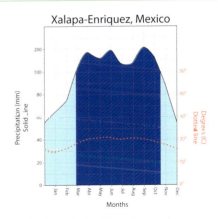

Xalapa-Enriquez, Mexico

True to its name, Mesoamerican Cloudforest is often cloaked in mist. © BEN KNOOT, TROPICAL BIRDING TOURS

PINE-OAK WOODLAND occupying areas more exposed to fire or more desiccating winds. Overall, Mesoamerican Cloudforest covers less than 1% of the area of Mexico. The cloudforests can be subdivided into **Lower Montane Cloudforest**, at 3300–8200 ft. (1000–2500 m) and **Upper Montane Cloudforest**, at 6600–11,500 ft. (2000–3500 m). Above 11,500 ft., up to 12,500 ft. (3800 m), this forest is severely stunted and analogous to the Elfin Forest of Central and South America. In Mexico, because it is so restricted and lacks distinct bird assemblages, **Elfin Forest** is treated as a subhabitat of Mesoamerican Cloudforest. The Lower Montane Cloudforest subhabitat differs from the Upper Montane Cloudforest subhabitat in having some trees with minor buttress roots and having fewer mosses, bromeliads, and other epiphytes and more vines than the latter.

The canopies of this evergreen forest are lower than those of the rainforest—cloudforest trees rarely grow taller than 80 ft. (25 m) —and branches extend much lower on the trunk than in trees of MESOAMERICAN LOWLAND RAINFOREST or MESOAMERICAN SEMI-EVERGREEN FOREST. Because of the constant landslides, the forest is disjointed, with trees of different ages and heights forming a noncontiguous canopy that lets far more light hit the understory than in lowland rainforest. Most of the trees are close relatives of species found in rainforest, such as Remiendo (*Oreomunnea mexicana*), though some, like the Mexican Hand Tree (*Chiranthodendron pentadactylon*), belong to genera endemic to the cloudforest. The forest is dominated by broad-leaved angiosperms, and a few of these species are very widespread in the s. and e. United States such as American Hornbeam (*Carpinus caroliniana*) and Sweetgum (*Liquidambar styraciflua*).

Some of the non-angiosperms first evolved before South America and Africa split from Antarctica about 180 million years ago, and therefore have strong Gondwanan affinities, such as the Tabla (*Podocarpus matudae*), which is a conifer, and the Mexican Tree Fern (*Alsophila firma*). Overall, pioneer species like the extremely fast-growing cecropias make up a much higher proportion of the canopy than in more stable forests. Bromeliads are also a major component of the cloudforest canopy, and it is rare to see an old tree that is not enveloped by bromeliads and draping mosses.

Because of the open nature of the canopy, there is a strong and irregular subcanopy as well as a very thick brush layer. In contrast with rainforest, the undergrowth in the cloudforest is extremely thick, made up of many broadleaf saplings and massive-leaved bushes such as *Gunnera* spp., whose leaves can approach 10 sq. ft. (1 m²) in area. Heliconias (which resemble banana plants) are very common in light gaps. Mexican Climbing Bamboo (*Chusquea coronalis*) forms dense thickets on the ground up to 10 ft. (3 m) tall, and species of climbing bamboos reach up into the canopy, though the stands here are nowhere near as dominant as they are in the cloudforests of the Andes or se. Brazil. Due to the thick understory, it is nearly impossible to walk through cloudforest away from a trail without a machete to cut a path.

WILDLIFE: The habitat's great range of elevation and its growth in many isolated side ranges have produced huge biodiversity, resulting in many localized endemics. Frog and reptile diversity is very high below 4000 ft. (1200 m), but above this elevation the forest gets cold, and species diversity drops dramatically. Very few venomous snakes make it above 5000 ft. (1500 m), and frog diversity is reduced, often to just localized endemics.

In stark contrast to the bird assemblages (described below), many of the larger mammals found in the cloudforests are widespread in North America, so species such as Virginia Opossum, Nine-banded Armadillo, Southern Flying Squirrel, Coyote, American Hog-nosed Skunk, Common Raccoon, and White-tailed Deer will be familiar to many visitors. More distinctly Neotropical mammals like Northern Tamandua, Kinkajou, and White-nosed Coati also occur here. The Kinkajou is one of the larger mammals with a more southerly provenance, occurring through much of n. South America. Almost all cat species (certainly all American cat species) live in a wide variety of habitats, so cats are found throughout the Neotropics. Jaguarundi, Ocelot, Margay, and Jaguar can all occur in the cloudforests but are rarely encountered. Puma (aka Mountain Lion) is the most habitat- and climate-tolerant of all cat species, found from the Yukon, at 52°N, to Patagonia, at 55°S—that whopping 107° latitude variation is the greatest natural latitudinal range of any mammal other than humans.

Some of the other mammals found here are also very catholic in habitat choice, also found in lowland rainforests and deciduous forests, with examples including Mexican Cottontail, Mexican Gray Squirrel, Hooded Skunk, Long-tailed Weasel, and Ringtail. Goldman's Broad-clawed Shrew is one of the few mammals endemic to the cloudforests of Mexico. There are many bat species here and numerous mice, such as Mexican Spiny Pocket Mouse, various species of giant deer mice, and Aztec Mouse. There is a distinct lack of primates in the Mesoamerican Cloudforest of Mexico, though farther south this habitat has a few species including howler monkeys and capuchins.

Birdlife in the cloudforest is dominated by frugivorous families such as tanagers, New World barbets, and cotingas. Many of these canopy birds move in large mixed-species flocks, sometimes

Horned Guan is endemic to cloudforest on high mountain slopes in Chiapas, Mexico, and Guatemala.
© DANIEL ALDANA SCHUMANN

Opposite: **The Resplendent Quetzal is one of the most beautiful creatures on earth.** © BEN KNOOT, TROPICAL BIRDING TOURS

Right: **Garnet-throated Hummingbird often appears all dark in the low light of the cloudforest but is spectacular in sunlight.** © DANIEL ALDANA SCHUMANN

numbering hundreds of individuals. These flocks move as waves: First come the flock-leader species, often members of the various genera collectively called tanagers, such as Flame-colored and Yellow-winged Tanagers, as well as Squirrel Cuckoo, Blue-throated Motmot, and Spotted and Spot-crowned Woodcreepers. They are followed by a whole suite of species that wander great distances; this group is joined for short periods by species that are more loyal to one territory but will participate in the feeding frenzy in their area. All this means that flocking may last for hours and go for miles with a changing mix of species. There are also understory flocks that may move with the canopy flocks or independently of them. These undergrowth flocks are dominated by species such as Eye-ringed Flatbill, Middle American Leaftosser, Rufous-browed Wren, and several thrushes. Other birds in the forest that tend not to join flocks include the enigmatic Horned Guan, Highland Guan, Singing Quail, White-faced Quail-Dove, and Resplendent Quetzal, the males of which have wonderful, elongate tail feathers.

Hummingbird diversity is much higher in cloudforest than in lowland rainforest, and various species make up a significant portion of the bird assemblage; in El Triunfo reserve, of 101 regular bird species, 15 are hummingbirds, including common species such as Green-throated Mountain-gem, Garnet-throated Hummingbird, Rivoli's Hummingbird, Wine-throated Hummingbird, and Violet Sabrewing.

CONSERVATION: Conservation of the cloudforests in Mexico is difficult, with many challenges including population growth, illegal clearing for cash crops, and insufficient governance. To protect what remains, agencies and NGOs are undertaking a combination of protective measures such as sustainable land-use practices, research, and community engagement. Protected areas include El Triunfo Biosphere Reserve in Chiapas, which encompasses cloudforest ecosystems.

DISTRIBUTION: The Mesoamerican Cloudforest is found as tiny enclaves dotted along mountain slopes as far north as 25°N in c. Mexico and becomes more dominant through s. Mexico. The habitat is common in Central America, though the bird assemblies change. Mesoamerican Cloudforests are also found in the Caribbean. They are widespread on the island of Hispaniola, though much more extensive in the Dominican Republic than in Haiti. They are also found in Puerto Rico, e. Cuba, and e. Jamaica.

WHERE TO SEE: El Triunfo Biosphere Reserve, Chiapas, Mexico; José Armando Bermúdez National Park, Dominican Republic.

Ne4B MESOAMERICAN SEMI-EVERGREEN FOREST

IN A NUTSHELL: A slightly drier version of Mesoamerican Lowland Rainforest (and often mistakenly referred to as lowland rainforest in Central America), differing in that some trees lose their leaves in drier periods of the year. **Global Habitat Affinities:** NEOTROPICAL SEMI-EVERGREEN FOREST; MALABAR SEMI-EVERGREEN FOREST; SOUTHEAST ASIAN SEMI-EVERGREEN FOREST; BRAHMAPUTRA SEMI-EVERGREEN FOREST. **Continental Habitat Affinities:** None. **Species Overlap:** MESOAMERICAN LOWLAND RAINFOREST; YUCATÁN DRY DECIDUOUS FOREST; PETÉN SWAMP FOREST; KARST FOREST MOGOTES AND CENOTES.

DESCRIPTION: Rainfall of the Mesoamerican Semi-Evergreen Forest is comparable to that of some lowland rainforests, approximately 48–75 in. (1200–1900 mm) annually, although the rainforests also receive much higher rainfall amounts. This forest's climate (Köppen **Awb**) has an uneven monsoonal distribution of precipitation, with a dry season of up to six months of reduced rainfall, including a few exceedingly dry months with almost no rain along with excessive evapotranspiration rates. So even though for much of the year it appears an ideal growing environment, the harsh months are the primary driver of this ecosystem.

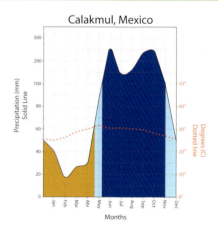

Calakmul, Mexico

Much of what is called rainforest in s. Mexico and Central America is actually this habitat type. The confusion arises because for much of the year, in the wet season, Mesoamerican Semi-Evergreen Forest appears very similar to MESOAMERICAN LOWLAND RAINFOREST. Both have tall trees that grow to around 130 ft. (40 m) in height, have large, laurel-shaped leaves, and are draped by numerous lianas. The typical trees that are evergreen, retaining their leaves throughout the year, include Jobillo (*Astronium graveolens*), which has a very straight trunk with large buttresses up to 6 ft. (2 m) tall and can sometimes be so dominant that the forest could be regarded as a Jobillo forest. Other common canopy evergreen trees that are also found in surrounding rainforests include Sapodilla (*Manilkara zapota*), Santa Maria or Jacareúba (*Calophyllum brasiliense*), and possibly the strangest named of any of the rainforest trees, the Horse Balls Tree (*Taberneaemontana donnell-smithii*), whose fruit is composed of two very large, separate carpels; botany would be so much easier if all plants were described so pertinently.

Mesoamerican Semi-Evergreen Forest covers a large part of the Yucatán Peninsula and conceals some massive ancient cities like Calakmul. © PHIL CHAON

The understory of Mesoamerican Semi-Evergreen Forest can be quite open during the dry season. © PHIL CHAON

In the drier (winter) months, however, this forest looks very different. With numerous bare branches on the deciduous trees, the semi-evergreen nature becomes evident, although only 30% of the canopy trees are deciduous, losing their leaves in the dry season. The deciduous nature become very obvious when the main emergent tree of the forest, the Kapok Ceiba (*Ceiba pentandra*), loses its leaves, revealing the large pods hanging from the bare branches. Other deciduous canopy trees include Hormigo (*Platymiscium dimorphandrum*) and Ramon (*Brosimum alicastrum*), the latter of which can lose its leaves twice a year. Another significant proportion of the canopy trees are semi-evergreen, losing their leaves only in years when rainfall is reduced to a degree that stresses them; these include Honduran Mahogany (*Swietenia macrophylla*) and Cuban Cedar (*Cedrela odorata*).

The Mesoamerican Semi-Evergreen Forest is a little more open than lowland rainforest, with upper canopy coverage at around 80%, which allows for an overall two-canopy structure, including a distinct and complete middle canopy. Some of the middle-canopy trees are also deciduous, such as Pink Poui (*Tabebuia rosea*), but many are evergreen, including Allspice (*Pimenta dioica*) and Holywood (*Guaiacum sanctum*), the latter sometimes becoming a very dominant mid-canopy tree.

Many of the less conspicuous middle-canopy tree species are microphyllous (having small, narrow leaves) rather than deciduous and are more similar to the species of the YUCATÁN DRY DECIDUOUS FOREST than to lowland rainforest trees.

These lower-level trees tend to flower in the dry season, and the combination of a colorful lower canopy and a more barren upper canopy makes this forest easier to identify at this time of the year. Epiphytes and mosses are not as numerous as in MESOAMERICAN LOWLAND RAINFOREST or MESOAMERICAN CLOUDFOREST, which becomes obvious only when you are inside the forest looking up. Palms, such as Escobo (*Cryosophila stauracantha*), are common in the understory, though because they usually grow to only around 22 ft. (7 m) tall, they are not obvious in the mid-canopy. Guarumo (*Cecropia peltata*) is a very common and conspicuous tree with hand-shaped leaves. It is one of the first colonizers in an area that is exposed, such as a road cutting or light gap (opening in the forest caused by natural occurrence such as tree-fall), and is usually replaced by other trees over time. Undergrowth in the Mesoamerican Semi-Evergreen Forest is diminished due to the heavy lower canopy, so walking around in this forest feels similar to walking in lowland rainforest.

Various parrot snake species can be found hunting high in the trees of these forests. © PHIL CHAON

One of the fascinating aspects of these forests in this part of Mesoamerica is that they may have been extremely denuded by the Maya in the very recent past. Many of the prime examples of these forests are in areas surrounding deserted Mayan cities such as Tikal and Calakmul, where seemingly timeless forests have formed on fallow land in recent soils derived from denuded hillsides. No doubt some of the forests cut by the Maya were lowland rainforests, but the extent to which the existing forests can be seen as advanced secondary rainforests or climax semi-evergreen forests is in need of further research.

WILDLIFE: Although its vegetation is distinctly different, Mesoamerican Semi-Evergreen Forest is remarkably similar to MESOAMERICAN LOWLAND RAINFOREST in terms of wildlife. Most mammal species freely use both when the two habitats are adjacent. Amphibian numbers are lower in semi-evergreen forests, while lizards become relatively more common.

Birdlife is similar in the two habitats, with some of the same families represented, but overall species numbers are lower in the semi-evergreen forests of Mexico than in the lowland rainforest, with fewer "rainforest guilds"—groups of birds with similar feeding strategies such as obligate antbirds, barbets, puffbirds, and gnateaters—relative to the more humid forests. The star bird of this habitat in Mexico is the magnificent Ocellated Turkey, whose wattles are so bright and grotesque they look like they were finger-painted by a toddler. Other ground birds include Thicket Tinamou, Great Curassow, and Red-throated and Red-crowned Ant-Tanagers. There are far fewer hummingbirds than are present in MESOAMERICAN CLOUDFOREST, but Wedge-tailed Sabrewing and Buff-bellied and White-bellied Hummingbirds are regulars. Compared to the nearby YUCATÁN

The bizarre Ocellated Turkey is often found around protected temples on the Yucatán Peninsula. © PHIL CHAON

Ornate Hawk-Eagle with prey in Calakmul Biosphere Reserve. © PHIL CHAON

DRY DECIDUOUS FOREST, Mesoamerican Semi-Evergreen Forest has many more parrots, such as White-fronted Parrot and Olive-throated Parakeet; antbirds, such as Barred Antshrike and Mayan Antthrush; and tanagers, such as the Red-legged Honeycreeper. Other birds found in this habitat include Black-headed, Collared, and Gartered Trogons, Squirrel Cuckoo, Ivory-billed Woodcreeper, Northern Bentbill, Eye-ringed Flatbill, Bright-rumped Attila, Spot-breasted Wren, and Montezuma Oropendola.

CONSERVATION: While large areas of this habitat were transformed to thornscrub in Mayan times, and cleared for farmland in colonial times, vast areas still exist and are at least partially protected in some massive biosphere reserves such as Calakmul, which borders the huge Maya Biosphere Reserve in Guatemala. Problems exist in these biosphere reserves, with natural population growth and immigration, and until those conflicts can be resolved, the habitat remains threatened.

DISTRIBUTION: Mesoamerican Semi-Evergreen Forest is found in s. Mexico along the Caribbean coast through Central America. It also occurs in many of the Caribbean islands, where it can be the dominant lowland humid forest type.

WHERE TO SEE: Calakmul Biosphere Reserve, Campeche, Mexico.

Ne4C KARST FOREST MOGOTES AND CENOTES

IN A NUTSHELL: The natural limestone or marble towers (mogotes) and sinkholes (cenotes) of Mesoamerica and the Caribbean. **Global Habitat Affinities:** INDO-MALAYAN LIMESTONE FOREST. **Continental Habitat Affinities:** MESOAMERICAN SEMI-EVERGREEN FOREST; MESOAMERICAN CLOUDFOREST. **Species Overlap.** MESOAMERICAN SEMI-EVERGREEN FOREST; MESOAMERICAN CLOUDFOREST; PETÉN SWAMP FOREST; YUCATÁN DRY DECIDUOUS FOREST; CARIBBEAN THORNSCRUB.

Above left: **Many cenotes have deep pools linked to subterranean rivers, though some may be forested.**

Left: **Karst Forest occurs on complex terrain often riddled with limestone caves.**

DESCRIPTION: It may seem incongruous that this one habitat encompasses both hills and sinkholes, but these microhabitats are aspects of karst topography, which develops when soluble minerals such as calcium carbonate and gypsum are removed from rocks such as limestone (a calcareous sedimentary rock), dolomite (a calcareous-magnesium sedimentary rock), and very rarely—and not in Mesoamerica—sandstone (a silica-rich sedimentary rock). The minerals are chemically weathered (broken down) and eroded (removed) by water percolating in the rocks to create underground caves. In the lowlands, these caves can connect to underwater flows that

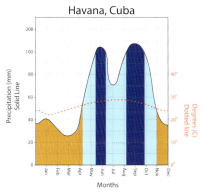

may move many feet per day, and the caves can join each other, sometimes falling in to cause sinkholes, called cenotes, which are linked to each other through the waterway and cave system. The sinkholes can have large open-water pools over 100 ft. (30 m) wide, though most cenotes have flooded soil and vegetation at the base, which can be up to 50 ft. (15 m) below the surrounding ground surface, and look like sunken forests.

When this process occurs in higher areas, the base level of water is much lower, and most importantly, the rock system has a lot of vertical jointing (cracks) that allows water to percolate quickly; the erosion of the cave system can become extreme, with rectangular blocks of the

Imposing mogotes are a conspicuous feature in parts of Cuba. © CHRIS SLOAN

overlying rock falling to the base and rolling away. When most of the original level of the landscape has been removed, only the towers, called mogotes in the Caribbean, remain. In cenotes, the vegetation is governed by the underground hydrological cycle, while in mogotes, the vegetation is determined by the edaphic nature of the soils caused by the calcareous bedrock; in neither of these environments is the climate a primary factor in vegetation development.

In Mesoamerica, and particularly in the Yucatán, the general landscape around the top of a cenote can have CARIBBEAN THORNSCRUB or MESOAMERICAN SEMI-EVERGREEN FOREST, though the most common vegetation type is YUCATÁN DRY DECIDUOUS FOREST, its small trees and shrubs dominated by the kapok tree Pochote (*Ceiba aesculifolia*), along with Gumbo-limbo (*Bursera simaruba*), Cuban Cedar (*Cedrela odorata*), and Spanish-elm (*Cordia alliodora*). The plant growth on the sides and base of the sinkholes has more in common with vegetation typical of PETÉN SWAMP FOREST, so in the driest areas of Yucatán, the difference between the surface ground layer and the sinkhole forest can be very stark, with the cenote containing tall trees, while these have mainly been removed for agriculture at the surface. These include Sapodilla (*Manilkara zapota*), Honduran Mahogany (*Swietenia macrophylla*), Campeche Logwood (*Haematoxylum campechianum*), Black Poisonwood (*Metopium brownei*), and Yax-nik (*Vitex gaumeri*), but they are generally much shorter and thinner here than they are in the Petén Swamp Forest, rarely topping 50 ft. (15 m). Because of the lack

Opposite: **Cenotes have deep clear pools at the bottom, which are often connected to Limestone Caves and Subterranean Rivers.**
© BEN KNOOT, TROPICAL BIRDING TOURS

of direct sunlight at the base of the cenote, the forest grows with a more open canopy, and the understory and ground cover are much thicker than in normal swamp forest, composed of trees such as West Indian Elm (*Guazuma ulmifolia*), Pimientillo (*Xilopia frutescens*), and Dysentery-bark (*Simarouba glauca*). Karst formations are also an important feature of MESOAMERICAN CLOUDFOREST in c. and s. Mexico.

On the mogotes, the forest forms on lithosols (poorly developed soils) on the slopes or cliffs of the dolomite and limestone towers. In these steeper and drier settings, the trees have to adapt to harsh conditions of water scarcity and nutrient deficiency; coping mechanisms include deciduous, sclerophyllous, and/or microphyllous leaves, or pachycaulous (bottle-shaped) trunks—or being a cactus. The canopy of the mogote forest is very open and usually below 30 ft. (9 m) tall, though sometimes up to 50 ft. (15 m), but at the base of mogote slopes, those same trees can have a canopy around 60 ft. (20 m) tall and can be covered by mosses and epiphytes.

There are many endemic plant species in this habitat throughout the Caribbean, but in Cuba, the karst forest is dominated by Cuban Frangipani (*Plumeria emarginata*), Barbados Cherry (*Malpighia emarginata*), Strawberry Guava (*Psidium cattleianum*), Bastard Lime (*Trichilia havanensis*), and Hammock Velvetseed (*Guettarda elliptica*). The cliffs are dominated by *Agave tubulata* and the cycad Cork Palm (*Microcycas calocoma*). Palms such as Palmita de Jumagua (*Hemithrinax ekmaniana*) and the Brittle Thatch Palm (*Leucothrinax morrisii*) grow in better-watered areas.

WILDLIFE: Karst formations within MESOAMERICAN CLOUDFOREST in Oaxaca and Veracruz are the sole habitat for the cave-dwelling Nava's Wren (IS) and Sumichrast's Wren (IS). Fan-tailed Warblers are also strongly associated with karst, and Maroon-fronted Parrots are reliant on limestone cliffs for nesting sites. Depending on the amount of forest on the sides and bottom, the bottoms of cenotes tend to hold the same types of birds as the PETÉN SWAMP FOREST and the MESOAMERICAN SEMI-EVERGREEN FOREST, with species such as Thicket Tinamou, Red-throated and Red-crowned Ant-Tanagers, Barred Antshrike, Mayan Antthrush, Wedge-tailed Sabrewing, Buff-bellied and White-bellied Hummingbirds, and Black-headed, Collared, and Gartered Trogons. The tops of cenotes have the more typical CARIBBEAN THORNSCRUB species such as Turquoise-browed Motmot, Golden-fronted Woodpecker, White-fronted Parrot, and Olive-throated Parakeet. The hummingbirds expected at the cenote rim include Canivet's Emerald and Cinnamon Hummingbird.

The mogotes of the Caribbean have a surprising lack of endemic birds given that so many of the plants have such restricted ranges. The birds tend to be generalists, and even though they are

endemic to an island or found only in the Caribbean, they can also be found in surrounding YUCATÁN DRY DECIDUOUS FOREST and MESOAMERICAN SEMI-EVERGREEN FOREST. A bird assemblage from Cuba would be expected to include species such as Cuban Oriole, Cuban Pygmy-Owl, Cuban

Sumichrast's Wren is a true specialist of karst habitat, often disappearing underground to forage in deep limestone recesses.
© PHIL CHAON

Fan-tailed Warbler is often found in dark vine tangles in Mexico.
© GORDON KARRE

Tody, Cuban Trogon, Cuban Vireo, Fernandina's Flicker, Giant Kingbird, Yellow-headed Warbler, Great Lizard-Cuckoo, West Indian Woodpecker, La Sagra's Flycatcher, and Olive-capped Warbler.

CONSERVATION: Given that mogotes tend to be in rugged terrain of limited potential for agriculture, they have fared better than MESOAMERICAN LOWLAND RAINFORESTS, which are on flat land with good soil. Many mogotes are within national parks and are protected for their spectacular beauty. Cenotes are more restricted and often surrounded by farmland. These ecosystems are prone to poisoning through chemical runoff from agriculture, and the famous ones suffer from being "loved to death" by visitors.

DISTRIBUTION: Cenotes are found throughout the limestone lowlands of the Yucatán Peninsula of se. Mexico, where over 6000 sinkholes have been mapped, but they can be found in lower numbers throughout the Caribbean islands. Mogotes are a Caribbean habitat and are found throughout Cuba, though they are much more prominent in the island's western region, where the majority of the endemic plants are found. Karst terrains with similar soils and vegetation are found generally below 2000 ft. (600 m) elevation in Jamaica, Dominican Republic, and Puerto Rico.

WHERE TO SEE: Viñales Valley, Pinar del Río, Cuba; Coto Sur, Puerto Rico, US.

Ne4D MESOAMERICAN LOWLAND RAINFOREST

IN A NUTSHELL: One of the hottest, wettest, tallest, and thickest-canopied habitats in the world. **Global Habitat Affinities:** AMAZON TERRAFIRMA; AFROTROPICAL LOWLAND RAINFOREST; AUSTRALASIAN TROPICAL LOWLAND RAINFOREST; SOUTHEAST ASIAN LOWLAND RAINFOREST. **Continental Habitat Affinities:** PETÉN SWAMP FOREST. **Species Overlap:** MESOAMERICAN SEMI-EVERGREEN FOREST; MESOAMERICAN CLOUDFOREST; PETÉN SWAMP FOREST.

DESCRIPTION: A must-see for anyone with the vaguest interest in nature, this is the luxuriant habitat that many people think of when they first imagine the Neotropics.

We tend to think of lowland rainforest as a single entity, yet this habitat is unexpectedly heterogeneous with a mélange of different forest microhabitats depending on localized hydrology, slope, soil fertility, and underlying rock type, as well as temporal factors such as disturbance due to flooding, hurricanes, fire, and landslides. There are variations within the forest microhabitat type at any one locality, but taken as a whole, the habitat and the bird assemblages in it remain fairly constant over large areas, so the bird lists for locations in s. Mexico will be fairly similar to those of lowland rainforest in Costa Rica. However,

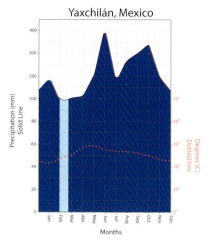

the experience of being in the lowland rainforest at the local scale varies greatly depending on where you are in the canopy profile.

High amounts of precipitation, between 48 in. (1200 mm) and 80 in. (2000 mm) annually, occur as relatively regular rainfall without long dry seasons or intense drought periods, and relatively constant temperatures (Köppen **Ama**) result in a surprisingly uniform leaf structure in canopy trees: medium-size leaves, often with drip tips, that appear similar to those of temperate trees from the laurel family.

Conifers are notably rare in Mesoamerican Lowland Rainforest. The northern conifers such as spruce, fir, larch, and juniper are all missing from these tropical forests; Tabla (*Podocarpus matudae*), which is mainly a cloudforest tree but grows down to 2600 ft. (800 m), at the upper limits of rainforest, and other podocarps are from the Southern Hemisphere. These ancient conifers are remnants from when Gondwanan forests dominated throughout South America, Africa, Australia, India, and Antarctica.

Deciduous trees are rare in this forest, a notable exception being the kapok trees, such as Pochote (*Ceiba aesculifolia*) and other *Ceiba* spp., which occur as emergents, rising above the rest of the canopy, so while they are not dominant, they are certainly obvious.

Mesoamerican Lowland Rainforest is a dense and lush habitat. © BEN KNOOT, TROPICAL BIRDING TOURS

With no drought or temperature extremes, deciduous species had no reason to evolve here, and nearly all the trees are broadleaf evergreens, most of which lose their old leaves and grow new ones throughout the year. The few trees that do drop all their leaves at once do so at random times and are not triggered by drought or season, unlike many trees of MESOAMERICAN SEMI-EVERGREEN FOREST. The lowland rainforest canopy is very dense and tall, to 100 ft. (30 m) with occasional emergent trees up to 150 ft. (45 m), with multiple layers (or strata) of plant growth. The uniform nature of leaf size and texture in the canopy masks remarkable diversity, though the forest may superficially look no richer than a deciduous forest of the e. United States in summer. Typical canopy trees include Chiche Colorado (*Aspidosperma megalocarpon*), Guapaque (*Dialium guianense*), Sapodilla (*Manilkara zapota*), Gavilán (*Pentaclethra macroloba*), Cacaotillo (*Miconia robinsonia*), *Cassipourea elliptica*, and the very fast-growing *Vochysia guatemalensis*. Palms make up only a minor fraction of the rainforest canopy and are noted more for being easily recognizable than for their abundance.

Although from a distance the forest may look uniform, underneath it is far from homogeneous. The rainforest understory, which includes the subcanopy and lower strata, is lush, with a variety of smaller trees, most of which have oversize leaves with large drip tips. Below the subcanopy, which is almost always over 15 ft. (5 m) high, this habitat is very open with a lot of exposed ground.

When canopy trees fall and create an opening in the forest, plants like Guarumo (*Cecropia obtusifolia*), Mexican Pepperleaf (*Piper auritum*), and Alligatorwood (*Guarea glabra*) rapidly fill the light gap. Over time, saplings of the canopy trees, lying in wait on the forest floor, grow through the pioneer cecropias and others and reestablish the closed forest canopy.

The higher ground of the rainforest, where it is not prone to inundation, is often referred to as terrafirma, and away from the dense forest edge and any light gaps, you will be surprised by just how dark, cool, and open the ground level is under the thick, closed canopy and multiple subcanopies. This is in stark contrast to the cloudforests, where the understory and ground cover can be extremely dense.

Palms are not particularly common in the terrafirma, but in the lower-lying swampy areas, there are patches of species such as Trooli Palm (*Manicaria saccifera*) and the raffia palm Yolilla (*Raphia taedigera*), which form thick, almost impenetrable groves. These groves have different bird assemblages and are always worth exploring, though you'll need to stand on the terrafirma and look in.

You can spend many days in lowland rainforest and each day concentrate on a new environment with its own suite of species; you will have diverse experiences and find different species in the understories and canopies of the forest edges and light gaps, the palm forest, and the dry terrafirma.

A highlight of any visit to these humid forests is to come across an army ant swarm. It can be well argued that the understory habitat changes during a swarm to a completely different environment, and an ant-swarm area could be regarded as an extremely temporal microhabitat (see sidebar 7).

Much has been written about lowland rainforest soil types, but rainforests will grow on soils formed over most rock types, other than the extremely nutrient-deficient quartzites (which can be pretty close to pure glass), though the amount of rainfall required for growth may differ; generally, the more productive the soil's parent material (the rock or sediment the soil is forming in), the lower the rainfall required for rainforest formation. In environments with very nutrient-rich bedrocks such as igneous basalts (or gabbros) or alluvial sediments, red-brown soils form easily, and rainforest growth is possible with only 1200 mm of rainfall. At the other extreme, with metamorphic rocks such as gneiss, or igneous rocks such as granites and rhyolites, rainforest forms only in very

SIDEBAR 7   ARMY ANT SWARMS: THE MOST TEMPORARY OF HABITATS

Swarms of the nomadic Eciton Army Ant (*Eciton burchellii*) are an important feature of Neotropical humid lowland forests, and because their impact can be so extreme for such a short time, their location can be thought of as a temporal habitat. During the time the swarm is present in a small area, all hell breaks loose; these ants are highly organized, exhibit a remarkable level of collective intelligence and coordination, and perform very efficient raids.

Eciton Army Ants are nomadic, constantly on the move, and don't have a permanent nest like many other ant species. Instead, they fashion a temporary nest, called a bivouac, out of the live bodies of the worker ants, which lasts two to three weeks and serves as a protective layer while inside the queen breeds. The bivouacs are usually under logs, crammed into buttress roots, or sometimes low in trees; they can be over 3 ft. (90 cm) tall and 2 ft. (60 cm) wide, and contain several hundred thousand ants. While in the stationary breeding phase, the hunters undertake hunting raids around the bivouac, quickly depleting local food sources.

The Eciton Army Ant hunting strategy is highly effective; the ants form wide raiding fronts, sometimes stretching over many feet, to hunt and scavenge for food. This front moves forward in a coordinated fashion, the ants using their sheer numbers and coordinated attacks to consume thousands of prey items per day. Their primary victims are terrestrial insects and other arthropods. However, they will take anything they can overpower, including small mammals, birds, amphibians, and reptiles. Birds that nest on the ground or within a few feet of the ground are particularly vulnerable to these swarms, and once under attack, young birds have an extremely small chance of survival.

The role of these ants in the system is so profound that a whole guild of birds has evolved to be army-swarm obligates or to take advantage of the chaos of insects fleeing from these marauding hordes. Larger bird species can walk in front of the army, feeding on fleeing animals, while smaller species, such as antbirds, perch just high enough above the troops to remain protected and pluck off prey that seek refuge up tree trunks and small branches. Even mammals, such as tamanduas, coatis, and opossums, follow ant swarms.

An Army Ant swarm sweeps through a forest in Panama.

Geoffroy's Spider Monkey, aided by a prehensile tail, moves easily through the Mesoamerican Lowland Rainforest. © PHIL CHAON

stable environments where soil development is faster than erosion and rainfall is very high. Given the right conditions, weathering of a granite will provide the nutrients required for luxuriant growth, but because the minerals in a granite weather much more slowly than in a basalt, they need much longer to wear down and release their nutrients.

WILDLIFE: In the Neotropics, most primates have prehensile tails, are arboreal and very agile, and are predominantly fruit eaters. New World primates are found mostly in rainforest canopies, whereas Old World primates use a wider variety of habitats and many species are fairly terrestrial. To best experience mammals in the Mesoamerican Lowland Rainforest canopy, you need to be on a small ridge or, preferably, a canopy tower. From such a vantage, you might see Geoffroy's Spider Monkey, Guatemalan Black Howler, and Mantled Howler hanging out at a fruiting tree. Visits to the canopy may result in an encounter with a rare Silky Anteater, which is the canopy cousin of the better-known mainly terrestrial Giant Anteater. Herps are well represented in the rainforest, and frogs make up a much larger percentage of the assemblage than they do in higher MESOAMERICAN CLOUDFOREST or in drier MESOAMERICAN SEMI-EVERGREEN FOREST.

Most bird families and subfamilies that typify lowland rainforest have at least some members that are also found in cloudforest or semi-evergreen forest, but a greater number of species are found in this habitat. These include Long-billed and Stripe-throated Hermits (a subfamily of hummingbirds), with very long and decurved bills, as well as smaller-billed hummingbirds such as Rufous-tailed Hummingbird and Purple-crowned Fairy. There are smaller frugivores such as White-collared

Great Curassow is frequently hunted and remains only in well-protected areas.
© BEN KNOOT, TROPICAL BIRDING TOURS

Despite its large size and brilliant colors, Keel-billed Toucan is often detected by its yelping call.
© BEN KNOOT, TROPICAL BIRDING TOURS

and Red-capped Manakins; and medium-size frugivores, like Lovely Cotinga, Rufous Piha, and Cinnamon Becard. There are many tanagers, which comprise a family of frugivores ranging in size from very small to medium-size birds, including Black-throated Shrike-Tanager and Crimson-collared, Scarlet-rumped, Yellow-winged, and Golden-hooded Tanagers. Toucans are iconic to this habitat, and Northern Emerald-Toucanet, Collared Aracari, and Keel-billed Toucan are regular species. Canopy hunters include White-necked and White-whiskered Puffbirds and Rufous-tailed Jacamar.

In the understory, army ants on the move (see sidebar 7) attract a suite of both ant-swarm obligates (birds that feed only at ant swarms) and birds that take advantage of the mayhem caused during a swarm. You may find Dusky Antbird as well as terrestrial birds feeding on the first wave of insects fleeing the marauding army ants. Woodcreepers, ant-tanagers, and a host of different types of flycatchers feast on these many escapees. Other ant-swarm specialists perch on sapling stems or low vines a few feet above the ground, just out of danger from the ants but close enough to have a full buffet of small invertebrates.

CONSERVATION: The vast majority of Mesoamerican Lowland Rainforest has been cleared from Mexico. What remains is in reserves that protect MESOAMERICAN CLOUDFOREST or occurs in small patches surrounded by MESOAMERICAN SEMI-EVERGREEN FOREST in the massive Calakmul Biosphere Reserve. As this is the northernmost extension of a habitat that is found throughout Central America, the forest is better protected in countries to the south such as Costa Rica and Panama. Much of what is mapped as rainforest in the Caribbean is actually secondary forest or very degraded rainforest better described as ruderal rainforest.

Theoretically, much of the remaining primary forest is preserved in national parks or ecological reserves, but there is little real protection where large-scale African Oil Palm plantations have been developed. The situation is bleak.

DISTRIBUTION: The Mesoamerican Lowland Rainforest runs from Mexico south of 25°N through Chiapas and Central America to Panama. Remnants of lowland rainforest can be found on some islands of the Caribbean including Jamaica, Hispaniola, Cuba, and Puerto Rico. Much of this habitat has already been destroyed in s. Mexico and the Caribbean, and much of what people experience is secondary rainforest.

WHERE TO SEE: Bonampak Archaeological Zone, Chiapas, Mexico; La Encrucijada Biosphere Reserve, Chiapas, Mexico.

Ne4E PETÉN SWAMP FOREST

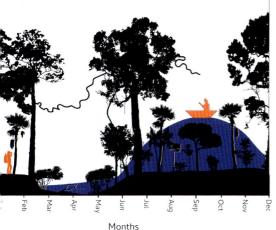

Water levels are highly variable through the seasons, and are usually slightly delayed from rainfall.

IN A NUTSHELL: Lowland rainforest that is completely flooded for at least part of the year, supporting a similar though subtly different set of wildlife than nonflooded forest. **Global Habitat Affinities:** VÁRZEA FLOODED FOREST; ASIAN PEAT SWAMP FOREST. **Continental Habitat Affinities:** MESOAMERICAN LOWLAND RAINFOREST. **Species Overlap:** MESOAMERICAN LOWLAND RAINFOREST; MESOAMERICAN MANGROVES; MESOAMERICAN SEMI-EVERGREEN FOREST.

DESCRIPTION: The Mesoamerican sister habitat of VÁRZEA FLOODED FOREST of South America, this habitat consists of forest that is completely flooded for at least part of the year. It generally lies either in broad lowland valleys with impeded drainage or on the freshwater end of an estuarine system, and forms the ecotone between MESOAMERICAN LOWLAND RAINFOREST on the elevated areas and MESOAMERICAN MANGROVES closer to the coast. The climate here is similar to that of MESOAMERICAN SEMI-EVERGREEN FOREST (Köppen **Ama**), with annual precipitation of 35–56 in. (900–1400 mm), concentrated between May and October; the

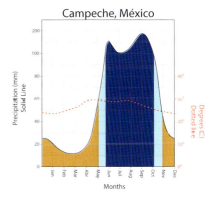

Campeche, México

different habitats are a result of geomorphology impeding drainage, producing flooding, and promoting the development of gleysols (or histisols, saturated, gray-colored soils).

This habitat looks like a swamp when inundated and a rainforest when dry, although it has a profoundly different botanical composition from normal Mesoamerican Lowland Rainforest.

The structure of the forest changes with drainage and salinity; in freshwater areas with better drainage, the canopy of swamp forest is lower than that of rainforest, averaging 65–80 ft. (20–25 m) and with emergent trees up to 150 ft. (45 m) tall. With only 50% canopy cover, the overstory is much more open than that of lowland rainforest. Many trees have aerial roots, and some have stilt roots, reminiscent of mangroves. Typical canopy trees include some trees also typical of other humid forests such as Sapodilla (*Manilkara zapota*) and Honduran Mahogany (*Swietenia macrophylla*), as well as others such as Campeche Logwood (*Haematoxylum campechianum*), Black Poisonwood (*Metopium brownei*), Santa Maria or Jacareúba (*Calophyllum brasiliense*), and Yax-nik (*Vitex gaumeri*).

The understory is dominated by stunted broadleaf trees and palms around 25–50 ft. (8–15 m) tall. Given the amount of light, it is a surprise that the undergrowth is not thicker than it is, but this is due to the relatively constant flooding, which prevents most bushes from growing. Species present include Wild Cinnamon (*Croton nitens*), Simpson's Stopper (*Myrcianthes fragrans*), False Birch (*Coccoloba spicata*), Pigeon-plum (*Coccoloba diversifolia*), Black Olive (*Terminalia buceras*), Saffron Plum (*Sideroxylon celastrinum*), Black Ironwood (*Krugiodendron ferreum*), and Yucatán Wattle (*Senegalia gaumeri*). Even in the light gaps, grasses and the like do not grow well, though Swamp Sawgrass (*Cladium mariscus*) is often present. Lianas are prominent and also tend to grow on the many trees that lean over in this forest.

In more poorly drained areas, secondary areas, and closer to the mangroves, the forest takes on a shrubbier appearance, with a bunch of small trees at different heights (generally reaching up to 40 ft./12 m), not forming a canopy and without a distinct understory. Some of the species, such as *Vochysia hondurensis* and West Indian Elm (*Guazuma ulmifolia*), can grow up to 60 ft. (20 m) tall, though most are shrubs and small trees such as *Hirtella* spp., *Mouriri* spp., Pimientillo (*Xilopia frutescens*), Dysentery-bark (*Simarouba glauca*), and *Miconia racemosa*, a New World species that has become a serious invasive in Australia.

Petén Swamp Forest is inundated during the rainy season. © JOSE LUIS PEREZ DE CASTRO

Agami Heron Is a rare and secretive visitor to Petén Swamp Forest during the wet season.
© KEITH BARNES, TROPICAL BIRDING TOURS

The palms include the climbing palm *Desmoncus orthacanthos*, Chocho Palm (*Astrocaryum mexicanum*), Savanna Palm (*Sabal mauritiiformis*), and the inornate but interestingly named Vampire Palm (*Calyptrogyne ghiesbreghtiana*), which is pollinated by bats.

WILDLIFE: This habitat supports a similar set of wildlife to MESOAMERICAN LOWLAND RAINFOREST. The major difference in avifauna occurs during the wet season, when a wide variety of swamp-loving species appears in the Petén Swamp Forest. Among these seasonal visitors are Agami and Boat-billed Herons, Sungrebe, Russet-naped Wood-Rail, Ruddy Crake, Limpkin, Black-collared Hawk, and American Pygmy, Ringed, and Amazon Kingfishers. Unfortunately, wildlife-watching here is difficult as these swamp forests are challenging to access.

CONSERVATION: These alluvial forests are easily exploited, and where the soil is good for agriculture, such as non-calcareous soils, the forest has been mostly removed.

DISTRIBUTION: In continental North America, Petén Swamp Forest is limited to tropical areas of Mexico south of Veracruz and on the Yucatán Peninsula; it extends south through Central America to the Darién Gap on the Central–South American border. It is widespread in lowland areas of the larger Caribbean islands.

WHERE TO SEE. Calakmul Biosphere Reserve, Campeche, Mexico.

A Sungrebe swims silently between roots in flooded swamp forest. © KEITH BARNES, TROPICAL BIRDING TOURS

Ruddy Crake Is one of the many birds found in Petén Swamp Forest while the habitat is flooded. © PHIL CHAON

Ne4F WET 'ŌHI'A LEHUA–KOA FOREST

IN A NUTSHELL: A moist subtropical broadleaf forest found on the Hawaiian Islands and dominated by 'Ōhi'a Lehua and Koa trees. **Global Habitat Affinities:** TEMPERATE ANDEAN CLOUDFOREST; NEW ZEALAND RATA FOREST; STUNTED CLOUDFOREST; SUNDA MONTANE RAINFOREST; PHILIPPINE MONTANE RAINFOREST. **Continental Habitat Affinities:** MESOAMERICAN CLOUDFOREST. **Species Overlap:** MAMANE-NAIO DRY FOREST.

DESCRIPTION: Wet 'Ōhi'a Lehua–Koa Forest is an extremely moist montane broadleaf forest found at elevations between 2400 and 7800 ft. (750–2400 m) on the windward slopes of the high islands of Hawai'i. These forests are characteristically steep and muddy, shrouded in clouds, with a low tree canopy and an abundance of epiphytes. The area receives huge amounts of rainfall, anywhere between 60 and 350 in. (1500–8900 mm) per year. Mount Wai'ale'ale on Kaua'i is one of the wettest places on earth and in 1982 recorded an astonishing 681 in. (17,300 mm) of precipitation. Fog drip also makes a significant contribution to the total annual precipitation and is responsible for as much as 40 in. (1000 mm). The Wet

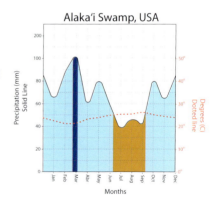

Alaka'i Swamp, USA

'Ōhi'a Lehua–Koa Forest is generally cool, and annual temperatures vary little. Typical wintertime temperatures range from 50 to 75°F (10–24°C), and summer temperatures increase slightly to an average of 60–82°F (16–28°C). Near the upper elevational limits, Wet 'Ōhi'a Lehua–Koa Forest can be quite cold, and most species at this altitude are frost-resistant. The forest here naturally experiences little disturbance except for occasional openings caused by large storms. In areas with recent volcanic activity, Wet 'Ōhi'a Lehua–Koa Forest occurs in isolated islands or hammocks, called *kīpuka*, generally surrounded by unvegetated lava flows.

As the name implies, 'Ōhi'a Lehua (*Metrosideros polymorpha*) and Koa (*Acacia koa*) are the dominant trees in this habitat. However, the structure and relative abundance vary with elevation. At lower elevations, Koa is the dominant species, forming a moderately open canopy above a well-

Wet ʻŌhiʻa Lehua–Koa Forest is found at high elevations on the Hawaiian Islands. © PHIL CHAON

stratified understory of ʻŌhiʻa Lehua and other trees. These forests are typically of intermediate height, the canopy reaching 50–80 ft. (15–25 m). As the elevation increases, ʻŌhiʻa Lehua becomes more common, and the canopy grows denser and decreases in stature. By the time you reach tree line, this habitat is entirely dominated by moss- and epiphyte-laden ʻŌhiʻa Lehua trees only about 10 ft. (3 m) tall. Other common tree species here include Kāwaʻu (*Ilex anomala*), ʻAlani (*Melicope clusiifolia*), Olomea (*Perrottetia sandwicensis*), ʻŌhiʻa ha (*Syzygium sandwicense*), ʻŌlapa (*Cheirodendron* spp.), and ʻoheʻohe (*Polyscias* spp.) as well as the tree fern known as Hāpuʻu (*Cibotium menziesii*).

Naturally, the understory is moderate to dense and full of a wide variety of ferns, mosses, woody plants, and forbs. In many areas, the understory is choked with thick stands of invasive Kahili Ginger (*Hedychium gardnerianum*). Common native shrubs include ʻApeʻape (*Gunnera petaloidea*), ʻōhā wai (*Clermontia* spp.), Olopua (*Nestegis sandwicensis*), Hame (*Antidesma platyphyllum*), hāhā (*Cyanea* spp.), Kamakahala (*Labordia hirtella*), Kanawao (*Broussaisia arguta*), ʻĀkala (*Rubus hawaiensis*), Kāmanamana (*Adenostemma lavenia*), Hōʻawa (*Pittosporum* spp.), and Olonā (*Touchardia latifolia*). Interestingly, many of the plants here have lost defenses against herbivory. The ʻĀkala (or Hawaiian Raspberry) has no thorns, and the Honohono (or Hawaiian Mint, *Haplostachys haplostachya*) lacks the minty scent and taste of other mints.

WILDLIFE: Learning about the native fauna on Hawaiʻi is often a fascinating and heartbreaking endeavor for ecologists and naturalists. Here, on the most isolated archipelago on the planet, an incredible array of unique species arose over several million years. Catastrophically, most of these species have vanished over the past several centuries. The ones that remain are mostly found in the Wet ʻŌhiʻa Lehua–Koa Forest.

'I'iwi is still common at high elevations on the islands of Hawai'i and Maui. © PHIL CHAON

Due to the archipelago's extreme isolation, the Wet 'Ōhi'a Lehua–Koa Forest is home to a single native mammal species, the endangered Hawaiian Hoary Bat. Several invasive mammal species may also be encountered in these forests, including feral cats, feral hogs, Black-tailed Deer, Axis Deer, Black Rat, Polynesian Rat, and Brown Rat.

All of Hawai'i's remaining native forest birds, apart from the Palila (see MAMANE-NAIO DRY FOREST), can be found in Wet 'Ōhi'a Lehua–Koa Forest. Most of these birds are rare and generally occur above the "mosquito line" (4500 ft./1300 m), where malaria-transmitting mosquitoes do not occur. While most native birds are rare, some are still readily observed. In particular, Omao, Hawai'i 'Amakihi, O'ahu 'Amakihi, 'Apapane, Hawai'i 'Elepaio, and Kaua'i 'Elepaio can all be quite abundant. The Hawai'i 'Amakihi is the only species of Hawaiian honeycreeper that has shown some malarial resistance. The brilliant red 'I'iwi is also still fairly common at high elevations on Maui and Hawai'i, and the 'Anianiau is also readily found at similar elevations on Kaua'i. Many of these species are most easily observed around flowering 'Ōhi'a Lehua trees and often travel together in noisy mixed-species flocks. The 'Io, or Hawaiian Hawk, is a generalist that is still widespread on the island of Hawai'i. From April to November, Newell's Shearwaters, Hawaiian Petrels, and Band-rumped Storm-Petrels all return to breed in burrows on forested slopes. While they spend the day at sea, these birds return to the burrows at night and are easily detected by their wailing or braying calls.

The rest of the native songbirds on the Hawaiian Islands are quite rare and are encountered only in the most remote and well-protected reaches. Since 1788, over half of Hawai'i's 73 native forest birds have gone extinct. These are among the most recent avian extinctions on the planet, with 7 since 1980, including 'Alalā (Hawaiian Crow) in 2002 and Po'ouli in 2004. Of the remaining native birds in Wet 'Ōhi'a Lehua–Koa Forest, 'Ākohekohe, Maui Parrotbill, 'Akeke'e, Puaiohi, and 'Akikiki are critically endangered. At the time of writing, there are 5 'Akikiki remaining, and this honeycreeper will presumably be extinct in the wild by the time of publication. O'ahu 'Elepaio, 'Akiapola'au, Hawai'i Creeper, Maui 'Alauahio, and Hawai'i 'Akepa are all endangered.

The red flowers of ʻŌhiʻa Lehua are an important food source for many birds including the Hawaiʻi ʻAmakihi.
© PHIL CHAON

Numerous non-native birds are also easily found in Wet ʻŌhiʻa Lehua–Koa Forest. Warbling White-eyes are particularly abundant and are often found at flowering ʻŌhiʻa Lehua with native honeycreepers. Kalij Pheasant, Red-vented Bulbul, Japanese Bush Warbler, Chinese Hwamei, Red-billed Leiothrix, White-rumped Shama, and Common Waxbill are also found throughout the Wet ʻŌhiʻa Lehua–Koa Forest.

There are no native reptiles or amphibians in Hawaiʻi's forests, though escaped oddities like Gold Dust Day Gecko and Jackson's Chameleon can occasionally be found.

There are hundreds of invertebrates endemic to Hawaiʻi, and new species are constantly being discovered. Of particular note are the *kāhuli*, or Hawaiian tree snails. A spectacular example of adaptive radiation, nearly 100 species of these small colorful snails were once found throughout the islands, particularly on Oʻahu. Less than half of these species remain, and many of those remaining have as few as 50 individuals. Their survival is threatened by the highly predatory and invasive Rosy Wolf Snail. Adding to their vulnerability, the native snails don't reach sexual maturity until they are five years of age, and then adults produce only about 10 live young.

CONSERVATION: The ecological history of the Hawaiian Islands is one of the great modern tragedies in the natural world. A critically endangered habitat, Wet ʻŌhiʻa Lehua–Koa Forest is truly making a last stand. Destruction of native forests began with the arrival of the first humans on the Hawaiian Islands, however, the bulk of forest loss occurred during the 19th century after the arrival of European colonists. A valuable source of timber, most of the old-growth Koa was quickly logged. Smaller, less valuable forests were cleared for grazing and the introduction of cattle and goats. By 1900, nearly all the forest was lost. Goats and cattle prevented the regeneration of forests, while alien weeds quickly colonized any available areas. The non-native Banana Poka Vine (*Passiflora tarminiana*) has smothered over 70,000 acres (28,000 ha) of prime native forest. Feral hogs continue to destroy the understory of intact forests, accelerating erosion and introducing invasive plants into the forest interior. Most recently, rapid ʻŌhiʻa death, caused

The 'Akikiki is possibly the rarest bird on the planet and may be extinct in the wild by the time of this book's publication. © PHIL CHAON

by the fungal pathogen *Ceratocystis*, has emerged as the greatest threat to the forest; since its first detection in 2010, it has killed over a million 'Ōhi'a Lehua trees, sometimes destroying a stand in a matter of days.

The loss of native forest is surpassed only by the faunal extinctions this habitat has experienced. As with many isolated islands, first human contact on the Hawaiian archipelago was swiftly followed by the extinction of many large or flightless bird species. Most small arboreal species survived until European colonization. At this point a wave of habitat destruction and invasive species began to erode the island's fauna. Over the past 200 years, innumerable invasives from Electric Ants to Indian Gray Mongoose have wrought untold destruction. Black Rats and feral hogs have been especially destructive to birds, though not nearly as destructive as the introduction of avian malaria.

Starting in 1903, much of Hawai'i's remaining native Wet 'Ōhi'a Lehua–Koa Forest was placed into reserves. Today 20% of remaining native forest is protected, with efforts underway to increase that to 30% by 2030. The battle to save Hawai'i's native fauna is a complex and multifaceted effort with dozens of public agencies and private conservation organizations all working on different aspects of the problem. Widespread fencing seeks to exclude non-native mammals, especially pigs and goats, from the most pristine forests. Within protected areas there is also active lethal control of non-native predators like feral cats, Black Rats, and Barn Owls. Captive-breeding facilities have been established for *kāhuli* snails and several of the rarest species of birds. 'Alalā (Hawaiian Crow) has been extinct in the wild since 2002, but several individuals remain alive in captivity. The same will soon be true for 'Akikiki. However, captive-breeding efforts are only a stopgap without the elimination of avian malaria from native forests. Trials for landscape-level mosquito control on Hawai'i began in 2023. The efforts rely on the release of male mosquitoes infected with a strain of *Wolbachia* bacteria that will render the next generation of their offspring sterile. Despite the numbers already lost, there is still much left to save. Hopefully, conservation efforts will come in time for Hawai'i's remaining species.

DISTRIBUTION: Found on the islands of Hawai'i, Maui, Moloka'i, Lāna'i, O'ahu, and Kaua'i, Wet 'Ōhi'a Lehua–Koa Forest is restricted mostly to steep montane ridges in isolated or protected areas of the islands, largely on the wet, windward sides of islands where there is high rainfall. Typically, the lower elevational limits are bounded by anthropogenic ruderal forests and human habitation or pastureland. On dry, leeward sides of islands, this habitat will transition to MAMANE–NAIO DRY FOREST. On most islands, 'Ōhi'a Lehua–Koa Forest occupies the highest elevations, but on the high peaks of Maui and Hawai'i, the forest disappears by 7800 ft. (2400 m) and is replaced by HAWAIIAN GRASSLANDS.

WHERE TO SEE: Hakalau Forest National Wildlife Refuge, Hawai'i, US; Kōke'e State Park, Hawai'i, US.

Geological and evolutionary processes are generally slow, and ongoing processes may even appear to have halted completely, such as the evolution of lampreys (a group of jawless fishes that still exist today) or the rocks of the Canadian Shield, which are up to 4 billion years old. We generally think of the evolution of birds as playing out on an already existing geological tapestry; this is not always the case, and in places such as the Galápagos or the Hawaiian Islands, the relationship between hotspot volcanism and the biogeography of bird distributions and species richness showcases a fascinating interplay between geology and biology that is playing out in real time.

The earth's mantle, the malleable layer beneath the crust, contains regions of heightened thermal activity called hotspots. As the Pacific tectonic plate drifts over one such hotspot, the immense heat causes the mantle to melt, forming magma. This magma rises through the oceanic crust and erupts on the ocean floor, forming volcanoes. Over time, as repeated eruptions occur, the volcanoes grow until they form volcanic islands. The eruptions are episodic, so there are periods of no volcano formation, as the Pacific Plate continues its northwest motion; newer islands form in succession, while older islands stop forming and start to erode. They continue to erode and subside until they are no longer islands but seamounts below the ocean surface. This process has resulted in the formation of the Hawaiian archipelago, with the oldest islands in the northwest and the youngest in the southeast, near the current position of the hotspot.

When an island forms, it is initially barren basalt, which gradually will be weathered, forming soil, and be colonized by both plants and animals over time from distant lands, carried over by winds or currents or by hitching a ride on floating debris. Once they arrive, these species begin to adapt to the unique conditions of the island, often evolving into entirely new species—a process known as adaptive radiation.

Rosefinches, a group of birds mainly from Asia, arrived to the now-submerged proto–Hawaiian Islands about 7.2 MYA and radiated on the early islands between 5.7 and 7.2 MYA. The oldest (of the recently living) lineage diverged about 5.7–5.8 MYA, which was when Ni'ihau and Kaua'i were starting to form. Most of the highly distinctive lineages originated after the formation of O'ahu but before the formation of Maui, so most genus radiation occurred on O'ahu, with speciation occurring later on Maui and Hawai'i (the Big Island). This ongoing process has led to a dynamic distribution of honeycreepers (and other bird species) across the Hawaiian archipelago. Some birds and even genera are found in only one habitat on specific islands, having evolved in isolation and adapted to the unique conditions; some have spread across multiple islands in very specific habitats; and some have become generalists, adjusting to varied habitats within one island and/or on multiple islands. This is how one species of rosefinch, which is a very uniform group of birds through temperate North America and Eurasia, has evolved in the Hawaiian Islands into over 50 species of honeycreepers with extreme variations in bill shapes and life histories. Knowing this history makes it all the more painful to watch in real time as most of these species go extinct.

HAWAIIAN ISLAND HOTSPOT VOLCANISM AND HONEYCREEPERS

Ancestors of Hawaiian honeycreepers arrived from Asia to (now submerged) islands 7.2 - 5.7 MYA.

Most honeycreeper lineages evolved on Oahu before formation of Maui.

All honeycreeper lineages evolved before formation of Hawaii, but new genera evolved on Big Island.

Hawaii 0.7 MYA-Present

Niihau & Kauai 5.6-4.9 MYA

Oahu 3.4 MYA-10k YBP

Maui 1.3 MYA-Present

Direction of plate movement

MANTLE

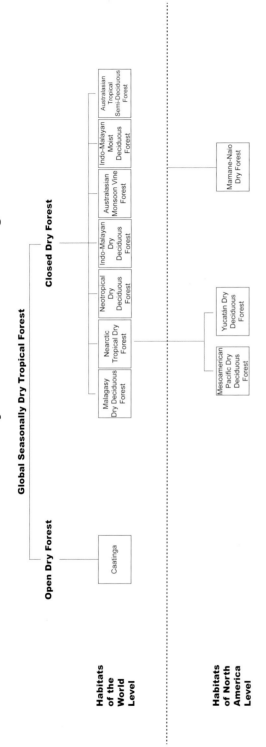

DRY DECIDUOUS FORESTS

Ne5A MESOAMERICAN PACIFIC DRY DECIDUOUS FOREST

IN A NUTSHELL: Dry tropical forest that appears lush in the wet season but stark in the dry season, when the canopy loses many of its leaves. **Global Habitat Affinities:** SOUTHEAST ASIAN DRY DECIDUOUS FOREST; INDIAN DRY DECIDUOUS FOREST; MALAGASY DECIDUOUS FOREST; NEOTROPICAL PACIFIC DRY DECIDUOUS FOREST; AGRESTE CAATINGA. **Continental Habitat Affinities:** CENTRAL MEXICAN SUCCULENT MATORRAL; YUCATÁN DRY DECIDUOUS FOREST; MESOAMERICAN SEMI-EVERGREEN FOREST. **Species Overlap:** CENTRAL MEXICAN SUCCULENT MATORRAL; YUCATÁN DRY DECIDUOUS FOREST; SONORAN DESERT; MADREAN ENCINAL; TAMAULIPAN MEZQUITAL.

DESCRIPTION: There are few tropical habitats that experience the incredible transformations seen in the Mesoamerican Pacific Dry Deciduous Forests. While rainfall is variable throughout this habitat, the average dry season is seven months long and sees less than 3.5 in. (90 mm) of rainfall in total. At the height of the dry season, the forest is mostly leafless, and large columnar cacti are often the most prominent feature on the landscape. Wildlife is easy to spot during this time of year, as the habitat is much more open, and the presence of animals is often revealed by the loud crunching of dry leaves. The wet season is also variable, with 18–55 in. (450–1400 mm) of rain falling between June and September. During and immediately after the rainy season, Pacific Dry Deciduous Forest is lush and humid, with a dense canopy covered in tangled vines, resembling MESOAMERICAN SEMI-EVERGREEN

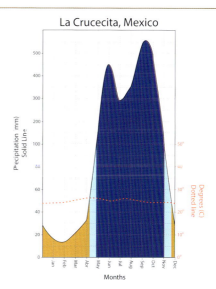

La Crucecita, Mexico

A Mesoamerican Pacific Dry Deciduous Forest after the rains; it looks completely different late in the dry season. © PHIL CHAON

FOREST. This habitat is generally found from sea level to 5000 ft. (1500 m), though it occurs slightly higher in the Balsas River drainage and Chiapas Depression.

The canopy of Pacific Dry Deciduous Forest is usually closed and reaches a height of 35–80 ft. (10–25 m). Many of the trees in this habitat are very distinctive and give the environment an alien, Dr. Seussian feel. In particular, the massive kapoks (*Ceiba* spp.) with their spiky, bulbous trunks, green bark, and puffy white flowers seem like they're out of a storybook. Other common canopy trees include burseras (*Bursera* spp.), Dagame (*Calycophyllum candidissimum*), Geiger Tree

During the dry season, the large cacti found in the Mesoamerican Pacific Dry Deciduous Forest are much more evident. © PHIL CHAON

(*Cordia sebestena*), Black Sapote (*Diospyros nigra*), devil's-ears (*Enterolobium* spp.), figs (*Ficus* spp.), Red Frangipani (*Plumeria rubra*), and Periquillo (*Thouinidium decandrum*). Many of the trees are heavily covered in epiphytes; this is especially obvious during the dry season.

The understory of this forest is thick and viny and can often feel impenetrable. Some areas surveyed found that lianas account for 20% of all stems in the forest, adding to the dense, tangled feel. Large columnar cacti are also an important component; some like Candelabro (*Pachycereus weberi*) can reach 50 ft. (16 m) in height and actually join the canopy. The rest of the understory is composed of a diverse array of small trees and evergreen shrubs. Often this habitat feels like CARIBBEAN THORNSCRUB with a canopy overlaying it. Many of the understory shrubs are thorny. The understory typically lacks grasses, and small herbaceous plants are sparse, except for a short time during the rainy season.

WILDLIFE: This habitat is one of the world's biodiversity hotspots, though it may not seem like it at first glance. It is home to a rich array of mammals found nowhere else in the world. In the Jalisco, Mexico, dry forests alone, there are 10 endemic mammalian genera that include such species as Mexican Shrew, Trumpet-nosed Bat, Michoacán Deer Mouse, Allen's Woodrat, and Magdalena Rat. Widespread species like White-tailed Deer, Collared Peccary, Virginia Opossum, Nine-banded Armadillo, Mexican Gray Squirrel, Northern Tamandua, Gray Fox, Jaguarundi, Ocelot, Kinkajou, and White-nosed Coati occur as well.

The birdlife is just as divergent. Many widespread dry forest specialists occur, including Russet-crowned Motmot, Streak-backed Oriole, Yellow Grosbeak,

Above: **Russet-crowned Motmot sits motionless in the midstory for long periods of time.** © PHIL CHAON

Right: **Lesser Ground-Cuckoo is a shy terrestrial resident of Pacific Dry Deciduous Forest.**
© ALVARO GUTIERREZ PHOTOGRAPHY

The colors of Orange-breasted Bunting are truly electric.
© GLENN BARTLEY PHOTOGRAPHY

Lesser Ground-Cuckoo, Lesser Roadrunner, Nutting's Flycatcher, White-lored Gnatcatcher, Orange-breasted Bunting, Red-breasted Chat, and Citreoline Trogon. These species are joined by an array of localized endemics. In the Balsas River basin of Michoacán and Guerrero, the dry forests have Banded Quail, Balsas Screech-Owl and Black-chested Sparrow. Nayarit is home to Mexican Parrotlet, Mexican Woodnymph, and San Blas Jay. The narrow and windy Isthmus of Tehuantepec holds one of the Nearctic region's most beautiful birds—the Rose-bellied Bunting, the plumage of which reflects every color of the setting sun from vibrant orange to those last dusky blues.

Reptiles are conspicuous and abundant here. Common species include Long-tailed Spiny Lizard, Western Spiny-tailed Iguana, Black-nosed Lizard, Least Gecko, Pacific Patch-nosed Snake, Western Lyre Snake, Middle American Indigo Snake, and Pacific Coast Parrot Snake. After the rains, amphibians seem to appear from nowhere—Mexican Leaf Frog, Marbled (or Wiegmann's) Toad, Sabinal Frog, and Mexican Burrowing Toad all emerge after a dormant dry season.

This region encompasses several Endemic Bird Areas and is home to nearly one-third of Mexico's 120-plus endemic bird species. Major areas of endemism include the Balsas River basin, the Isthmus of Tehuantepec, and the Pacific slope of nw. Mexico.

CONSERVATION: Pacific Dry Deciduous Forest is one of the most extensive habitats in Mexico, covering much of the Pacific slope. Mexico contains more tropical deciduous forest than any other country in the Americas. Despite this, only about 26% of the original Pacific Dry Deciduous Forest remains

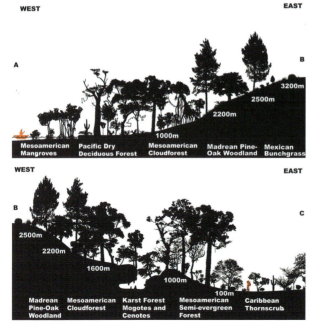

Fig. 8. West–east cross section of southern Mexico

intact, and less than 10% of that is under formal protection. Major threats include land clearing for agriculture (especially cattle grazing) and climate change. Climate models predict that the area is at high risk for desertification and high-intensity fires. Wildfires (both natural and anthropogenic) are increasingly common in this habitat, as rainfall becomes less substantial and more sporadic. Major protected areas include the Chamela-Cuixmala, Sierra de Manantlán, La Sepultura, and Sierra de Huatula Biosphere Reserves, as well as Cañón del Sumidero, El Tepozteco, Huatulco, and Lagunas de Chacahuan National Parks.

DISTRIBUTION: Pacific Dry Deciduous Forest is one of the most widely distributed habitats in w. Mexico, stretching from s. Sonora to the border of Guatemala in a wide band adjacent to the Pacific coast. These forests are also found in low inland valleys along the Balsas River and in the Chiapas Depression. Figure 8 depicts the habitat transitions as one moves from the Pacific (west coast) across Mexico to the Yucatán Peninsula (east coast).

WHERE TO SEE: Huatulco National Park, Oaxaca, Mexico; Xochicalco archaeological site, Morelos, Mexico; San Blas, Nayarit, Mexico.

Ne5B YUCATÁN DRY DECIDUOUS FOREST

IN A NUTSHELL: Dry tropical forest that loses its leaves in the dry season; it occurs as an ecotone between semi-evergreen forest and thornscrub. **Global Habitat Affinities:** INDIAN DRY DECIDUOUS FOREST; MALAGASY DECIDUOUS FOREST. **Continental Habitat Affinities:** MESOAMERICAN PACIFIC DRY DECIDUOUS FOREST. **Species Overlap:** MESOAMERICAN SEMI-EVERGREEN FOREST; CARIBBEAN THORNSCRUB.

DESCRIPTION: Because these dry deciduous forests of the Yucatán Peninsula exist in a savanna climate (Köppen **Awa**), they vary greatly throughout the year, parched in the dry season and lush during the wet season. Found in the same areas that may have MESOAMERICAN SEMI-EVERGREEN FOREST, Yucatán Dry Deciduous Forest occurs in parts that have poorer soils, mainly on the very calcareous soils of the central peninsula.

It is not known whether, prior to intense cultivation by the Maya, much of this region was semi-evergreen forest, and this dry deciduous forest is a response to environmental degradation. The same is also true on the other end of the spectrum, where CARIBBEAN THORNSCRUB that exists now may be a response to degradation of this dry deciduous forest. However, these forests have a high percentage of plant endemism, so the extent of cover may have changed during the Holocene, but this forest has been a feature of the Yucatán for a very long time.

Despite looking very different from each other, the dry deciduous forests and savannas occur in the same monsoonal climate, with an intense wet season alternating with long periods with little rainfall, including a few months of near-total drought that is enough to kill most large evergreen trees in areas of nutrient-deficient soils. In the summer wet season (May–October) this habitat appears very similar to MESOAMERICAN SEMI-EVERGREEN FOREST or MESOAMERICAN LOWLAND RAINFOREST: water abounds, the canopy appears thick (though close inspection shows that the leaves are generally smaller than those in rainforest), and there is abundant, lush undergrowth. Visiting the forest during the winter dry season (February–April) gives a very different impression: many of the plants have lost their leaves, the ground is covered with a thick layer of dry, brittle leaves, and the layer of brush at head height seems almost impenetrable. These dry

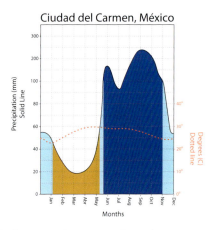

Ciudad del Carmen, México

forests are highly susceptible to destruction through fire (as are semi-evergreen forests).

The canopy of deciduous trees sits at a height of 40–65 ft. (12–20 m) and is generally very open, with less than 50% cover during the wet season. The open nature of the canopy lets light penetrate the forest and allow for a thick lower midstory of evergreen trees. When this habitat is more

open during the dry season, you can see that most trees are stout, quite thick for their height, and not as straight as trees in wetter forests. They are usually angled and gnarled, with branches starting much closer to the base of the trunk, than in rainforest. The trees have a variety of canopy forms, with many of the smaller-leaved trees having a flatter shape than trees of closed forests. The canopy is dominated by Gumbo-limbo (*Bursera simaruba*), Cuban Cedar (*Cedrela odorata*), and Spanish-elm (*Cordia alliodora*). One of the prominent features of this kind of forest, even notable in the wet season, is the abundance of baobab-like kapok trees such as Pochote (*Ceiba aesculifolia*) and other *Ceiba* spp., which store water in their trunk. Kapoks dominate the forest and are usually higher than the surrounding trees as well as much broader. The canopy has fewer vines and epiphytes than rainforest canopy, but because of the deciduous nature of this forest, they are often more conspicuous than their rainforest counterparts.

The understory usually consists of small evergreen trees and shrubs, such as the very distinctive Elephant's-foot Tree (*Beaucarnea pliabilis*), Bastard Logwood (*Gymnopodium floribundum*), Cucumber Tree (*Parmentiera aculeata*), Florida Fish-poison Tree (*Piscidia piscipula*), and Frangipani Blanco (*Plumeria obtusa*), along with a few younger deciduous canopy trees. Areas of thornbushes form a microhabitat within this forest (similar to the surrounding CARIBBEAN THORNSCRUB) that is dominated by legumes such as the Yucatán Wattle (*Senegalia gaumeri*), Feather Vachellia (*Vachellia pennatula*), and Collins's Acacia (*Vachellia collinsii*), which occur as both subcanopy trees and shrubs. It seems incongruous to have cacti and palms together, but in this forest, Mexican Organ Pipe Cactus (*Pterocereus gaumeri*) and Dagger Cactus (*Stenocereus griseus*) occur alongside Florida Thatch Palm (*Thrinax radiata*).

Grasses and herbaceous plants are limited, distinguishing dry deciduous forest from woodland habitats such as MESOAMERICAN SAVANNA AND GRASSLAND. Because of the thick undergrowth, walking through this habitat away from trails is generally difficult, especially in the wet season. In the dry season you can see the ground ahead for 20–50 ft. (6–15 m); in the wet season, ground visibility is limited to 10–20 ft. (3–6 m). At head height, visibility is limited year-round due to the thick understory.

Yucatán Dry Deciduous Forest is quite lush after the rainy season.
© RONI MARTINEZ

Rose-throated Tanager is endemic to the Yucatán Peninsula. © PHIL CHAON

WILDLIFE: While Yucatán Dry Deciduous Forest is visually distinct from adjacent habitats, its wildlife overlaps broadly with CARIBBEAN THORNSCRUB and MESOAMERICAN SEMI-EVERGREEN FOREST. The usual array of lowland tropical mammals is found here, including White-nosed Coati, Southern Opossum, Ocelot, Jaguarundi, and Geoffroy's Spider Monkey.

Generally, the avifauna of dry deciduous forest has representatives of most Neotropical bird families, although fruit-eating groups such as toucans, barbets, and cotingas are not well represented. Furnariids such as woodcreepers, foliage-gleaners, and spinetails make up a larger proportion of the avian assemblage than in wetter areas. Many regional endemics are found in this habitat including Yucatán Woodpecker, Yucatán Flycatcher, Yucatán Jay, and Rose-throated Tanager. White-fronted Parrots are abundant here and are major seed-dispersers in the region.

CONSERVATION: The dry forests of the Yucatán Peninsula have undergone substantial deforestation as a consequence of subsistence agriculture, deliberately set fires, agave cultivation, and cattle-ranching activities.

DISTRIBUTION: The main area of this forest is on the Yucatán Peninsula of se. Mexico from sea level to around 2000 ft. (600 m); a small patch of severely degraded habitat occurs near Veracruz, Mexico (**Veracruz Dry Deciduous Forest** subhabitat).

WHERE TO SEE: Chichen Itza, Yucatán, Mexico.

Singing Quail are inconspicuous until they burst into loud fits of group singing. © PHIL CHAON

Ne5C MAMANE-NAIO DRY FOREST

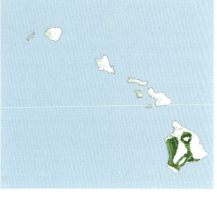

IN A NUTSHELL: A dry, high-elevation woodland found on the island of Hawai'i. **Global Habitat Affinities:** MALAGASY DECIDUOUS FOREST. **Continental Habitat Affinities:** CARIBBEAN THORNSCUB. **Species Overlap:** WET 'ŌHI'A LEHUA–KOA FOREST.

DESCRIPTION: The Mamane-Naio Dry Forest is a short and shrubby evergreen forest found on the high and dry slopes of Mauna Kea, on the island of Hawai'i. The temperature varies little throughout the year, with highs of 60–70°F (16–21°C) and lows of 45–50°F (7–10°C). The area receives 15–25 in. (400–650 mm) of rain, with the majority coming between the months of February and April. Due to the high elevation and intense sun, this habitat feels like many other arid

Mamane-Naio Dry Forest occurs only on the leeward side of the island of Hawai'i. © KEITH BARNES, TROPICAL BIRDING TOURS

thornscrubs and dry forests found globally; 70°F can feel shockingly hot in full sun at 8000 ft. (2500 m).

Two tree species, Mamane (*Sophora chrysophylla*) and Naio (*Myoporum sandwicense*), compose the canopy of Mamane-Naio Dry Forest. These forests are rarely more than 25 ft. (7.5 m) tall and become increasingly short and sparse as you move upslope. The canopy is quite open, and the forest often grows in small dense patches with sizable gaps. 'Ōhi'a Lehua (*Metrosideros polymorpha*) is present around the periphery of the habitat but is never a key component.

The shrub component is also dominated by Mamane and especially Naio, and the distinction between tall shrubland and short forest often feels blurred. Other common native shrubs include 'A'ali'i (*Dodonaea viscosa*), Pūkiawe (*Leptecophylla tameiameiae*), and 'Akoko (*Chamaesyce olowaluana*). The understory is interspersed with unvegetated areas of cinder and volcanic rock. Vegetated areas are usually dominated by introduced grasses, especially Fountain Grass (*Pennisetum setaceum*), Kikuyu Grass (*Pennisetum clandestinum*), and Buffel Grass (*Pennisetum ciliaris*).

In all but the driest times of year, the Mamane is adorned with strands of golden flowers and long pale-green pods that are magnets for birds, especially Hawai'i 'Amakihi and Warbling White-eye.

WILDLIFE: The Mamane-Naio Dry Forest is the sole location for the critically endangered Palila, reduced to fewer than 1000 individuals. The last living dry-forest endemic bird in the Hawaiian archipelago, Palila was once extremely common throughout dry forests on the island of Hawai'i. The best way to locate this bird is to move slowly, listening for its pleasant, cheery whistle or the soft crunching of seedpods being consumed. Palila feeds almost exclusively on Mamane pods and seeds, which are extremely toxic to most species. The seeds have been known to kill House Finches within minutes of consumption! The only other native birds found in this habitat are the abundant Hawai'i 'Amakihi and the occasional 'Io (Hawaiian Hawk).

A wide variety of non-native species occur in this habitat, largely introduced game birds like Black Francolin, California Quail, and Ring-necked Pheasant. Commonly seen passerines include a cosmopolitan mix of House Finch, Warbling White-eye, Yellow-fronted Canary, Zebra Dove, Northern Cardinal, and Northern Mockingbird.

There are no other native vertebrates found in this habitat. Feral goats, feral hogs, and Mouflon are the most commonly encountered large mammals. Black Rat and Indian Gray Mongoose are also present in large numbers and frequently predate nestlings and eggs of Palila.

CONSERVATION: The Mamane-Naio Dry Forest is a severely threatened habitat suffering from a myriad of different threats. While habitat degradation began with the arrival of the first people on Hawai'i, around 1000–1200 CE, the vast majority of the damage occurred in the 19th century when upward of 90% of the forest was cleared for cattle ranching. Also during this time, the introduction of invasive plants and non-native grasses began to alter the fire regime, resulting in intense stand-clearing fires. Overbrowsing by goats and Mouflon (released for hunting in the 1960s) have caused severe damage to the remaining Mamane-Naio stands, especially saplings and seedlings. Most recently, the Naio Thrip has become a major source of concern. Since its first detection in 2009, the insect has spread throughout the habitat, causing widespread mortality of Naio trees. In the long term, persistent drought driven by climate change is a looming threat.

Palila is a rare and declining bird found only in this habitat. © ALEX WANG

The Mamane-Naio Dry Forest was the battleground for the landmark *Palila v. Hawaii Department of Land and Natural Resources* federal court case, which ruled that the protections afforded the Palila by the US Endangered Species Act superseded the state's right to maintain sheep and goats for hunting within a state game management area. Several large tracts of Mamane-Naio Dry Forest are protected by fencing that excludes grazing ungulates. Within these fenced areas, invasive-species removal and propagation of native trees are taking place.

DISTRIBUTION: Mamane-Naio Dry Forest is limited to dry areas, mostly on the leeward side of Mauna Kea on the island of Hawai'i. While historically occurring at lower elevations, all remaining Mamane-Naio habitat is found between 6000 and 9000 ft. (1800–2750 m).

WHERE TO SEE: Palila Discovery Trail at Ka'ohe Game Management Area, Hawai'i, US.

North American Savannas Dendrogram

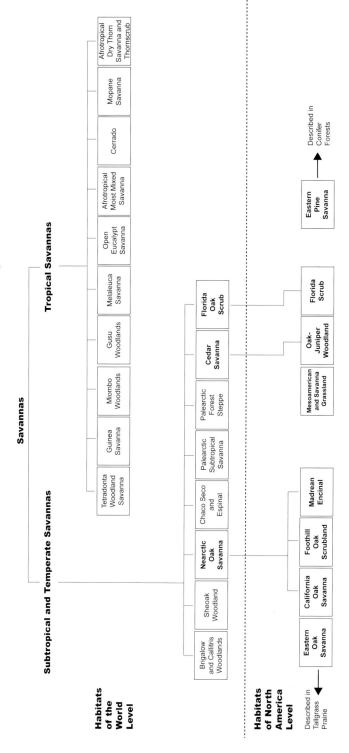

SAVANNAS

Ne6A NEARCTIC OAK-JUNIPER WOODLAND

IN A NUTSHELL: An open, dry savanna of small oaks and junipers (largely Ashe Juniper). **Global Habitat Affinities:** OAK DEHESA; BRIGALOW; AUSTRALASIAN CALLITRIS EUCALYPT THICKET; MAGHREB BROADLEAF WOODLAND. **Continental Habitat Affinities:** MADREAN ENCINAL; PINYON-JUNIPER WOODLAND. **Species Overlap:** MADREAN ENCINAL; CALIFORNIA OAK SAVANNA; CHIHUAHUAN DESERT; SHORTGRASS PRAIRIE; EASTERN MESQUITE.

DESCRIPTION: Oak-Juniper Woodland is a dry and patchy, oak and juniper savanna located on steep and rocky limestone or dolomitic soils of the Texas Hill Country and a few other outlying pockets in the sc. United States and n. Mexico. The structure of the habitat varies with topography but comprises short grasses with scattered small trees, low shrubs, and rocky outcroppings. Occurring in a semiarid subtropical zone, the region has a highly seasonal climate, with moderately cold winters and hot summers. Typical winter low temperatures are between 25 and 35°F (–4 and 2°C), and average

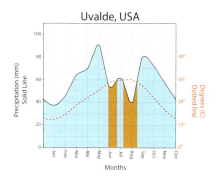

summer highs are around 90–95°F (32–35°C). The region receives about 30 in. (750 mm) of annual precipitation, with peak precipitation falling in May and June.

The Oak-Juniper Woodland habitat comprises two major subhabitats. **Ne6A-1 Edwards Plateau Oak-Juniper Scrubland** is an open, shrubby savanna dominated by small Ashe Juniper (*Juniperus ashei*), Eastern Redcedar (*Juniperus virginiana*), and Redberry Juniper (*Juniperus pinchotii*). Small scrubby oaks are present but rarely dominate. Canopy trees here rarely surpass 20 ft. (6 m) in height, and canopy cover is usually less than 30%. This subhabitat has a well-developed shrub and understory layer. The midstory of this savanna is a smattering of sapling canopy trees and small shrubs, including Texas Persimmon (*Diospyros texana*), Agarito (*Berberis trifoliolata*), Texas Mountain Laurel (*Dermatophyllum secundiflorum*), Honey Mesquite (*Prosopis glandulosa*), and pricklypears (*Opuntia* spp.). While generally sparse, the density of the shrub layer (particularly Honey Mesquite) can increase with overgrazing, choking out the normally dominant understory of Little Bluestem (*Schizachyrium scoparium*), Side-oats Grama (*Bouteloua curtipendula*), Texas Wintergrass (*Nassella leucotricha*), Curly Muhly Grass (*Muhlenbergia setifolia*), and gramas

Edwards Plateau Oak-Juniper Scrubland is a distinctive subhabitat.
© SAM WOODS, TROPICAL BIRDING TOURS

(*Bouteloua* spp.). This subhabitat naturally experiences frequent low-intensity fires that maintain the open grassy structure.

The other subhabitat, **Ne6A-2 Edwards Plateau Oak-Juniper Woodland**, has a much more forested feel. Often occurring in dense copses called mottes, this subhabitat is strongly dominated by a variety of oaks. Post Oak (*Quercus stellata*), Blackjack Oak (*Quercus marilandica*), Lacey Oak (*Quercus laceyi*) Buckley Oak (*Quercus buckleyi*), and especially Plateau Live Oak (*Quercus fusiformis*), along with Cedar Elm (*Ulmus crassifolia*) and hackberries (*Celtis* spp.), are the primary canopy trees. Junipers and cedars (*Juniperus* spp.) are regularly present but rarely dominant and often occur as a mid-canopy or shrub layer. This is still a relatively short woodland, with most canopy trees growing to a height of only 30–40 ft. (10–12 m). Canopy cover ranges from 30 to 70%. The shrub and understory layers are generally poorly developed but contain similar species to Edwards Plateau Oak-Juniper Scrubland. In this subhabitat, fires are naturally less frequent and more intense than in the scrubland. These fires clear out shrubs while leaving the canopy intact.

WILDLIFE: Located at a biotic crossroads between TEMPERATE DECIDUOUS FOREST, TALLGRASS PRAIRIE, and CHIHUAHUAN DESERT shrubland, the Oak-Juniper Woodland holds an interesting mix of mammal and bird species. Large mammals like White-tailed Deer, Collared Peccary (in Texas), and feral hogs are common due to the abundance of grazing land and acorn-rich oak forests. Pumas are still found in the Texas Hill Country, and a few remain in the Wichita Mountains of Oklahoma, while smaller carnivores like Bobcat, Coyote, Gray Fox, Ringtail, Common Raccoon, Striped Skunk, Western Spotted Skunk, and American Badger are more widespread and common. Other mammals found in this habitat include Black-tailed Jackrabbit, North American Porcupine, Virginia Opossum, Nine-banded Armadillo, and a large array of rodents. Perhaps the most spectacular mammal-viewing opportunities are afforded by the massive colonies of Mexican Free-

Golden-cheeked Warbler nests exclusively in Nearctic Oak-Juniper Woodland.
© BEN KNOOT, TROPICAL BIRDING TOURS

tailed Bats that live in the limestone caves throughout the region. On spring and summer evenings, colonies numbering in the millions can be seen exiting these maternity caves to feed, while raptors like Red-tailed, Harris's, and Swainson's Hawks, Merlin, and Peregrine Falcon take advantage of this plentiful food source.

Common birds in the Oak-Juniper Woodland of Texas and the Wichita Mountains include Northern Bobwhite; Wild Turkey; White-winged and Mourning Doves; Greater Roadrunner; Black-chinned Hummingbird; Ladder-backed, Golden-fronted, and Red-headed Woodpeckers; Scissor-tailed Flycatcher; White-eyed Vireo; Black-crested and Tufted Titmice; Cliff and Cave Swallows; Bewick's Wren; Lesser Goldfinch; Field, Lark, and Rufous-crowned Sparrows; and Painted Bunting. Among nocturnal species, Common Poorwill, Common and Lesser Nighthawks, Chuck-will's-widow, and Eastern Whip-poor-will use Oak-Juniper Woodland—a large array of nightjars for a single habitat. The two undoubted avian stars of this habitat are the endangered Golden-cheeked Warbler (IS) and vulnerable Black-capped Vireo (IS), which are endemic and near-endemic breeding birds, respectively. Black-capped Vireo prefers the open, juniper-dominated Edwards Plateau Oak-Juniper Scrubland, while Golden-cheeked Warbler breeds in the denser Edwards Plateau Oak-Juniper Woodland. Reliably found in spring and early summer, these birds are largely dependent on Oak-Juniper Woodland for food and nesting. Strips of Ashe Juniper bark are a particularly important material in construction of vireo nests, and oaks host a wide variety of caterpillars that are the primary food for chicks of these species.

A range of reptiles and amphibians can be found in Oak-Juniper Woodland. Great Plains Rat Snake, Eastern Milk Snake, Flat-headed Snake, Copperhead, Prairie Racerunner, Eastern Fence Lizard, and Eastern Collared Lizard are common.

Black-capped Vireo prefers the juniper-dominated scrublands within Oak-Juniper Woodland.
© SAM WOODS, TROPICAL BIRDING TOURS

CONSERVATION: Less than 1% of this biologically diverse habitat is currently protected. The urban centers of Austin and San Antonio are in the heart of Oak-Juniper Woodland and are rapidly expanding. The human population in this area has doubled over the past 30 years, and residential development is rampant. Much of the region has also been altered, particularly for ranching. Overgrazing leads to encroachment from Honey Mesquite and other shrubs and grasses. This can alter the fire regime, leading to higher fuel loads and more intense fires. Despite the many challenges in the region, Black-capped Vireo was removed from the endangered species list in 2018 after populations surpassed 5000 adult males, up from a low of fewer than 300 individuals. A combination of prescribed burns, removal of Brown-headed Cowbirds, and extensive cooperation with private landowners aided in the dramatic recovery. Golden-cheeked Warbler generally needs more mature, intact habitat, and its recovery has been a slower process.

DISTRIBUTION: In the sc. United States, Oak-Juniper Woodland is found mostly on the rugged limestone escarpments of the Edwards Plateau in Texas Hill Country. This core area stretches from San Antonio north and east to Waco and as far west as the edge of the Rio Grande valley. Away from this core area, there are a few outlying pockets in n. Coahuila in Mexico and the Wichita Mountains of Oklahoma.

WHERE TO SEE: Balcones Canyonlands National Wildlife Refuge, Texas, US; Kerr Wildlife Management Area, Texas, US; Wichita Mountains Wildlife Refuge, Oklahoma, US.

SIDEBAR 9   GHOSTS OF THE PLEISTOCENE

Somewhere along the Red River of Oklahoma, a large bumpy green fruit falls to the ground. This brain-like, viridian Osage-orange (*Maclura pomifera*) will lie here until it eventually rots away. Why would a tree expend so much energy producing a fruit that seems to serve no purpose? Like all fruits, the purpose of the Osage-orange is to entice animals that will consume the seeds and spread the fruit over distances the immobile plant cannot. Unfortunately for the Osage-orange, all the animals that would have eagerly entered into this partnership have been dead for millennia.

The great Pleistocene extinction saw the demise of dozens of species of megafauna that roamed North America. Among the many animals to vanish at this time were the mammoths (*Mammuthus* spp.) and ground sloths (*Megalonyx* spp.). For thousands of years, North American trees had developed large fruits, specifically for animals of such a massive size. Kentucky Coffee-tree (*Gymnocladus dioicus*), Honey Locust (*Gleditsia triacanthos*), and pawpaws (*Asimina* spp.) are all trees with large fruiting bodies that lack a living disperser and likely relied on megafauna that is now extinct. The Kentucky Coffee-tree is also armed with large brittle thorns that are too widely spaced to effectively deter herbivory from deer but would have posed a serious impediment to a large-mouthed ground sloth.

The 11,000 years that Osage-orange has spent without dispersers is just a blink in evolutionary time, but in that short period, seven out of eight species in the genus *Maclura* have disappeared completely, and the Osage-orange occupies only a tiny natural range. In the face of a rapidly changing climate, dispersal is an important survival tool for many plants. Animal partnerships allow plants to reach new and favorable areas as former homes become inhospitable. As the landscape changes, and many frugivorous animals decline, the relationship between plants and dispersers will be critical for the continued survival of entire forests in the coming decades.

Ne6B CALIFORNIA OAK SAVANNA

IN A NUTSHELL: A habitat characterized by widely spaced oaks with an understory of grasses and forbs, found along the western edge of the United States and Baja California, Mexico. **Global Habitat Affinities:** OAK DEHESA. **Continental Habitat Affinities:** MADREAN ENCINAL; TALLGRASS PRAIRIE (Eastern Oak Savanna subhabitat); OAK-JUNIPER WOODLAND. **Species Overlap:** PACIFIC CHAPARRAL; PONDEROSA PINE FOREST.

DESCRIPTION: California Oak Savanna occurs adjacent to the Pacific coast, typically in transitional zones between grassland and forest habitats. This habitat is characterized by widely spaced broad-crowned oaks growing with an understory of grasses and forbs. Most California Oak Savannas have a Mediterranean climate. Average precipitation is 15–32 in. (400–800 mm), falling mostly as rain during the winter months (November–March). The summers can be extremely hot and dry, with daytime temperatures reaching 90–110°F (32–43°C). Winter temperatures are generally pleasant, with daytime highs of 45–70°F (7–21°C) and lows rarely below freezing. These open,

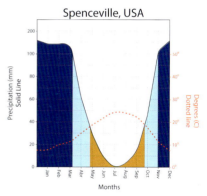

parklike environments are easy to walk in and are a great place to observe wildlife, especially during mast years (large seeding events).

The California Oak Savanna is the most diverse of the North American oak savannas and includes over a dozen oak species. Trees in this habitat are typically 20–60 ft. (6–18 m) tall, and canopy cover varies from 10 to 50%, with denser groupings of trees occurring at higher elevations. Coast Live Oak (*Quercus agrifolia*), Valley Oak (*Quercus lobata*), Interior Live Oak (*Quercus wislizenii*), California Black Oak (*Quercus kelloggii*), Engelmann Oak (*Quercus engelmanni*), and Blue Oak (*Quercus douglasii*) are dominant species in this habitat. Other trees, such as Pacific Madrone (*Arbutus menziesii*), California Bay (*Umbellularia californica*), Gray Pine (*Pinus sabiniana*), and Ponderosa Pine (*Pinus ponderosa*), are also present in small numbers. The shrub layer is typically sparse or absent, but commonly occurring shrubs include buckbrushes (*Ceanothus* spp.), manzanitas (*Arctostaphylos* spp.), and Western Poison Oak (*Toxicodendron diversilobum*).

The understory of California Oak Savanna is usually a subset of grasses and forbs from adjacent grassland habitats, often dominated by non-native grasses like Cheatgrass (*Bromus tectorum*) and Wild Oats (*Avena fatua*). The **Ne6B-1 California Grasslands** subhabitat was formerly a major component of this ecoregion and formed a broad matrix with California Oak Savanna. Once dominated by Giant Wild Rye (*Leymus condensatus*), Torrey's Melica (*Melica torreyana*), and needlegrasses (*Nassella* spp.), this subhabitat has been virtually eliminated through conversion to agriculture and introduction of invasive species.

California Oak Savannas occur in areas where the amount of precipitation is intermediate between that of adjacent grasslands and forests, or in areas with sandy or otherwise poor soil. In the Coast Ranges, California Oak Savanna often forms on exposed ridgetops above NEARCTIC TEMPERATE RAINFOREST in areas called bald hills.

Fire is crucial to the maintenance of the open, parklike nature of California Oak Savanna.

WILDLIFE: While lacking a unique set of mammals, this habitat, with its open nature and wealth of food, is a great place to see wildlife. California Oak Savanna attracts an abundance of grazing animals, with large populations of Mule Deer and Elk. Squirrels and ground squirrels (especially California Ground Squirrel) are common and provide a large prey base for the Coyotes, Bobcats, and American Badgers that are all readily seen here. Ringtail is abundant relative to its presence in other habitats.

The oak savannas of California have a distinctive subset of birds, several of which are near-endemic. Oak Titmouse (IS), Nuttall's Woodpecker (IS), and Yellow-billed Magpie are found almost exclusively in this habitat. Acorn and Lewis's Woodpeckers, Phainopepla, and Lark Sparrow are also especially common. Other readily seen birds include Wild Turkey, California Quail, Ash-throated Flycatcher, White-breasted Nuthatch, Bushtit, Bewick's Wren, California Scrub-Jay, Black-throated Gray Warbler, and California Towhee. During large winter mast events, sizable flocks of Band-tailed Pigeons may be found in the area.

California Oak Savanna is the dominant habitat in the foothills of California. © BEN KNOOT, TROPICAL BIRDING TOURS

The abundance of small mammals makes California
Oak Savanna a great place to look for Bobcats.
© BEN KNOOT, TROPICAL BIRDING TOURS

Nuttall's Woodpecker is endemic
to California and Baja California.
© BEN KNOOT, TROPICAL BIRDING TOURS

California Oak Savannas are typically too dry to support many amphibian species, but Western Toad, Pacific Tree Frog, California Slender Salamander, and Arboreal Salamander are all present. Lizards are decidedly more abundant in this habitat, and Western Skink, Western Fence Lizard, Southern Alligator Lizard, and Northern Alligator Lizard are particularly common. With a large mammalian and amphibian prey base, snakes are numerous; Sharp-tailed Snake, Ring-necked Snake, California Kingsnake, Gopher Snake, Pacific Rattlesnake, and Western Terrestrial Garter Snake are among the most common.

The small pockets of California Oak Savanna found on the Channel Islands are home to the endemic Island Scrub-Jay and the diminutive endemic Island Fox.

The Oak Titmouse was formerly
known as the Plain Titmouse,
for obvious reasons.
© BEN KNOOT, TROPICAL BIRDING TOURS

CONSERVATION: California Oak Savanna is still a fairly common habitat on the landscape for the time being, despite large losses due to residential, industrial, and agricultural development. Major threats to oak savannas include clearing for grazing, increased fire mortality due to changes in fire frequency and intensity, persistent drought, and sudden oak death caused by the pathogen *Phytophthora ramorum*. California Oak Savannas have also experienced relatively poor recruitment (i.e., successful establishment) of young trees, especially Blue Oak. Increased herbivory and the proliferation of feral hogs on the landscape are significant factors in poor recruitment. Very little of the California Oak Savanna is within protected areas.

While California Oak Savannas are still relatively common, the associated perennial **California Grasslands** have been decimated. Non-native grasses are favored heavily during drought periods, and native grasses like Giant Wild Rye, Torrey's Melica, and needlegrasses are found only in tiny remnant fragments. Efforts to restore native grasses have been entirely unsuccessful.

DISTRIBUTION: California Oak Savanna forms a long interior strip from n. Baja California, Mexico, northward through California, Oregon, and Washington. It also occurs coastally and around the margins of the Central Valley in California. This habitat occurs primarily at elevations of 200–2000 ft. (60–600 m) in the Coast Ranges, and in a ring around the Central Valley in the foothills of the Sierra Nevada and Coast Ranges. The savannas are situated between annual grasslands at lower elevations and MONTANE MIXED-CONIFER FOREST or PONDEROSA PINE FOREST at higher elevations.

WHERE TO SEE: Spenceville Wildlife Area, California, US.

Ne6C MADREAN ENCINAL

IN A NUTSHELL: An oak-dominated habitat located below the Madrean Pine-Oak Woodland and varying from open savanna to dense woodland. **Global Habitat Affinities:** OAK DEHESA. **Continental Habitat Affinities:** CALIFORNIA OAK SAVANNA; FOOTHILL OAK SHRUBLAND. **Species Overlap:** CHIHUAHUAN DESERT GRASSLAND; CHIHUAHUAN DESERT; SONORAN DESERT; CENTRAL MEXICAN SUCCULENT MATORRAL; MADREAN PINE-OAK WOODLAND; MESOAMERICAN PACIFIC DRY DECIDUOUS FOREST.

DESCRIPTION: Madrean Encinal occurs in a mid-elevational band, directly below the MADREAN PINE-OAK WOODLAND and usually above xeric shrublands or grasslands, generally occurring between 4000 and 6000 ft. (1200–1800 m). The habitat is dry and pleasant for much of the year, though summers can be quite hot. Encinal varies with latitude in a long gradient between its northern and southern forms. In the north it is structurally like other oak savannas, with widely spaced trees, broad spreading crowns, and a dense understory of grasses. Southward, it generally becomes more of a closed woodland and eventually dense and shrubby. In s. Mexico it is often part of a well-blended ecotone between the lower-elevation thornscrub and dry deciduous habitats and the higher pine-oak woodlands.

Sierra Vista, USA

The Madrean Encinal at the northern end of its range is usually open and savanna-like and heavily dominated by Emory Oak (*Quercus emoryi*). Arizona White Oak (*Quercus arizonica*), Felt Oak (*Quercus chihuahuensis*), and Mexican Blue Oak (*Quercus oblongifolia*) are also regularly present. The northern encinal has few shrubs, mostly small oaks and scattered junipers (*Juniperus* spp.).These savannas have a grassy understory generally comprising

Madrean Encinal is found in the lower elevations of Arizona's "sky islands." © BEN KNOOT, TROPICAL BIRDING TOURS

species from arid shrublands and grasslands downslope, especially gramas (*Bouteloua* spp.) and muhlys (*Muhlenbergia* spp.).

By the time the encinal reaches the southern end of its range it is mostly chaparral. A dense, shrubby woodland, this form of encinal feels more like a dwarf form of PACIFIC DRY DECIDUOUS FOREST or a tall thornscrub. A diverse array of oaks still dominates the canopy, with up to a dozen species occurring in a single stand. Mexican Red Oak (*Quercus castanea*), Netleaf Oak (*Quercus rugosa*), and Chilillo Oak (*Quercus crassifolia*) are common, along with a variety of thorny leguminous trees. The understory can be quite viny, and there are scattered cacti, but the forest floor is usually bare aside from a dense layer of oak leaves. The oaks in this form are often covered in a staggering number of small epiphytes, especially bromeliads in the genus *Tillandsia*. Many of these bromeliads are endemic to specific valleys and basins within this system.

WILDLIFE: While lacking a unique set of mammals, this habitat, with its open nature and abundance of food, is a great place to see wildlife. Madrean Encinal attracts an abundance of grazing animals, with large populations of White-tailed and Mule Deer. Squirrels and ground squirrels are common and provide a substantial prey base for the Coyotes, Bobcats, and American Badgers that are all readily seen here. Farther south this habitat is home to Jaguarundi, White-nosed Coati, Collared Peccary, and Gray Fox. Ringtail and Hooded Skunk are common throughout.

The birdlife of the Madrean Encinal is strongly influenced by surrounding habitats. Wild Turkey, Acorn Woodpecker, Phainopepla, and Lark Sparrow are common in the northern encinal. Bridled Titmouse (IS) and the stunning Montezuma Quail (IS) are also characteristic of this habitat, especially in more savanna-like areas. Montezuma Quail are nearly invisible in grassy habitats,

Titmice are most common in oak-dominated habitats, and the Bridled Titmouse is no exception.
© BEN KNOOT, TROPICAL BIRDING TOURS

often freezing before flushing right under foot. The best way to detect them is by listening for a buzzy descending whistle, though this too is extremely difficult to pinpoint. In s. Mexico, the dense shrubby encinal is the primary habitat for several endemic species including Ocellated Thrasher (IS), Dwarf Vireo (IS), Oaxaca Sparrow (IS), and Bridled Sparrow. These species are also skulkers and difficult to find. Listening for rustling in the dense dry leaf litter is a good strategy.

Snakes and lizards are especially numerous in the encinal. Black-tailed Rattlesnake (IS) is common throughout the entirety of this habitat. Mexican Pygmy Rattlesnake, Short-tailed Horned Lizard, Middle American Gopher Snake, and a wide variety of spiny lizards (*Sceloporus* spp.) are found in the south. Sonoran Whipsnakes are abundant in the north.

CONSERVATION: Madrean Encinal is a relatively well-preserved habitat with few endemics. Many of the same threats present in other savanna habitats are found here—especially overgrazing, fire suppression, and invasive grasses. Oak wood is a valuable fuel source, and cutting for firewood is common.

DISTRIBUTION: Madrean Encinal occurs patchily as a transition between CHIHUAHUAN DESERT GRASSLAND, or other arid shrubland and thornscrub communities, and MADREAN PINE-OAK WOODLAND. It is found in se. Arizona south of the Mogollon Rim, sw. New Mexico, and w. Texas in the United States. In Mexico it occurs in both the Sierra Madre Occidental and Sierra Madre Oriental, as well as in large dry valleys, like the Oaxaca valley as far south as the Isthmus of Tehuantepec. Its range in the humid Sierra Madre Oriental is much more limited than in the arid Pacific ranges.

WHERE TO SEE: Miller Canyon, Arizona, US; Teotitlán, Oaxaca, Mexico.

The gorgeous Montezuma Quail is a seldom-seen resident in the Madrean Encinal.
© BEN KNOOT, TROPICAL BIRDING TOURS

Ne6D FLORIDA SCRUB

IN A NUTSHELL: A dry, open shrubland found on sandy soils in peninsular Florida. **Global Habitat Affinities:** RESTINGA. **Continental Habitat Affinities:** None. **Species Overlap:** EASTERN PINE SAVANNA; TEMPERATE DECIDUOUS FOREST.

DESCRIPTION: This hot, arid, open habitat is restricted to small areas of Florida, in the se. United States, and holds some unique fauna despite its small range. Florida Scrub occurs on the sandy, nutrient-poor soils of inland ancient dune ridges as well as interior coastal dunes. The white-sand soils are incredibly well drained, and despite the 50–60 in. (1250–1500 mm) of rain received a year, this habitat remains very dry.

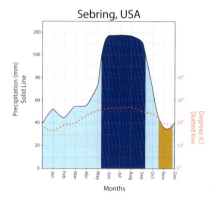

Florida Scrub rarely has any trees, and the few that do occur are small and scattered Sand Pines (*Pinus clausa*), which grow to a height of only 30 ft. (10 m). The majority of the vegetation occurs in the shrub layer, which is open to moderately dense and rarely more than 6 ft. (1.8 m) tall. Myrtle Oak (*Quercus myrtifolia*) or Sandhill Oak (*Quercus inopina*) are the two most dominant species. Sand Live Oak (*Quercus geminata*), Chapman Oak (*Quercus chapmanii*), Crooked-wood (*Lyonia ferruginea*), pricklypears (*Opuntia* spp.), and Florida Rosemary (*Ceratiola ericoides*) are usually present as well, and Saw Palmetto (*Serenoa repens*) is often abundant.

The herbaceous layer is sparse, and the ground cover is largely exposed sand. Scattered grasses and forbs do occur, with Bushy Bluestem (*Andropogon glomeratus*), Gopher-apple (*Licania michauxii*), and Sandyfield Beaksedge (*Rhynchospora megalocarpa*) the most prominent species. This habitat is home to a high concentration of endangered plants (15 species), including the beautiful Florida Bonamia (*Bonamia grandiflora*), the large purple-and-white flowers of which were once a common sight.

WILDLIFE: The fauna of Florida Scrub is a rather limited set due to the nutrient-poor nature of this habitat and its limited range. Despite that, a large fraction of the wildlife here is unique to the area. White-tailed Deer, American Black Bear, Common Raccoon, Bobcat, and Nine-banded Armadillo all

Florida Scrub exists mostly on sandy soils in the interior of the peninsula. © JARED MIZANIN

spend time foraging in Florida Scrub, though there aren't the resources for them to live exclusively in this habitat. One of the only permanent resident mammals is the endemic and endangered Florida Mouse. The only member of its genus, this large mouse lives in burrows constructed within large Gopher Tortoise burrows.

The bird community is also sparse. The star attraction is Florida Scrub-Jay (IS), an endangered species not found outside of this habitat. Florida Scrub-Jays rely largely on the acorns found in this habitat for food, and cached acorns are an important method of seed dispersal. Common birds include Mourning Dove, Burrowing Owl, Chuck-will's widow, White eyed Vireo, and Eastern Towhee.

In a productive season, a Florida Scrub-Jay can cache thousands of acorns for later consumption. These birds have been observed cooperatively hunting for snakes.
© JARED MIZANIN

Gopher Tortoise creates large burrows that are used by other animals including Burrowing Owls and Eastern Indigo Snakes. © JARED MIZANIN

The reptile communities are the most unique aspect of this habitat. The endangered Gopher Tortoise is relatively abundant and important in creating burrows utilized by the highly local Gopher Frog. Florida Scrub Lizard (IS), Blue-tailed Mole Skink, and Florida Sand Skink (IS) are all endemic to Florida Scrub. Eastern Coachwhip, Mole Kingsnake, and Eastern Indigo Snake are also regularly encountered. Florida Crowned Snake (IS) and Short-tailed Snake (IS) are Florida Scrub specialists. Florida Worm Lizard, a limbless and mostly blind reptile, is also endemic. This bizarre reptile is part of a group of fossorial lizards called amphisbaenians. Also called the Thunderworm, it is usually seen aboveground only when its burrows are flooded during major storms.

CONSERVATION: Florida Scrub is one of the most endangered habitats in North America, as over 90% has been lost to agricultural and residential development. It is a fire-dependent ecosystem, relying on high-intensity but infrequent fires every 20–50 years. Natural fires burn patchily, creating a mosaic of different-aged shrub stands. Fire suppression leads to overcrowding of plants and the loss of key species. Thankfully, the majority of remaining habitat is in protected areas that are being managed for its continued survival.

DISTRIBUTION: Florida Scrub is found on isolated sandy pockets throughout peninsular Florida, especially on Lake Wales Ridge and the Big Scrub region of Ocala National Forest. This habitat often occurs within a matrix of EASTERN PINE SAVANNA.

WHERE TO SEE: Ocala National Forest, Florida, US; Lake Wales Ridge National Wildlife Refuge, Florida, US.

Ne6E FOOTHILL OAK SHRUBLAND

IN A NUTSHELL: A dense foothill shrubland in the Rocky Mountains dominated by Gambel Oak. **Global Habitat Affinities:** OAK DEHESA. **Continental Habitat Affinities:** MADREAN ENCINAL. **Species Overlap:** PONDEROSA PINE FOREST; MONTANE MIXED-CONIFER FOREST; WESTERN RIPARIAN WOODLAND; SAGEBRUSH SHRUBLAND.

DESCRIPTION: Foothill Oak Shrubland occurs as a transitional habitat between lowland and montane habitats on the edge of the Rocky Mountains and in the Great Basin. These distinctive shrublands are arid or semiarid and dominated by drought-tolerant plants. They receive most of their annual 10–27 in. (250–700 mm) of precipitation as snow, and patches of snow will linger here long after they have melted on the surrounding hillside.

The oaks of this shrubland will retain dead leaves for much of the winter. © PHIL CHAON

This habitat is heavily dominated by dense, uniform stands of Gambel Oak (*Quercus gambelii*) that typically reach 3–8 ft. (1–2.5 m) in height. Occasionally, Gambel Oak will also occur as a small tree, giving this habitat a multilayered appearance. Typically, there are few other shrubs in this habitat, though Big Sagebrush (*Artemisia tridentata*), Alder-leaf Serviceberry (*Amelanchier alnifolia*), mountain mahoganies (*Cercocarpus* spp.), and Antelope Bitterbrush (*Purshia tridentata*) are frequently present. Foothill Oak Shrubland often occurs in a matrix of grasslands, with dominant species depending on neighboring habitats. Most dominant grasses are shared with MIXED-GRASS PRAIRIE or SHORTGRASS PRAIRIE.

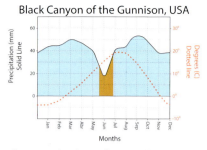

Black Canyon of the Gunnison, USA

Foothill Oak Shrublands provide good cover and nesting habitat in otherwise open country. The abundant oaks also provide a good source of acorns, a nutritious food source for wildlife.

WILDLIFE: Foothill Oak Shrubland has no true endemic animals, but many species are present here in above-average numbers. It is a particularly good place to find animals from adjacent habitats, especially during mast years when acorns are plentiful. Mule Deer, Elk, and American Black Bear seek out this habitat, and Abert's Squirrel, Rock Squirrel, and Least Chipmunk are among the wide variety of squirrels found here.

Dusky Grouse is abundant and is often seen displaying here in the spring months. Sharp-tailed Grouse will visit frequently in winter. Wild Turkey, Band-tailed Pigeon, Woodhouse's Scrub-Jay, Steller's Jay, and Lewis's Woodpecker arrive for the bounty of acorns. In summer, Virginia's

Acorns are an important food source for Mule Deer. © BEN KNOOT, TROPICAL BIRDING TOURS

Warbler is especially abundant in Gambel Oak. Other common species include Downy Woodpecker, Hairy Woodpecker, Mountain Chickadee, Green-tailed Towhee, and Spotted Towhee.

This is a cold montane ecosystem and mostly lacks reptiles and amphibians.

CONSERVATION: Foothill Oak Shrubland is not threatened and doesn't hold any rare or endemic animals. This habitat is very tolerant of disturbance and flourishes after fires. Fire suppression and drought are the primary concerns, along with urban development.

Above: **Dusky Grouse moves from Montane Mixed-Conifer Forest down into Foothill Oak Shrubland during the winter.** © PHIL CHAON

Right: **Spotted Towhee is abundant in many western habitats.** © BEN KNOOT, TROPICAL BIRDING TOURS

DISTRIBUTION: Widely distributed in the foothill zone of the s. Rocky Mountains in Utah, Colorado, Arizona, New Mexico, and Idaho, this habitat usually occurs from 6500 to 8000 ft. (2000–2500 m) elevation. Limited patches in the Trans-Pecos Mountains of w. Texas generally occur at higher elevations. Foothill Oak Shrublands are transitional between several habitats, including PONDEROSA PINE FOREST and MONTANE MIXED-CONIFER FOREST above it, and PINYON-JUNIPER WOODLAND and SAGEBRUSH SHRUBLAND below it. Arid oak shrublands and chaparrals are also found in many areas of Mexico but are more closely related to MADREAN ENCINAL and CHIHUAHUAN DESERT habitats.

WHERE TO SEE: Black Canyon of the Gunnison National Park, Colorado, US.

Ne6F MESOAMERICAN SAVANNA AND GRASSLAND

IN A NUTSHELL: A mosaic of thick grasses, groves of thorny scrub, and scattered trees. **Global Habitat Affinities:** AUSTRALASIAN OPEN EUCALYPT SAVANNA; AFRICAN MOPANE. **Continental Habitat Affinities:** TAMAULIPAN MEZQUITAL; MADREAN ENCINAL. **Species Overlap:** MESOAMERICAN SEMI-EVERGREEN FOREST; CARIBBEAN THORNSCRUB; TAMAULIPAN MEZQUITAL.

DESCRIPTION: The Mesoamerican Savanna and Grassland habitat is something of a catchall for several microhabitats in a mosaic of dense grasses and scattered trees that could be parsed out but occur in such a fine and complex mélange that they are almost impossible to tease apart, in some areas forming groves, sometimes thickets, and even treed savanna parkland with patches of flooded grassland. The savannas have an anthropogenic influence in that they are probably much more widespread now than in prehuman times, and the proto-savannas may have been limited to the seasonally flooded areas and very sandy soils. The savannas on the richer soils are likely derived from cleared or burned MESOAMERICAN PACIFIC DRY DECIDUOUS FOREST or YUCATÁN DRY DECIDUOUS FOREST, and overall the sandier soils tend to have a more open feel than the groves occurring on loamier and nutrient-rich soils.

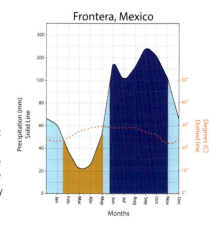

Frontera, Mexico

With an annual average temperature range of 72–82°F (22–28°C), this is generally a warm to hot, monsoonal, seasonally dry habitat (Köppen **Awa**) that has a wide range of precipitation variation from almost semiarid in the north to wet in the south, and much of the 30–63 in. (750–1600 mm)

Coastal savanna and grassland is dotted with palms and floods seasonally. © PHIL CHAON

of rain falls during an intense summer rainy season between May and October. Coastal areas tend to be slightly cooler due to the influence of the ocean, while inland areas may experience higher temperatures.

Mesoamerican Savanna and Grassland is clinal, gradually transitioning from north to south. In the north, the savanna is dominated by microphyllous (small-leaved) and sometimes thorny trees that give it the look of the Espinal of South America or the arid EASTERN MESQUITE from the north, and although it includes broadleaf components, broadleaf trees never dominate the way they do in MADREAN ENCINAL. In the north of the range, wooded groves are dominated by Honey Mesquite (*Prosopis glandulosa*), which forms an open canopy 10–20 ft. (3–6 m) tall and is mixed with Texas Ebony (*Ebenopsis ebano*), Desert Hackberry (*Celtis ehrenbergiana*), Wild Cashew Tree (*Curatella americana*), Bluewood Condalia (*Condalia hookeri*), Nance (*Byrsonima crassifolia*), and Calabash Tree (*Crescentia cujete*). The Mexican Calabash (*Crescentia alata*), a tree that grows to 25 ft. (7.5 m) tall as an emergent in this environment, was very rare when Europeans arrived; it has gourd-like fruits (hence the name calabash) with a very hard shell protecting the pulp that could be opened only by long-extinct megafauna. They are now opened by horses and humans, and for that reason the tree seems abnormally common around farm fields.

The understory and shrub layer are dominated by palms such as Sombrero Palm (*Brahea dulcis*) along with shrubs and small trees such as Wild Lime (*Zanthoxylum fagara*), Texas Persimmon (*Diospyros texana*), and Texas Hog Plum (*Colubrina texensis*). Cacti are represented by the seemingly ubiquitous Engelmann's Pricklypear (*Opuntia engelmannii*) and the Desert Christmas Cactus (*Cylindropuntia leptocauli*).

Although grasses occur extensively in the north of the range, in the south, where the habitat changes from a semiarid one to a fully moist tropical environment, the habitat is dominated more by thick grasslands with palms. Grasses in the drier and/or sandier wooded areas grow 4–5 ft. (1.2–1.5 m) tall and tend to be the same species as in the more open areas. These grasslands are dominated by Little Bluestem (*Schizachyrium scoparium*), Red Lovegrass (*Eragrostis secundiflora*), Texas Grama (*Bouteloua rigidiseta*), and Shore Little Bluestem (*Schizachyrium littorale*) in the north. In the south, Hooded Windmill Grass (*Chloris cucullata*), Silver Beardgrass (*Bothriochloa laguroides*), and Hooded Finger Grass (*Trichloris pluriflora*) are more common. In the areas that are prone to partial flooding during the year, Gulf Dune Paspalum (*Paspalum monostachyum*) and Pan American Balsamscale (*Elionurus tripsacoides*) become more common, and thick fields of Brownseed Paspalum (*Paspalum plicatulum*) reach 12 ft. (4 m) in height and are much more reminiscent of the flooded grasslands of India or the Pantanal of South America than of the dry grasslands of Mesoamerica.

Fire is a major component of these savannas, and in the absence of overgrazing or cutting, the habitat could be regarded as a sere (ecological stage) in the succession to a climax community of dry woodland. The grasslands can last up to 20 years without fire before becoming a woodland, though there is burning usually around every 5 years; this contrasts markedly with the grasslands of w. Africa or n. Australia, which are prone to more frequent burning. During the middle stages of development, between 20 and 50 years, fire frequency diminishes, and the woodlands attain a climax community dominated by Honey Mesquite, Texas Ebony, and Wild Cashew. This fire regime frequency and succession is now being changed through human intervention; the shrub understory of the groves and the grasslands is prone to destruction through overgrazing, and thickets can form with a canopy monoculture of Honey Mesquite and an understory of Engelmann's Pricklypear and Bluewood Condalia. The overall appearance merges with that of TAMAULIPAN MEZQUITAL.

In the Caribbean region, the **Ne6F-1 Caribbean Savanna** subhabitat of Mesoamerican Savanna and Grassland habitat is more prevalent as a dense and thorny shrubland about 6–20 ft. (2–6 m) high, rather than a treed savanna, though it does have palm trees throughout. It occurs over a wide variety of substrates, rather than the predominantly sandy soils of the Mexican savannas; it is particularly prevalent over iron-rich soils derived from the Cuban serpentinite belt, a series of metamorphic rocks formed from the baking of mafic and ultramafic rocks such as basalts. Over other substrates such as sedimentary rocks, it is probably mainly derived from the degradation of dry forests. Although the Caribbean Savanna is dominated by microphyllous trees, it differs from continental Mesoamerican Savanna and Grassland and from CARIBBEAN THORNSCRUB in that cacti are rare, although Royen's Tree Cactus (*Pilosocereus royenii*) can be found in most thickets; even more surprising than its occurrence is this plant's alternative name, Dildo Cactus, which leaves this author both perplexed and rather disturbed. Other shrubs indicative of this subhabitat include Puerto Rico Ceboruquillo (*Thouinia striata*), Cuban Torchwood (*Jacquinia shaferi*), and the widespread Common Myrtle (*Myrtus communis*). There are small palm trees such as Fragrant Cuban Thatch Palm (*Coccothrinax fragrans*), Blue Star Palm (*Hemithrinax rivularis* var. *savannarum*), Cuban Blue Star Palm (*Hemithrinax rivularis*), and vines such as the morning glory *Ipomoea carolina*.

PREVIOUS TWO PAGES:

Left: **Lesser Yellow-headed Vulture is an open-country specialist that has benefited from the conversion of forested habitats to grassland and savanna.** © BEN KNOOT, TROPICAL BIRDING TOURS

Right: **Fork-tailed Flycatcher seeks prominent perches in this habitat.** © BEN KNOOT, TROPICAL BIRDING TOURS

Double-striped Thick-knee
is inconspicuous despite
its large size.
© BEN KNOOT, TROPICAL BIRDING TOURS

WILDLIFE: The small groves and parkland areas of Mesoamerican Savanna and Grassland host many species familiar in southern areas of the United States including Plain Chachalaca, Northern Bobwhite, Inca Dove, Vermilion Flycatcher, Golden-fronted Woodpecker, Brown Jay, and Orchard Oriole, as well as most of the Neotropical migrant warblers that pass through Mexico to breed in temperate North America. However, these small patches of trees also hold many species much more typical of the Neotropics including Red-billed Pigeon, Green-breasted Mango, Ladder-backed Woodpecker, Zone-tailed Hawk, Barred Antshrike, Rose-throated Becard, Yellow-bellied Elaenia, Brown-crested and Fork-tailed Flycatchers, Rufous-naped, Band-backed, and Giant Wrens, Altamira and Hooded Orioles, Yellow-winged Tanager, Indigo Bunting, Painted Bunting, Cinnamon-rumped Seedeater, Buff-bellied Hummingbird, and Groove-billed Ani. These savannas are where Northern Mockingbird and Tropical Mockingbird not only overlap but hybridize, leading to some interesting identification challenges.

The dry grasslands between the groves have a suite of North America and Neotropical residents including Lesser Yellow-headed Vulture, Common and Plain-breasted Ground Doves, Double-striped Thick-knee, Aplomado Falcon, Eastern Meadowlark, Melodious Blackbird, Grassland Yellow-Finch, Blue-black Grassquit, and Morelet's Seedeater. Many of the temperate breeding sparrows winter here including Grasshopper, Savanna, and Lincoln's Sparrows. The moist grasslands often have pools of both permanent and ephemeral wetlands that attract most of the usual freshwater wetland birds expected in the United States.

CONSERVATION: It is difficult to appreciate how truly endangered this "natural" habitat is because it is at once both heavily modified to grazing land and subsistence farming, and looks extensive because cleared rainforests, dry forests, and other woodlands all take on the appearance of grasslands. Many of the original species can somewhat adapt to the newer ruderal savanna and grassland.

DISTRIBUTION: Most of these savannas are on sandy alluvial plains that have been eroded by water to form low rolling hills. On Mexico's east coast they occur in isolated patches from the Texas-Tamaulipas border, becoming widespread in central s. Tamaulipas, down to the Yucatán Peninsula. In the c. Mexico rangelands, they also occur as far north as Zacatecas and south through e. Oaxaca to Chiapas. This habitat continues south to Central America, where pines also become more common, and the bird assemblage changes. The Caribbean Savanna subhabitat is a prominent feature in Cuba and Puerto Rico, though it occurs as an anthropogenic habitat on many of the smaller islands.

WHERE TO SEE: Western Veracruz (state), Mexico.

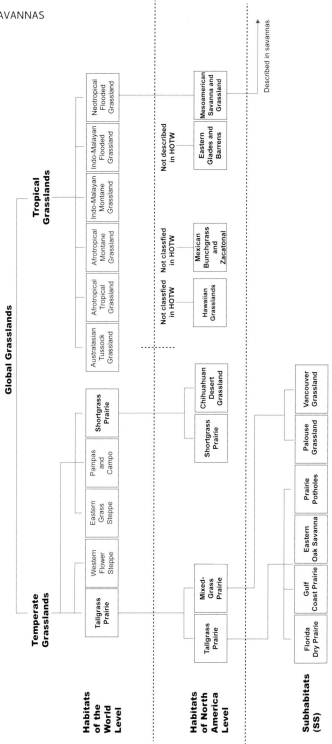

North American Grasslands Dendrogram

Global Grasslands

Temperate Grasslands

Tropical Grasslands

Described in savannas

Habitats of the World Level

Tallgrass Prairie | Western Flower Steppe | Eastern Grass Steppe | Pampas and Campo | Shortgrass Prairie

Australasian Tussock Grassland | Afrotropical Tropical Grassland | Afrotropical Montane Grassland | Indo-Malayan Montane Grassland | Indo-Malayan Flooded Grassland | Neotropical Flooded Grassland

Not classified in HOTW | Not classified in HOTW | Not described in HOTW

Habitats of North America Level

Tallgrass Prairie | Mixed-Grass Prairie | Shortgrass Prairie | Chihuahuan Desert Grassland

Hawaiian Grasslands | Mexican Bunchgrass and Zacatonal | Eastern Glades and Barrens | Mesoamerican Savanna and Grassland

Subhabitats (SS)

Florida Dry Prairie | Gulf Coast Prairie | Eastern Oak Savanna | Prairie Potholes | Palouse Grassland | Vancouver Grassland

GRASSLANDS

IN A NUTSHELL: A dry, open grassland with grasses rarely more than 6 in. (15 cm) tall. **Global Habitat Affinities:** EUROPEAN SALT STEPPE. **Continental Habitat Affinities:** MIXED-GRASS PRAIRIE; TALLGRASS PRAIRIE; CHIHUAHUAN DESERT GRASSLAND; SAGEBRUSH SHRUBLAND; EASTERN MESQUITE. **Species Overlap:** MIXED-GRASS PRAIRIE; CHIHUAHUAN DESERT GRASSLAND; SAGEBRUSH SHRUBLAND.

DESCRIPTION: Shortgrass Prairie is a stark, low grassland occurring in the w. Great Plains in the arid rain shadow of the Rocky Mountains in the c. United States and sc. Canada. This habitat is dominated by low-growing grasses and a high diversity but low density of forbs; woody vegetation makes up less than 1% of the landscape. The Great Plains Shortgrass Prairies experience cool winters and warm summers, with minimum temperatures ranging from 5°F (−15°C) in the north to 39°F (4°C) in the south, and maximum temperatures ranging from 74°F (23°C) in the north to 100°F (38°C) in the south. Much of the annual

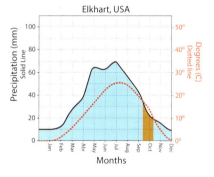

precipitation occurs during the spring and summer months, generally falling during a small number of intense events. The average rainfall for the region is 15 in. (400 mm), with amounts generally increasing in the southern and eastern parts of the habitat's range. Growth of grasses is slow due to limited rainfall, and regrowth typically takes two to three years.

The Shortgrass Prairie is dominated by two low-growing warm-season grasses: Blue Grama (*Bouteloua gracilis*) and Buffalograss (*Bouteloua dactyloides*). These two species make up the vast majority of the landcover, while a variety of forbs, succulents, and dwarf shrubs provide the majority of plant diversity in this habitat. Common shrubs and forbs include yuccas (*Yucca* spp.), pricklypears (*Opuntia* spp.), Prairie Zinnia (*Zinnia grandiflora*), Scarlet Globemallow (*Sphaeralcea coccinea*), Plains Blackfoot Daisy (*Melampodium leucanthum*), Slimflower Scurfpea (*Psoralidium tenuiflorum*), and Skunkbrush (*Rhus aromatica*). The presence of Honey Mesquite (*Prosopis glandulosa*), a common invasive shrub, and Tree Cholla (*Cylindropuntia imbricata*) are generally signs of overgrazing. In the wetter eastern sections of the Shortgrass Prairie, taller graminoids like Side-oats Grama (*Bouteloua curtipendula*) and Little Bluestem (*Schizachyrium scoparium*)

The flatlands of the Shortgrass Prairie are a vast and open landscape, home to Pronghorns. © DAVE SPANGENBURG

can be found, though Blue Grama and Buffalograss still dominate. With the exception of a few plants, such as yuccas, the vast majority of vegetative ground cover on Shortgrass Prairie reaches a maximum height of 10 in. (25 cm) and rarely exceeds 5 in. (13 cm). On sandy soils in the southern extent of this habitat's range, Shortgrass Prairie is found mixed with large areas of low Shinnery Oak (*Quercus havardii*) shrub and patches of exposed dune.

Variations in habitat structure and habitat maintenance are largely attributed to precipitation and grazing. Frequent droughts mean there is wide variation in the productivity and height of vegetation from year to year. Historically, this area was grazed by large herds of migratory herbivores, with American Bison being especially critical to the structure and annual maintenance of the Shortgrass Prairie. Along the habitat's southern border, changes in grazing and fire regimes have led to rapid incursion from Honey Mesquite and loss of Shortgrass Prairie. Unsuccessful cultivation efforts leading up to the Dust Bowl agricultural disaster of the 1930s also leave large scars on the landscape.

WILDLIFE: Shortgrass Prairies were once home to the largest herds of herbivores in North America, and these animals are still a major feature of the landscape. While the vast herds of American Bison that shaped this habitat were extirpated long ago, 20th-century reintroduction efforts have established herds in protected areas throughout the Shortgrass Prairie's range. In addition to this landscape-altering bovid, the prairie provides forage for Pronghorn, Mule Deer, and White-tailed Deer. Another landscape engineer, Black-tailed Prairie Dog is still an important feature. Dog towns numbering in the millions are a thing of the past, but modern-day colonies provide prey and shelter for predators like American Badger, Coyote, the endangered Swift Fox (IS), and critically endangered Black-footed Ferret. Other common mammals on the Shortgrass Prairie

Swift Fox is a rare resident of large intact Shortgrass Prairie.
© JOSHUA COVILL

include Black-tailed Jackrabbit, Thirteen-lined Ground Squirrel, Northern Pocket Gopher, and a variety of less-conspicuous small mammals.

The Shortgrass Prairie has limited bird diversity due to a dearth of cover and resources, especially during the winter months. Only a hardy few are common year-round

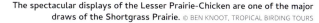

residents; among them are Mourning Dove, Northern Harrier, American Kestrel, Loggerhead Shrike, Horned Lark, and Western Meadowlark. Raptors such as Golden Eagle, Ferruginous Hawk, and Prairie Falcon are present year-round in small numbers. In summer, a larger variety of birds can be found, including Killdeer; Long-billed Curlew; Upland Sandpiper; Swainson's Hawk; Burrowing Owl; Common Nighthawk; Say's Phoebe; Western and Cassin's Kingbirds; Vesper, Grasshopper, Cassin's, and Lark Sparrows; and Lark Bunting. The region holds a variety of gallinaceous birds, including Sharp-tailed Grouse, Lesser Prairie-Chicken, Scaled Quail, and Northern Bobwhite.

The spectacular displays of the Lesser Prairie-Chicken are one of the major draws of the Shortgrass Prairie. © BEN KNOOT, TROPICAL BIRDING TOURS

Despite its name, Mountain Plover is endemic to the Shortgrass Prairie. © JOACHIM BERTRANDS

Lesser Prairie-Chicken (IS) is endemic to the region, and Mountain Plover (IS) and Thick-billed Longspur (IS) are both breeding endemics or near-endemics. Most of these species winter in CHIHUAHUAN DESERT GRASSLAND.

Prairie Racerunner, Greater Short-horned Lizard, Prairie Rattlesnake, Western Massasauga, and Gopher Snake are common and conspicuous reptile residents of this habitat.

CONSERVATION: All the North American grasslands have been heavily altered, and completely unaffected areas are quite rare. In fertile areas with adequate rainfall, former prairies are now largely cropland. In more arid grasslands, the habitat is often heavily dependent on grazing, which is sometimes unsustainable. Shortgrass Prairie is not heavily cultivated, and around 50% remains as grassland in some form. Despite this, many species here are rare and declining. Mountain Plover and Lesser Prairie-Chicken, two species of high concern, have declined precipitously over the past few decades. Mountain Plovers are affected by conversion to cropland, overgrazing, and elimination of prairie dogs. Lesser Prairie-Chickens are strongly affected by fragmentation and overgrazing, and climate change poses a major threat, as extended droughts lead to low reproductive efforts, and high temperatures and hailstorms contribute to chick mortality. In the southern part of the prairie-chicken's range, Shinnery Oak is important as a refuge from scorching temperatures and allows the bird to survive in areas that are otherwise too hot. Increasingly, summer temperatures can be fatally high, even with adequate shade. Eighty-five percent of Shortgrass Prairie exists on privately owned lands, and cooperation with ranchers and other stakeholders is vital to the preservation of this habitat.

DISTRIBUTION: Located in the Great Plains of North America, the Shortgrass Prairie is bounded to the west by the Rocky Mountains and extends from s. Alberta and Saskatchewan in the north to c. New Mexico and w. Texas in the south. The eastern boundary of Shortgrass Prairie is ill defined, as it blends with the MIXED-GRASS PRAIRIE in a long, dynamic, and complex ecotone. Pure Shortgrass Prairie occurs as far east as w. North Dakota in the north and the New Mexico–Texas line in the south. It also exists as small pockets on the adjacent Mixed-Grass Prairie, especially on exposed ridges.

SIDEBAR 10	PRE-COLUMBIAN HABITAT MODIFICATION

It is a commonly held misconception that the North American landscape before Europeans arrived was an untouched, untamed wilderness. Europeans encountered many areas of climax forest that appeared pristine in the absence of active management. However, the "untouched" nature of these lands was triggered by the widespread loss of Indigenous populations resulting from epidemics of introduced disease, forcible removal, warfare, and other active forms of genocide. In truth, much of the continent was carefully managed in precontact times, and entire landscapes were altered for production of food, building materials, and medicine. Management practices encompassed nearly all terrestrial habitats and were as diverse as the hundreds of cultures present.

The use of controlled burns and other forms of land-clearing are the most widespread and notable of Indigenous land-management practices. In many areas of the eastern forests, small low-intensity fires were set every one to three years. These fires resulted in an abundance of small grasslands and savannas that were incredibly productive for hunting and agriculture. Controlled burns were of critical importance for the maintenance of open habitats, especially the TALLGRASS PRAIRIE and its Eastern Oak Savanna and Gulf Coast Prairie subhabitats, EASTERN GLADES AND BARRENS, and CALIFORNIA OAK SAVANNA. The use of controlled burns opened the forest and woodland understory, allowing for easier travel and favoring the growth of many fruiting plants. Tree-girdling was a common practice for creating forest openings for agriculture, and millions of acres were likely cleared for planting of corn, squash, and beans as well as hundreds of less well-known regional crops.

Active silviculture was another a major landscape feature of precolonial North America. Forests that appeared unmanaged to Europeans were often the result of careful tree selection and planting. Forests with unnaturally high concentrations of nut- and fruit-producing plants were a common feature, especially in the e. United States and on the Yucatán Peninsula. Breadnut (*Brosimum alicastrum*), American Hazelnut (*Corylus americana*), American Chestnut (*Castanea dentata*), Pawpaw (*Asimina triloba*), and walnuts (*Juglans* spp.) are among the dozens of species of trees selectively planted for food. The planting or management of food crops also included many fruiting shrubs in the understory and herbaceous plants with nutritious roots on the forest floor. Rotation of smaller agricultural plots also increased the variation of forest ages and successional stages.

This subject is worth significant exploration, and one could easily fill many volumes with information relevant to each region of the continent. For further information, a few resources the authors recommend include: *Tending the Wild: Native American Knowledge and the Management of California's Natural Resources*, by M. Kat Anderson; *Fire, Native Peoples, and the Natural Landscape*, edited by Thomas Vale; and *Imperfect Balance: Landscape Transformations in the Pre-Columbian Americas*, edited by David Lentz.

The Shortgrass Prairie is the overwhelmingly dominant terrestrial habitat throughout its entire range. A scattering of Prairie Pothole (see sidebar 14) and PLAYA wetlands dot the region, which is also crisscrossed by narrow bands of WESTERN RIPARIAN WOODLAND. Apart from these isolated habitats, the Shortgrass Prairie is an unbroken habitat transitioning to SAGEBRUSH SHRUBLAND in Montana, Wyoming, and Colorado; to MIXED-GRASS PRAIRIE on its eastern border; and to CHIHUAHUAN DESERT GRASSLAND in Texas and New Mexico.

WHERE TO SEE: Pawnee National Grassland, Colorado, US.

Ne7B TALLGRASS PRAIRIE

IN A NUTSHELL: A tall, dense grassland with tall grasses and abundant flowering forbs. **Global Habitat Affinities:** WESTERN GRASS STEPPE; WESTERN FLOWER STEPPE. **Continental Habitat Affinities:** EASTERN GLADES AND BARRENS; MIXED-GRASS PRAIRIE. **Species Overlap:** MIXED-GRASS PRAIRIE; EASTERN PINE SAVANNA; SEDGE AND GRASSLAND MARSHES; EASTERN GLADES AND BARRENS; TAMAULIPAN MEZQUITAL; FLORIDA SCRUB.

DESCRIPTION: The Tallgrass Prairie is a dense and towering grassland habitat that historically stretched from Oklahoma in the sc. United States to Manitoba, Canada; it is the great Nearctic grassland of the e. Great Plains. A few tall species of grasses dominate, producing 80% of the biomass, while a diverse array of flowering plants makes up the remaining 20% of the prairie flora. While generally cooler and wetter than the Shortgrass Prairie to its west, this habitat has such a broad latitudinal spread that it experiences a massive range of temperatures, from –31°F (–35°C) to 80°F (27°C) in the north, and 22°F (–6°C) to over 110°F (43°C) in the south. Despite these extremes, the region is overall temperate and receives a moderate amount of rainfall, 20–40 in. (500–1000 mm) annually, concentrated in intense storms in spring and early summer.

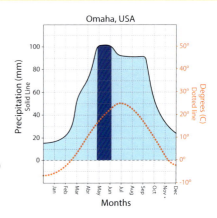

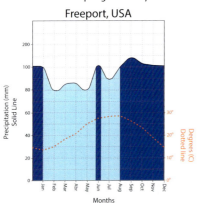

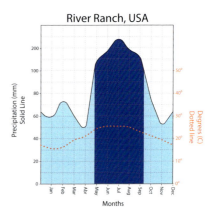

Tallgrass Prairies have an abundance of bright flowers amid grasses that can reach towering heights.
© TONY IFLAND, USFWS

Known as "the four horsemen of the prairie," Big Bluestem (*Andropogon gerardii*), Switchgrass (*Panicum virgatum*), Indiangrass (*Sorghastrum nutans*), and Little Bluestem (*Schizachyrium scoparium*) are the core species of this habitat. These grasses are generally 2–3 ft. (0.6–0.9 m) tall, though at the end of the growing season healthy prairies are often 5–6 ft. (1.5–1.8 m) in height, and some can reach 10 ft. (3 m). In late summer, it is easy to disappear in the Tallgrass Prairie, and visibility can be nil. Growing among these core species of grasses is a bountiful collection of wildflowers, including Annual Sunflower (*Helianthus annuus*), Leadplant (*Amorpha canescens*), scurfpeas (*Psoralidium* spp.), Purple Coneflower (*Echinacea purpurea*), milk vetches (*Astragalus* spp.), blazingstars (*Liatris* spp.), and White Heath Aster (*Symphyotrichum ericoides*), which transform the prairies into colorful patchworks during the spring and summer months. Historically rare away from permanent water, woody plants like Eastern Redcedar (*Juniperus virginiana*), buckbrushes (*Ceanothus* spp.), Bur Oak (*Quercus macrocarpa*), Common Hackberry (*Celtis occidentalis*), Plains Cottonwood (*Populus deltoides* ssp. *monilifera*), and Eastern Redbud (*Cercis canadensis*) have encroached as fire regimes have changed.

We have chosen to include several more-limited grassland subhabitats under the umbrella of Tallgrass Prairie. While generally smaller and more isolated than the principal Tallgrass Prairie, these grasslands share many of the same characteristic plants and wildlife.

Ne7B-1 Eastern Oak Savanna occurs in transitional zones between TEMPERATE DECIDUOUS FOREST and Tallgrass Prairie. This open savanna has an understory dominated by Tallgrass Prairie grasses and forbs and an overstory consisting largely of Bur Oak (*Quercus macrocarpa*), Northern Pin Oak (*Quercus ellipsoidalis*), and Black Oak (*Quercus velutina*). Historically, these habitats were maintained by fire and rarely had canopy cover greater than 25%.

Ne7B-2 Florida Dry Prairie is a very rare grassland found on the Florida peninsula. Once the dominant habitat in c. Florida, this habitat is all but gone. Frequent spring fires and summer flooding once maintained this habitat and prevented the growth of EASTERN PINE SAVANNA. The habitat is shrubbier than most Tallgrass Prairies. Saw Palmetto (*Serenoa repens*) is a common element along with Southern Wiregrass (*Aristida beyrichiana*), Little Bluestem (*Schizachyrium scoparium*), Toothache Grass (*Ctenium aromaticum*), Lopsided Indiangrass (*Sorghastrum secundum*), and Splitbeard Bluestem (*Andropogon ternarius*).

Ne7B-3 Gulf Coast Prairie is the most extensive of these subhabitats, extending along the coastal plain from Mississippi to Tamaulipas in Mexico. Gulf Coast Prairies are dominated by the big four Tallgrass Prairie grasses along with Brownseed Paspalum (*Paspalum plicatulum*) and Savanna Hairgrass (*Muhlenbergia expansa*). These prairies are wetter than most Tallgrass subhabitats, and tree growth is restricted mostly by the dominance of dense clay soils. This subhabitat is frequently interspersed with SALT MARSH and SEDGE AND GRASSLAND MARSHES.

The **Prairie Potholes** (see sidebar 14) is a region of Tallgrass and MIXED-GRASS PRAIRIE dotted with a high density of small freshwater wetlands.

WILDLIFE: Tallgrass Prairie was once dominated by massive herds of grazing animals, but these habitat-shaping species are largely gone. While Elk and Pronghorn are extirpated from the region, White-tailed Deer remains abundant, and American Bison is being reintroduced to numerous

American Bison used to roam across the Tallgrass Prairie in great numbers. © DAVE SPANGENBURG

larger tracts of protected prairie. Smaller carnivores like Coyote, Red Fox, Bobcat, American Badger, and Long-tailed Weasel remain common, feeding off abundant rodents such as Thirteen-lined Ground Squirrel, Plains Pocket Gopher, Prairie Vole, Eastern Woodrat, and Western Harvest Mouse. Larger carnivores including Gray Wolf and Puma (Mountain Lion) are largely extirpated from the prairies, but sporadic individuals have been returning as overall population trends increase. Collared Peccary, Nine-banded Armadillo, and Ocelot are found in the southern Tallgrass subhabitats.

The Tallgrass Prairie has a relatively low avian diversity but very high densities of birds in the summer months, especially in the northern portion. During winter, the prairie is dominated largely by raptors such as Northern Harrier, American Kestrel, Red-tailed and Rough-legged Hawks, and Short-eared Owl. Northern Bobwhite and Greater Prairie-Chicken are found on the prairie year-round, and the springtime displays of Greater Prairie-Chicken are one of the great spectacles on the continent. In summer, the Tallgrass Prairie comes alive with grassland-breeding specialists including Upland Sandpiper (IS); Bobolink (IS); Sedge Wren; Henslow's (IS), Grasshopper, LeConte's, and Vesper Sparrows; Eastern and Western Meadowlarks; and Dickcissel (IS). While prairie birds are lacking in color, their songs and flight displays are a delightful and impressive feature of the landscape. An abundance of insect prey makes Eastern and Western Kingbirds and Scissor-tailed Flycatcher (in the south) ubiquitous in the warmer months.

Many of the smaller habitat subhabitats lack at least some subset of Tallgrass specialists, though Eastern Meadowlark and Grasshopper Sparrow are often good indicators. Eastern Oak Savanna is home to large numbers of Red-headed Woodpeckers, Wild Turkeys, and Lark Sparrows (IS). Florida Dry Prairie is home to several endemic subspecies including Florida Burrowing Owl, Florida Sandhill Crane, and Florida Grasshopper Sparrow. Crested Caracara and White-tailed Kite are also features of this subhabitat. The endangered Attwater's Prairie-Chicken and Aplomado Falcon are both found in Texas sections of Gulf Coast Prairie. The wet nature of Gulf Coast Prairie means it is also important wintering habitat for many waterbirds and grassland birds including Black Rail, Yellow Rail, LeConte's Sparrow, and Henslow's Sparrow.

The northern Tallgrass Prairie, known as the Prairie Pothole region, is dotted with numerous small wetlands that are critical breeding areas for North American waterfowl. Blue-winged Teal, Northern Shoveler, Gadwall, Mallard, Northern Pintail, Canvasback, Redhead, and Lesser Scaup are commonly found nesting in the cover of upland Tallgrass Prairie adjacent to these wetlands.

A hyperabundance of flowering plants makes the Tallgrass Prairie a very productive region for insects in the summer months. A number of rare butterflies are Tallgrass Prairie specialists, including Ottoe, Arogos, and Dakota Skippers; Karner Blue; and Poweshiek Skipperling. Other butterflies characteristic of Tallgrass Prairie include Great Spangled Fritillary, Regal Fritillary, Gorgone Checkerspot, Black Swallowtail, and Monarch.

CONSERVATION: The Tallgrass Prairie was formerly subjected to sweeping disturbance that regularly cleansed the area and prevented the encroachment of trees. Rapid fires would tear through the grasses, recycling nutrients and renewing the habitat. The large herds of American Bison that once grazed here provided more localized disturbance and variation in vegetation height. Efforts are being made in remaining Tallgrass Prairie sites to restore and maintain these historical methods of disturbance, with regular burns occurring at most locations and active reintroduction of bison to larger tracts of protected land.

Unfortunately, the deep, fertile soils of the Tallgrass Prairie made for excellent agricultural land, and an estimated 96–99% of this habitat has been destroyed, to be replaced, largely, by soybean and corn monocultures. The largest remaining tracts exist on rocky or less arable soils in the Flint Hills of Oklahoma and Kansas, and the Sandhills of Nebraska. There are major Tallgrass Prairie restoration projects ongoing throughout the region; two examples are the the Midewin National Tallgrass Prairie in Illinois, which has revegetated an area of 20,000 acres (8000 ha) and actively hosts a herd of 50 bison; another impressive project is the Nature Conservancy's Flint Hills Tallgrass Prairie Preserve.

Less than 1% of the Gulf Coast Prairie remains in pristine condition, with most of the habitat lost to agriculture and development. Florida Dry Prairie is also incredibly endangered and is most threatened by development, fire suppression, and the invasive Cogon Grass (*Imperata cylindrica*). These two prairies are home, respectively, to the endangered subspecies Attwater's Prairie-Chicken and Florida Grasshopper Sparrow. While there are active conservation programs for these two birds, only the Grasshopper Sparrow initiative is meeting with much success thus far, whereas the Attwater's Prairie-Chicken effort has suffered due to lack of habitat, extreme weather events, and invasive species. Aplomado Falcon reintroduction efforts have been more successful, and this species is now resident in Gulf Coast Prairies in s. Texas and n. Tamaulipas.

DISTRIBUTION: Located on the east side of the North American Great Plains from the sc. United States to sc. Canada, the Tallgrass Prairie stretches from n. Texas and Oklahoma in the south to Manitoba in the north, where it transitions to ASPEN FOREST AND PARKLAND or BOREAL CONIFER FOREST. The western edge of the Tallgrass Prairie is ill defined, as it slowly blends with MIXED-GRASS PRAIRIE in a long, dynamic, and complex ecotone. To the east, the prairie slowly transitions to the Eastern Oak Savanna subhabitat, then to forest. Historically, Tallgrass Prairie occurred in pockets as far east as w. Ohio and Kentucky, though little remains of these isolated eastern patches.

Other regions of the e. Nearctic have small, isolated pockets of prairie that have similar flora and wildlife to those of the Tallgrass Prairie; these are covered in EASTERN GLADES AND BARRENS.

WHERE TO SEE: Joseph H. Williams Tallgrass Prairie Preserve, Oklahoma, US; Tallgrass Prairie National Preserve, Kansas, US; Midewin National Tallgrass Prairie, Illinois, US. FLORIDA DRY PRAIRIE—Kissimmee Prairie Preserve State Park, Florida, US. EASTERN OAK SAVANNA—Pleasant Valley Conservancy State National Area, Wisconsin, US.

Ne7C MIXED-GRASS PRAIRIE

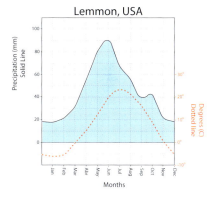

IN A NUTSHELL: A diverse transitional grassland occurring in the c. Great Plains between the Tallgrass Prairie and the Shortgrass Prairie. **Global Habitat Affinities:** EASTERN GRASS STEPPE; WESTERN GRASS STEPPE. **Continental Habitat Affinities:** TALLGRASS PRAIRIE; SHORTGRASS PRAIRIE; EASTERN GLADES AND BARRENS. **Species Overlap:** TALLGRASS PRAIRIE; SHORTGRASS PRAIRIE; SAGEBRUSH SHRUBLAND.

DESCRIPTION: Mixed-Grass Prairie is a broad transitional habitat occurring between the TALLGRASS PRAIRIE and the SHORTGRASS PRAIRIE. It occurs as a long ecotone with Tallgrass plants dominating to the east and Shortgrass dominating to the west. It also occurs as a mosaic with Tallgrass dominating in low wet swales and Shortgrass occupying dry exposed ridges. Despite the intermediate nature of this habitat, it has a unique feel and hosts several endemic species. The Mixed-Grass Prairie stretches from n. Texas all the way to c. Alberta and spans a wide range of temperatures. The amount of precipitation, 15–25 in (400–650 mm) annually, is the defining climatic feature of this habitat. Anything much above or below this produces Tallgrass or Shortgrass, respectively.

Mixed-Grass Prairie is a structurally pleasant grassland, intermediate between the stark, unbounded Shortgrass and the impenetrable, towering Tallgrass. This grassland typically reaches a height of 2–3 ft. (0.6–0.9 m) and occurs on flat or gently rolling terrain. While a very high diversity of grasses can be found here, Needle-and-thread Grass (*Hesperostipa comata*) and Western Wheatgrass (*Pascopyrum smithii*) are diagnostic species throughout most of the habitat's range. The exception is in the north, where this habitat is dominated by fescues (*Festuca* spp.). Other common grasses throughout the habitat's range include Side-oats Grama (*Bouteloua curtipendula*), Blue Grama (*Bouteloua gracilis*), Indiangrass (*Sorghastrum nutans*), and Little Bluestem (*Schizachyrium scoparium*). The mixture of warm- and cool-season grasses means there are two peaks of plant growth in this habitat, one occurring early in spring and a second one in late summer.

This grassland naturally has more woody species than the other two prairie types and can be quite shrubby. As with many grassland systems, Mixed-Grass Prairie has been frequently invaded by woody shrubs due to overgrazing and fire suppression. These prairies are typically overrun by Eastern Redcedar (*Juniperus virginiana*) in the northeast, Ponderosa Pine (*Pinus ponderosa*) in the northwest, and Honey Mesquite (*Prosopis glandulosa*) in the south.

Mixed-Grass Prairie is the dominant habitat in Badlands National Park, South Dakota. © DAVE SPANGENBURG

The **Ne7C-1 Palouse Grassland** of Idaho, Oregon, and Washington was very much like the Mixed-Grass Prairie but more heavily dominated by cool-season bunchgrasses like Bluebunch Wheatgrass (*Pseudoroegneria spicata*) and Idaho Fescue (*Festuca idahoensis*). Very little of this region remains as viable grassland.

The **Ne7C-2 Vancouver Grassland**, found in the Georgia Depression of the Pacific northwest, is also closely related to this habitat. This grassland exists mostly as an association with Garry Oak (*Quercus garryana*) savannas and has significant overlap with animals found in other oak savanna environments.

WILDLIFE: The wildlife on Mixed-Grass Prairie overlaps broadly with the adjacent TALLGRASS PRAIRIE and SHORTGRASS PRAIRIE ecosystems. Historically, this habitat was strongly defined by large grazing herds of American Bison and massive towns of Black-tailed Prairie Dogs. While some large prairie dog colonies still remain in this habitat, bison are almost entirely restricted to large national parks and reserves. Mule Deer, White-tailed Deer, and Pronghorn are still common here. Texas Kangaroo Rat is endemic to this habitat.

Black-tailed Prairie Dogs form huge colonies with underground burrows that are important to many other species including Black-footed Ferrets and Burrowing Owls. © PHIL CHAON

The bird communities of the Mixed-Grass Prairie have many typical grassland species. Tallgrass species found here that are absent from the adjacent Shortgrass Prairie include Greater Prairie-Chicken and Dickcissel. Mountain Plover, usually a Shortgrass endemic, will use areas heavily grazed by prairie dogs, bison, or cattle. Long-billed Curlew, Swainson's Hawk, Upland Sandpiper, Lark Bunting, Bobolink, Western Meadowlark, Grasshopper Sparrow, and Scissor-tailed Flycatcher are common in the Mixed-Grass habitat. Baird's Sparrow (IS), Chestnut-collared Longspur (IS), and Sprague's Pipit (IS) are rare and declining species near-endemic to the Mixed-Grass Prairie. Harris's Sparrow (Canada's only endemic breeding bird) winters almost exclusively in this habitat, especially in riparian corridors and shrubby areas.

The Prairie Potholes (see sidebar 14) region lies within the Mixed-Grass Prairie and is dotted with many small REEDBED MARSHES and SEDGE AND GRASSLAND MARSHES. These incredibly productive wetlands, combined with some of the most intact prairie systems on the continent, make this a fantastic area for wildlife-viewing in spring or summer. In June the abundance of nesting birds can be truly staggering.

Baird's Sparrow breeds exclusively in the Mixed-Grass Prairie. © PHIL CHAON

CONSERVATION: About 30% of the Mixed-Grass Prairie is still intact. The vast majority of the habitat in the south has been lost, largely to agriculture. However, the northern Mixed-Grass Prairies, preserved in several massive national parks and private reserves, are some of the most extensive and best-protected grasslands on the continent. In Theodore Roosevelt National Park and Fort Pierre National Grassland, Mixed-Grass Prairies have been the sites of the majority of Black-footed Ferret reintroductions, though these animals convert the immediate areas around their towns to SHORTGRASS PRAIRIE. The population of Black-footed Ferrets is currently estimated to be close to 1300 individuals, up from a low of just 18 in 1985. Just as importantly, this area has seen the development of some major programs to commercially raise bison or graze cattle in a way that mimics natural grazing regimes. There has been an increase in good quality Mixed-Grass Prairie on private lands over the past few decades. Baird's Sparrow, Chestnut-collared Longspur, Long-billed Curlew, and many other grassland birds are species of special concern, however, and still in decline.

DISTRIBUTION: The distribution of this habitat is rather ill-defined as it has long ecotones with SHORTGRASS PRAIRIE to the west and TALLGRASS PRAIRIE to the east. Traditionally, Mixed-Grass Prairie begins south of the BOREAL CONIFER FOREST of Alberta, Saskatchewan, and Manitoba, with its eastern edge passing through the middle of the Dakotas and c. Nebraska before reaching its southern limit in n. Texas, as far south as the Edwards Plateau. The western boundary covers the w. Dakotas, ne. Wyoming, and e. Montana. Isolated patches of Mixed-Grass Prairie occur on the Sandhills of Nebraska and e. Colorado in areas that are normally part of the Shortgrass Prairie. Mixed-Grass Prairie habitat is crossed by ribbons of WESTERN RIPARIAN WOODLAND and some patches of SAGEBRUSH SHRUBLAND and PONDEROSA PINE FOREST in the west. The Palouse

SIDEBAR 11   BADLANDS

Badlands, such as those at Badlands National Park, South Dakota, are regions where underlying, poorly consolidated sedimentary rocks such as soft shales, silts, and claystones are exposed through removal of topsoil or regolith (rotten rock and soil) carapaces such as laterite and, as a result, undergo significant erosion. This erosion develops a stark landscape with extensive bare gullies and ravines with very steep interfluves (ridges) where there is little difference in resistance to erosion between rock types, or buttes (flat-topped, steep-sided towers) and hoodoos (mushroom-shaped rocks) where there is a carapace of more resistant material. The overall appearance is similar to a sand pile that was differentially eroded after a rainstorm, leaving towers with pebble caps that keep them from eroding.

Badlands National Park has some of the most spectacular examples of these formations in North America.
© PHIL CHAON

For badlands to form, there needs to be a combination of desert or grassland environment in an upland area dominated by either unconsolidated sediments and ashfall, or highly weathered or altered rocks, with an infrequent but very intense rainfall pattern. Basically, erosion is infrequent but very rapid when occurring. In some regions, the conversion from normal upland regions to badlands can be rapid, and once the vegetation is first removed, by overgrazing or intense drought, and then followed by massive heavy rainfall, areas of localized gully erosion can join to start a self-perpetuating badlands system that stops only when the erosion base level is achieved, and the area becomes a lower gentle slope.

Grassland formerly occupied much of the Columbia Basin in w. Idaho, e. Washington, and ne. Oregon but is almost entirely gone. The Vancouver Grassland is limited to the Georgia Depression on Vancouver Island.

WHERE TO SEE: Badlands National Park, South Dakota, US; Fort Pierre National Grassland, South Dakota, US; Theodore Roosevelt National Park, North Dakota, US; Grasslands National Park, Saskatchewan, Canada.

Ne7D EASTERN GLADES AND BARRENS

IN A NUTSHELL: Isolated grasslands on poor soils associated with the Appalachian, Ozark, and Ouachita Mountains. **Global Habitat Affinities:** EUROPEAN WET GRASSLANDS. **Continental Habitat Affinities:** TALLGRASS PRAIRIE. **Species Overlap:** TALLGRASS PRAIRIE; MIXED-GRASS PRAIRIE; TEMPERATE DECIDUOUS FOREST.

DESCRIPTION: Eastern Glades and Barrens occur in isolated pockets throughout the mountainous areas of the e. United States. In many ways, this habitat represents relict pockets of TALLGRASS PRAIRIE that have been maintained by fire and rocky soils. The climate, similar to that of surrounding forest types, experiences distinct seasons with cold winters, hot and humid summers, and significant rainfall. Winter lows vary from 30 to −15°F (−1 to −26°C), while summer highs are in the range of 80–95°F (27–35°C). Precipitation falls consistently year-round as either rain or snow and totals 30–60 in. (750–1500 mm).

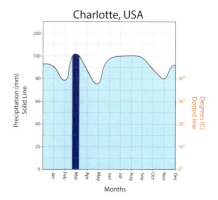

Charlotte, USA

The grasslands of this habitat are generally small—oftentimes occupying only a few acres. The dominant grasses, which overlap broadly with those of the Tallgrass Prairie, are Big Bluestem (*Andropogon gerardii*), Indiangrass (*Sorghastrum nutans*), and Little Bluestem (*Schizachyrium scoparium*). In the Ozarks and Ouachitas, Side-oats Grama (*Bouteloua curtipendula*) is also important. Glades and barrens are shrubbier than other North American grasslands, and small Eastern Redcedar (*Juniperus virginiana*), Ashe Juniper (*Juniperus ashei*), various oaks (*Quercus* spp.), and Eastern Redbud (*Cercis canadensis*) are common plants. The barrens in the Ozark and Ouachita Mountains are relict patches of OAK-JUNIPER WOODLAND, like those in c. Texas, and share many similar plants.

Eastern Glades and Barrens are strongly associated with thin soils and specific bedrock types, especially in the Appalachian, Ozark, and Ouachita Mountains. These grasslands often occur in mafic environments, which have bedrocks high in magnesium and iron, such as gneiss and dolomite. Glades and barrens also occur on calcareous environments with limestone, chalk, or other minerals high in calcium carbonate. These underlying bedrocks tend to form nutrient-poor, acidic soils that are difficult for tree growth and have allowed grasslands to survive. The mafic and calcareous soils support a large variety of specialized herbaceous plants, and the diversity and endemism of

An open glade in the Allegheny Mountains of Pennsylvania. © NICHOLAS A. TONELLI/CREATIVE COMMONS (CC BY 2.0)

flowering plants is huge. Many of the glades share herbaceous plants with BOREAL BOG AND FEN and with pocosins and other boggy areas of EASTERN PINE SAVANNA.

Outside of mafic and calcareous soils, the grasslands of glades and barrens need frequent disturbance, or they will quickly be swallowed up by the surrounding TEMPERATE DECIDUOUS FOREST. Historically, this disturbance came in the form of fire; the occasional fire was the result of lightning strikes, but most were controlled burns. Fire-management practices by Indigenous peoples were crucial to the health and maintenance of grasslands in the Piedmont Prairie, a region with high concentrations of this habitat. The forcible removal of these peoples along with overhunting of important grazing animals like White-tailed Deer and Elk led to massive declines in glades and barrens throughout the 18th, 19th, and 20th centuries. More recently, reclaimed mine sites and associated disturbed, rocky soils will also pass through a grassland phase that is similar to Eastern Glades and Barrens. Without fire maintenance, this is often just a short successional step on the way to becoming a forest.

WILDLIFE: Mammals in the Eastern Glades and Barrens overlap broadly with those found in surrounding forest habitats, and there are no true endemics. Small mammals like Texas Mouse and Fulvous Harvest Mouse occur in isolated pockets of this habitat in the Ozark and Ouachita Mountains. This habitat formerly supported Elk and American Bison, which were important in maintaining grasslands in areas requiring disturbance.

Above: **A small population of Eastern Collared Lizards occupies the hilltop barrens of the Ozark Mountains.**
© RANDY JONES, USFWS

Left: **Henslow's Sparrow is found in isolated patches of grassland in the midwestern United States.**
© JARED MIZANIN

The birdlife here overlaps broadly with that of both TALLGRASS PRAIRIE and early successional TEMPERATE DECIDUOUS FOREST, depending on the ratio of grass to shrubland. Northern Bobwhite, Northern Harrier, Loggerhead Shrike, Eastern Meadowlark, Grasshopper Sparrow, and Henslow's Sparrow are specialty birds generally present only in Eastern Glades and Barrens in forested areas of the east, though they are more widespread. Other birds that are notably more abundant here than in surrounding habitats include Wild Turkey, Indigo Bunting, Blue Grosbeak, Yellow-breasted Chat, and Prairie Warbler. Bachman's Sparrow is also occasionally associated with this habitat. The barrens in the Ozarks and Ouachitas host some birds that are more typical of arid western habitats, including Greater Roadrunner and, rarely, Rock Wren and Rufous-crowned Sparrow.

Eastern Glades and Barrens share many reptiles and amphibians with surrounding forests but also have some unique or uniquely abundant species. Slender Glass Lizard is found in this habitat. The barrens and glades of the Ozarks and Ouachitas have an endemic subspecies of Eastern Collared Lizard that is brilliant turquoise and saffron. Several other species reach the eastern extent of their distribution here, including Prairie and Six-lined Racerunners, Flat-headed Snake, and Eastern Coachwhip.

CONSERVATION: Eastern Glades and Barrens has always been a rare habitat, and it has declined precipitously over the past several centuries. The primary cause of decline is fire suppression, which has resulted in habitat loss to forest encroachment. Conversion to agriculture and localized mining have also led to declines. Many of the birds found here have broad distribution but are quite rare regionally. Cooperatives like the Virginia Grassland Bird Initiative and the Southeastern Grasslands Initiative seek to protect remaining Eastern Glades and Barrens as well as to restore areas

Indigo Bunting prefers brushy, overgrown areas in Eastern Glades and Barrens.
© BEN KNOOT, TROPICAL BIRDING TOURS

SIDEBAR 12   MICROHABITAT: LIMESTONE ALVAR

Found in tiny, isolated pockets within the Nearctic and w. Palearctic, Limestone Alvar is a sparse and barren grassland found on broad expanses of calcareous bedrock. In the Nearctic this habitat is found exclusively around the Great Lakes in areas with thin mineral soils less than 3 in. (10 cm) deep. Limestone Alvars are prone to both flooding and drought. Their flora and fauna are similar to assemblages characteristic of TALLGRASS PRAIRIE or MIXED-GRASS PRAIRIE.

The basic and nutrient-poor soils of Limestone Alvar provide habitat for many rare plants that would be poor competitors elsewhere, including orchids like Ram's-head Lady's-slipper (*Cypripedium arietinum*) and Alaska Orchid (*Platanthera unalascensis*) and carnivorous plants like Common Butterwort (*Pinguicula vulgaris*). The nearly 70 species of plants that are found almost exclusively on alvars are joined by disjunct populations of plants from the prairie and Arctic regions. Little Bluestem (*Schizachyrium scoparium*), Prairie Smoke (*Geum triflorum*), and Prairie Dropseed (*Sporobolus heterolepis*) are all common.

Grassland birds like Bobolink, Eastern Meadowlark, Upland Sandpiper, Eastern Towhee, Brown Thrasher, and Short-eared Owl make their homes in alvars with deeper soils. Large Limestone Alvars are also the primary habitat of Loggerhead Shrike and Eastern Massasauga in Ontario, where they are both endangered. Limestone Alvars are particularly notable for their high diversity of butterflies, many of which are rare or declining outside of this floristically rich environment. The high availability of calcium in the limestone-based environment also means that alvars are home to dozens of rare or endemic snail species, like the Carinate Pillsnail.

Limestone Alvars are fragile, naturally range-restricted, and easily developed for commercial quarry operations. While many are protected, remaining alvars are threatened by road construction, off-road vehicle use, invasive species, and trampling of vegetation.

of the Piedmont Prairie. The naturally limited nature of these grasslands makes restoration efforts less expensive than they are in the TALLGRASS PRAIRIE, where restoration will have to encompass massive areas to be effective.

DISTRIBUTION: Eastern Glades and Barrens are found in widely scattered areas of the c. and s. Appalachian Mountains, the Ozark Mountains, and the Ouachita Mountains. They also occur broadly in the Piedmont region, which runs in a broad band between the Appalachian Mountains and the Atlantic coastal plain from c. Virginia to n. Alabama. Often glades and barrens occur on hills and ridgetops, especially those with rocky domes and mafic or calcareous soils. This habitat is broadly surrounded by TEMPERATE DECIDUOUS FOREST and occasionally TEMPERATE MIXED FOREST.

WHERE TO SEE: Valley View Glades Natural Area, Missouri, US; Shenandoah National Park, Virginia, US.

Ne7E CHIHUAHUAN DESERT GRASSLAND

IN A NUTSHELL: A sparse and open grassland dominated by bunchgrasses and dotted with yuccas and cacti. **Global Habitat Affinities:** WESTERN DESERT STEPPE. **Continental Habitat Affinities:** SHORTGRASS PRAIRIE; MIXED-GRASS PRAIRIE; CHIHUAHUAN DESERT. **Species Overlap:** CHIHUAHUAN DESERT; SHORTGRASS PRAIRIE; EASTERN MESQUITE; MEXICAN BUNCHGRASS AND ZACATONAL.

DESCRIPTION: This sparse and open grassland habitat is found in the valleys and basins of the Chihuahuan Desert in the sw. United States and n. and c. Mexico. It is dominated by multiple species of warm-season bunchgrasses of varying heights, scattered among a mixture of bare earth and low-growing shrubs, cacti, yuccas, and forbs. In many places, human degradation has increased the number of shrubs and turned these grasslands into shrub savannas. Chihuahuan Desert Grassland occurs in a region with warm, humid summers and cool, dry

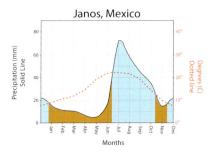

winters. The grasslands receive 9–24 in. (230–600 mm) of rain in a typical year, the majority falling in late summer in intense monsoon thunderstorms. The climate is strongly seasonal—summer highs regularly reach 105°F (41°C), while winter lows of 0°F (−18°C) are not unusual.

Opposite: **Chihuahuan Desert Grassland experiences intense storms in the late summer months.** © DAVE SPANGENBURG

Dozens of species of bunchgrasses can be found in Chihuahuan Desert Grassland, but the most widespread and dominant species are Black (*Bouteloua eriopoda*) and Blue Gramas (*Bouteloua gracilis*), Bush Muhly (*Muhlenbergia porteri*), dropseeds (*Sporobolus* spp.), three-awns (*Aristida* spp.), Giant Sacaton (*Sporobolus wrightii*), and Tobosa (*Hilaria mutica*). While the majority of these grasses reach only 1–2 ft. (0.3–0.6 m) in height, Giant Sacaton can form large bunches up to 6 ft. (2 m) tall. Among the grasses is a scattering of small shrubs and succulents, including mesquites (*Prosopis* spp.), Creosote (*Larrea tridentata*), American Tarbush (*Flourensia cernua*), Winterfat (*Krascheninnikovia lanata*), pricklypears (*Opuntia* spp.), barrel cacti (*Echinocactus* spp.), agaves (*Agave* spp.), yuccas (*Yucca* spp.), chollas (*Cylindropuntia* spp.), and Ocotillo (*Fouquieria splendens*). These shrubs and succulents, which may reach heights of 10 ft. (3 m), provide important cover for wildlife.

While shrubs are a natural part of this landscape, Chihuahuan Desert Grasslands have undergone widespread transition to shrublands over the past two centuries. This is largely due to overgrazing, soil loss, conversion to agriculture, and fire suppression. Only an estimated 15% of Chihuahuan Desert Grassland remains healthy and intact.

WILDLIFE: This habitat does not support many large animals but does hold a diverse assemblage of reptiles, birds, and small mammals. Pronghorn is the most successful large mammal in the Chihuahuan Desert Grassland but Mule Deer, Collared Peccary, and Bighorn Sheep can also be found in small numbers. The primary mammalian predators here are Bobcat and Coyote, though a few Pumas (aka Mountain Lions) occur as well as small carnivores like Kit Fox, American Badger, and American Hog-nosed Skunk. The bulk of mammalian diversity is found among rodents and rabbits, which can reach astronomical numbers under favorable conditions. Desert Cottontail, Black-tailed and White-sided Jackrabbits, numerous species of kangaroo rats, Chihuahuan Pocket Mouse, Spotted Ground Squirrel, and Mexican Prairie Dog are all common small mammals in the Chihuahuan Desert Grassland. Black-tailed Prairie Dogs are common in the northern half of the habitat's range, where they form massive dog towns, though many have been exterminated by cattle ranchers.

Chihuahuan Desert Grassland birdlife is at its most diverse in winter. It is the only habitat where many grassland specialties can be seen away from their northern breeding grounds. Common birds include Scaled Quail, Turkey Vulture, Northern Harrier, Mourning Dove, Inca Dove, American Kestrel, Cassin's Kingbird, Loggerhead Shrike, Chihuahuan Raven, Horned Lark, and Western and Chihuahuan Meadowlarks (IS). This area is particularly important to wintering birds like Golden Eagle; Burrowing and Short-eared Owls; Mountain Plover; Say's Phoebe; Sprague's Pipit (IS); Baird's (IS), Grasshopper, Botteri's, Cassin's, and Vesper Sparrows; Lark Bunting; and Chestnut-collared and Thick-billed Longspurs. This is the primary habitat for the endangered Chihuahuan population of Aplomado Falcon and the critically endangered Worthen's Sparrow (IS), which numbers fewer than 150 individuals. Efforts to reintroduce this sparrow into Chihuahuan Desert Grassland in Texas and New Mexico have been unsuccessful.

The reptile community here is generally a smaller subset of the species found in CHIHUAHUAN DESERT shrubland and SHORTGRASS PRAIRIE. Common species include Prairie Rattlesnake, Coachwhip, Desert Grassland Whiptail, and Desert Spiny Lizard.

CONSERVATION: Chihuahuan Desert Grassland is an imperiled habitat of high conservation concern with only 5% remaining in suitable condition for obligate species. Centuries of heavy grazing have caused widespread encroachment of shrubs, especially Honey Mesquite (*Prosopis glandulosa*); however, total lack of grazing, with the complete removal of cattle without natural grazers replacing them, can also be harmful. Recently, huge swaths in the state of Chihuahua have been converted to cropland. Drought and invasive grasses are also a major threat to the integrity of this habitat. An estimated 90% of northern grassland obligate breeding birds spend their winters in Chihuahuan Desert Grassland. Protecting this habitat is just as crucial for their continued survival as management of breeding sites. Declines in these grasslands are tied to major declines in birds like Sprague's Pipit and Baird's Sparrow.

While conservation of Chihuahuan Desert Grassland has historically lagged behind the conservation of northern prairie habitats, major conservation efforts are currently underway. Conservation organizations are partnering with private landowners to create conservation easements and reserves and to promote sustainable land-use practices. Removal of mesquite and restoration of grasslands are important steps in this process.

DISTRIBUTION: Chihuahuan Desert Grassland is patchily distributed throughout the CHIHUAHUAN DESERT. From its northern limits in the United States, in se. Arizona, s. New Mexico, and w. Texas, the desert extends south into Mexico, across n. Sonora, and through the states of Chihuahua and Coahuila. Within its broader distribution, Chihuahuan Desert Grassland occurs mostly in valleys and basins between mountains and in lower foothills close to valley floors.

WHERE TO SEE: Las Cienegas National Conservation Area, Arizona, US; Marfa Grasslands, Texas, US; Janos Biosphere Reserve, Chihuahua, Mexico; Altiplano Mexicano Nordoriental, Zacatecas, Mexico.

Ne7F MEXICAN BUNCHGRASS AND ZACATONAL

IN A NUTSHELL: A high-montane grassland of the volcanic belt in Mexico, often occurring as small parklike meadows. **Global Habitat Affinities:** AFROTROPICAL MONTANE GRASSLAND; SHOLA GRASSLANDS. **Continental Habitat Affinities:** HAWAIIAN GRASSLANDS; ALPINE TUNDRA. **Species Overlap:** MADREAN PINE-OAK WOODLAND; CHIHUAHUAN DESERT GRASSLAND.

DESCRIPTION: Mexican Bunchgrass and Zacatonal is a rare subalpine grassland limited to the highest mountains in the Sierra Madre Occidental and the Trans-Mexican Volcanic Belt. Typically occurring at elevations from 8000 to 13,000 ft. (2400–4000 m), these grasslands can, in rare cases, reach the alpine zone, as high as 15,500 ft. (4800 m). This habitat is a cold and semiarid environment with the upper elevations regularly experiencing temperatures well below freezing. In many ways this habitat is a transitional habitat intermediate between NEARCTIC ALPINE TUNDRA and the Paramo of South America.

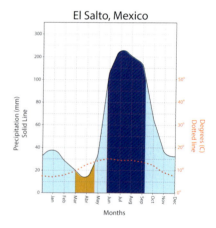

The habitat transitions from Mexican Bunchgrass to Zacatonal as you travel upslope. At the lower and middle elevations, this grassland exists as small parklike meadows within the upper reaches of MADREAN PINE-OAK WOODLAND. Mexican Bunchgrass clearings are surrounded by savanna-like stands of Montezuma Pine (*Pinus montezumae*) and dominated by Toluca Fescue (*Festuca tolucensis*), muhly (*Muhlenbergia quadridentata*), and Peruvian Feathergrass (*Jarava ichu*), the last of which grows in large tussocks 3–5 ft. (1.0–1.5 m) tall with flower spikes reaching even higher. The grasses make the terrain uneven and hummocked—especially difficult to traverse for a grassland. At higher elevations of 12,500–13,800 ft. (3800–4200 m), Zacatonal ascends above tree line and becomes significantly more uniform, losing the heavily tussocked bunchgrass appearance. Toluca Reedgrass (*Calamagrostis tolucensis*) is the dominant species at these elevations before it is replaced by a short alpine fescue (*Festuca livida*) near the upper limits of vegetative growth.

WILDLIFE: As with many subalpine and alpine habitats, the diversity of mammals in Mexican Bunchgrass and Zacatonal is rather limited. Widespread species include Bobcat, Coyote, Gray Fox, Mexican Cottontail, White-tailed Deer, and American Badger. There are several rare, endemic small

Mexican Bunchgrass and Zacatonal with Iztaccíhuatl volcano in the background. © PHIL CHAON

mammals in this habitat including Mexican Volcano Mouse, Volcano Harvest Mouse, and Volcano Rabbit. The critically endangered Volcano Rabbit is the second-smallest rabbit in the world. Similar to a pika, it will issue a loud, high-pitched shriek to alert other rabbits of danger.

The grasslands found in this habitat are quite isolated and limited and cannot support a diverse community of specialized birds. Widely distributed species found in Mexican Bunchgrass include Montezuma Quail, Striped Sparrow, Savanna Sparrow, and Chihuahuan Meadowlark. Mexican Bunchgrass meadows are the habitat of the endemic Sierra Madre Sparrow (IS), which is restricted to a few isolated sites near Mexico City and in Durango, only totaling

The Sierra Madre Sparrow is restricted to a few small areas of bunchgrass in c. Mexico.
© JOSE HUGO MARTINEZ GUERRERO/
CREATIVE COMMONS (CC BY-SA 4.0 DEED)

about 27 sq. mi. (70 km²). The extremely high Zacatonal grasslands have even fewer birds, and Yellow-eyed Junco and Common Raven are two of the only species seen at this elevation.

Mexican Bunchgrass and Zacatonal supports surprisingly diverse reptile and amphibian communities. Endemic species include Anahuacan Bunchgrass Lizard, Dusky Rattlesnake, and Longtail Alpine Garter Snake. Brown's Bunchgrass Lizard, Mexican Plateau Horned Lizard, and Twin-spotted Rattlesnake are also found in this habitat.

CONSERVATION: Mexican Bunchgrass and Zacatonal were always limited in range—accounting for 0.02% of Mexico's naturally occurring land cover. The area they occupy also overlays many densely populated areas, including Mexico City with its population of over 20 million people. These grasslands have been prized grazing land for centuries and are frequently burned to maintain pasture. As a result, many of the remaining patches of this habitat are degraded or not fully developed. Climate change is also of pressing concern, as is the case with many habitats limited to isolated mountaintops. Mexican Bunchgrass and Zacatonal has a high level of endemism in plant, reptile, amphibian, and insect communities and is critical habitat for the endangered Volcano Rabbit and Sierra Madre Sparrow.

DISTRIBUTION: Limited to high-montane areas of Mexico and Guatemala, this habitat occurs patchily above 8000 ft. (2400 m) and more consistently above 10,000 ft. (3000 m). Zacatonal occurs mostly in the Sierra Madre Occidental in w. Mexico and on high volcanic peaks in the south. The area above this habitat is dominated by GLACIERS AND SCREE, while MADREAN PINE-OAK WOODLAND replaces it at lower elevations.

WHERE TO SEE: Iztaccíhuatl-Popocatépetl National Park, Puebla, Mexico; El Tepozteco National Park, Mexico, Mexico.

Ne7G HAWAIIAN GRASSLANDS

IN A NUTSHELL: A pair of highly endangered shrubby grasslands found in either the subalpine zone or the dry lowlands of the Hawaiian Islands. **Global Habitat Affinities:** AFROTROPICAL MONTANE GRASSLAND. **Continental Habitat Affinities:** MEXICAN BUNCHGRASS AND ZACATONAL; CHIHUAHUAN DESERT GRASSLAND. **Species Overlap:** None.

DESCRIPTION: Hawaiian Grasslands are a formerly widespread habitat located on high mountaintops and arid lowlands on the leeward sides of islands. Principally occurring on Hawai'i and Maui, this habitat comprises two distinct subhabitats.

The **Ne7G-1 Hawaiian Lowland Dry Grassland** subhabitat is found in the rain shadows of towering volcanos on Hawai'i and Maui, as well as on the small islands of Lāna'i and Kaho'olawe. This habitat is typically warm, sunny, and dry. The lowland dry grasslands receive most of their annual rain during the winter months. Precipitation ranges from 4 to 30 in. (100–750 mm) annually, the amount increasing as you move upslope. Under natural conditions, this grassland was dominated by Pili Grass (*Heteropogon contortus*), which grows in tussocks up to 5 ft. (1.5 m) tall. There are scattered low shrubs, such as the native Broadleaf Hopbush (*Dodonaea viscosa*) and Yellow 'Ilima (*Sida fallax*), as well as the invasive Huisache (*Vachellia farnesiana*), Brazilian Peppertree (*Schinus terebinthifolius*), and Common Lantana (*Lantana camara*). Currently, invasive grasses like Fountain Grass (*Pennisetum setaceum*), Broomsedge Bluestem (*Andropogon virginicus*), Barbed-wire Grass (*Cymbopogon retractus*), and Guinea Grass (*Megathyrsus maximus*) are a major part of this habitat.

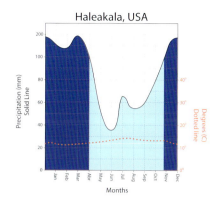

The **Ne7G-2 Hawaiian Subalpine Grassland** subhabitat is found on the highest slopes of Hawai'i and Maui. This environment is often cold and windy with blowing fog. Hawaiian Subalpine Grasslands range from mesic to semiarid, depending on their position on the mountain, and

Grasslands occur on Hawaiian islands near the coast and on high mountain peaks. © KEN LUND/WIKIMEDIA COMMONS (CC BY-SA 2.0)

The recovery of the Nene is one of the great conservation success stories of the 20th century. © PHIL CHAON

rainfall can range anywhere from 16 to 90 in. (400–2300 mm), falling evenly throughout the year. This habitat is dominated by dense bunchgrasses and low shrubs, usually about 3 ft. (1 m) tall. Important native species include Alpine Hairgrass (*Deschampsia nubigena*), Hawaiian Bracken Fern (*Pteridium aquilinum* var. *decompositum*), Pūkiawe (*Leptecophylla tameiameiae*), ʻĀheahea (*Chenopodium oahuense*), dwarf ʻŌhiʻa Lehua–Koa (*Metrosideros polymorpha*), and ʻŌhelo ʻai (*Vaccinium reticulatum*) in wet areas. More xeric native grasslands are characterized by Purple Lovegrass (*Eragrostis atropioides*) and Mountain Pili (*Panicum tenuifolium*) with broad overlap in shrubs. Kikuyu Grass (*Pennisetum clandestinum*), Buffel Grass (*Pennisetum ciliare*), and European Gorse (*Ulex europaeus*) are a few of the invasive species that dominate this habitat.

The Hawaiian Lowland Dry Grassland system has seen many changes to its natural fire regime from increased burning by native Hawaiians to fire suppression under European colonists and eventually increased fire due to invasive grasses. Currently this habitat is experiencing larger, more frequent, and more intense fires due to invasive fire-adapted grasses. These fires threaten not only native grasslands but also adjacent MAMANE-NAIO DRY FOREST.

WILDLIFE: In many ways these habitats are living ghosts. Much of the wildlife that may have inhabited them went extinct shortly after the arrival of Polynesians in the archipelago around 1000–1200 CE. There were never any native mammals found in this habitat due to the remoteness of the archipelago. Currently, the Hawaiian Grasslands are home to numerous introduced cattle, feral goats, Axis Deer, feral hogs, and Mouflon.

The extant birdlife here is more diverse but still limited. Before the arrival of humans on the islands, they were home to numerous species of giant flightless and semi-flightless geese. Like the giant moas of New Zealand, these large birds likely filled a niche usually filled by ungulate mammals on continental landmasses. There is still a smattering of native birds found in this habitat. Hawaiian Petrels nest in Hawaiian Subalpine Grasslands on Maui and Hawai'i. The Pueo (or Hawaiian Short-eared Owl) is found in both Hawaiian Subalpine and Lowland Dry Grasslands as well as a variety of agricultural habitats. A relatively recent arrival to the islands, it is the only raptor on the islands, living or extinct, that doesn't show some degree of specialization for avian prey. The establishment of Pueo is theorized to be tied to the introduction of the Polynesian Rat as a prey item 1000 years ago. The Nene (IS) (or Hawaiian Goose), a grassland specialist, is the only extant large grazing bird endemic to the islands. Historically, Nene spent most of their time in the Subalpine Grassland subhabitat, moving to the Lowland Dry Grassland in winter when fresh grass growth occurred. Currently, Nene use a mix of native grasslands and anthropogenic open areas. They are thriving on Kaua'i, where there is no remaining native grassland and, like many geese, are quite at home on a golf course. The grasslands are also utilized occasionally by migrant shorebirds including Bristle-thighed Curlew and Pacific Golden-Plover. The remaining avifauna of Hawaiian Grassland comprises introduced bird species. Many game birds, such as Wild Turkey, Black Francolin, Erckel's Spurfowl, and California Quail are common. There are more Erckel's Spurfowl on Hawai'i than there are in the entirety of the species' native range. Mixed flocks of small seed-eating birds, a common sight in the grasslands, often contain African Silverbill, Scaly-breasted Munia, Chestnut Munia, Common Waxbill, Red Avadavat, Yellow-fronted Canary, and Saffron Finch. Eurasian Skylark and Western Meadowlark have also been introduced to this habitat.

Bristle-thighed Curlew winters in coastal grasslands on Hawai'i.
© PHIL CHAON

Many rare endemic insects have co-evolved with the diverse flora in these habitats. The Fabulous Green Sphinx (*Tinostoma smaragditis*) is the sole pollinator of Kopiko (*Psychotria grandiflora*). The moth was thought to be extinct for many years until it was rediscovered in 1998. Due to the rarity of the pollinator, most of the 200–300 remaining Kopiko are pollinated by hand.

CONSERVATION: Both Hawaiian Grassland subhabitats are highly endangered, and Lowland Dry Grasslands have already been eliminated from several islands. The principal threats are invasive species, including invasive ungulate grazers. Climate change is a lesser threat, but lower rainfall and increased temperatures do threaten both subhabitats, especially mesic Subalpine Grasslands.

More than half of the remaining Hawaiian Grasslands are found on state or federal lands with some degree of protection. There have been many attempts to control invasives and restore native grasslands, and these have had some success. Fencing and ungulate control combined with weed eradication have led to a slight increase in native grasslands over the past several decades. However, the tide is always against fragile native habitats, and without increased conservation measures, these habitats will likely be lost.

On a positive note, the Nene is one of the great conservation success stories on the Hawaiian Islands. Due to hunting and invasive predators, the population of this goose was reduced to 30 individuals in 1952, with no birds left in the wild. Thanks to captive breeding efforts and invasive species control, the current population is nearly 4000 birds and rapidly increasing. Initial reintroductions took place in remote Subalpine Grassland wilderness areas, but since then these birds have spread to a variety of habitats, including lawns and golf courses, on all four major islands.

DISTRIBUTION: Hawaiian Grasslands occur patchily and are often degraded. With the wide array of invasive species and large areas of cleared pasture, the line between native Hawaiian Grasslands and anthropogenic ruderal grasslands can often feel blurry.

The Hawaiian Lowland Dry Grassland subhabitat is found on the leeward side of the islands of Hawai'i and Maui, away from the immediate coastal areas and up to 3200 ft. (1000 m). These grasslands also occur on the small dry islands of Lāna'i and Kaho'olawe. They were formerly found in w. Moloka'i and along the far western coastal plain of Kaua'i. Above 3200 ft. (1000 m), this habitat is usually replaced by MAMANE-NAIO DRY FOREST.

The Hawaiian Subalpine Grassland subhabitat is found on the high mountain slopes of Hawai'i and Maui from 3000 to 10,000 ft. (900–3000 m). More common at higher elevations, this grassland is generally found above Mamane-Naio Dry Forest (at relatively lower elevations) and above WET 'ŌHI'A LEHUA–KOA FOREST (at relatively higher elevations).

WHERE TO SEE: Hawai'i Volcanoes National Park, Hawai'i, US.

MEDITERRANEAN SHRUBLAND

IN A NUTSHELL: A diverse and highly fire-dependent shrubland with a Mediterranean climate and largely sclerophyllous vegetation. **Global Habitat Affinities:** EUROPEAN MAQUIS; EUROPEAN GARRIGUE; MAGHREB MAQUIS; MAGHREB GARRIGUE; MIDDLE EASTERN OAK JUNIPER; ASIAN GARRIGUE. **Continental Habitat Affinities:** SAGEBRUSH SHRUBLAND. **Species Overlap:** CALIFORNIA OAK SAVANNA; MOJAVE DESERT; SAGEBRUSH SHRUBLAND.

DESCRIPTION: Pacific Chaparral is the only truly Mediterranean habitat in the Nearctic. Chaparral experiences mild winters, when the temperature rarely drops below 32°F (0°C) and the vast majority of annual precipitation falls, accumulating an average of 10–17 in. (250–430 mm). The summers are hot and dry, with little to no rainfall and temperatures reaching upward of 110°F (43°C).

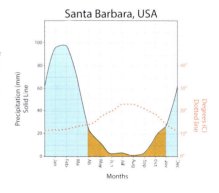

Santa Barbara, USA

This habitat occurs mostly on steep slopes with well-drained, rocky soils, blanketing foothills and coastal bluffs in a nearly impenetrable thicket. The woody shrubs that dominate this habitat grow 5–15 ft. (1.5–4.5 m) tall and are mostly evergreen and sclerophyllous.

Pacific Chaparral is an incredibly botanically diverse habitat, containing well over 1400 documented plant species. With such high diversity, chaparral communities display a huge variation in species composition. Chamise (*Adenostoma fasciculatum*) is the most widespread and common shrub, and the closest to a defining botanical feature. Other shrubs usually present include manzanitas (*Arctostaphylos* spp.), buckbrushes (*Ceanothus* spp.), oaks (especially California Scrub Oak, *Quercus berberidifolia*), Western Poison Oak (*Toxicodendron diversilobum*), mountain mahoganies (*Cercocarpus* spp.), and Toyon (*Heteromeles arbutifolia*). The diversity of herbaceous plants here is staggering, and postfire annuals account for nearly 20% of species in California's flora.

Pacific Chaparral is famously fire-dependent. Under optimal conditions, this habitat experiences low-intensity ground fires every 5–20 years and high-intensity stand-replacing fires every 30–100 years. The characteristic flora is well adapted to these periodic burns and responds to fire in one of two ways. Re-sprouters have large subsoil burls, and the entire shrub regrows from this established root system after the destruction of aboveground vegetation. Obligate-seeders produce large quantities of seeds that remain dormant for long periods between fires. When exposed to fire and heat, these seeds germinate, replacing the parent plants consumed in the fire. A few species employ a mixture of these two strategies. Recovery is rapid postfire, and it takes only a few years for Pacific Chaparral to regrow a closed canopy.

One exception to this fire tolerance is the **Ne8A-1 California Coastal Scrub** subhabitat, a short (2–6 ft./0.5–2.0 m), dense shrub community found in the coastal lowlands. This "soft chaparral" subhabitat is composed primarily of sages and buckwheats, especially California Sagebrush (*Artemisia californica*), California Black Sage (*Salvia mellifera*), California White Sage (*Salvia apiana*), California Buckwheat (*Eriogonum fasciculatum*), Coyote Brush (*Baccharis pilularis*), Coast Brittlebush (*Encelia californica*), and Golden Yarrow (*Eriophyllum confertiflorum*). These species are adapted for low-frequency and low-intensity fires. As fire frequency and intensity increase, many of these characteristic species die out and are replaced by dense stands of Laurel Sumac (*Malosma laurina*), pricklypear (*Opuntia* spp.), and Lemonade Berry (*Rhus integrifolia*).

Pacific Chaparral is found largely in the coastal foothills of California. © JUSTIN PURNELL

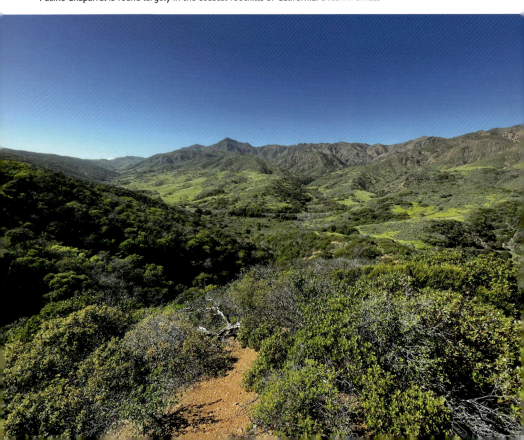

While Pacific Chaparral is well adapted to fire, the human cohabitants of the area are not. This habitat surrounds some of the most densely populated areas in the Nearctic, with destructive and dangerous consequences. Fast-moving intense fires in summer and fall are often followed by heavy winter rains and rapid erosion of the now-unstable soil. This fire-flood-landslide cycle is all too familiar in s. California and n. Baja California and means that careful management of this habitat, including regular and well-timed prescribed burns, is crucial for the well-being of the human population.

WILDLIFE: Pacific Chaparral is home to a high diversity of mammals, with over 50 species recorded, though none are found exclusively here. Columbian Black-tailed Deer, California Ground Squirrel, and Brush Rabbit are among the most visible mammals. There is a high diversity of small mammals; Santa Cruz Kangaroo Rat, California Deer Mouse (IS), and White-eared Pocket Mouse (IS) are rare species largely restricted to chaparral environments. This habitat is a great place to see carnivores. Coyote, Bobcat, and Gray Fox are all widespread and common, and this habitat supports remarkably high concentrations of Puma (aka Mountain Lion) and Ringtail.

Compared to the mammalian fauna, the bird communities of Pacific Chaparral are relatively species-poor. The omnipresent Wrentit (IS) and California Thrasher (IS) are strongly associated with Pacific Chaparral. Anna's Hummingbird, Greater Roadrunner, California Scrub-Jay, Bushtit, California and Spotted Towhees, and Lazuli Bunting are very common as well. A specific subset of birds prefers recently burned chaparral, and Costa's Hummingbird, Bell's and Black-chinned Sparrows, and Lawrence's Goldfinch are readily found in chaparral for several years after a fire. The coastal subspecies of California Gnatcatcher (IS) is found in the California Coastal Scrub of s. California

Above right: **Wrentit has an extremely small territory and may never leave the small patch of chaparral it was born in.** © DORIAN ANDERSON, TROPICAL BIRDING TOURS

Right: **California Thrasher's long and varied song is an important part of the chaparral soundscape.** © DORIAN ANDERSON, TROPICAL BIRDING TOURS

and n. Baja California. The most famous avian resident is the gargantuan, critically endangered California Condor. The majority of the world's population can be seen soaring over the chaparral-covered peaks of the coastal mountains of c. California.

A good diversity of reptiles is found in Pacific Chaparral, including several specialties. Western Fence Lizard, Common Side-blotched Lizard, Western Whiptail, Gopher Snake, Pacific Rattlesnake, and Eastern Racer are common and widespread species. Coast and Blainville's Horned Lizards; Coastal, Southern, and Northern Rubber Boas; Coastal Rosy Boa; Striped Racer; Two-striped Garter Snake; and Garden Slender Salamander also occur in Pacific Chaparral.

The floristic diversity here is accompanied by similar insect diversity, especially among pollinators. Over 300 species of bees are found in the chaparrals of San Diego County alone. This habitat is home to many endemics, including the endangered El Segundo Blue and Palos Verdes Blue butterflies.

CONSERVATION: Pacific Chaparral is a severely neglected habitat of high conservation priority. Overlapping with some of the most densely populated areas on the continent, chaparral is often viewed as a worthless shrubland and a dangerous fire hazard and treated as such. In California, nearly 75% of the Pacific Chaparral has been replaced by agricultural expansion or urban development. This figure is closer to 90% in the California Coastal Scrub.

Furthermore, the regions of California with a Mediterranean climate have responded with particular volatility to climate change. Reduced rainy seasons and higher temperatures have resulted in a nearly year-round fire season in the chaparral. This leads to both destructive fire regimes and more active destruction of the habitat for fire-prevention in developed areas. Changes in ocean temperatures have reduced the frequency of coastal fog, which is important for the maintenance of California Coastal Scrub.

The incredible diversity and high levels of endemism found in this habitat make the need for preservation especially important. Dozens of threatened and endangered plants are found in the chaparral, many with exceedingly small ranges. California Condor, coastal California Gnatcatcher, San Clemente Bell's Sparrow, Santa Cruz Kangaroo Rat, and Island Fox are all species of special concern found within this habitat.

Extensive tracts of chaparral are found in several national forests and coastal military bases, where they are protected from development. The endangered species protections associated with several chaparral species are also a safeguard against further development in the area. However, there are no formal policies promoting fire practices that benefit chaparral.

DISTRIBUTION: Pacific Chaparral is found locally in the w. United States, from sw. Oregon through California, south to nw. Baja California, Mexico, in the Transverse and Peninsular coastal mountain ranges and the foothills of the Sierra Nevada. California Coastal Scrub is limited to the coastal lowlands of c. and s. California and nw. Baja California as well as small pockets on the Channel Islands. Pacific Chaparral dominates areas that have shallow rocky soil or have experienced major disturbance (especially fire). At higher elevations, regular frost excludes many chaparral species, and the habitat usually transitions to PONDEROSA PINE FOREST or SAGEBRUSH SHRUBLAND. In areas with deep, well-formed soils, Pacific Chaparral is replaced by CALIFORNIA OAK SAVANNA over time.

WHERE TO SEE: Pinnacles National Park, California, US; Angeles National Forest, California, US.

Opposite: **Thanks to reintroduction efforts, California Condor can once again be found soaring above the Pacific Chaparral of the California coast.** © OWEN SINKUS

North American Tundras Dendrogram

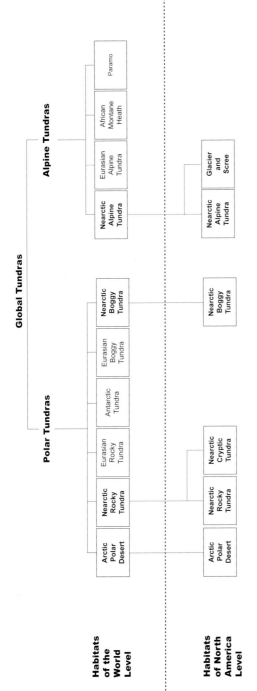

Global Tundras

Polar Tundras

Alpine Tundras

Habitats of the World Level

- Arctic Polar Desert
- Nearctic Rocky Tundra
- Eurasian Rocky Tundra
- Antarctic Tundra
- Eurasian Boggy Tundra
- **Nearctic Boggy Tundra**
- **Nearctic Alpine Tundra**
- Eurasian Alpine Tundra
- African Montane Heath
- Paramo

Habitats of North America Level

- Arctic Polar Desert
- Nearctic Rocky Tundra
- Nearctic Cryptic Tundra
- Nearctic Boggy Tundra
- Nearctic Alpine Tundra
- Glacier and Scree

TUNDRAS

IN A NUTSHELL: This is the habitat at the very edge of where life is possible on earth. There is almost no vegetation of any kind. **Global Habitat Affinities:** This habitat extends into Europe and Asia. **Continental Habitat Affinities:** None. **Species Overlap:** CRYPTIC TUNDRA; ROCKY TUNDRA.

DESCRIPTION: The northernmost vegetated area is one of both bitter cold and aridity (Köppen **ET**). The polar desert receives less than 10 in. (250 mm) of precipitation per year and never has a month when temperatures average over 50°F (10°C). What truly separates this climate regime from others is not the bitter winters, because the tundra to its south also has those, but rather the cold summers. The ice may melt for a very short period of summer, allowing photosynthesis to start at about 36°F (2°C), but there is no prolonged period of growth before temperatures drop to 23°F (–5°C) and photosynthesis halts, so plant life is severely limited to the hardiest of species.

The ground is sparsely covered, with no closed vegetation cover, and over 90% of the surface is bare rock. The region's biota, found in protected areas in cracks and hollows, consists mainly of crustose (flat-lying) lichens such as *Ochrolechia frigida*, though some free-standing (fruticose) lichens such as *Stereocaulon rivulorum* survive in the most protected areas. Mosses, and very rarely forbs such as Regel's Chickweed (*Cerastium regelii*), Pygmy Saxifrage (*Saxifraga hyperborea*), and Purple Saxifrage (*Saxifraga oppositifolia*), and graminoids (grasses and similar plants) such Ice Grass (*Phippsia algida*), Adam's Whitlow-grass (*Draba pauciflora*), and Northern Wood-rush (*Luzula confusa*) occur only where fine soils and moisture have accumulated in the best-protected areas.

Because of the low temperatures and lack of water, there is almost no chemical weathering of the rocks here, and most of the disintegration of rock material is through frost and wind abrasion;

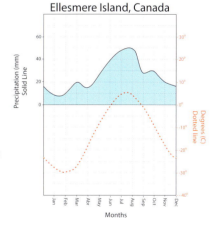

Ellesmere Island, Canada

Arctic Polar Desert is a land of rock and ice. © IAIN CAMPBELL, TROPICAL BIRDING TOURS

few nutrients are available to sustain growth, and there is rarely a relationship between flora and underlying rock type. Nutrients are derived either from the rotting of existing flora or the occasional input from defecation or rotting of seabirds and the occasional mammal such as Walrus or Polar Bear.

WILDLIFE: There are no endemic animals in this region. The few birds and other animals that do occasionally arrive here are present in the tundras to the south. Birds use cliffs for nesting but do not rely on the limited vegetation for food, and no resident bird species can survive. No land mammals reside here, though seals, Walrus, and Polar Bear use the fringes of the land as haul-outs. In the true polar desert environment, no insects or reptiles can exist; however, a few insects live in transitional areas between Arctic Polar Desert and CRYPTIC TUNDRA on Baffin Island.

CONSERVATION: Increasing global temperatures will result in CRYPTIC TUNDRA and ROCKY TUNDRA encroaching into the polar desert, and because this is the coldest environment in the Northern Hemisphere, there is nowhere for this habitat to move. Increased transportation through the Arctic Ocean is likely to result in development and further pollution along the coastlines of the Arctic.

DISTRIBUTION: This habitat is limited to n. Greenland; Baffin Island, Canada; and some other islands north of continental North America.

WHERE TO SEE: This habitat is difficult to access because there is little human habitation where it occurs; a cruise through the Northwest Passage offers the best opportunity.

Walrus occupies coastal areas fringing the Arctic Polar Desert. © IAIN CAMPBELL, TROPICAL BIRDING TOURS

Ne10B NEARCTIC ROCKY TUNDRA

IN A NUTSHELL: The low, dry or spongy heathlands in Arctic North America, which pass three months of the year in frozen and almost complete darkness and three months in daylight. **Global Habitat Affinities:** Almost identical to EURASIAN ROCKY TUNDRA. **Continental Habitat Affinities:** CRYPTIC TUNDRA. **Species Overlap:** CRYPTIC TUNDRA; BOGGY TUNDRA; SHRUB TUNDRA.

DESCRIPTION: The feel of the Rocky Tundra varies markedly through the seasons. It is covered with snow or wind-driven snow for most of fall, winter, and early spring. From late May through late June, the landscape is bright green with a low covering of forbs, mosses, and grasses. By midsummer, it is a blend of earthy oranges, olive greens, and browns of mosses and lichens along with dying annuals from earlier in the season. Rocky Tundra has a very low-lying, two-layered ground cover with few bare patches over rock. There are places where only lichens and mosses grow, but over most of the area where soil has been able to develop, there are shrubs and a few taller grasses and flowers. There are fewer plant species here than in more temperate regions, but because of the large range of microhabitats caused by dramatic landscapes with uneven snow distribution, many microhabitats exist, allowing for more biodiversity than otherwise expected.

Rocky Tundra has sparse vegetation, with 20–50% cover in gullies and snow beds, and less on headlands, ridgelines, and steeper scree slopes where this habitat merges with CRYPTIC TUNDRA and GLACIER AND SCREE. In the north of the tundra, permafrost thawing is very limited, and the vegetation is dominated by lichens such as Reindeer Lichen (*Cladonia rangiferina*), mosses such as Woolly Feather Moss (*Tomentypnum nitens*), and sedges such as Curly Sedge (*Carex rupestris*), Short-leaved Sedge (*Carex fuliginosa*), and Spike Sedge (*Carex nardina*). In areas with significant wintertime snow beds over slightly better-drained ground, the vegetation is dominated by Arctic Willow (*Salix arctica*) and Dwarf Birch (*Betula nana*) groves with a canopy ranging from just 1–2 in. (2–5 cm) to 24 in. (60 cm) tall, mixed with plants like White Dryas (*Dryas octopetala*), Purple Saxifrage (*Saxifraga oppositifolia*), and, on Greenland, Arctic Dandelion (*Taraxacum arcticum*).

In the southern regions of the Rocky Tundra, a deeper thawing of the permafrost, to 20 in. (50 cm), occurs, peat formation is possible, and vascular plants become more common. The

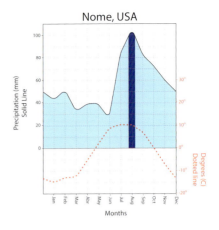

Nome, USA

Flowers proliferate on the Rocky Tundra during the brief Arctic summer. © BEN KNOOT, TROPICAL BIRDING TOURS

vegetation comprises mainly perennial plants, often no higher than 12 in. (30 cm) aboveground, especially dwarf shrubs such as Arctic White Heather (*Cassiope tetragona*), along with Lingonberry (*Vaccinium vitis-idaea*), Northern Labrador Tea (*Rhododendron tomentosum*), and Black Crowberry (*Empetrum nigrum*), as well as mosses, lichens, and Bigelow's Sedge (*Carex bigelowii*). The Rocky Tundra is being encroached upon by the SHRUB TUNDRA from the south, with many of the herbs and forbs being replaced by shrubs.

Though there is a general rule that tundra lies north of the 50°F (10°C) summer isotherm, much of the Rocky Tundra is restricted to areas of permafrost. The growing environment of this habitat is extremely harsh. With winter average highs of −4 to 8°F (−20 to −13°C), mean annual temperatures of 30–44°F (−1 to 7°C), and three months of night, three of day, and much of the year in twilight, growth is limited to around half the year. At these high latitudes, growth periods are cool, with average summer high temperatures between 36 and 53°F (2–12°C). With annual precipitation of 12–24 in. (300–600 mm), the Rocky Tundra should be very arid, but with such low temperatures, the effective evapotranspiration rates allow for a (seemingly) humid environment in areas protected from desiccating winds with abundant surface water in early summer. Some areas may be snow-free for only a month of the year, allowing vegetation to start growing only at the end of July after the snowbanks have melted off.

The weathering in these harsh environments is much more mechanical than chemical, resulting in lithosols with limited humic (organic-matter containing) layers; the high importance of soil parent

In winter, Muskox will move to Rocky Tundra along ridgelines where shallower snows allow it to graze. © PHIL CHAON

material in these immature soils means that changes in underlying rock chemistry from acid to alkaline can play important roles in determining the individual plants that grow there—but it is not as important as in Cryptic Tundra, because in Rocky Tundra, many more nutrients are derived from defecation of birds and mammals, generally missing from Cryptic Tundra.

During the Pleistocene, from 2.5 million to 11,800 YBP, cold ice-age conditions ranged over most of North America, creating "Mammoth Steppe" habitat. Much colder and drier than today's Rocky Tundra and BOGGY TUNDRA, these steppes supported mainly grasses over well-drained soils, more akin to an extreme version of a North American SHORTGRASS PRAIRIE or Asian Temperate Desert Steppe. During these exceptionally cold and dry periods, the Rocky and Boggy Tundras were more associated with warmer refugia, such as existed in Beringia on the dry land along the strait between Siberia and Alaska, at a time when glaciers existed on either side of the strait but the strait itself was dry.

WILDLIFE: Around half of the insect species of the Rocky Tundra are flies and mosquitoes (Diptera), which account for nearly 800 species in the combined Rocky, Boggy, and Shrub Tundras. As anyone who has spent time in the Arctic in summer can attest, midges are everywhere, representing 155 species; when combined with mosquitoes, they comprise around half of the tundra insect biomass. The other groups of insects, in decreasing abundance, are bees and wasps, butterflies and moths, and some beetles. It is notable that beetles account for over 40% of global insects but only 13% of Rocky Tundra insects. There are no ants in the North American Rocky Tundra.

It is the burst of insect life in spring that induces vast numbers of birds to head to the tundra for the short summer season, because apart from Common Raven and Snowy Owl, very few birds are resident in the Rocky Tundra habitat. In summer, millions of shorebirds arrive to breed and gorge themselves on the astounding hatches of insects. While more species tend to breed in the BOGGY TUNDRA, several specialize in this drier, rockier counterpart. Rock

Above left: **Pacific Golden-Plover breeds in the High Arctic but spends the winter in grassy areas in Hawai'i and Australia.**
© BEN KNOOT, TROPICAL BIRDING TOURS

Left: **Rock Ptarmigan is one of the only resident birds in the Nearctic Rocky Tundra.**
© BEN KNOOT, TROPICAL BIRDING TOURS

Ptarmigan, Black-bellied Plover, American (IS) and Pacific Golden-Plovers, Western and Baird's Sandpipers, Sanderling (IS), Long-tailed Jaeger (IS), and Snowy Owl select dry and rocky areas of the tundra. Snow Bunting and Lapland Longspur are abundant breeders and often the only passerines seen in this rocky habitat. On St. Matthew Island, Alaska, a large portion of breeding McKay's Buntings selects rocky sites, and in w. Alaska, Northern Wheatear also prefers this habitat.

Arctic regions are too frigid in winter to support any reptiles or amphibians. Most mammals found on Rocky Tundra are unable to migrate and have had to find ways of dealing with this environment for the eight months of the year when it is inhospitable. The larger grazing mammals such as Caribou and Muskox do not hibernate, so they need a large fat layer beneath the skin and two fur layers. Beneath the coarser outer fur layer is a much finer, denser undercoat that traps body heat. In the summer months, the larger mammals molt their fur for a much lighter coat to prevent overheating in the mild temperatures of summer. Arctic Fox is notable in this habitat in that it can almost be regarded as a marine species because it is so closely related to coastal environments. It is becoming rarer in the southern edge of the Rocky Tundra habitat with global warming, as Red Fox moves north into the Arctic zone.

Rocky Tundra is home to plenty of smaller mammals that are also widely distributed in the more southerly SHRUB TUNDRA such as Arctic Hare, Arctic Ground Squirrel, Ungava and Richardson's Collared Lemmings, North American Brown Lemming, and Singing and Tundra Voles. The abundance of many of the smaller mammals relates to the number of snowbanks during winter. Areas with limited snow and snowbanks are generally depauperate in smaller mammals because they provide little protection against bitter winter temperatures. These small mammals spend the winter in snowbanks, where they can seek protection from the frigid winds, but do not hibernate. Rather, they continue to search for food throughout the winter, and some species store food in preparation for the harder times. Both voles and lemmings have fluctuating populations; vole numbers are controlled by predators whereas lemming numbers are controlled by food supply. Voles eat mainly fast-growing grasses, which continue to be replenished throughout the summer, and their populations rise and fall with predation. Lemmings feed mainly on mosses, and there is evidence to suggest that lemming numbers rise a little faster than vole numbers in areas where moss is abundant; then the lemmings overgraze, exhausting the moss supply, and their population drops suddenly. Population explosions of voles and lemmings trickle through the food chain and affect predators like Arctic Fox, Long-tailed and Pomarine Jaegers, and Snowy Owl.

CONSERVATION: Throughout the Pleistocene, there have been many glacial (stadial) periods, or ice ages, and interglacial (interstadial) periods. Each of these events had profound effects on the distribution of mammals within the Nearctic tundra, with local and complete extinctions opening the opportunity for expansion and evolution of remaining species. Even within the glacial periods, there were many, sometimes rapid, minor climate fluctuations. An exemplar is the Younger Dryas "mini ice age" of 12,000 YBP, with a drop of 18°F (10°C), which happened rapidly, in a couple of decades, causing population bottlenecks resulting in extinctions, although the temperatures were not as cold as at glacial maxima.

Animals have survived the multiple cooling and warming events in the earth's recent history by moving southward or to the Beringian refugia during glacial times and moving northward during the interstadials. With the current rising planetary temperatures, it is the speed of change that causes most alarm.

While increasing temperature should result in more plant growth in humid environments, because precipitation is low and temperatures are low, much of the Rocky Tundra has the illusion of humidity. A minor rise in temperatures of a few degrees without a corresponding increase in precipitation will

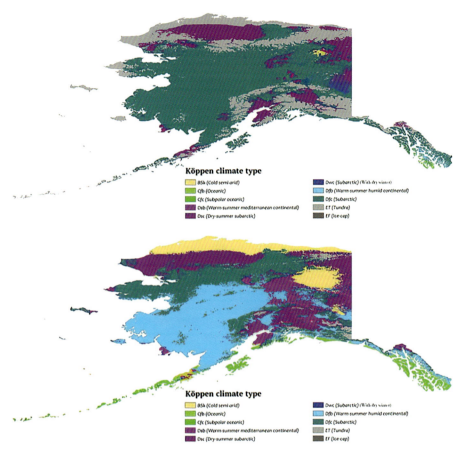

Fig. 9. Köppen climate maps for Alaska, 2020 (upper) and 2070 (lower). H. E. BECK, N. E. ZIMMERMANN, T. R. MCVICAR, N. VERGOPOLAN, A. BERG, AND E. F. WOOD (2018), PRESENT AND FUTURE KÖPPEN-GEIGER CLIMATE CLASSIFICATION MAPS AT 1-KM RESOLUTION, *SCIENTIFIC DATA* 5: 180214. BOTH LICENSED UNDER CC BY 4.0 DEED.

greatly increase plant stress and spur a likely change to a more steppe-like environment. Where there is sufficient water, shrubs will likely increase in dominance. It seems that much of the Rocky Tundra habitat is doomed due to increasing temperatures regardless of the water regime.

In one model of future climate for the Arctic region (depicted in fig. 9), we see that the tundra regions of the Alaskan Arctic in 2020 contain areas of ET and Dwc Köppen climate classifications, which equate to the climate conditions that produce ROCKY and BOGGY TUNDRA (with very little CRYPTIC TUNDRA). The prediction for 2070 has the Boggy Tundra of Utqiagvik (Barrow) replaced by Bsk, which is the climate conducive to a dry SUBARCTIC WOODLAND at this time, and the Rocky Tundra of Nome replaced by climates conducive to BOREAL CONIFER FOREST and TEMPERATE DECIDUOUS FOREST. From the map, it is clear that animals that are endemic breeders to the tundra habitats have no new areas to colonize and may go extinct. The transition from one habitat to another will not be smooth, as most of the Arctic plants have a very specific relationship with their pollinators. With the life cycles of pollinating insects being disrupted by temperature changes, it is expected that there will be a significant and rapid breakdown in the relationships between insects and host plants, including plants with obligate pollinators and plants with insect enemies. Note that the predictions are extremely loose, and while we know that there will be major disruptions, we don't know the exact nature of those; we cannot assume that all plants will behave as expected and move north.

DISTRIBUTION: Rocky Tundra occurs across a huge swath of Arctic continental North America from the Seward Peninsula in Alaska, across the north of the Brooks Range, to Hudson Bay in Canada. In the islands to the north, it is replaced by CRYPTIC TUNDRA, and in the south it merges with SHRUB TUNDRA or open SUBARCTIC WOODLAND. It is often in the same areas as BOGGY TUNDRA, where Rocky Tundra occupies the better-drained areas and Boggy Tundra the poorly drained areas.

WHERE TO SEE: Nome, Alaska, US; Baffin Island, Nunavut, Canada.

Ne10C NEARCTIC CRYPTIC TUNDRA

IN A NUTSHELL: Circumpolar at very high latitudes, an almost plantless environment with only very short mosses, lichens, and similar growth. **Global Habitat Affinities:** It is the North American expression of the EURASIAN CRYPTIC TUNDRA. **Continental Habitat Affinities:** ROCKY TUNDRA. **Species Overlap:** ROCKY TUNDRA; ARCTIC POLAR DESERT; PELAGIC WATERS (Arctic).

DESCRIPTION: Cryptic Tundra, "cryptogram barren," and High Arctic Vegetation (HAV) are terms describing the circumpolar habitat at the extreme north of North America, Europe, and Asia, as well as higher-elevation areas, such as ridgelines of the ROCKY TUNDRA. Most of the surface area of the regions around the pole has no vegetation, so this habitat exists as a mosaic with glaciers and barren rock fields. This is a very uniform habitat where no trees or woody plants are able to grow. Vascular plants such as forbs, grasses, cushion plants, and rosette plants make up less than 10% of botanical species and only 2% of the biomass, with the remainder dominated by fungi, algae, lichens, mosses, and liverworts.

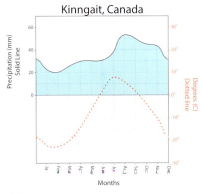

Kinngait, Canada

The structure of the tundra can be divided into the three layers. The "canopy" is a prostrate dwarf shrub layer less than 2 in. (5 cm) high; through this shrub canopy, the occasional emergent grasses or forbs grow to as high as 4 in. (10 cm). Much of the ground is completely bare, but where there is a ground covering, the so-called cryptogram layer makes up 60% of it; generally about 1 in. (3 cm) high, it includes most of the fungi, algae, lichens, and mosses.

With the exception of ARCTIC POLAR DESERT and ice cap, this is the most inhospitable environment in the world. The very low polar angles of sunlight mean essentially three months

Most of the sparse vegetation in the Cryptic Tundra is made up of lichens and mosses. © BEN KNOOT, TROPICAL BIRDING TOURS

of complete darkness and three months of total light, and less than four months with air temperatures above freezing; with little snowmelt much below the surface, permafrost (frozen soil) is a defining feature, and the growing season in these regions is extremely short. The Köppen climate classification, ET, is an indication of just how extreme this area is. These tundras experience very low temperatures throughout the year; winters are particularly cold, with average temperatures well below freezing, and often as low as –22°F (–30°C). Summer temperatures are relatively milder but still remain very cold, with average temperatures rarely above 40°F (5°C). Summer temperatures of the Alaskan tundras are determined by latitude, with the north being colder than the south. This is very different from the warmer European Arctic, which is moderated by temperate ocean currents, or the much more severe climates of Siberia and Canada, where the coldest temperatures are affected by extreme continentality. This is why Cryptic Tundra is much farther south in c. Canada than in Alaska or the eastern seaboard.

Regions of Cryptic Tundra are usually very dry, receiving around 12 in. (300 mm) of precipitation annually, most of it from snow, which paradoxically does not usually fall in winter. This low precipitation level in most locations on the planet would dictate that the habitats be deserts, but the low evapotranspiration rates mean that some surface waters are usually present in summer and the habitat can give off the impression of being humid. In contrast with the Rocky Tundra, even the better-protected snowbanks cannot support shrubs.

Extremely little chemical weathering occurs here, and almost all weathering is mechanical, such as freeze-thaw weathering and abrasion, resulting in lithosols where changes in underlying rock chemistry from acid to alkaline are the main determinant of the individual plants that grow there. Calcareous rocks such as limestones are dominated by Woolly Feather Moss (*Tomentypnum nitens*) and the fork moss *Dicranum spadiceum*. On more acidic soils formed on igneous rocks such as granites or metamorphic rocks such as schist, the fruticose (free-standing) lichens *Cetrariella delisei*, *Cladonia mitis*, and *Cetraria nivalis* are dominant.

Caribou is the only large mammal that can metabolize lichens, which comprise some 70% of its winter diet. © BRAD JAMES WILDLIFE PHOTOGRAPHY

WILDLIFE: There are very few mammal species in the Cryptic Tundra, and no amphibians or reptiles are able to survive here. Only 0.3% of the world's terrestrial mammal species can survive in this environment. For mammals to survive they have to be either species that hunt on the ice floes, such as Polar Bear or Arctic Fox, or small mammals that, to survive the winter, burrow into snowbanks, where temperatures remain stable at just under freezing even when outside temperatures are much colder. The small mammals that occur here include North American Brown Lemming, American Ermine, and Tundra Stoat (a subspecies of Eurasian Stoat).

Muskox, a massive bovine that looks like a short-legged, long-haired bison with downward sloping horns, used to occur through much of the High Arctic, and therefore Cryptic Tundra, but has been exterminated in most of that range. It has been reintroduced to a few areas of ROCKY TUNDRA, such as around Nome, Alaska, and today can be found on the Cryptic Tundra of Banks Island, Canada. Caribou occur over vast areas, though in much lower densities in Cryptic Tundra than in Rocky Tundra habitats to the south.

Gray Wolves hunt the Caribou and Muskox and readily feed on Arctic Hare and Northern Collared Lemming. Given that Muskox has been exterminated from most of its traditional range, the wolf's adaptability has meant that it still has a large range over the Cryptic Tundra. Polar Bears are found throughout Cryptic Tundra where it is close to coastline, but these animals also extend hundreds of miles inland. One of the authors once found very fresh scat miles from the coastline and had a very long hike back to the car—one of those naturalist moments when you truly realize where you lie in the food chain.

The birdlife of the Cryptic Tundra on the islands to the north of continental North America tends to be an impoverished version of the assemblage of the Rocky Tundra. Birds north of continental Canada and the United States include Snow Goose, Canada Goose, Baird's Sandpiper, Long-Tailed Jaeger, Rough-legged Hawk, Lapland Longspur, and Snow Bunting.

Left: **Snow Bunting breeds in a wide variety of tundra habitats.**
© PHIL CHAON

Below: **Red Knots engage in spectacular migrations, flying up to 20,000 mi. (32,000 km) a year. One individual known as B95, or "Moonbird," had flown an estimated 650,000 mi. (over 1 million km) as of 2024.**
© IAIN CAMPBELL, TROPICAL BIRDING TOURS

Where Cryptic and Rocky Tundra occur together, such as the hills around Nome, Alaska, species such as Surfbird, Red Knot, and Rock Sandpiper prefer the Cryptic Tundra, while most species prefer the denser Rocky Tundra. Surfbirds have elaborately mottled backs, and when on this territory, the birds blend in almost perfectly with the lichens and mosses on the rocky terrain. Red Knots tend to nest close to rocks with extensive patches of orange lichens.

CONSERVATION: The Arctic is the region most affected by climate change because the temperature is rising here more than twice as fast as in the tropical and subtropical parts of the world, a phenomenon known as Arctic amplification. Because the Arctic region is bound by the Arctic Ocean, there is little room for Cryptic Tundra to expand north, while it will be replaced by ROCKY TUNDRA and SHRUB TUNDRA to the south. Although it is an extremely cold environment, it is also a very dry one, and only a slight increase in temperature will result in more of the plants here undergoing water stress. Some models suggest that there may be an increase in snow cover, but most models suggest a drying environment. Increasing temperatures will open up much of this terrain to human colonization as well as increased exposure to extraction industries such as mining and oil production.

DISTRIBUTION: Nearctic Cryptic Tundra skirts the edges of Greenland and covers most of the smaller islands to the north of continental Canada, the northern side of Baffin Island and Victoria Island, and most of Banks Island. On continental Canada is it confined to Melville Peninsula, to the northwest of Hudson Bay. In Alaska it is confined mainly to the very northern coast around Utqiagvik (Barrow), where it occurs with BOGGY TUNDRA. There are smaller patches of Cryptic Tundra on the Seward Peninsula, where it occurs on the drier ridgelines and can be accessed from Nome.

WHERE TO SEE: Most extensive around Banks and Baffin Islands, Canada. Found on ridges of the Council Road and Teller Highway near Nome, Alaska, US; and at Barrow Point, Utqiagvik (Barrow), Alaska, US.

Ne10D NEARCTIC BOGGY TUNDRA

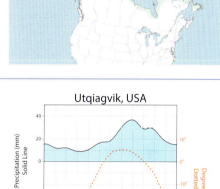

IN A NUTSHELL: A low, marshy and boggy tundra with scattered meltwater pools. **Global Habitat Affinities:** EURASIAN BOGGY TUNDRA. **Continental Habitat Affinities:** BOREAL BOG AND FEN. **Species Overlap:** ROCKY TUNDRA.

DESCRIPTION: This habitat is closely associated with ROCKY TUNDRA, occurring in the same zones with the same climate. The only significant difference between the two is drainage. Boggy Tundra, with its bogs, marshes, and lagoons, resembles the bogs that exist in the BOREAL CONIFER FOREST to the south, but here this wet habitat covers vast areas of the tundra belt. Much of this landscape is very flat, promoting the concentration of water. The bogs can have a grassy cover of sedges and cotton grasses, along with water-loving mosses.

Utqiagvik, USA

Precipitation (mm) Solid Line

Degrees (C) Dotted line

Months

Nearctic Boggy Tundra is dotted with small shallow pools in the summer. © BEN KNOOT, TROPICAL BIRDING TOURS

Palsa mounds, sometimes called pingos, are raised areas of the bog formed in areas where gradual accumulation of ice in the permafrost causes the ground to swell and rise above the surrounding terrain. They are usually elevated only a few feet but can be up to 25 ft. (7.5 m) high. These elevated areas have a different microhabitat than the surrounding areas, and while the less well-drained areas have marsh that is similar to more temperate wetlands with rushes, the raised areas can be windblown and desiccated in the winter, resulting in plants more typical of Rocky Tundra, such as Reindeer Lichen (*Cladonia rangiferina*), Woolly Feather Moss (*Tomentypnum nitens*), and sedges such as Curly Sedge (*Carex rupestris*), Short-leaved Sedge (*Carex fuliginosa*), and Spike Sedge (*Carex nardina*), all growing around a blanket of sphagnum mosses, such as Rusty Bogmoss (*Sphagnum fuscum*), which form a barrier to the underlying permafrost. On the sides of the palsa mounds, and especially where snowbanks form in winter, the grasses are thicker and are accompanied by Arctic Dandelion (*Taraxacum arcticum*), Purple Saxifrage (*Saxifraga oppositifolia*), and White Dryas (*Dryas octopetala*). In the wettest areas, plants such as Highland Rush (*Oreojuncus trifidus*) are dominant.

The terrain of the Boggy Tundra is fascinating in that it is far more rolling than initial impressions in early spring suggest, with very irregular drainage patterns. In late May, most of the terrain is covered in snow, with only the high palsa mounds snow-free. As the snow begins to melt in early June, and the Arctic Ocean is still frozen, the snow on the mainland melts but forms ephemeral lakes that may exist for only a week before they dry out to form drier tundra. When visiting tundra areas such as those around Utqiagvik (Barrow), Alaska, a naturalist may find an area with a foot of water and hundreds of ducks one day, and the same area dry and replete with shorebirds starting to breed the next. As the melt continues, the permanent lakes start to thaw, and by the end of June, the terrain has uplands with the driest tundra, gentle slopes with extensive sphagnum moss, and the marshlands.

WILDLIFE: Wet and marshy in summer and buried in comparatively deep snows in winter, Boggy Tundra has even fewer species of mammals than ROCKY TUNDRA. Collared lemmings, North American Brown Lemming, and Tundra Vole are the only true resident mammalians in this habitat.

The Arctic Fox will trade its white winter coat for a shorter dark gray one in the summer months. © PHIL CHAON

On its tundra breeding grounds, Pectoral Sandpiper engages in spectacular flight displays.
© BEN KNOOT, TROPICAL BIRDING TOURS

Polar Bear and Arctic Fox can also be found foraging here during the summer and fall months but will return to the coast and extensive pack ice during winter and spring.

While mammal diversity is lower, the number of birds breeding in the Boggy Tundra is much higher than in adjacent rocky habitat. More insects, open water, and denser cover all drive the higher abundance and variety of species found here. Most Arctic breeding waterfowl use this habitat, and the Boggy Tundra is the summer home to Steller's, King, and Spectacled Eiders and Long-tailed Duck (IS)—all easily among the most spectacular ducks in the world. Emperor, Ross's (IS), Snow, and Greater White-fronted Geese all nest here in clustered colonies. Ross's and Snow Geese form particularly dense and large colonies that can be heard from great distances; with their grazing, these geese alter the slow-growing tundra and can cause permanent damage and widespread loss of vegetation. In the areas surrounding these colonies, birds nesting in Boggy Tundra have shown significant declines in density in response to these habitat changes. Yellow-billed (IS), Red-throated, Pacific, and Arctic Loons; Parasitic and Pomarine Jaegers; and over 25 species of shorebirds breed here as well. While shorebirds are often considered drab and skittish on migration and on wintering grounds, the breeding shorebirds of the Arctic are a completely different animal. Many obtain bright and intricately patterned alternate plumage that is utilized both in display and as camouflage. Male Buff-breasted Sandpipers perform elaborate dances to groups of potential mates; Dunlins sing complex warbling songs in flight that can last for minutes on end; and Red Knots flutter and soar in an upward spiraling display.

The breeding season here is incredibly short, and many shorebirds arrive, nest, and leave in less than five weeks' time. While adults will provide some preliminary care and protection, shorebird chicks are left to fend for themselves long before they are capable of flight. This leads to oddly staggered migrations and even different migratory routes

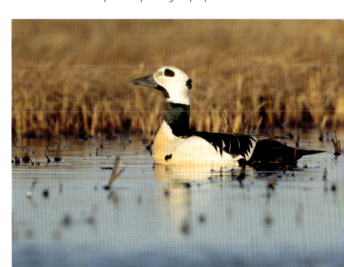

Steller's Eider breeds in small meltwater ponds in the coastal Boggy Tundra. © PHIL CHAON

between adults and juveniles. Juvenile Sharp-tailed Sandpipers (a Eurasian-breeding shorebird) will often detour thousands of miles east to Alaska before heading to their wintering grounds in Australia. For this reason, juvenile Sharp-tailed Sandpipers are a regular vagrant to the United States, while adults are almost never seen.

CONSERVATION: Boggy Tundra occurs in the same general bands as the ROCKY TUNDRA, and increasing temperatures impose the same pressures. The changed environment will result in a far more continental climate with much reduced snowfall and melt. The reduction in permafrost will change the geomorphology of the pingo environment and the local hydrology of the tundra, resulting in a far drier terrain with fewer ephemeral ponds and more lakes, similar to NEARCTIC REEDBED MARSHES. And while Rocky Tundra may be able to move north and colonize parts of the northernmost continent that are now covered in CRYPTIC TUNDRA, this boggy habitat may not have room to expand north, and certainly the habitat's breeding birds have nowhere to move. The Boggy Tundra of n. Alaska is a highly endangered habitat, and the future looks incredibly bleak for those shorebirds and waterbirds relying on it.

DISTRIBUTION: The distribution of Boggy Tundra mostly overlaps that of ROCKY TUNDRA, stretching from w. Alaska across the northern tier of Canadian provinces to e. Newfoundland. This habitat is more common coastally and in low-lying areas.

WHERE TO SEE: Utqiagvik (Barrow), Alaska, US.

Ne10E NEARCTIC SHRUB TUNDRA

IN A NUTSHELL: This low, shrubby and mossy habitat with patches of taller shrubs passes most of the year under snow but has a spectacular burst of insects and birdlife in summer. **Global Habitat Affinities:** EURASIAN SHRUBBY TUNDRA. **Continental Habitat Affinities:** None. **Species Overlap:** ROCKY TUNDRA; SUBARCTIC WOODLAND.

DESCRIPTION: The flora of Shrub Tundra can grow several feet high, but it is generally made up of taller versions of the same plant species that grow in more exposed areas, such as Dwarf Birch (*Betula nana*) and Tea-leaved Willow (*Salix planifolia*), combined with a lower layer of Gray Willow (*Salix glauca*).

One's first impression of tundra in midsummer is a blend of earthy oranges, olive greens, and browns of the mosses and lichens, along with the previous year's dead growth. Shrub Tundra is the more densely vegetated, slightly taller (1–4 ft./30–120 cm), Ericaceae-dominated tundra that grows in the better

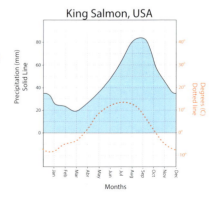

King Salmon, USA

Precipitation (mm) Solid Line

Degrees (C) Dotted line

Months

Nearctic Shrub Tundra is the dominant habitat on the Pribilof and Aleutian Islands. © BEN KNOOT, TROPICAL BIRDING TOURS

protected, thicker soils (where there is permafrost), as well as farther south (where there is not permafrost), than surrounding ROCKY TUNDRA. The growing season for most of the Shrub Tundra is only four months a year, when there are up to 24 hours of sunlight, and the rest of the year the habitat remains dormant; for 200 days, it is buried under snow cover (which protects the plants from desiccating winds). Perennials and shrubs tend to flower early in the growing season, while annuals or plants without substantial biomass in their root systems flower and seed later in the season and wither away at the short summer's end, spending the winter as seeds.

Therefore, the plants of this habitat, rather than simply resistant to extremely cold conditions, are adapted to a very short growing season with long periods of daylight, and can withstand the intense drought (through desiccation) of the winter months as well as the exposure to winds when there is no snow cover. Temperature alone would intuitively seem to be the main factor determining vegetation limitations of this habitat, but that is not the case; temperatures in the BOREAL CONIFER FOREST can be much colder than those of Shrub Tundra.

However, Shrub Tundra can be very windy, and at extreme temperatures in areas of permafrost, these winds cause rapid transpiration and desiccation of plant life with no chance of replenishment, as all water is frozen. So it is the dry wind rather than temperature that causes microenvironments in the most northerly areas, where the Shrub Tundra takes hold in protected areas and the surrounding areas are shrubless Rocky Tundra. Farther south, in areas such as the Aleutian Islands and mainland Alaska west of Anchorage, where there is no permafrost, the situation is reversed.

Here the Shrub Tundra is on the exposed tops of plateaus and ridgelines and on islands, whereas the more protected areas have SUBARCTIC RIPARIAN WOODLAND.

The Shrub Tundra habitat is dominated by shrubs that grow several feet high, generally taller versions of the same plant species that grow in more exposed areas, such as European Blueberry (*Vaccinium myrtillus*), Dwarf Birch, Tea-leaved Willow, Snowbed Willow (*Salix herbacea*), Black Crowberry (*Empetrum nigrum*), and Bog Bilberry (*Vaccinium uliginosum*). The ground cover is dominated by rushes such as Highland Rush (*Oreojuncus trifidus*) and grasses like Viviparous Sheep's-Fescue (*Festuca vivipara*). Between the shrubs, rushes, and grasses, the rocks and soils are almost completely covered by mosses such as Dusky-fork Moss (*Dicranum fuscescens*) and Woolly-fringe Moss (*Racomitrium lanuginosum*) and lichens such as *Nephromopsis cucullata* and *Cetraria ericetorum*.

WILDLIFE: Most of the mammals found on Shrub Tundra are not able to migrate and have had to find ways of dealing with this environment for the six months of the year when it is inhospitable. Caribou do not hibernate (nor did the Woolly Mammoth before them), so they need a large fat layer beneath the skin, as well as two fur layers, a coarser outer layer and a much finer, denser undercoat that traps body heat. In the summer months, the Caribou molt their coat for a much cooler coat to prevent overheating in the mild temperatures of summer.

Brown (aka Grizzly) Bears use the Shrub Tundra on continental North America, and although they tend not to hibernate in this habitat, they range widely through it in summer. Gray Wolves also occur in high density during the summer months, where they hunt on the tundra and scour the coastline, hunting pinnipeds such as Walrus.

Gray-crowned Rosy-Finch is found in low coastal environments in the far north.
© BEN KNOOT, TROPICAL BIRDING TOURS

Shrub Tundra is home to plenty of smaller mammals. Lemmings such as Northern Collared Lemming and voles such as Tundra Vole are widely distributed. Both the lemmings and voles spend the winter in snowbanks, where they seek protection from the bitter winds but do not hibernate (for more on their survival strategies, see ROCKY TUNDRA).

The biggest change in animal numbers comes with the invertebrate ephemeral breeders such as mosquitoes and midges, which burst into life in early summer, have phenomenal growth over a very short time, and provide the food source for the bulk of migratory birds. Many shorebirds migrate north to exploit this food source with its feeding opportunities. The Shrub Tundra will come alive with species like American Golden-Plover, Wandering Tattler, Surfbird, and Whimbrel. Along with the shorebirds are a handful of passerines, such as Horned Lark, American Pipit, Snow Bunting, Lapland Longspur, and Gray-crowned Rosy Finch. Willow Ptarmigan is one of the few birds that live in this harsh environment year-round.

CONSERVATION: Shrub Tundra is well protected from farming. Because of climate

Lapland Longspur is among the most common birds in the Arctic during the summer.
© BEN KNOOT, TROPICAL BIRDING TOURS

Rock Sandpiper nests in Shrub Tundra on the Pribilof Islands. © BEN KNOOT, TROPICAL BIRDING TOURS

change and the warming plant, it is expanding at the expense of the ROCKY TUNDRA in the north of its range. The threat of encroachment by SUBARCTIC RIPARIAN WOODLAND AND BOREAL SHRUBLAND MOSAIC is the main threat to this habitat in the south of its range.

DISTRIBUTION: Shrub Tundra is circumpolar, found in the European and Asian Arctic as well as North America. It is very prominent on the Aleutian Islands and in the Katmai region of Alaska. In Canada, it is much less extensive than other tundras but found around Hudson Bay, the far northeast coast, and around the uplands and coastlines of Newfoundland.

WHERE TO SEE: St. Paul Island, Alaska, US; Katmai National Park, Alaska, US; Newfoundland, Canada.

Ne10F NEARCTIC ALPINE TUNDRA

IN A NUTSHELL: An open, spongy habitat with low forbs and grasses found above tree line in temperate and subarctic regions. **Global Habitat Affinities.** EUROPEAN ALPINE TUNDRA; ASIAN ALPINE TUNDRA; AUSTRALIAN ALPINE TUNDRA. **Continental Habitat Affinities:** ROCKY TUNDRA. **Species Overlap:** ROCKY TUNDRA; HIGH-ELEVATION PINE WOODLAND; GLACIER AND SCREE.

DESCRIPTION: Alpine Tundra offers a glimpse into the polar regions. When ascending in elevation, after passing through the high-mountain forests and scrubby krummholz zones (see HIGH-ELEVATION PINE WOODLAND), one meets this treeless, windswept landscape, the last vegetated habitat on the tops of higher mountains. Above this is the snow line, beyond which snow and ice persist year-round, preventing even the scant growing season experienced on the Alpine Tundra.

Alpine Tundra is above tree line, the exact elevation of which varies with latitude. Climatically, this is one of the harshest environments in which plants survive. A suite of adaptations allows for plant growth despite high winds, frequent disturbance, poor soils, and frigid temperatures. The sedges, grasses, and forbs that dominate the landscape rarely grow more than 12 in. (30 cm) tall. Many of the woody cushion plants form tight, ground-hugging mats that are 1 in. (2.5 cm) or less above surface level. Areas sheltered from intense winds can hold small willows and taller meadow grasses but are also prone to retaining snow for longer periods, which further shortens the growing season. Furthermore, Alpine Tundras generally do not benefit from the endless summer sunshine of high-latitude tundras. To counteract the truncated growing season, perennial plants here keep a reserve of nutrients that allow for rapid growth under favorable conditions. Some of these plants are capable of growing, blooming, and producing seeds within a few short weeks.

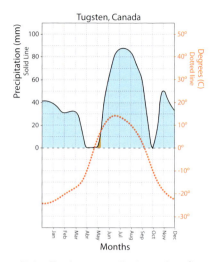

Alpine Tundra is similar to Rocky Tundra but occurs at high elevations. © DAVE SPANGENBURG

In addition to their short stature, many plants of the Nearctic Alpine Tundra have tomentose stems and leaves—covered in dense, woolly hairs that retain moisture and trap air, protecting the stems and leaves from frost. A red pigment (anthocyanin) prevalent in many tundra plants is visible at either end of the growing season. Anthocyanin helps the plant absorb ultraviolet radiation, which is converted into heat, allowing the plant to photosynthesize at very low temperatures.

WILDLIFE: Nearctic Alpine Tundra is an incredibly harsh environment with few permanent residents. The hardy few include Yellow-bellied and Hoary (IS) Marmots and Collared and American (IS) Pikas. The marmots will spend upward of eight months of the year hibernating to escape the dire winters. The pikas spend the summer creating large hay piles of grasses and wildflowers, which they subsist on in subterranean burrows all winter long. In the summer months, the Alpine Tundra is high-quality grazing land, and Mountain Goat, Elk, Bighorn Sheep, and Dall's Sheep come from lower elevations to feed. Wolverine and Brown (aka Grizzly) Bear will also visit Alpine Tundra periodically.

While every year, the ROCKY TUNDRA and BOGGY TUNDRA of the Arctic serve as breeding grounds for tens of millions of migratory birds, Alpine Tundra does not. Surfbird is the lone shorebird that breeds on Nearctic Alpine Tundra, returning annually to this habitat in the North Slope of Alaska. American Pipit is the only other long-distance migrant that returns to breed here. Brown-capped, Black, and Gray-crowned Rosy-Finches spend time feeding on high-elevation tundra in summer, preferring to nest around rocky outcrops and snowfields. Common Raven and Golden Eagle will both hunt on the open grassy elements of Alpine Tundra but prefer to nest on cliffs. White-tailed Ptarmigan (IS) is the only true Nearctic Alpine Tundra specialist, spending the entirety of its life in this habitat throughout the Rocky Mountains and northwest to Anchorage. Farther north and across the top of the continent, Rock and Willow Ptarmigans are also present.

While there are no reptiles or amphibians in this habitat, there is a surprisingly high diversity of butterflies. Multiple species, like Uncompahgre Fritillary, are endemic to isolated pockets of tundra habitat. Other butterflies like Common Alpine, Uhler's Arctic, and Great Arctic are widespread in the Arctic tundras and exist in disjunct patches in the alpine zone.

CONSERVATION: Alpine Tundras are fragile habitats that are easily threatened due to their limited range and long recovery times.

Mountain Goat occurs in Alpine Tundra in Glacier National Park, Montana, US. © DAVE SPANGENBURG

Wolverines den in areas where deep snow persists into the summer months.
© JARI PELTOMAKI, FINNATURE

Recreational activities like hiking and camping can damage thin and delicate layers of plant life, and the recovery can take centuries. The main threats come from climate change. Vegetation from lower elevations can already be seen encroaching upslope, pushing tundras higher toward mountain peaks. Limited to the tops of mountains, with nowhere else to go, many patches of Alpine Tundra could be eliminated before the end of the 21st century. Increased temperatures and reduced snowfall also make tundras vulnerable to fires in the future. As Alpine Tundras are reduced in extent, their connectivity is also reduced, creating small populations and genetic bottlenecks for species with limited dispersal. These stressors also make local extinctions more likely. In recent years the White-tailed Ptarmigan has become extirpated from sites at the southern end of its range. Though active reintroduction efforts are taking place in New Mexico, the habitat may not be able to support viable populations.

DISTRIBUTION: Alpine Tundra has a wide distribution at fairly low elevations throughout c. Alaska and Canada's Yukon and Northwest Territories. Farther south, its distribution follows the Rocky Mountains, Coast Mountains, Cascades, and Sierra Nevada. In Mexico, Alpine Tundra is restricted to the heights of a few towering stratovolcanoes in the south. In the ne. United States, Alpine Tundra is limited to a few square miles in the Presidential Range in the White Mountains of New Hampshire. In terms of elevational distribution, Nearctic Alpine Tundra occurs near sea level at 70°N; at 4500 ft. (1350 m) at 50°N; at 9200 ft. (2800 m) at 40°N; and at 13,000 ft. (4000 m) at 20°N.

WHERE TO SEE: Rocky Mountain National Park, Colorado, US; Mt. Rainier National Park, Washington, US.

White-tailed Ptarmigan is found in Alpine Tundra but not in other tundra habitats.
© BEN KNOOT, TROPICAL BIRDING TOURS

SIDEBAR 13   ICE EROSION AND DEPOSITION

Ice erosion and deposition occur through the action of glaciers, which are large masses of ice that flow like rivers, albeit at a glacial pace; stable continental ice sheets that are "cold-based" with frozen bottoms move a few inches a year, while "warm-based" glaciers with meltwater at the base during warmer periods can cover over 3 mi. (10 km) a year. These processes shape landscapes, carving out valleys and depositing material as glaciers advance and retreat.

There are a few types of glacial erosion and resulting landscapes. Abrasion occurs when moving glaciers carry debris, ranging from fine silt to boulders, which acts like sandpaper and grinds down, grooves, and polishes the underlying bedrock. This type of erosion is common on the cold-based glaciers. Plucking occurs when the base of the glacier thaws, producing meltwater that seeps between rocks or into cracks within the underlying rock. When the water freezes again, it expands and loosens the rock material, so as the glacier moves, it plucks this material out of the bedrock. The rock surface underlying warm-based glaciers can be very jagged. Bulldozing is when the movement of the glacier pushes loose rock material in its path. Cirque erosion occurs when snow accumulates in depressions or hollows on mountainsides and forms small circular glaciers; the rotational movement forms a bowl-shaped depression known as a cirque. U-shaped valley formation occurs as glaciers move down V-shaped river valleys, eroding the sides more than the base, changing the form into U-shaped glacial valleys.

What gets moved must get dropped, so as glaciers melt, they deposit the transported sediment, which ranges from silt-size to massive boulders. Till is the sediment that is deposited directly by the melting ice of the glacier. It is characteristically unsorted because, unlike rivers and especially calm lakes, glacial ice does not promote the differential settling and sedimentation of various-size fragments, holding instead one big mesh of boulders with cobbles, sand, and silt, all together. When till accumulates into mounds or ridges, it is referred to as a moraine. If the till is deposited at the end of the glacier, it is called a terminal moraine; once the glaciers have retreated this deposit can impede the drainage of rivers to form massive wetlands. If the till is at the side of the glacier, it is called a lateral moraine, and when two glaciers meet, their lateral moraines join to form a medial moraine. Drumlins are teardrop-shaped hills of till with a tapering end, showing the direction of the glacier's movement. Recessional moraines form when retreating glaciers have periods of stabilization and the accumulation glacial till occurs. Eskers are ridges formed between the former channels of meltwater under warm-based glaciers and are composed mainly of sand and gravel. Kames are like inverted bowls of sediment that form on the top of a glacier but are deposited as small, conical hills with the glacial retreat. Outwash plains are areas in front of glaciers where glacial meltwater deposits sands and gravels. In stark contrast with tills, the sediments are well-sorted because of the action of the flowing water.

Kettle lakes form from large blocks of ice left behind by retreating glaciers and buried by glacial outwash; when the ice melts, the depressions fill with water. This is how many of the shallow lakes formed in the Prairie Pothole region from Alberta, Canada, to Iowa, US. Along with terminal moraines, kettle lakes are incredibly important habitat drivers.

Ne10G NEARCTIC GLACIER AND SCREE

IN A NUTSHELL: A largely unvegetated habitat composed almost entirely of rock and ice found at high elevations and high latitudes with regular snowfall.
Global Habitat Affinities: NIVAL ROCKY TUNDRA.
Continental Habitat Affinities: ROCKY TUNDRA; CRYPTIC TUNDRA; ALPINE TUNDRA; ROCKY CANYON.
Species Overlap: ALPINE TUNDRA; ROCKY TUNDRA.

DESCRIPTION: Found in the high latitudes of the Arctic and on towering mountain peaks farther south, Glacier and Scree is one of the most visually stunning habitats found on the continent. This habitat structurally comprises two principal elements—permanent, slow-moving bodies of dense ice (glaciers) and unstable fields of loose, broken rock (scree). There are glaciers without scree and scree without glaciers, but the conditions required for each frequently co-occur. Despite their related nature, it is easier to describe the dynamics and formation of each of the two aspects separately.

The term "scree" is applied both to an unstable steep mountain slope composed of rock fragments and other debris, and to the mixture of rock fragments and debris itself. For our purposes, "scree" also refers to talus (material directly at the base of a rock face) and colluvium (material transported by gravity downslope), which form by slightly different processes with the same end result—a big pile of rocks. Glacial scree occurs in areas that are mechanically unstable because plant growth is particularly slow in these frigid environments. This means scree typically forms in areas that are either particularly cold or particularly dry. In the case of co-occurrence with glaciers, it is almost always the former.

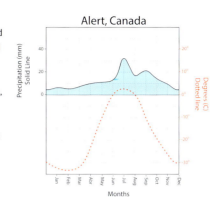

Scree can accumulate to an extent that it halts the movement of the source material. When this happens, the scree or talus stabilizes and eventually will degrade and be covered by encroaching vegetation. However, the presence of glaciers provides constant disturbance via glacial movement and glacial runoff, which keeps scree slopes from stabilizing and degrading. Weathering of scree is almost entirely mechanical, as it is broken down bit by bit through abrasion, frost fracturing,

and other physical processes. Frost fracturing occurs when water enters minute cracks in rocks and freezes, causing a roughly 9% increase in volume that fractures the rock a little. In periods of fluctuating freeze-thaw activity, the process is repeated often with dramatic effect (think frozen pipes). In extreme climates, such as the High Arctic, this process is uncommon because temperatures remain below freezing for many months on end, and in ARCTIC POLAR DESERT, it is not appreciable due to a lack of water to freeze.

In contrast to more tropical environments, chemical weathering is extremely limited in Glacier and Scree environments. The lichens and other growth that occur here create their own nutrient source through biotic breakdown rather than uptake of soil nutrients from rocks. This may seem esoteric, but it means that the soils that form on these deposits usually have very little relationship to the underlying geological parent material, something that is a major habitat determinant in warmer environments.

Exploring Kenai Fjords National Park, Alaska, US, is a great way to experience glaciers.
© BEN KNOOT, TROPICAL BIRDING TOURS

Scree is often found between glaciers and Alpine Tundra. © BEN KNOOT, TROPICAL BIRDING TOURS

The formation of glaciers is simple—the amount of snow accumulating needs to exceed the amount of snow lost on an annual basis so that compaction occurs. There is no single combination of elevation, latitude, temperature, or precipitation that produces a glacier, but typically, you can expect a glacial habitat to have extremely cold, snowy winters and relatively low temperatures in summer. Many areas that seem like they should hold glaciers are simply too dry, and vast areas of the Arctic remain ice-free POLAR DESERT.

In a growing glacier, snow accumulates over many years and is compressed into dense glacial ice. As the weight of snow and ice builds at the head of the glacier, it will begin to flow downward, literally at a glacial pace, or outward through a geological weakness—often a gap in the mountains. While scouring new paths, through abrasion of the underlying rock, flowing glaciers create dramatic landscapes such as U-shaped valleys, hanging valleys, and cirques. Many glacial flows slowly diminish as they move downslope, but some terminate more dramatically as they flow directly into the sea. These tidewater glaciers and their sudden end produce spectacular ice walls and a constant stream of icebergs. The calving of tidewater glaciers is a minor source of sea ice found in Arctic PELAGIC WATERS.

While mixed areas of Glacier and Scree habitat can be utilized by wildlife, massive glaciers generally cannot. When conditions appropriate for glacier formation occur over large contiguous areas, they lead to the formation of ice sheets. Ice sheets cover a minimum of 19,000 sq. mi. (50,000 km^2) and can be more than a mile thick. In modern times, ice sheets are found only in polar regions, but during the last glacial maximum (20,000 years ago) the Laurentide Ice Sheet covered 5 million sq. mi. (13 million km^2) and stretched from the Arctic Circle to as far south as Indianapolis. The remnants of this massive ice sheet still exist today on Greenland.

WILDLIFE: Among the harshest environments on the continent, Glacier and Scree sees few animals and none that would be considered resident.

Among mammals, Collared and American Pikas den within the subterranean spaces of rocky scree and talus slopes, but they are still reliant on adjacent tundra habitats for food. In the late summer, many Brown (aka Grizzly) Bears will head upslope to feast on giant congregations of Army Cutworm Moths that arrive on the scree slopes, consuming upward of 40,000 moths per day. Mountain Goats, Caribou, and Muskox will venture into the scree zone to forage on lichens.

Birds are generally absent from this environment. Black, Gray-crowned, and Brown-capped Rosy Finches are the alpine champions of the North American avian world and nest almost exclusively on cliffs and scree slopes at the tops of mountains. The nearby glaciers and snowfields are important for foraging, as insects are easy prey against a contrasting white background. American Pipits will often leave the ALPINE TUNDRA to forage in this zone. In Alaska, where there

American Pika makes its home in between the loose rocks of scree fields. © BEN KNOOT, TROPICAL BIRDING TOURS

Kittlitz's Murrelet nests in scree fields on the edge of tidewater glaciers. © ERIC MCCABE, WILDSCOTPHOTOS

are many coastal areas of Glacier and Scree, Kittlitz's Murrelet is closely tied to this habitat, nesting and laying its eggs on scree slopes and foraging in shallow, turbid freshwater at the base of tidewater glaciers.

CONSERVATION: Due to its remote and inhospitable nature, Glacier and Scree is almost entirely free of threats from development and invasive species. Despite this, the habitat remains critically threatened by anthropogenic climate change and natural interglacial cycles. A worldwide survey of 19,000 glaciers predicts an average reduction in volume of 33–60% by 2100. This average is skewed by large numbers of high-latitude glaciers. Glaciers at the edge of their range are much more at risk, and most glaciers south of the Canadian border are likely to disappear in the next century. Glacier National Park in Montana exemplifies the problem, currently retaining just 26 out of the 150 glaciers present during the late 19th century.

DISTRIBUTION: Most of the glaciers in the Nearctic occur at high latitudes in the Arctic around Greenland, upland areas of the Arctic Archipelago in Canada, and mountainous areas of Alaska. Greenland alone holds 12% of the world's total glacial mass. Farther south, the distribution is spottier, with glaciers occurring at high elevations in Washington, Oregon, California, Montana, Wyoming, Colorado, and Nevada. In Mexico, glaciers are found on the three tallest mountains— Citlaltépetl (Pico de Orizaba), Popocatépetl, and Iztaccíhuatl.

WHERE TO SEE: Glacier National Park, Montana, US; Kenai Fjords National Park, Alaska, US.

FRESHWATER HABITATS

Ne11A NEARCTIC REEDBED MARSHES

IN A NUTSHELL: Freshwater marshes dominated by tall, dense emergent vegetation, particularly Broad-leaved Cattail and Common Tule. **Global Habitat Affinities:** NORTH AFRICAN TEMPERATE WETLAND; AUSTRALASIAN TEMPERATE FRESHWATER WETLAND; EUROPEAN REEDBEDS. **Continental Habitat Affinities:** SEDGE AND GRASSLAND MARSHES. **Species Overlap:** OPEN WATER; SEDGE AND GRASSLAND MARSHES; LOWLAND RIVERS.

DESCRIPTION: The gently bobbing seed heads of the Broad-leaved Cattail (*Typha latifolia*) are a familiar sight to anyone who has spent time near fresh water in the Nearctic. These tall and impenetrable reedbeds are home to many secretive marsh birds, and listening carefully is often

Nearctic Reedbed Marshes are dense habitats harboring many secretive birds best detected by voice.

© BEN KNOOT, TROPICAL BIRDING TOURS

Black-polled Yellowthroat is endemic to a few reedbed marshes in c. Mexico. © PHIL CHAON

crucial to detecting wildlife here. Viewing can be quite difficult, and Reedbed Marshes are often best viewed from open edges or boardwalks.

This habitat is one of the hardiest and most widespread wetland types on the continent. A wetland of shallow, stagnant, and permanent or semipermanent waters, it often occurs on the shallow margins of lakes, ponds, artificial ditches, or seasonally flooded depressions. As a habitat of intermediate water depth, these marshes are frequently bound by OPEN WATER on the lowland side and a variety of habitats on the upland edge. The surface is flooded for most of the year, though key plant species can survive in muddy soil without standing water.

The most conspicuous feature of these marshes is towering and uniform emergent vegetation that is frequently dominated by a single species. Throughout most of the range it is the Broad-leaved Cattail that occupies this role, though several other species of cattails are present, especially in the southern range of this habitat. In the western part of the habitat's range, the Common Tule or Hard-stem Bulrush (*Schoenoplectus acutus*) fills this role. Throughout North America, non-native Common Reed or Phragmites (*Phragmites australis*) is a frequent component, eventually replacing cattails and tules. In Europe, Common Reed creates an analogous habitat with many of the equivalent animal niches.

Despite the uniform appearance of Reedbed Marshes, a diverse array of wetland plant life is hidden in the understory or around the margins. Associated species include Woolgrass (*Scirpus cyperinus*), arrow arums (*Peltandra* sp.), bur-reeds (*Sparganium* spp.), Sensitive Fern (*Onoclea sensibilis*), Spotted Jewelweed (*Impatiens capensis*), Pickerelweed (*Pontederia cordata*), wapatos or arrowheads (*Sagittaria* spp.), beggar-ticks (*Bidens* spp.), smartweeds (*Polygonum* spp.), and duckweeds (Lemnoideae). These plants are often important forage for animals living here, as cattail and tule are largely inedible.

Because of their hardiness, many wetland plants have become destructive and invasive throughout much of their range. Nutrient-rich runoff and low-disturbance water regimes allow *Typha* and *Phragmites* to flourish at the expense of more sensitive freshwater plants. Within these already resilient systems, the invasive species Common Reed, Narrow-leaved Cattail (*Typha angustifolia*), and Purple Loosestrife (*Lythrum salicaria*) are frequently a major problem, crowding out native cattails and tules. Despite this, a notable portion of the habitat's wildlife communities can persist in these invaded habitats.

WILDLIFE: Many mammals will utilize Reedbed Marshes for foraging and as a source of water, but few are expressly tied to it. Mammals with a strong affinity for wetlands include Marsh Rabbit, Swamp Rabbit, Common Muskrat, North American Beaver, and American Mink.

By contrast, Nearctic Reedbed Marshes are one of the most productive habitats for birds on the continent. In summer, wetlands in northern latitudes host hordes of breeding ducks, herons, grebes,

American Bitterns will remain motionless for hours, relying on their camouflage to fool both predators and prey. © JARED MIZANIN

rails, wrens, sparrows, and blackbirds. Redhead, American Wigeon, Blue-winged Teal, Pied-billed Grebe, Clark's Grebe, Double-crested Cormorant, American Bittern, Least Bittern, Virginia Rail, King Rail, American Coot, Franklin's Gull, Black Tern, Marsh Wren, Common Yellowthroat, Swamp Sparrow, Yellow-headed Blackbird, and Red-winged Blackbird are just a few wetland breeding birds endemic to the Nearctic. In winter, these same species head south to join resident wetland birds in more temperate climates. Flocks of tens of thousands of Snow Geese, Ross's Geese, Sandhill Cranes, American Wigeons, Northern Shovelers, Northern Pintails, and many more species are not uncommon in winter—especially on isolated wetlands in the west. While these birds will often utilize OPEN WATER, the surrounding Reedbed Marshes are crucial for forage and cover. The dense, matted reedbeds provide a secure microclimate with warmer temperatures, insects, and hidden liquid water. Many rodents and half-hardy passerines will spend much of the winter nestled in these hidden refugia.

The subtropical Reedbed Marshes of the se. United States and Mexico hold their own resident avifauna, including many species shared with the Neotropics. Masked Duck, Neotropic Cormorant, Anhinga, Purple Gallinule, Little Blue Heron, Tricolored Heron, and Wood Stork are all birds more typical of s. Nearctic Reedbed Marshes.

Purple Gallinule can be difficult to spot despite its bright colors. © BEN KNOOT, TROPICAL BIRDING TOURS

The banjo-like twang of a Green Frog is a common sound in Reedbed Marshes. © JARED MIZANIN

Nearctic Reedbed Marshes hold a large percentage of the continent's reptiles and amphibians. American Alligator is an iconic giant and the largest predator in many southern freshwater wetlands, while the smaller Spectacled Caiman is a feature of this habitat in Mexico. Water snakes (*Nerodia* spp.), garter snakes (*Thamnophis* spp.), Cottonmouth, Mud Snake, Rough Green Snake, and Black Swamp Snake are all wetland specialists. Most of the Nearctic's frogs and turtles breed here, and the sounds of American Bullfrog, Green Frog, and Northern Leopard Frog are omnipresent in the summer months. Newts (*Notophthalmus* spp.), dwarf sirens (*Pseudobranchus* spp.), mudpuppies (*Necturus* spp.), and amphiumas (*Amphiuma* spp.) are salamanders that spend most of their lives in freshwater wetlands.

The Central Mexican Marshes EBA encompasses a few wetlands near Mexico City that are home to Black-polled Yellowthroat and Aztec Rail. This habitat was the former home of the extinct Slender-billed Grackle. Yellowthroats are particularly sedentary, and Belding's and Altamira Yellowthroats are endemic to Reedbed Marshes in the Baja peninsula and ne. Mexico, respectively.

CONSERVATION: In general, freshwater wetlands are among the most threatened habitats on the planet. Over the past two centuries, more than 50% of all wetlands, including millions of acres of Nearctic Reedbed Marshes, have been drained. These wetlands have been destroyed primarily for agriculture and development, and continue to be lost at a rate of 60,000 acres (24,000 ha) per year. Reedbed Marshes are also plagued by invasive plants like Common Reed, Purple Loosestrife, and Common Water-hyacinth (*Eichhornia crassipes*), which outcompete native plants. Invasive animals like Asian Carp, Island Apple Snail, Nutria, and American Bullfrog (in places) predate and outcompete native species and alter vegetation on large scales. Reedbed Marshes are also susceptible to pollution, hypersalination, and extensive drought, often exacerbated by climate change.

Despite these challenges, this is a tenacious habitat, and Reedbed Marshes are capable of existing in highly disturbed fragments. From roadside ditches to parking-lot retention ponds, copses of swaying cattails full of Red-winged Blackbirds, Common Muskrats, and Soras are still a common sight. Major efforts to conserve wetlands have been made over the past few decades. The North American Wetlands Conservation Act (1989) affords special protections to wetlands and provides money for conservation easements on private land. The Ramsar Convention on Wetlands of International Importance (1971) recognized wetlands of global importance and made provisions for the conservation and sustainable use of these sites; 140 Ramsar sites (8% of the world total) are found in Mexico, more than the number in the United States and Canada combined. The US National Wildlife Refuge system has created and preserved millions of acres of Reedbed Marshes, mostly through taxes levied on recreational equipment and the "duck stamp" permits purchased annually by waterfowl hunters.

DISTRIBUTION: Nearctic Reedbed Marshes are found patchily throughout the continent, interspersed among a huge array of habitats. They occur in all but the highest latitudes and those well below the Tropic of Cancer. Reedbed Marshes are found in low-lying and flat areas, coastal plains, near large rivers, and around the Great Lakes. In areas with abundant water, many artificial Reedbed Marshes have been created by the US National Wildlife Refuge system. These provide recreational areas for waterfowl hunters and important habitat for hundreds of nongame species as well. An auto tour through a refuge is a great way to see a huge abundance and diversity of wildlife, particularly birds.

WHERE TO SEE: Horicon Marsh, Wisconsin, US; Great Swamp National Wildlife Refuge, New Jersey, US; Ciénegas del Lerma, Mexico (state), Mexico.

Ne11B NEARCTIC SEDGE AND GRASSLAND MARSHES

IN A NUTSHELL: A freshwater wetland habitat dominated by short, dense stands of grasses and sedges, usually seasonally dry. **Global Habitat Affinities:** TERAI FLOODED GRASSLAND; SOUTHEAST ASIAN FLOODED GRASSLAND; EUROPEAN REEDBEDS. **Continental Habitat Affinities:** None. **Species Overlap:** MIXED-GRASS PRAIRIE; MESOAMERICAN SAVANNA AND GRASSLAND; REEDBED MARSHES; EASTERN GLADES AND BARRENS; TALLGRASS PRAIRIE; SALT MARSH; OPEN WATER.

DESCRIPTION: Nearctic Sedge and Grassland Marshes are widely distributed across the continent, especially in the n. Great Plains and se. United States. Most of these wetlands are shallow and seasonal, most often inundated in late spring and early summer after snowmelt or spring rains. They rarely have standing water year-round. Like REEDBED MARSHES, these wetlands frequently occur around the margins of lakes and ponds, as well as bogs and in low-lying areas of grasslands. Unlike Reedbed Marshes, they usually have short vegetation (<3 ft./1 m) that provides little cover for larger birds and animals.

Sedge and Grassland Marshes are common in the prairies. © BEN KNOOT, TROPICAL BIRDING TOURS

American Mink is a voracious predator usually found near fresh water. © PHIL CHAON

Sedge and Grassland Marshes are botanically diverse and dominated by graminoid plants. While the dominant species vary throughout the habitat's range, sedges (*Carex* spp.) are almost always an important component. Widespread sedges found in this habitat include Tussock Sedge (*Carex stricta*), Beaked Sedge (*Carex utriculata*), and Bladder Sedge (*Carex vesicaria*). Bluejoint grasses (*Calamagrostis* spp.), Prairie Cordgrass (*Spartina pectinata*), and woolgrasses (*Scirpus* spp.) are also relatively common. During dry years, Sedge and Grassland Marshes are often invaded by grasses from nearby upland habitats. There are rarely any shrubs present in this habitat; when there are, they are typically small willows (*Salix* spp.).

Ne11B-1 Sawgrass Marsh is a unique subhabitat of this habitat restricted to s. Florida. Unlike most other Sedge and Grassland Marshes, it is dominated by a single species, Sawgrass (*Cladium mariscus*). Sawgrass is not a true grass but a member of the sedge family. Unlike most sedges in other Sedge and Grassland Marshes, Sawgrass can reach towering heights, often surpassing 10 ft. (3 m). Sawgrass Marshes are inundated for most of the year, with the soil exposed for only a few months at a time. Fire is important for the maintenance of Sawgrass Marsh, and succession by maples (*Acer* spp.) and willows (*Salix* spp.) occurs in its absence.

WILDLIFE: There are few resident mammals in Sedge and Grassland Marshes, and most species found here are common in adjacent upland habitats. American Mink and Common Muskrat are both abundant in this habitat. Marsh Rabbit and Round-tailed Muskrat are common in Sawgrass Marsh.

This habitat has broad overlap in birdlife with other freshwater communities in North America but also can host grassland species. This is the preferred breeding habitat of several birds, including

LeConte's Sparrow prefers Sedge and Grassland Marsh on both the breeding and wintering grounds. © ANDREW CANNIZZARO/CREATIVE COMMONS (CC BY 2.0 DEED)

Yellow Rail (IS), Black Rail (IS), LeConte's Sparrow (IS), Nelson's Sparrow (IS), and Sedge Wren. Other widespread wetland birds found here include a variety of dabbling ducks, Northern Harrier, Short-eared Owl, Sora, Virginia Rail, Wilson's Snipe, Marbled Godwit, Wilson's Phalarope, American Bittern, Common Yellowthroat, Swamp Sparrow, and Red-winged Blackbird. In fall and winter, this habitat is often dry and very similar to adjacent upland grasslands. In the winter, many of the aforementioned species migrate to Sedge and Grassland Marshes on the Gulf of Mexico. Sawgrass Marshes have fewer resident bird species overall and more overlap with REEDBED MARSHES due to structural similarity. Some specialty birds found in Sawgrass Marsh include Limpkin and Snail Kite.

Sedge and Grassland Marshes are important breeding grounds for many amphibians as they often provide a fish-free environment for raising young. Northern Leopard Frog, Blanchard's Cricket Frog, Northern Cricket Frog, Spotted Chorus Frog, and Little Grass Frog are all commonly associated with this habitat. This habitat is also crucial for the endangered Eastern Massasauga, a small, wetland-loving rattlesnake.

Right: **The Eastern Massasauga is a rare rattlesnake found in wet grassy areas as far north as Ontario, Canada.** © JARED MIZANIN

Below: **American Alligator is common in the Sawgrass Marsh of Everglades National Park, Florida, US.** © DAVE SPANGENBURG

| SIDEBAR 14 | MICROHABITAT: PRAIRIE POTHOLES |

As the North American ice sheets (part of an event known as the Wisconsin Glaciation) retreated 10,000 years ago, they left behind innumerable depressions and irregularities across the landscape. The scars of this hasty glacial retreat are especially prominent in the n. Great Plains, where they have resulted in tens of thousands of small, shallow wetlands called Prairie Potholes.

While some consider this landscape to be a discreet habitat, the authors consider the Prairie Potholes region to be a distinctive mosaic of habitats that occur over a wide geographic area. A mix of VERNAL POOLS AND EPHEMERAL WETLANDS, REEDBED MARSHES, OPEN WATER, MIXED-GRASS PRAIRIE, TALLGRASS PRAIRIE, and SEDGE AND GRASSLAND MARSHES co-occur in the region. A diverse array of permanent and ephemeral, vegetated and unvegetated, these wetlands are filled by meltwater, precipitation, or groundwater in spring. Some may remain dry for years, but most are wet during critical periods for nesting wetland birds.

Often called "America's Duck Factory," the pothole wetlands are home to 60% of North America's Gadwalls, Mallards, Northern Pintails, Blue-winged Teals, Redheads, Northern Shovelers, and Canvasbacks. This is especially impressive considering these wetlands account for only 10% of the breeding range of these species. Of course, the Prairie Potholes are home to more than just ducks. Other birds found here include Eared Grebe, American White Pelican, American Bittern, Least Bittern, Virginia Rail, Yellow Rail, American Avocet, Upland Sandpiper, Marbled Godwit, Western Willet, Black Tern, Franklin's Gull, Short-eared Owl, Sedge Wren, Chestnut-collared Longspur, Baird's Sparrow, LeConte's Sparrow, Nelson's Sparrow, Dickcissel, Yellow-headed Blackbird, and Bobolink. The abundance of life here can be jaw-dropping in the early summer months.

Over the past two centuries, many Prairie Pothole wetlands have been lost to agricultural development, and the surrounding grassland matrix is even more imperiled. Loss of wetlands to development has slowed, though it remains a threat. The most serious looming threat is climate change, as drought will lead to the loss of many more wetlands. Additionally, early season drying events can result in phenological mismatches that find many birds returning from winter grounds too late to take advantage of the many short-lived potholes. The recognition of Prairie Pothole wetlands as sites of great importance for breeding waterfowl has led to extensive conservation efforts and many partnerships between private landowners and government agencies. These conservation agreements are increasingly important as federal oversight and environmental protections have continued to weaken in recent years.

In Sawgrass Marsh, American Alligators, Florida Banded Water Snake, Green Water Snake, Florida Cricket Frog, and Southern Leopard Frog are common. The invasive Burmese Python is frequently found in Sawgrass Marsh and has caused massive declines in populations of native mammals and large birds.

CONSERVATION: Nearctic Sedge and Grassland Marshes are rare and declining. As a seasonal wetland associated with grasslands, the habitat is vulnerable to agricultural activities. Many of these wetlands are small and easily disturbed and exist only on the margins of larger freshwater bodies. In more arid areas of w. North America, Sedge and Grassland Marshes are largely found on river floodplains and have declined due to damming, drought, and channelization of rivers.

Many Sedge and Grassland Marshes are home to endemic and endangered plants and invertebrates in addition to a few rare obligate breeding birds. Yellow Rail has experienced major declines in the past century, though its cryptic nature makes the true cause difficult to discern.

Sawgrass Marshes have largely been destroyed by development, both from urban centers and for growing sugarcane. Remaining Sawgrass Marshes are found mostly in protected areas like Everglades National Park, though even in these areas, invasive species remain a persistent threat.

DISTRIBUTION: Sedge and Grassland Marshes are widely distributed throughout North America. The largest concentrations are found in the Prairie Potholes region of TALLGRASS PRAIRIE and MIXED-GRASS PRAIRIE. These marshes are also abundant in grasslands in the boreal zone. In arid western areas of the continent, this habitat largely occurs in narrow bands along the margins of ponds, lakes, and rivers. Sawgrass Marsh is restricted to s. Florida, from the Lake Okeechobee basin to the southern end of the peninsula.

WHERE TO SEE: Everglades National Park, Florida, US; Beaverhill Lake, Alberta, Canada; Minot region, North Dakota, US.

Ne11C NEARCTIC BOREAL BOG AND FEN

IN A NUTSHELL: Freshwater wetlands with peat accumulation and strongly acidic or alkaline soils. **Global Habitat Affinities:** AUSTRALASIAN MONTANE BOGS AND FENS; EUROPEAN PEATLANDS, FENS, BOGS, AND MIRES. **Continental Habitat Affinities:** None. **Species Overlap:** BOREAL CONIFER FOREST; TEMPERATE MIXED FOREST; SUBARCTIC RIPARIAN WOODLAND; SUBARCTIC WOODLAND; EASTERN PINE SAVANNA (Pocosin subhabitat).

DESCRIPTION: Nearctic Boreal Bog and Fen is a unique wetlands habitat that is widely distributed throughout temperate and boreal regions of the continent. While bogs and fens can be quite rare in middle latitudes, boreal bogs, often called muskegs, are a large component of the BOREAL CONIFER FOREST. Variable in form and formation, bogs and fens share one major feature—the presence of peat. Peat is a dense accumulation of partially decayed plant material that forms in anaerobic or acidic conditions. The formation of peat facilitates the formation of bogs by absorbing large amounts of water, creating a spongy and saturated environment. In turn, many plants in bogs and fens facilitate the creation of peat by excreting acidic tannins that preserve plant material.

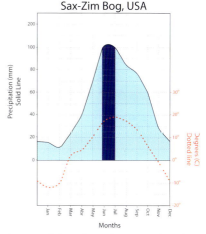

Sax-Zim Bog, USA

A diverse set of wetlands, bogs can take many forms. In general, bogs have deep peat deposits (>12 in./30 cm), are nutrient-poor and strongly acidic (pH <5.5), and are derived from lakes and precipitation, not groundwater. Bogs usually form on poorly drained soils in valleys or on plateaus and often evolve slowly from other wetland types as peat accumulates and acidification occurs. The vast muskegs of the boreal and Arctic zones form above clay soils or permafrost. Most bogs outside of the boreal zone are quaking bogs, composed of floating mats of peat and sphagnum. Quaking bogs are often associated with deep kettle lakes created by retreating glaciers; these bogs form slowly around the margins of the lake and grow inward. The bog mat is usually quite thick (2 ft./0.6 m), and the entire surface moves like a waterbed when you walk on it. In kettle lake bogs, floating mats of vegetation insulate the lake and create a cool microclimate that often has isolated pockets of boreal vegetation. Bogs have a wide array of plants, many of them rare species adapted to acidic and nutrient-poor environments. Most bogs include a ground mat dominated by sphagnum mosses (*Sphagnum* spp.) and various sedges (*Carex* spp.), especially Few-seed Sedge (*Carex oligosperma*). Shrubs in the family Ericaceae are abundant in bogs—this includes Bog Laurel (*Kalmia polifolia*), Cranberry (*Vaccinium macrocarpon*), Small Cranberry (*Vaccinium oxycoccos*), Lingonberry (*Vaccinium vitis-idaea*), and Bog Bilberry (*Vaccinium uliginosum*). Bogs are often ringed in small, stunted trees like Black Spruce (*Picea mariana*), White Spruce (*Picea glauca*), and Tamarack Larch (*Larix laricina*). Many bog plants have overcome the nutrient-poor conditions by becoming carnivorous or insectivorous, including sundews (*Drosera* spp.), pitcher plants (*Sarracenia* spp.), and bladderworts (*Utricularia* spp.). Orchids have also adapted to this environment by using mycorrhizal fungi to extract nutrients from peat. The majority of temperate and boreal orchids are found in bogs and fens.

While bog formation occurs under a variety of conditions, the conditions needed to create fens are much more specific. Fens typically form in areas where the water table is very close to the surface. The water is often supplied by mineral-rich groundwater that flows slowly across the surface in a sheet. The waterlogged soil creates anaerobic conditions that allow for the accumulation of thin layers of peat. The mineral-rich groundwater is often associated with

Bogs are often found in the Boreal Conifer Forest. © LIANNA PEVAR

Boreal Bog and Fen is home to many carnivorous plants, including Green Pitcher Plant.
© GARY PEEPLES USFWS

Mourning Warbler is a common breeding bird in shrubby bogs.
© GLENN BARTLEY PHOTOGRAPHY

marl or limestone bedrocks that are heavy in carbonate minerals like calcium, magnesium, and potassium. These minerals in solution create the alkaline conditions associated with "rich" fens. As peat accumulates, it can create a buffer between mineral-rich groundwater and soils. This allows for increased growth of sphagnum, which leads to acidification. Acidified, or "poor," fens have plant life much more similar to bogs and over time can transition into bogs. Plants typically associated with alkaline fens include Shrubby Cinquefoil (*Dasiphora fruticosa*), Woolly-fruit Sedge (*Carex lasiocarpa*), and a variety of brown mosses (*Calliergon, Campylium, Drepanocladus*). Fens also differ from bogs in having a notable lack of sphagnum mosses and ericaceous shrubs like blueberries and cranberries. Fens are often associated with SEDGE AND GRASSLAND MARSHES, EASTERN GLADES AND BARRENS, and LIMESTONE ALVARS (see sidebar 12).

Pocosins are peat-forming bogs that are found in the se. United States, mostly within EASTERN PINE SAVANNA. These bogs are similar to boreal bogs in many ways but are usually dominated by evergreen shrubs like Shining Fetterbush (*Lyonia lucida*), Gallberry (*Ilex glabra*), and Swamp Titi (*Cyrilla racemiflora*). Trees are more common in pocosins than in other bog types, and Pond Pine (*Pinus serotina*) and Longleaf Pine (*Pinus palustris*) are often present.

WILDLIFE: Bogs and fens, especially their margins, are highly attractive to wildlife, and the abundance of fruit-bearing and broadleaf shrubs makes them a good area to look for wildlife, especially compared to the surrounding BOREAL CONIFER FOREST. Common mammals in bog environments include Moose, North American Beaver, Common Muskrat, American Black Bear, and American Mink. Snowshoe Hares and Southern Bog Lemmings occur in bogs well south of their normal range.

The birds found in association with bogs and fens are similar to those occurring in Boreal Conifer Forest. Palm Warbler (IS), Rusty Blackbird (IS), and Lincoln's Sparrow are strongly associated with bogs, especially muskegs. American Woodcock, Wilson's Snipe, Lesser Yellowlegs, Solitary Sandpiper, Yellow Rail, Black-backed Woodpecker, Yellow-bellied Flycatcher, Canada Jay, Boreal Chickadee, Ruby-crowned Kinglet, Common Yellowthroat, Tennessee Warbler, and Wilson's Warbler are also regularly found in bogs and fens. Olive-sided Flycatcher, Mourning Warbler, and Canada Warbler are common members of the bog bird community and breed in disjunct populations associated with bogs south of the boreal zone.

Bog Turtle, the smallest turtle in North
America, lays only three eggs a year.
© GARY PEEPLES, USFWS

Boreal Bog and Fen has a high diversity of
dragonflies including the diminutive Elfin Skimmer.
© JUDY GALLAGHER/WIKIMEDIA COMMONS (CC BY 2.0 DEED)

Bogs and fens are the home of the critically endangered Bog Turtle—North America's smallest turtle species. Spotted Turtle, another small and attractive species, is primarily found in kettle lake bogs and pocosins. Fens have many of the same amphibians as SEDGE AND GRASSLAND MARSHES, while bogs are home to Western Chorus Frog, Gray Tree Frog, Mink Frog, Wood Frog, and Blue-spotted Salamander. Many rare insects are found in bogs and fens, and this is one of the most diverse habitats for damselflies and dragonflies—Sphagnum Sprite, Ringed Boghaunter, Lake Darner, and the minuscule Elfin Skimmer are endemic to bogs.

CONSERVATION: Boreal Bogs and Fens are fragile wetland systems that are easily disturbed. While northern bogs like the muskeg are relatively intact, southern bogs and fens are quite endangered. Once disturbed, these wetlands can take hundreds or even thousands of years to recover, due to the slow formation of peat. Commercial activities that threaten bogs and fens include the harvesting of peat and the commercial production of cranberries. Huge areas of bog in the Arctic are deteriorating as permafrost melts in response to climate change. Muskegs and other peatlands are the single largest form of carbon storage on the planet, and loss of bogs threatens to further accelerate climate change.

Bogs and fens are home to many endangered species of plants and insects as well as a few rare vertebrates like Bog and Spotted Turtles. While the majority of southern bogs were lost during the 19th and early 20th centuries, a large number of remaining bog and fen systems are protected by a mixture of public and private entities. The small size of most subboreal bogs and fens makes protecting them a relatively achievable goal.

DISTRIBUTION: Boreal Bog and Fen habitat is distributed across the boreal zone in Canada and the n. United States and widely overlaps with BOREAL CONIFER FOREST. Smaller, more isolated bogs and fens are found in kettle and moraine formations around the Great Lakes as well as mountainous areas of New England and as far south as West Virginia. Alkaline fens are associated with limestone soils around the Great Lakes, the Ozark and Appalachian Mountains, and parts of the TALLGRASS and MIXED-GRASS PRAIRIES. Pocosins and other southern bogs are distributed in EASTERN PINE SAVANNA habitat on the coastal plain from Maryland south to Florida and west to e. Texas.

WHERE TO SEE: Ferd's Bog, New York, US; Sweetbay Bogs Preserve, Mississippi, US; Algonquin Provincial Park, Ontario, Canada; White River Marsh State Wildlife Area (fen), Wisconsin, US.

Ne11D NEARCTIC OPEN WATER

IN A NUTSHELL: A freshwater habitat with still water that is too deep for the growth of emergent vegetation. **Global Habitat Affinities:** AFRICAN LAKES AND PONDS; ANDEAN ALPINE FRESHWATER LAKES; EURASIAN FRESHWATER LAKES, DAMS, AND PONDS. **Continental Habitat Affinities:** None. **Species Overlap:** UPLAND RIVERS; LOWLAND RIVERS; REEDBED MARSHES; PELAGIC WATERS.

DESCRIPTION: Found throughout North America, Open Water is a habitat with few common threads. This habitat is generally more common in wetter areas, though large reservoirs, water treatment plants, and other man-made lakes and ponds are present throughout even hyperarid areas of the continent. Open Water habitats range in size from bodies less than an acre (0.4 ha) in area to the massive Lake Superior (31,700 sq. mi./82,100 km²). Often other types of freshwater wetlands occur along the shallower margins of Open Water.

Some benthic, nonemergent aquatic vegetation does grow in areas too deep for emergent vegetation but with enough light to promote plant growth. Depending on water clarity, this zone is generally 3–12 ft. (1–4 m) deep. Common aquatic plants include eelgrasses (*Vallisneria* spp.), coontails (*Ceratophyllum* spp.), water milfoils (*Myriophyllum* spp.), and waterweeds (*Elodea* spp.). Many types of algae are also present in open water; green algae (Chlorophyta), red algae (Rhodophyta), blue-green algae (Cyanobacteria), and diatoms (Bacillariophyta) are all integral parts of this habitat.

A mountain lake in California is a good example of an oligotrophic body of water. © PHIL CHAON

Open Water can be generally divided into two useful groups—oligotrophic and eutrophic. Oligotrophic bodies of water are usually clear, with rocky or sandy bottoms, few nutrients, little algal growth, and high oxygen content. Many high-mountain lakes are oligotrophic—Lake Tahoe is a famous North American example. Lakes Michigan, Huron, and Superior are also considered oligotrophic. Eutrophic bodies of water, by contrast, are very biologically productive. They usually have soft, mucky bottoms, cloudy water, lots of aquatic plants and algal growth, and low oxygen content. Many Open Water areas will tend toward eutrophication over time as sediments accumulate and nutrients are deposited by runoff. Rapid eutrophication is often the result of pollution as sewage, agricultural fertilizers, and untreated wastewater add massive amounts of phosphorous and nitrogen to the system.

Rivers share many characteristics with Open Water and have overlaps in ecology and wildlife. LOWLAND RIVERS tend toward being eutrophic while UPLAND RIVERS are generally oligotrophic, though these tendencies vary with latitude and elevation.

WILDLIFE: There are no mammals confined to Open Water in North America. North American River Otters will hunt in the open water, and many mammals are capable of crossing through this habitat. The head of an otherwise submerged Moose crossing a northern lake is a shocking though not uncommon sight.

Many birds are found on Open Water, mostly in winter and during migration. Open Water is the realm of the diving ducks, and Greater and Lesser Scaup, Redhead, Canvasback, Red-breasted Merganser, Common Goldeneye, Bufflehead, Long-tailed Duck, and occasionally scoters are among those found here. Almost all other species of waterfowl utilize Open Water, and it is not uncommon to see over 20 species of ducks, geese, and swans on a single lake. Other birds preferring deep Open Water include Horned, Eared, and Red-necked Grebes; Common and Yellow-billed Loons; most gulls; Common and Caspian Terns; and Double-crested Cormorant. Osprey and Bald Eagle are also commonly seen hunting over Open Water. This habitat is a great area to seek out wayward waterbirds, and typically pelagic species like jaegers, Sabine's Gull, and even boobies can be found with some regularity. A spotting scope will come in handy.

Most of the life in Open Water is, unsurprisingly, underwater. Few amphibians are found, as they generally prefer areas with access to more terrestrial habitats, but Common Mudpuppy is a fully aquatic salamander found in lakes and ponds. Many turtles spend time in Open Water, and Spiny Softshell, Common Snapping Turtle, Northern Map Turtle, and various sliders (*Trachemys* spp.) are common. In northern latitudes, turtles will spend the winter buried in the mud of eutrophic lakes while the surface is frozen.

The diversity of fish in open water is again hard to capture and varies strongly with latitude and between oligotrophic and eutrophic lakes. Prominent fish in oligotrophic lakes include Lake Sturgeon, Northern Pike, Yellow Perch, Walleye, Freshwater Drum, and salmonids such as whitefishes, ciscoes, Lake Trout, graylings, chars, and others. Eutrophic lakes are more diverse and are dominated by species tolerant of lower oxygen levels. Centrarchids such as Largemouth Bass, Smallmouth Bass, and smaller relatives Green Sunfish and Pumpkinseed; carps; pickerels; and bullheads and other catfishes are more common in eutrophic waters.

OPPOSITE:

Top: **The yodeling of the Common Loon is an iconic sound on northern lakes during the summer months.** © BEN KNOOT, TROPICAL BIRDING TOURS

Middle: **Red-necked Grebe moves awkwardly on land but is incredibly graceful in the water.** © BEN KNOOT, TROPICAL BIRDING TOURS

Bottom: **A wide variety of ducks and geese frequent Open Water, making this habitat great for birding.** © JARED MIZANIN

| SIDEBAR 15 | INVASIVE SPECIES: ZEBRA MUSSEL |

Soon after a small mussel from freshwater lakes in s. Russia first appeared in the Great Lakes system in 1988, many of the largest freshwater bodies in North America were changed forever. Rapidly spreading from Lake St. Clair to the neighboring Great Lakes, the Mississippi Basin, and smaller bodies of water, these short-lived and abundant bivalves filter out tiny particles from the water column with cascading effects. The massive amount of water filtration by Zebra Mussels has increased water clarity and shaken up the entire trophic structure of large aquatic systems. Higher water clarity means more light penetration deeper in the water column, which transfers available nutrients to lower strata of lakes. Additionally, Zebra Mussels selectively filter certain algae while allowing blue-green algae to flourish, often resulting in toxic blooms that lead to massive fish die-offs. Zebra Mussels reproduce faster than native freshwater mussels and attach to almost any hard surface, including native mussels, and have catastrophic effects on native species, over 70% of which are extinct or endangered. The growth of Zebra Mussel colonies is so prolific that the native mussels' movement, feeding, and reproductive behaviors are stifled. While the filtration of toxins and pollutants by Zebra Mussels could be beneficial, it in fact creates a deadly sink for any organism feeding on the mussels. Toxins transferred to birds either directly or through fish, especially the invasive Round Goby, have led to major outbreaks of avian botulism, killing more than 80,000 birds in the Great Lakes since the 1999.

Of course, there is a spectrum with many intermediate (or mesotrophic) species occurring in both the oligotrophic and eutrophic ends of the range.

CONSERVATION: Open Water habitats are common and resilient despite the many threats currently posed to them. Drought and overuse for irrigation have led to the rapid depletion of many reservoirs throughout the w. United States. Pollution, especially from sewage and agricultural runoff, can lead to hyper-eutrophication and large algal blooms that deplete the water of oxygen and kill aquatic animals. One of the most complex threats to Open Water is the myriad invasive species introduced throughout the habitat's range. Most large bodies of water have multiple introduced species of fish, often introduced as sport fish. Asian carps, Alewife, various salmonids, and Largemouth and Smallmouth Basses have all been introduced well outside of their natural ranges. Trout were widely stocked in North American alpine lakes throughout the 20th century. Rainbow Trout deplete mountain lakes of invertebrate larvae and limit food availability to alpine species like rosy-finches. Trout are also responsible for direct predation on many species including the endangered Mountain Yellow-legged Frog. Zebra and Quagga Mussels are found widely, especially in the Great Lakes, where they can create landscape-level changes in hydrology (see sidebar 15). In the past, overfishing was a major issue, and Deepwater, Longjaw, and Blackfin Ciscoes all went extinct in the 20th century as a result. Most commercial fisheries in Open Water habitats are now small and well regulated.

DISTRIBUTION: Open Water habitats are found throughout the continent. There are especially large numbers of lakes in subarctic Canada. In the arid west, most Open Water is associated with man-made reservoirs.

WHERE TO SEE: Lake Superior, US–Canada; Pyramid Lake, Nevada, US.

Ne11E NEARCTIC VERNAL POOLS AND EPHEMERAL WETLANDS

IN A NUTSHELL: Seasonal depressional wetlands that appear after winter rains or spring snowmelt. **Global Habitat Affinities:** None. **Continental Habitat Affinities:** PLAYAS. **Species Overlap:** TEMPERATE DECIDUOUS FOREST; TEMPERATE MIXED FOREST; SEDGE AND GRASSLAND MARSHES; REEDBED MARSHES.

DESCRIPTION: Vernal Pools and Ephemeral Wetlands form in small depressions, frequently over areas with near-surface bedrock or hardpan clay that prevents drainage. Pools are filled during prolonged periods of precipitation and/or by melting snow, runoff, or rising groundwater. In the w. United States, this usually occurs in late winter and early spring (December–March), while in the east, these wetlands are most active between February and May. Vernal Pools and Ephemeral Wetlands are not connected to permanent water sources, and they undergo complete drying for long periods.

Eastern Vernal Pools do not have a distinctive array of plants and often exist with little or no associated plant growth. They often occur as a wetland element within eastern temperate forests including TEMPERATE DECIDUOUS FOREST, TEMPERATE MIXED FOREST, BALD CYPRESS-TUPELO GUM SWAMP, and EASTERN PINE SAVANNA. Red Maple (*Acer rubrum*), Silver Maple (*Acer saccharinum*), American Beech (*Fagus grandifolia*), and Black Tupelo (*Nyssa sylvatica*) are trees commonly found around Vernal Pools. Other common plants found around these habitats in the east include buttercups (*Ranunculus* spp.), sedges (*Carex* spp.), pondweeds (*Potamogeton* spp.), Skunk Cabbage (*Symplocarpus foetidus*), and various ferns.

In the w. United States, Vernal Pools are often found within PACIFIC CHAPARRAL, CALIFORNIA OAK SAVANNA, and PASTURELAND AND RANGELAND. Due the relative scarcity of water in these habitats, western Vernal Pools have a more unique herbaceous plant community. Over 100 species of plants, many of these threatened or endangered, are endemic to Vernal Pool systems in California. Calico flowers (*Downingia* spp.) are a group showing a particular affinity for Vernal Pools and a high degree of endemism.

WILDLIFE: While at first glance these wetlands may appear to be little more than puddles, Vernal Pools are vital for the survival of dozens of species. After the first warm rains of spring, hundreds of salamanders can be seen plodding their way across roads in search of these precious ephemeral nurseries.

Due to the fleeting nature of these wetlands, there are no birds or mammals strongly associated with them. However, high concentrations of food make Vernal Pools popular feeding areas for a variety of wading birds, including Green Heron, Great Blue Heron, and Great Egret. Ephemeral Wetlands occurring

Vernal Pools are formed by melting snow and spring rains.

Spring Peepers emerge after the first early spring rains.
© JARED MIZANIN

outside of forested areas (particularly in California) can be stopover habitat for dabbling ducks and migrating shorebirds.

The brief period of inundation and the lack of connection to permanent water sources mean that Vernal Pools and Ephemeral Wetlands are free of predatory fish. This relative safety is the driving factor behind the mass migrations undertaken by breeding amphibians annually. Amphibians strongly tied to Vernal Pools in the east include Wood Frog, Eastern Spadefoot Toad, Eastern Tiger Salamander, Spotted Salamander, Jefferson Salamander, Marbled Salamander, and many other species of mole salamanders (*Ambystoma*). In Missouri and Arkansas, the Ringed Salamander is an autumnal breeder, migrating to small pools after early fall rains. In California, California Tiger Salamander is a breeding obligate of Vernal Pools. Many other semiaquatic species of reptiles and amphibians will make use of these wetlands as well, and several species of garter snakes (*Thamnophis*) are frequently found feeding on larval amphibians.

Tadpole shrimp (Triopsidae) and fairy shrimp (Anostraca) are small crustaceans found throughout Vernal Pool systems. Living extremely brief lives, these crustaceans hatch when waters return to the pools. After feeding on algae for a matter of weeks (sometimes only days), females lay eggs in the rapidly drying pools. The eggs will survive on the dry surface of the depression and hatch the next time the pool fills. In the w. United States, many of these species are localized endemics, and three (Conservancy Fairy Shrimp, Longhorn Fairy Shrimp, and Vernal Pool Tadpole Shrimp) are federally endangered.

Spotted Salamander has a symbiotic relationship with a green alga that provides nourishment to its eggs through photosynthesis. © JARED MIZANIN

The Wood Frog utilizes Vernal Pools for breeding and occurs as far north as the Arctic Circle.
© JARED MIZANIN

CONSERVATION: In the e. United States, Vernal Pools and Ephemeral Wetlands are still abundant but fragile. Most are too small to receive any formal protection as a wetland, and they are susceptible to logging, development, and pollution from roads and agriculture. Vernal Pool–obligate amphibians are extremely vulnerable during migration, and large numbers often die crossing busy roads.

In California and Oregon, Vernal Pools are a critically endangered habitat with over 90% already lost. Major threats include development, agricultural runoff, overgrazing, and changes to hydrology. Extensive droughts due to climate change also pose severe risks for Vernal Pool flora and fauna.

Unfortunately, artificial ephemeral pools created as compensatory mitigation by developers tend to be unsuccessful and are rarely recolonized by amphibians. The exact reasons for the failure of these artificial wetlands remain unclear.

DISTRIBUTION: Vernal Pools and Ephemeral Wetlands are found mostly in glaciated areas of the c. and ne. United States as well as in areas of the west coast with Mediterranean climates. In the w. United States, most Vernal Pools occur in California, particularly the Central Valley. In the northeastern and midwestern states, Vernal Pools are largely found in glaciated areas that have gentle topography conducive to creating shallow depressions. In the se. United States, Vernal Pools largely occur on the coastal plain.

WHERE TO SEE: Mather Regional Park, California, US; Cuyahoga Valley National Park, Ohio, US.

Ne11F NEARCTIC UPLAND RIVERS

IN A NUTSHELL: Swift-flowing bodies of water draining from upland areas, typically with clear water and rocky or gravelly beds. **Global Habitat Affinities:** AFRICAN RIVERS; EURASIAN MOUNTAIN STREAMS AND RIVERS; SOUTH AMERICAN MOUNTAIN STREAMS. **Continental Habitat Affinities:** LOWLAND RIVERS. **Species Overlap:** LOWLAND RIVERS; OPEN WATER.

DESCRIPTION: At the most basic level, a river is a flowing body of water that drains the surrounding landscape. These bodies of water may be permanent, semipermanent, or seasonal, depending on the hydrology of the region, but for the purposes of this book, we are talking principally about permanent rivers. The terms "stream," "creek," and "river" are all used for these bodies of water, and though they do not have strict definitions, creek and stream tend to refer to smaller watercourses. Smaller streams join to form midsize streams, which in turn form rivers. The network of waterways forming a single terminal drainage point is termed a "watershed." Some watersheds can encompass tens of thousands of square miles of land. Creeks and streams that do not have any smaller bodies flowing into them are termed "headwaters." Headwaters tend to be relatively free of both pollution and predators and are important for specific wildlife.

In rivers, unlike most habitats in this book, the most important factors for wildlife are all abiotic—water flow, temperature, light, suspended matter, and bedrock define a river. Ecologically, rivers are typically divided into Upland Rivers and Lowland Rivers based on these abiotic factors. While most Nearctic Upland Rivers are mountainous in origin, they are not exclusively so. The most important factors in their formation are the velocity of water and the gradient of the slope the waterway follows. Upland Rivers have swift-flowing water and a relatively steep gradient. These features tend to produce a similar suite of characteristics including higher oxygen content in the water, cooler water temperatures, and a riverbed dominated by rocky surfaces. Upland rivers

also tend to be more structurally complex and frequently have an alternating pattern of riffles (fast-flowing shallow sections often with protruding rocks) and pools or glides (slow-flowing deep sections with a smooth surface). The surrounding topography and high velocity mean that upland rivers are likely to be more incised. (The level of incision refers to how much a river has eroded the surrounding bedrock.) Heavily incised rivers are key to the formation of steep canyons or gorges.

The swift-flowing nature means few aquatic plants can grow in Upland Rivers. Primary nutrient input for this system is usually in the form of algae growing on rocks exposed to adequate light. In Upland River systems covered by a canopy, falling detritus, especially leaf litter, is the primary nutrient input.

Waterfalls occur in areas where rivers flow over a vertical drop or a series of steep drops. These formations are a popular visual spectacle and provide important microenvironments in Upland River systems.

Upland Rivers are scenic but difficult to explore.
© BEN KNOOT, TROPICAL BIRDING TOURS

WILDLIFE: There are very few obligate mammal species in the Nearctic Upland River system, but many species visit them as a source of food or water. The Mexican Fishing Mouse and Thomas's Water Mouse are both endemic to small headwater streams in Mexico. Perhaps the most famous association between mammals and Upland Rivers is the large concentrations of Brown (aka Grizzly) Bears that congregate in these rivers during fall salmon runs.

Fewer species of birds are associated with Upland River systems in North America than on most continents, but several species can be considered near-obligate. The most classic Upland River bird is the American Dipper (IS), North America's only aquatic songbird and a common sight in mountainous waterways throughout the western half of the continent. Dippers can often be spotted bouncing and bobbing on exposed rocks in the riffle zone before plunging underwater to hunt aquatic insects. Harlequin Duck (IS) nests primarily along Upland Rivers, and Barrow's Goldeneye and Common Merganser are common in this habitat as well. Louisiana Waterthrush (IS) breeds along

The American Dipper is the only aquatic passerine in North America. © PHIL CHAON

Right: **Louisiana Waterthrush is found along swift, rocky streams in the e. United States.**
© BEN KNOOT, TROPICAL BIRDING TOURS

Below: **The Hellbender is an enormous aquatic salamander found in pristine Upland Rivers.**
© JARED MIZANIN

shady upland streams with heavy canopy cover in the e. United States. Black Swift (IS) and White-naped Swift (IS) nest on mossy vertical surfaces behind waterfalls.

Nearctic Upland Rivers are cold and tend to have very few reptiles. Queen Snake and Crayfish Snake are among the few to prefer this habitat, where they tend to hunt aquatic crustaceans. On the other hand, quite a few rare and unique amphibians prefer Upland Rivers and streams including the otherworldly Hellbender. Also known as the Snot Otter, Lasagna Lizard, or Grampus, Hellbender is a massive salamander found in pristine upland streams in the Ozark and Appalachian Mountains. Reaching nearly 2 ft. (0.6 m) in length, with a broad head, tiny eyes, and copious wrinkles, it is possibly the most spectacular amphibian on the continent. Many species of dusky salamanders (*Desmognathus* spp.) in the east and torrent salamanders (*Rhyacotriton* spp.) in the northwest congregate around the splash zone of waterfalls. The Coastal and Rocky Mountain Tailed Frogs (*Ascaphus* spp.) are found exclusively in frigid headwater streams in the west. Living in such a cold environment, these frogs develop extremely slowly and do not reach sexual maturity for at least four years—longer than any other known species of frog.

Upland Rivers are the habitat of trout and salmon, which need clear, cold, highly oxygenated water. The six species of Pacific salmon are anadromous and start and end their life cycle in Upland Rivers. Anadromous fishes hatch and spend the early part of their life in freshwater rivers before heading out into the open ocean to feed and grow. After several years the fish return to their natal Upland Rivers and begin a bizarre transformation. Upon entering a river, male ocean-form salmon transition to their brightly colored and patterned adult spawning form and may, depending on species, develop a large hump, long hooked jaws, and protruding fangs. Tens of thousands of salmon swim hundreds of miles upriver, breed, and die, in one of the planet's great migrations. Upland Rivers are also home to dozens of endemic species of wildly colorful darters (*Etheostoma* spp.) along with hogsuckers, madtoms, and many more fishes.

North American river systems are also home to over 300 species of freshwater mussels—the most diverse array in the world. Many of these species have vividly imaginative names

Spawning Sockeye Salmon migrate en masse from ocean waters to Upland Rivers to breed annually.
© DAVE SPANGENBURG

like Sugarspoon, Fat Pocketbook, Wabash Pigtoe, Carolina Heelsplitter, and White Wartyback. Unfortunately, 75% are threatened or endangered, and 23 species went extinct in the 20th century.

CONSERVATION: River ecosystems are in crisis on a global scale, and Upland Rivers are generally more fragile than LOWLAND RIVER systems. They face myriad threats including pollution, invasive species, and flow alteration.

Pollution was a major concern through the first half of the 20th century with massive quantities of pollutants entering rivers from industrial sources. The scale of contamination was hard to fathom and culminated in events like the Cuyahoga River in Ohio catching fire. Since the passage in the early 1970s of the Canada Water Act and the US Clean Water Act, and later a similar law (LGEEPA) in Mexico, point-source pollution has been strongly curtailed. Pollution remains a problem and a much more difficult one to control, as pollution sources are diffuse and come primarily from agricultural runoff, roads, and other areas of development. Erosion related to human activities can also result in large amounts of sediment runoff, which is itself a pollutant in upland systems.

Damming and flow alteration have also been incredibly damaging to Upland Rivers. There are over 90,000 dams in the United States alone. These structures permanently alter the structure of large stretches of river and create barriers to animal dispersal and migration. Dams have been an especially contentious issue in the w. United States, where they have largely restricted natural movements of salmon, and in the southeast, where they have resulted in widespread extinction of freshwater mussels.

There are dozens of endangered species in this habitat, most of which have declined for similar reasons. The Hellbender has declined precipitously in the past century due to sedimentation, impeded migration routes, destruction of riverine habitats by dams, pollution, disease, and overharvesting for commercial and scientific purposes. Restoration of Upland River habitats is difficult, and it is more effective to try to conserve remaining high-quality river systems. Decades of litigation have resulted in the removal of some major dams in the west, a step in the right direction for restoring Nearctic Upland Rivers. The world's largest dam-removal project is currently underway on the Klamath River in California.

DISTRIBUTION: Nearctic Upland Rivers are distributed widely across the continent. Present anywhere there are significant changes in topography, they are found mostly in association with mountainous areas and are common throughout all North American mountain ranges. Rivers that have upland headwaters tend to remain Upland Rivers even when flowing through relatively flat areas.

WHERE TO SEE: St. Mary River, Glacier National Park, Montana, US; White River, Missouri–Arkansas, US; Fraser River, British Columbia, Canada.

Ne11G NEARCTIC LOWLAND RIVERS

IN A NUTSHELL: Slow-moving bodies of water typically traversing alluvial plains, often with warm, turbid water and muddy or silty beds. **Global Habitat Affinities:** AFRICAN RIVERS; AUSTRALASIAN SANDY RIVERBEDS; EURASIAN FLOWING RIVER. **Continental Habitat Affinities:** UPLAND RIVERS; BALD CYPRESS–TUPELO GUM SWAMP. **Species Overlap:** OPEN WATER; REEDBED MARSHES; BALD CYPRESS–TUPELO GUM SWAMP; WESTERN RIPARIAN WOODLAND; PETÉN SWAMP FOREST; MESOAMERICAN MANGROVES.

DESCRIPTION: For a baseline on river ecological processes, see NEARCTIC UPLAND RIVERS.

Nearctic Lowland Rivers are the languid, muddy rivers of flat, low-lying areas of the continent. These rivers are often broad, with wide floodplains, lower oxygen levels, and silty, sandy, or muddy riverbeds. The aquatic aspects of these rivers are generally less complex than Upland Rivers, and riffles and glides are generally absent. Deep, slow-moving pools do form and are important to a variety of species. Unlike Upland Rivers, Lowland Rivers have regular aquatic vegetation and an abundance of submerged logs and protruding snags. The animals here are not adapted to swift current, and in many ways this aquatic system is more similar to eutrophic lakes and ponds (see OPEN WATER) than it is to Upland Rivers.

Lowland Rivers generally fall into two broad categories: whitewater and blackwater. The majority, including the massive Mississippi, are whitewater (aka brownwater) rivers. Not to be confused with turbulent whitewater rapids, whitewater rivers are pH-neutral and hold large amounts of suspended sediment, which gives them the color of milky coffee.

Blackwater rivers tend to be smaller waterways, and in North America are largely restricted to the se. United States. These rivers originate in flooded swamplands and bottomland forests and often have sandy bottoms. Their water is generally acidic and low in nutrients. It is heavily stained by tannins, and the color resembles a cup of strong tea. Lacking in dissolved minerals, blackwater systems don't have sufficient calcium for shell growth in mollusks and are usually lacking in snails and mussels.

Lowland Rivers are often highly variable in width, filling large river basins and regularly flooding huge areas. These rivers are typically associated with swamp forests and wetlands, including BALD CYPRESS–TUPELO GUM SWAMP, PETÉN SWAMP FOREST, MESOAMERICAN MANGROVES, and SEDGE AND GRASSLAND MARSHES.

WILDLIFE: The mammals of Lowland River systems are largely influenced by the surrounding forest and marshland habitats. No true obligate species are found here, but North American River Otter, Neotropical River Otter, and North American Beaver are common. West Indian Manatees are able to tolerate

Lowland Rivers are slow-moving and easily explored in a canoe or kayak. © MICHAEL RIVERA/WIKIMEDIA COMMONS (CC BY-SA 4.0 DEED)

Once rare, Bald Eagles have made a spectacular recovery and are again a common sight along many rivers. © JARED MIZANIN

a wide range of salinity and are frequently found in Lowland Rivers. During cold spells in Florida, manatees will congregate in relatively warm, spring-fed rivers—there is no better opportunity to observe this species.

The birds of Lowland Rivers are largely generalists or species associated with adjacent habitats. This is an important habitat for kingfishers, such as Belted, Ringed, Amazon, Green, and American Pygmy Kingfishers. A boat trip down a Lowland River is a great way to see wildlife, and Boat-billed Heron, Agami Heron, Black-collared Hawk, and Sungrebe are all best observed in this way. As these rivers tend to be very slow moving, many of the birds associated with OPEN WATER are found here as well.

Relatively few amphibians specialize in this habitat, but a wide variety of reptiles are found. American Alligator, Cottonmouth, and many species of water snakes (*Nerodia* spp.) utilize Lowland Rivers. Turtle diversity reaches its peak in this habitat, and there are dozens of endemic species. On sunny days, emergent snags and exposed banks can be packed with sunning turtles—especially various species of map turtles (*Graptemys* spp.), mud turtles (*Kinosternon* spp.), musk turtles (*Stenotherus* spp.), and softshell turtles (*Apalone* spp.). The prehistoric Alligator Snapping Turtle is found in this habitat. While it typically weighs around 45 lb. (21 kg), individuals have been known to reach 250 lb. (113 kg), and reportedly up to 400 lb. (180 kg), making it a contender for the world's largest freshwater turtle.

Above: **Northern Map Turtles are frequently seen basking on exposed logs along the edges of Lowland Rivers.** © JARED MIZANIN

Below: **Flathead Catfish can reach enormous size in slow muddy rivers.** © ERIC ENGBRESTON, USFWS

Lowland River habitat is home to some other prehistoric giants, and the largest freshwater fishes on the continent occur in these waters: American Paddlefish, Alligator Gar, and Blue Catfish are all endemic to this habitat. American Paddlefish has a giant, paddle-shaped rostrum and can reach 71 in. (1.8 m) in length and weigh up to 150 lb. (70 kg). The bizarre rostrum is covered in tens of thousands of electroreceptors that paddlefish use to detect zooplankton, which it captures through filter feeding. Paddlefish may also use the rostrum to detect and avoid obstacles in the dark, murky water. Fossils of paddlefish date back 120 million years.

CONSERVATION: Though less threatened than UPLAND RIVERS, Lowland Rivers are still a habitat of high conservation concern. A large percentage of North America's Lowland Rivers are part of the massive Mississippi River watershed. This area covers one of the largest intensive agricultural areas in the world, and pollution from fertilizers and soil runoff is a massive concern for aquatic wildlife here. Flood control is also a major issue, and natural flooding events have been largely eliminated, drastically changing the surrounding vegetation. Invasive species like Silver Carp have enormous populations in this habitat and regularly outcompete native fish.

Many large, long-lived species of this habitat are in decline, and American Paddlefish and Alligator Snapping Turtle are both endangered.

DISTRIBUTION: Lowland Rivers are widely distributed across the continent in flat, low-lying areas and alluvial plains. Most of these rivers are found in the Great Plains of the United States and Canada, the Atlantic coastal plain of the se. United States, and around the Gulf of Mexico. There are few Lowland Rivers in Mexico; most are in the states of Veracruz and Tabasco, on the Yucatán Peninsula, and in coastal areas of Chiapas.

WHERE TO SEE: Black River, South Carolina, US; Pascagoula River, Mississippi, US; Usumacinta River, Chiapas, Mexico.

Ne11H NEARCTIC LIMESTONE CAVES AND SUBTERRANEAN RIVERS

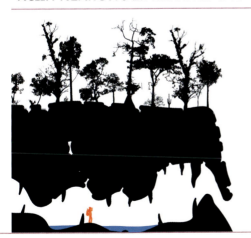

IN A NUTSHELL: A subterranean habitat found mostly in karst environments with both terrestrial and aquatic components. **Global Habitat Affinities:** None. **Continental Habitat Affinities:** KARST FOREST MOGOTES AND CENOTES. **Species Overlap:** KARST FOREST MOGOTES AND CENOTES; UPLAND RIVERS.

DESCRIPTION: While most of the habitats used by wildlife occur on the earth's surface, a small number of specialized organisms spend their entire lives underground in caves. A cave or cavern in the most basic sense is simply a natural void in the ground. These environments tend to maintain very stable temperature and humidity levels, and large caves stay at a nearly constant temperature throughout the year. In temperate zones, caves are cooler than the surface in the summer and warmer than the surface in the winter. The climatic stability of caves increases as you move in from the entrance.

Caves are typically divided into three zones—the entrance zone, the twilight zone, and the dark zone. The entrance zone occurs immediately in the vicinity of where a cave opens up to the surface. This area receives direct sunlight, experiences a highly variable climate, and often has photosynthetic plant growth. Many organisms not well adapted for life in caves will use this zone. The twilight zone lies inward of the entrance zone and receives only indirect sunlight. This zone usually has significant airflow and experiences large fluctuations in humidity. It is utilized by both cave-adapted organisms and some surface-dwelling animals. The dark zone receives no light and is the most climatically stable of the cave zones. This is the zone used by most true cave dwellers.

While caves form in numerous ways, most caves important to wildlife are solutional. These are not only the most common type of cave but are also the largest and most complex and typically are quite wet. Solutional caves form in rocks that are soluble in weak acidic mixtures. Typically, this means limestone, but

Right: **Caves are critical sites for breeding and hibernation for many bat species, including the Gray Myotis (pictured).** © ANN FROSCHAUER, USFWS

Below: **Large caves, like those in Carlsbad Caverns, New Mexico, US, may contain spectacular rock formations.** © MATHIEU LEBRETON/WIKIMEDIA COMMONS (CC BY 2.0)

solutional caves also occur in chalk, marble, and dolomite. Natural carbonic acid (H_2CO_3) present in groundwater will eat away at soluble rocks as it flows through fissures. Over time, these fissures widen to form caves and cave systems. Dissolved calcium carbonate present in the water will often precipitate over time to produce adornments called speleothems. The most familiar speleothems are stalactites and stalagmites, but other structures such as columns, flowstones, and soda straws may also form. Mammoth Cave in Kentucky is the world's longest solutional cave, with over 400 mi. (650 km) of surveyed passages.

Areas of the cave system that are below the water table will be flooded. These may be seasonally flooded passages or subterranean rivers. Subterranean rivers may flow underground from the surface or be entirely contained within cave systems. The two largest subterranean rivers in the world, inside the Sistema Sac Actun and Sistema Ox Bel Ha cave systems, are both found on Mexico's Yucatán Peninsula.

While weathering of limestone and similar rocks belowground produces caves and subterranean rivers, the same processes aboveground produce distinctive karst landscapes. Karst landscapes often have unique habitats associated with them, including the KARST FOREST MOGOTES AND CENOTES of Mexico.

WILDLIFE: Limestone Caves and Subterranean Rivers form a habitat that lacks many of the resources most animals require. A near-complete lack of sunlight and plant growth and a scarcity of food mean that cave-dwelling animals are low in both diversity and abundance. Despite these challenges, cave systems are still an important habitat with a high level of endemism.

Animals found in caves can be divided into three major categories based on their habitat usage. Trogloxenes, or "cave guests," are temporary cave residents that freely move in and out of the cave. They spend part of their lives in caves but never their entire life cycle. Troglophiles, or "cave lovers," are capable of spending their lives within caves and surviving within the dark zone of the cave but may also be found outside of caves. Finally, troglobites, or "cave dwellers," are animals that spend their entire life cycle within the dark zone and cannot survive outside of caves. Many troglobites lack pigment or external eyes.

There are very few North American birds associated with caves. Cave Swallows are occasionally trogloxenic and will nest within cave entrances.

North American mammals are also generally absent from caves. Common Raccoon, Ringtail, several species of skunks, American Black Bear, and Brown (aka Grizzly) Bear will use caves as den sites, torpor sites, and occasionally as natal dens.

While not true troglobites, bats in the order Microchiroptera spend much of their lives in caves, often well within the dark zone. Bats will use different caves as hibernacula (wintering roosts), migration roosts, and natal caves for birthing and raising young. In all three cases, bats tend to be picky; in most systems studied, bats will utilize only a small percentage of available caves within a region. The specific requirements for caves at different life-cycle stages vary by species, but important factors include temperature, humidity, structure, airflow, and volume.

Generally, hibernacula are deep caves with low temperatures, multiple entrances, and good airflow. Good hibernacula remain above freezing throughout the winter. These wintering roosts typically have higher numbers and densities of bats than summer caves. In summer, many bat species segregate by sex, with males using one cave and females using another to birth and rear young. Maternity caves tend to be much warmer than hibernacula and often have structures like domed ceilings that concentrate heat. Summer caves generally have smaller numbers of bats than hibernacula, but natal caves of some species can be enormous. The Mexican Free-tailed Bat colony at Bracken Cave in Texas holds nearly 15 million individuals—the largest concentration of mammals on earth!

Above: **The Western Grotto Salamander spends its entire life underground.**
© PETER PAPLANUS/CREATIVE COMMONS (CC BY 2.0)SEA

Right: **Like many troglobites, Mexican Tetras have lost their eyes and pigment.**
© GRAND DUC/WIKIMEDIA COMMONS (CC BY 2.0)

While not all bat species are associated with caves, 60 out of 139 bat species in Mexico and 18 out of 45 species in the United States and Canada rely substantially on caves as roosting and breeding sites. Some species strongly tied to caves include Gray Myotis, Indiana Myotis, Mexican Free-tailed Bat, Southeastern Myotis, Townsend's Big-eared Bat, Little Brown Bat, Big Brown Bat, and Northern Long-eared Bat.

Limestone Caves and Subterranean Rivers are also home to a variety of troglophilic and troglobitic salamanders. Troglophilic salamanders like Spotted-tail Salamander (aka Cave Salamander), Cave Splayfoot Salamander, and Green Salamander are often found in the twilight zones of caves and on nearby rocky outcroppings. Troglobitic salamanders are often geographically restricted. Many species are limited to a single cave system, and they are often endangered. Georgia Blind Salamander, Dixie Caverns Salamander, Southern Grotto Salamander, Texas Cave Salamander, Berry Cave Salamander, and Comal Blind Salamander are troglobitic. Other species like Barton Springs Salamander and San Marcos Salamander are not cave dwelling but are found only in waters issuing from extensive subterranean limestone aquifers. Salamanders in the genus *Hydromantes* are strongly associated with wet limestone outcroppings and caves in California. Most cave-dwelling salamanders are paedomorphic—retaining juvenile characteristics, in this case gills, as adults—and will spend their whole lives in water.

Other troglobites include about two dozen fish species and many arthropods, especially crayfish. The troglobitic fishes in North America come from eight different families and include Ozark Cavefish (Amblyopsidae), Mexican Tetra (Characidae), Phantom Blindcat (Ictaluridae), and Blind Swamp Eel (Synbranchidae). The Mexican Tetra and several other species have eyed surface-dwelling populations in addition to the eyeless, unpigmented troglobites.

CONSERVATION: While caves, as abiotic environments, are quite resilient, the organisms found in caves are often quite fragile and easily threatened. The largest threats to Limestone Caves and Subterranean Rivers are human pressures on aquifers, frequent human visitation, pollution, and the introduction of foreign organisms. Hydrologic disturbance is the most serious threat, as water usage, diversion, and damming may result in destructive drying or flooding of cave systems. The Edwards Aquifer in c. Texas serves several million people in a relatively arid environment, and usage for drinking water threatens species of cave fish and salamanders, especially the Texas Cave Salamander. Throughout North America, large chemical spills have caused major die-offs of aquatic cave-dwelling species. Human visitation to caves causes disturbance to both breeding and hibernating bats. The introduced fungal pathogen *Pseudogymnoascus destructans* causes white-

SIDEBAR 16	INVASIVE SPECIES: WHITE-NOSE SYNDROME

In 2007, researchers found dozens of dead and dying bats in a cave in New York. All the bats had a powdery white substance on their faces, and the disease was unlike anything seen before. The white substance was later identified as *Pseudogymnoascus destructans*—a previously undescribed fungus. Originating in Europe, the fungus was likely spread to North America in contaminated soil present on gear that had been used in European caves. The fungus has since spread to 38 US states and 7 Canadian provinces. It is currently not found in Mexico.

The fungus is not directly responsible for mortality. Instead, it infects hibernating bats, attacking exposed skin and causing severe irritation. As the fungus grows, it causes increased activity among them bats, leading them to expend precious energy during the winter months. Eventually, white-nose syndrome leads to starvation, dehydration, and often death. In some cases, white-nose syndrome may result in the deaths of 90–100% of individuals in a hibernaculum. Some caves that once hosted hundreds of thousands of bats are now virtually empty.

Since 2007, white-nose syndrome has killed more than 7 million bats, including 90% of Little Brown, Northern Long-eared, and Tricolored Bats. An additional 10 species, including the endangered Indiana Myotis and Gray Myotis, have been affected. Bats that do not hibernate and those that migrate long distances to warmer climates are not affected by the disease. Bats in Europe and Asia are also not affected by the fungus, explaining why the fungus was unknown within its native range.

There is currently no known cure for white-nose syndrome. Since the detection of the pathogen, there have been widespread closures of caves on public lands in the e. United States and Canada, though the disease has continued to spread. The public can help reduce its spread by respecting closures and by undergoing strict decontamination procedures between cave visits, even in areas where they are not mandated. *Pseudogymnoascus destructans* is very sensitive to UV exposure, and a motion-sensor triggered UV light at the entrance to hibernacula has been suggested as a possible solution. Other possible interventions include application of fungicidal chemicals or bacteria to hibernating bats. None of the suggested treatments offer a long-term solution, only the hope that bat colonies can survive long enough to develop resistance to the fungus as European and Asian bats have.

nose syndrome (see sidebar 16) in bats and has led to millions of deaths. Widespread efforts to conserve Limestone Caves and Subterranean Rivers include strict regulation of visitation, properly gating cave entrances, removal of trash and pollutants, and active removal of pest species.

DISTRIBUTION: Limestone Caves and Subterranean Rivers are widely spread throughout the continent. Large areas of limestone/karst harbor particularly high densities of cave systems. Most caves in Canada are found in British Columbia and s. Ontario. In the United States, large cave systems are concentrated in the Appalachian and Ozark Mountains, the Edwards Plateau of Texas, s. Indiana, w. Tennessee, and se. New Mexico. Mexico is home to the most extensive (many unexplored) cave systems in North America. The states of Coahuila, Nuevo León, Oaxaca, Puebla, San Luis Potosí, and Tamaulipas are all very cave rich, though many of these systems are dry. The Yucatán Peninsula is home to widespread and massive cave systems, many of which are partially or entirely filled with water.

WHERE TO SEE: Mammoth Cave National Park, Kentucky, US; Carlsbad Caverns National Park, New Mexico, US.

SALT-DOMINATED HABITATS

Ne12A MESOAMERICAN MANGROVES

IN A NUTSHELL: Tidal, salt and brackish, periodically flooded forests that form in coastal areas where wave action is limited. They often line the edges of beaches but are much more dominant in estuaries.
Global Habitat Affinities: NEOTROPICAL MANGROVES; AFROTROPICAL MANGROVE; AUSTRALASIAN MANGROVE FOREST; INDO-MALAYAN MANGROVE FOREST. **Continental Habitat Affinities:** PETÉN SWAMP FOREST. **Species Overlap:** MESOAMERICAN LOWLAND RAINFOREST; PETÉN SWAMP FOREST; TIDAL MUDFLAT.

DESCRIPTION: Mangroves are trees that are adapted to grow in an ephemerally saline flooded environment. Most grow in saline intertidal conditions, often in large inlets and tidal river systems, where fluctuations in water level can even exceed 16 ft. (5 m), though freshwater species do exist where the daily tidal flooding backs up the brackish waters. The habitat is not precipitation-driven, like other habitats, but it is still governed by temperature, occurring in tropical and subtropical regions.

There is considerable structural variation, both within and between species of mangroves, and different species tend to grow in slightly different conditions. In both tropical Mexico and subtropical Florida, the fringe mangroves closest to the sea face more tidal action and wave action than more distal stands. On the ocean side, mangrove stands are protected from the sea by smaller, 10–20 ft. (3–6 m) tall fringe mangroves, species such as Red Mangrove (*Rhizophora mangle*), Gentleman Mangrove (*Rhizophora harrisonii*), and in areas slightly more protected, *Rhizophora racemosa*, which can grow taller than the other *Rhizophora* spp. Generally, these species have prop roots that branch out spiderlike from the bottom quarter of the tree and give mangrove forests an eerie feel.

Some mangrove trees that are more protected from wave action have straight trunks going into the mud and can grow over 60 ft. (20 m) tall, even up to 120 ft. (40 m). These include the aforementioned Red Mangrove, Black Mangrove (*Avicennia germinans*), Button Mangrove (*Conocarpus erectus*), *Avicennia bicolor*, White Mangrove (*Laguncularia racemosa*), and a species with buttress roots that are more typical of a swamp forest, the Tea Mangrove (*Pelliciera rhizophorae*).

Within North America, species diversity is highest in s. Mexico and the Caribbean, where diverse mangrove forests also support several salt-tolerant plant species that are not classified as

Mangroves shelter an abundance of wildlife and are best explored by boat or boardwalk.
© BEN KNOOT, TROPICAL BIRDING TOURS

mangroves, such as Yolilla (*Raphia taedigera*) and Paurotis Palm (*Acoelorrhaphe wrightii*). These mangrove forests can also have plants such as orchids from surrounding rainforests, which grow as epiphytes on the trunks and branches of mangrove trees or on clumps of detritus caught at the tops of mangrove roots, along with Golden Leather Fern (*Acrostichum aureum*). In some of these forests, which are generally bordered on the land side by PETÉN SWAMP FOREST or MESOAMERICAN LOWLAND RAINFOREST, the change from mangrove forest to swamp forest can be imperceptible from the air, and it is only at ground level that the boundary between habitats is obvious, though some tree species, such as Mora (*Mora megistosperma*), exist in both habitats. Along the Pacific coastline and in the drier parts of the Yucatán, the situation is very different, and mangroves abruptly border deserts, thornscrubs, and savannas. With very little species overlap between mangroves and the surrounding mainland habitats, the stark differences in habitat are obvious.

Mangroves are pioneer plants that establish on otherwise unvegetated substrates; they can be successional, but without a change in wave dynamics, the system changes little over time. If the mangroves are moving into a mudflat, with extension of fringe mangroves, the habitat will change to "forest" mangrove, and potentially even to Petén Swamp Forest if elevated.

WILDLIFE: Mangroves, like many tidal environments, do not host a large array of mammals. The semiaquatic rice rats (*Oryzomys*) are the most abundant small mammals. Common Raccoons frequently forage and roost in mangroves, while the critically endangered Pygmy Raccoon of Mexico's Cozumel Island is found primarily in this habitat. Common Bottlenose Dolphin and West Indian Manatee visit deeper channels at high tide. In the Caribbean, many species of hutias (a

The Pygmy Raccoon is endemic to the island of Cozumel in Mexico. © PHIL CHAON

Mangrove Cuckoo is common in Mesoamerican Mangroves but generally secretive. © PHIL CHAON

type of rodent), including Cabrera's, Prehensile-tailed, and Desmarest's Hutias, can be found in mangroves, though not exclusively so.

Functioning both as wetland and forest, Mesoamerican Mangrove habitat is home to a variety of herons, egrets, cormorants, and at low tide, shorebirds. During the boreal winter, this insect-rich environment plays host to large numbers of wintering migrant passerines including American Redstart; Prairie, Black-and-white, and Prothonotary Warblers; and Northern Waterthrush. In many areas of the world, mangrove forests have a small set of specialist birds alongside the more generalist wetland and coastal species. In Mesoamerican Mangroves, Mangrove Cuckoo (IS), Mangrove Vireo, Rufous-necked Wood-Rail, Mangrove subspecies of Yellow Warbler (IS), Boat-billed Heron, and American Flamingo are the species most closely tied to the habitat.

The bizarre Boat-billed Heron forages in the dark using its sensitive bill to detect prey. © PHIL CHAON

Mesoamerican Mangrove is the preferred habitat of the American Crocodile, the top predator in this area. Several species of fish-eating snakes inhabit the mangroves; Banded Water Snake, Salt-marsh Snake, and Cottonmouth are the most common. During high tide, several species of sea turtles will feed in the mangroves, and Kemp's Ridley Sea Turtle shows a particular fondness for mangrove roots and associated vegetation. Mangroves are important as nurseries for many young oceanic fish.

CONSERVATION: Mesoamerican Mangroves have declined by an estimated 35% over the past 40 years. This habitat is severely threatened by coastal resort and housing development, aquaculture, and logging. It is estimated that 26% of mangrove forests worldwide are degraded by logging. Clearing of mangroves for shrimp culture contributes 38% of global mangrove loss, with other aquaculture accounting for another 14%. Mangroves may provide sites for heron and seabird rookeries. They are crucial sites for protecting coastlines, regulating nutrient flow in nearshore environments, and protecting human habitation from hurricanes and other intense storms. Sea-level rise caused by climate change is also a major threat to this habitat. The severity of storms and flooding in recent decades has prompted many areas to make more of an effort to protect and restore mangrove ecosystems.

DISTRIBUTION: Mesoamerican Mangroves are a diversified habitat found from coastal mudflats and offshore islands to far inland along large tidal rivers. They occur all the way around the Gulf of Mexico and Caribbean coastlines. They also occur along the Pacific coast, where the tidal range is more extreme than in the Caribbean, and extend farther up the river systems.

WHERE TO SEE: La Encrucijada, Chiapas, Mexico; Río Lagartos, Yucatán, Mexico; Sugarloaf Key, Florida, US.

Ne12B NEARCTIC TIDAL MUDFLATS

IN A NUTSHELL: Coastal areas of biologically rich soil that are exposed only at low tide or under favorable wind conditions. **Global Affinities:** AFRICAN TIDAL MUDFLATS AND ESTUARIES; AUSTRALASIAN MUDFLAT; SOUTH AMERICAN TIDAL MUDFLATS; MEDITERRANEAN TO CASPIAN TIDAL FLATS; ASIAN TEMPERATE TIDAL MUDFLAT. **Continental Affinities:** None. **Species Overlap:** PLAYAS; SALT MARSH; SANDY BEACH AND DUNES; MESOAMERICAN MANGROVES.

DESCRIPTION: Principally occurring at estuaries, bays, and lagoons, Tidal Mudflats are accumulations of rich organic material, sand, silt, and clay deposited by rivers or seawater/tidal influx. Coastal mudflats are one of the most biologically productive habitats on the planet, as the constant flood of nutrients produces a massive amount of life, especially in comparison to relatively sterile SANDY BEACH AND DUNES and ROCKY COASTLINE habitats. The unvegetated mudflats are exposed during low tides or when favorable winds result in the shifting of shallow waters. Once exposed, these open spaces, teeming with benthic invertebrates, become a crucial feeding area for masses of migratory birds and, to a lesser degree, resident coastal fauna.

In inland regions, mudflats are also associated with a variety of freshwater habitats, particularly where rivers and streams enter lakes. Mudflats also occur as a result of flooding in flat areas—especially agricultural sites and grasslands. These highly ephemeral inland mudflats, though less productive than their coastal counterparts, are also home to a wide array of migrant shorebirds.

WILDLIFE: Overall, coastal mudflats have little to offer mammals, though in British Columbia and Alaska, Brown (aka Grizzly) Bears are known to dig for the abundant mollusks found below the surface.

Shorebird ID is notoriously tricky—mudflats are a great place to practice. © SAM WOODS, TROPICAL BIRDING TOURS

Tidal Mudflats are incredibly important feeding areas for migratory, wintering, and resident birds. At specific times of year, tens of thousands of waders congregate at these sites, producing a diverse and spectacular congregation of species. The vast majority of North American shorebirds can be seen on Atlantic, Gulf, and Pacific coastal mudflats, though each coast holds a few species not shared with the others. Common birds include Black-bellied Plover; Willet; Long-billed and Short-billed Dowitchers; Lesser and Greater Yellowlegs; Least, Semipalmated, and Western Sandpipers; Marbled Godwit; Snowy Egret; and many more. The Atlantic coast holds huge concentrations of Red Knots at several key estuaries. Along the Gulf of Mexico and the Mexican Pacific coast, Reddish Egret is a mudflat specialist. In more temperate areas, exposed eelgrass beds are a popular grazing spot for Brant.

Apart from providing critical feeding grounds for migratory birds, the soft soils of Tidal Mudflats also serve as important spawning and nursery grounds for a wide array of fish when submerged. These areas are particularly important for flatfishes like flounders, soles, and dabs.

CONSERVATION: Mudflats worldwide are under threat from predicted sea-level rises, land claims for development, dredging for shipping lanes and harbors, and chemical pollution. Since 1980, an estimated 20% of the planet's Tidal Mudflats have been lost to development. Tidal Mudflats are critical habitat for migrating shorebirds, and loss of this stopover habitat is tied to the declines of many shorebird species.

DISTRIBUTION: Found locally along coastlines throughout the Nearctic.

WHERE TO SEE: Delaware Bay, Delaware–New Jersey, US; Humboldt Bay, California, US; Ensenada, Baja California, Mexico.

Behavior can be useful in shorebird ID—dowitchers, like this Short-billed, probe mudflats with a rapid "sewing-machine" motion. © BEN KNOOT, TROPICAL BIRDING TOURS

Ne12C NEARCTIC SALT MARSH

IN A NUTSHELL: Dense grassy marshes found in coastal lowlands, especially in sheltered areas. **Global Habitat Affinities:** AFRICAN TIDAL MUDFLATS AND ESTUARIES; AFRICAN SALT MARSH; AUSTRALASIAN COASTAL SALT MARSH; EUROPEAN COASTAL SALT MARSH. **Continental Habitat Affinities:** None. **Species Overlap:** TIDAL MUDFLAT; MESOAMERICAN MANGROVES; SEDGE AND GRASSLAND MARSHES; TALLGRASS PRAIRIE (Gulf Coast Prairie).

DESCRIPTION: Nearctic Salt Marsh habitat is found in low and sheltered coastal areas that receive regular tidal inundation. Found only in areas protected from strong wave action, Salt Marshes often grow around bays and estuaries, and on the leeward side of barrier islands. Calmer conditions and sediment from estuaries or tides allow for the accretion of soils on TIDAL MUDFLATS. As the mudflats increase in height, the rate and duration of tidal inundation decreases— this allows plants to become established on the exposed surfaces. Once plants are established, the rate at which sediment is trapped increases, and Salt Marshes can grow rapidly after the initial hurdle of establishment. These wetlands typically occur in temperate areas and are often found in conjunction with Tidal Mudflats and less commonly with SANDY BEACH AND DUNES.

In the Nearctic, Salt Marshes are dominated by halophytic (salt-loving) grasses. Height of the vegetation typically varies with distance from the waterline, with grasses decreasing in height from 4 ft. (120 cm) near the water's edge to 0.5–1.0 ft. (15–30 cm) far from water. Communities vary between the low marsh (areas that receive daily tidal flooding) and the high marsh (areas that flood only rarely). In **Ne12C-1 Atlantic and Gulf Coast Salt Marsh**, grasses tend to dominate, and shrubs are rare or absent. The primary plants found in this subhabitat are Saltgrass (*Distichlis spicata*), Smooth Cordgrass (*Spartina alterniflora*), Gulf Cordgrass (*Spartina spartinae*), Salt Hay (*Sporobolus pumilus*), Blackgrass (*Juncus gerardii*), and pickleweeds (*Salicornia* spp.).

Salt Marsh habitat is frequently threatened by coastal development. © BEN KNOOT, TROPICAL BIRDING TOURS

Ridgway's Rail spends most of its time in dense vegetation but will emerge at low tide to forage on exposed muddy banks. © BEN KNOOT, TROPICAL BIRDING TOURS

Ne12C-2 Pacific Coast Salt Marsh tends to be less grassy overall, supporting a mix of graminoid and succulent plants in the low marsh including Beachwort (*Batis maritima*), Lyngbye's Sedge (*Carex lyngbyei*), Saltgrass, and Common Spikerush (*Eleocharis palustris*). Common Glasswort (*Salicornia depressa*), Spear-leaved Orache (*Atriplex prostrata*), Iodine Bush (*Allenrolfea occidentalis*), and Alkali Heath (*Frankenia salina*) are small shrubs that dominate in the high marsh. Smooth Cordgrass is an invasive species in Pacific Coast Salt Marsh and in many areas has become the dominant vegetation.

Many Salt Marshes occur along estuaries, where salinity decreases as you move upstream. In many cases, these marshes will blend into freshwater wetlands like REEDBED MARSHES and SEDGE AND GRASSLAND MARSHES.

WILDLIFE: Nearctic Salt Marsh provides roosting habitat for many birds that feed on TIDAL MUDFLATS and is also home to a small but unique subset of specialist birds.

Salt Marsh is a very mammal-poor environment due to the regular tidal inundation, though a very few species, such as Common Raccoon and North American River Otter, will forage here. The Salt Marsh Harvest Mouse of San Francisco Bay, one of the only resident mammals, is an endangered Salt Marsh endemic that forages almost exclusively on pickleweed.

Best explored by boat, Salt Marsh can be teeming with waterbirds. Snowy and Great Egrets and Little Blue, Tricolored, and Great Blue Herons are abundant here within their ranges. Shorebirds from adjacent mudflat zones roost and forage in marshes during higher tides. On the Pacific coast, large, tightly clustered groups of Long-billed Curlew, Willet, Marbled Godwit, Western Sandpiper, Short-billed Dowitcher, and Greater and Lesser Yellowlegs are a common sight in their wintering ranges.

Salt Marsh also holds a few specialized birds, though finding them in the dense, muddy grasses can be a challenge. Atlantic and Gulf Coast Salt Marsh is the habitat of Seaside and Saltmarsh Sparrows, which can be found singing loudly from tall cordgrass stalks in spring before vanishing into the impenetrable depths. In winter, they are joined by Nelson's Sparrow. The habitat is also home to Clapper Rail (IS), which is easily located by walking along the edge of the grass at low tide or by listening for its raucous calls. Additionally, this is the primary habitat of the tiny Black Rail along the Atlantic and Gulf coasts. In winter,

Eastern Willets nest in Salt Marsh, while Western Willets typically nest in Sedge and Grassland Marsh. © PHIL CHAON

the Salt Marshes of the Texas Gulf coast are home to most of the world's population of the towering and spectacular Whooping Crane, and regular boat tours at Aransas National Wildlife Refuge are a great place to get a glimpse of this legendary bird. Pacific Coast Salt Marsh is home to Ridgway's Rail (IS)—a close relative of the Clapper Rail.

The Diamondback Terrapin (IS) and Salt-marsh Snake (IS) are both found mostly in this habitat on the Gulf and Atlantic coasts. Salt Marsh is also important nursery habitat for many species of pelagic fishes throughout its range.

CONSERVATION: Salt Marsh is moderately threatened on the Atlantic and Gulf coasts and severely threatened on the Pacific coast. Historically, the primary cause of decline was land reclamation or draining of wetlands to create upland areas for pasture and development. Currently, a wider range of threats includes urban development, climate-change-driven sea-level rise, and nitrogen loading due to industrial and agricultural runoff. On the Pacific coast invasive species, especially Smooth Cordgrass, are a major issue.

The Saltmarsh Sparrow is an endemic of especially high concern. This species has been declining rapidly for the past half century, and the probability of its extinction by 2050 is considered high. The Salt Marshes within this species' mid-Atlantic range are among the most damaged by development, and little of the habitat remains. More importantly, Saltmarsh Sparrows are extremely vulnerable to sea-level rise, and high tide/flood events regularly lead to near-complete nest failure.

DISTRIBUTION: Salt Marsh is widespread coastally but sporadic. It is more common on the s. Atlantic and Gulf coasts due to gentler topography and calmer seas. On other coasts it is more prolific where well protected, such as in Chesapeake Bay. Pacific Coast Salt Marsh is typically restricted to large bays and estuaries.

WHERE TO SEE: Aransas National Wildlife Refuge, Texas, US; Tijuana River Slough, California, US–Baja California, Mexico; Edwin B. Forsythe National Wildlife Refuge, New Jersey, US.

Seaside Sparrow is one of the few passerines that lives in Salt Marsh. © PHIL CHAON

Ne12D NEARCTIC SANDY BEACH AND DUNES

IN A NUTSHELL: Coastal areas with poor, sandy soil, usually lacking vegetation. **Global Habitat Affinities:** AFRICAN SANDY BEACH AND DUNES; EUROPEAN DUNES AND SANDY SHORES; ASIAN TROPICAL SANDY BEACH; AUSTRALASIAN SANDY BEACH; SOUTH AMERICAN SANDY BEACHES. **Continental Habitat Affinities:** None. **Species Overlap:** TIDAL MUDFLAT; SALT MARSH; SEACLIFFS AND OFFSHORE ISLANDS; PELAGIC WATERS.

DESCRIPTION: The most abundant of the Nearctic coastal habitats, Sandy Beach and Dunes encompasses everything from the cold windswept dunes on the Olympic Peninsula to the scenic sandy beaches of Florida and the Yucatán. This habitat is generally poorly vegetated except in the case of stabilized interior dunes. Sandy Beach and Dunes habitat is found throughout the continent but is most common along the s. Atlantic and the Gulf of Mexico. While most habitats without significant vegetation have a notable lack of animals, coastal environments are different, as they benefit from a constant input of biologically rich jetsam from the surrounding marine environments.

Sandy beaches usually form in areas where wave action has weathered adjacent landmasses and where currents and ocean topography allow for the material to be deposited on a gentle slope. Areas with steep topography, strong currents, or bedrock that is difficult to weather tend to produce ROCKY COASTLINE. These long sandy stretches will accumulate all manner of detritus brought in by the waves including seaweeds, dead fish, zooplankton, and other marine debris. The deep sands usually harbor filter feeders, including clams, mole crabs, marine isopods, and a wide

Sand Beaches may be interspersed along Rocky Coastline. © DAVE SPANGENBURG

Dunes lie just beyond the beach and are often partially stabilized by vegetation. © BEN KNOOT, TROPICAL BIRDING TOURS

variety of worms. While this habitat is less productive than TIDAL MUDFLAT, sandy beaches and sandflats can still attract a wide variety of migrant shorebirds, gulls, and terns.

In areas where the beach is wide enough and prevailing winds blow inland, wind-borne sand can accumulate into dunes. The primary dune, or foredune, receives all of its sand directly from the beach. Primary dunes are usually less vegetated than secondary dunes, which form from sands blown off primary dunes. Secondary dunes are often grassy or shrubby, and if relatively stable, interior dunes occasionally develop small, stunted forests, often dominated by Shore Pine (*Pinus contorta* var. *contorta*) on the Pacific coast and Pitch Pine (*Pinus rigida*) on the Atlantic coast. In the **Pacific Sandy Beach and Dunes** region, the sands are typically stabilized by American Dune Grass (*Leymus mollis*), Red Fescue (*Festuca rubra*), Beach Pea (*Lathyrus japonicus* var. *maritimus*), Oysterplant (*Mertensia maritima*), and Common Yarrow (*Achillea millefolium*). More stable dunes in the Pacific have a variety of shrubs including Dune Bush Lupine (*Lupinus chamissonis*), California Goldenbush (*Ericameria ericoides*), Salal (*Gaultheria shallon*), and Yellow Bush Lupine (*Lupinus arboreus*). Dunes in the **Atlantic Sandy Beach and Dunes** region are stabilized by American Beach Grass (*Ammophila breviligulata*), Bitter Panicgrass (*Panicum amarum*), Shore Little Bluestem (*Schizachyrium littorale*), Big Bluestem (*Andropogon gerardii*), and Bearberry (*Arctostaphylos uva-ursi*). Northern Bayberry (*Myrica pensylvanica*) and Beach Heather (*Hudsonia tomentosa*) are both important in northern dune systems, while Southern Wax Myrtle (*Myrica cerifera*) and Sea Oat (*Uniola paniculata*) are common farther south.

Large bodies of water away from the coast can form **Interior River and Lake Beach and Dune** systems. These sandy areas tend to have a smaller subset of the wildlife associated with other beach and dune systems and are largely found around the Great Lakes and the Missouri and Mississippi Rivers. Interior beach and dune systems are often stabilized by grasses from surrounding prairie habitats, though most beaches and dunes are also havens for large numbers of rare and endemic plants.

WILDLIFE: Mammals from nearby environments will use the coasts for foraging though are rarely resident. Pinnipeds such as Northern Elephant Seal, California and Steller's Sea Lions, and Harbor and Gray Seals use specific locales for massive haul-outs and as major pupping grounds where

The hulking Northern Elephant Seal breeds on a few select beaches along the Pacific coast.
© GLENN BARTLEY PHOTOGRAPHY

young are raised. Watching the daily lives of the multiton Northern Elephant Seals along the Pacific coast is a sight not to be missed.

These environments are great places to look for roosting flocks of terns, gulls, and shorebirds. Sanderling (IS) is especially common in this habitat, and small groups can be seen frantically running back and forth along the crashing surf. Black-bellied Plover, Semipalmated Plover, Willet, and Caspian Tern are also common throughout. The Atlantic, Gulf, and interior areas are crucial nesting habitat for Piping Plover (IS) and Least Tern (IS). The s. Atlantic, s. Pacific, and Gulf are also home to the Cyrano-esque Wilson's Plover and American Oystercatcher. Sandy Beach and Dune habitat is also the only breeding location for Snowy Plover along the Pacific coast. It is also a great place to find Black Skimmer, Royal and Sandwich Terns, Laughing and Western Gulls, and many other larids. Large piles of kelp are a good place to look for concentrations of shorebirds. Many small passerines will visit the beach to catch insects in the detritus, and American Pipits and Horned Larks are especially common. In the winter on the Atlantic, beaches and dunes are a great place to search for Snow Buntings and Snowy Owls.

Relatively few reptiles and amphibians are found in this environment. California Legless Lizard, Slender Glass Lizard, and Island Glass Lizard all favor dune environments. Sandy beaches are

Snowy Plover is well camouflaged for nesting with little cover in the open sand. © PHIL CHAON

The Black Skimmer flies low over the water using its exaggerated lower mandible to skim for fish near the surface. © BEN KNOOT, TROPICAL BIRDING TOURS

critical nesting habitat for all the world's sea turtle species. During the summer months, female sea turtles leave the ocean to dig nests on beaches at night, under cover of darkness. After laying between 50 and 350 eggs, the females return to the ocean. The eggs hatch about two months later, again, usually at night.

CONSERVATION: Nearctic Sandy Beach and Dunes is a threatened environment throughout its range. This habitat is one of the most popular for coastal development and human recreation. Crowded beaches, vehicle traffic, and off-leash dogs are a major threat to nesting birds and sea turtles. Large amounts of trash attract many scavengers, from feral dogs to Common Ravens, that also predate young terns and plovers. Least Tern and Wilson's, Snowy, and Piping Plovers are all threatened or endangered in much of their range. Invasive plants are also a major threat to dune systems, causing overstabilization that threatens many rare species that rely on frequent disturbance.

DISTRIBUTION: Sandy Beach and Dune habitat occurs in coastal areas throughout the Nearctic. Interior River and Lake Beach and Dune systems are found mostly around the Great Lakes and along the Missouri and Mississippi Rivers.

WHERE TO SEE: Cape May, New Jersey, US; Sleeping Bear Dunes, Michigan, US; Lanphere Dunes, California, US.

Ne12E NEARCTIC ROCKY COASTLINE

IN A NUTSHELL: Coastal areas with poor rocky soil, boulders, and outcroppings, usually lacking vegetation. **Global Habitat Affinities:** AFRICAN ROCKY SHORELINE; EURASIAN ARCTIC AND TEMPERATE ROCKY HEADLAND; ASIAN TEMPERATE ROCKY COASTLINE; AUSTRALASIAN ROCKY HEADLAND; SOUTH AMERICAN ROCKY COASTLINE. **Continental Habitat Affinities:** SEACLIFFS AND OFFSHORE ISLANDS. **Species Overlap:** TIDAL MUDFLAT; SALT MARSH; SEACLIFFS AND OFFSHORE ISLANDS; PELAGIC WATERS; SANDY BEACH AND DUNES; KELP FOREST.

DESCRIPTION: Large portions of Rocky Coastline habitat are intertidal, meaning they are regularly submerged at high tide but become exposed as the water recedes. While this is also true of SANDY BEACH AND DUNES, the stable substrate of Rocky Coastline allows for more development of visible fauna and vegetation. While sandy beaches may appear entirely barren, rocky coasts are rarely so. Rocks are often covered in a rainbow of different algae, as well as barnacles, mussels, oysters, snails, limpets, sea stars, and anemones. This habitat experiences a broad shift in temperatures as tides roll in and out and is constantly subjected to submersion, drying, and crashing waves. Animals that thrive here tend to be tough and are usually adapted for clinging tightly to rocks.

Rocky Coastline habitat is often divided into different zones based on how much exposure they typically receive. The spray zone is rarely ever submerged and instead is maintained by splashing water from constant wave action. The high-tide zone is submerged only during high tide and is typically dominated by limpets and barnacles, while the mid-tide and low-tide zones are underwater most of the time and can support more marine-adapted species like mussels, sea stars, anemones, and urchins. The intertidal zone encompasses the area between the high-tide and low-tide marks.

Large and diverse bands of seaweeds line the rocky intertidal zone with an array of forms in a wide variety of greens, browns, and reds. Though plantlike in appearance, seaweeds are taxonomically diverse in origin. Green algae (Chlorophyta) are considered part of the plant kingdom, while red algae (Rhodophyta) and brown algae (Phaeophyceae) are more closely related

Rocky Coastlines are stark but beautiful environments. © DAVE SPANGENBURG

to slime molds and amoebas than plants. Important seaweeds found on **Pacific Rocky Coastline** include sea lettuces (*Ulva* spp.), dead man's fingers (*Codium* spp.), corralline algae (*Corallina* spp.), and surfgrasses (*Phyllospadix* spp.). **Atlantic Rocky Coastline** typically occurs at higher latitudes than Pacific and is less extensive and less diverse. Common species here are Sugar Kelp (*Saccharina latissima*), Irish Moss (*Chondrus crispus*), sea lettuces, and Bladderwrack (*Fucus vesiculosus*).

WILDLIFE: Mammals from nearby environments will use Rocky Coastline for foraging though are rarely resident. Pinnipeds such as Northern Fur Seal, California and Steller's Sea Lions, and Harbor Seals on Pacific Rocky Coastline and Harbor and Gray Seals on Atlantic Rocky Coastline use specific locales for haul-outs and as major pupping grounds where young are raised.

These environments are great places to look for roosting flocks of terns, gulls, and shorebirds. **Pacific Rocky Coastline** is more extensive and has a larger subset of unique birds. The most notable are the "rockpipers," such as Black Turnstone (IS), Surfbird

Black Oystercatcher uses its chisel-like bill to extract mussels from rocks at low tide. © BEN KNOOT, TROPICAL BIRDING TOURS

(IS), Rock Sandpiper, Black Oystercatcher, and Wandering Tattler, which forage along boulders exposed at low tide. More widespread Pacific coastal species include Herring, Glaucous-winged, and Glaucous Gulls in the north, and Western and Heermann's Gulls and Royal and Elegant Terns in the south. The Yellow-footed Gull is found almost exclusively along the coast of the Baja California peninsula. Very few passerines use this environment, and among this group, crows and ravens are undoubtedly the most successful. The **Atlantic Rocky Coastline** also has its own set of birds, found mostly in the winter. Purple Sandpiper (IS) is the most closely tied to this habitat, but Harlequin and Long-tailed Ducks, American Oystercatcher, and many gull species can also be found here.

Its position in the intertidal zone means this area receives a large dose of nutrients twice daily on the rising tide as well as ocean detritus and plankton. Rocky Coastline is a highly productive habitat, and the rocks may be entirely coated in barnacles, limpets, mussels, and marine snails. Flat rocky areas can form spectacular tide pools at low tide.

Least Auklet breeds in crevices on the boulder-strewn coasts of the Bering Sea. © PHIL CHAON

Typically occurring in the mid- and low-tide zones, these sites allow people to access all manner of nearshore marine wildlife without having to put on a wetsuit. Numerous species are endemic to this intertidal zone, and exploring these tiny marine havens can reveal various crustaceans, fishes, sea stars, urchins, anemones, nudibranchs (or sea slugs), and even the occasional octopus. Northern Clingfish, moray eels, and a diverse array of sculpins and gobies occur here as well. Different sets of animals are active in tide pools depending on water depth, seasonal ocean temperature, and time of day. A nighttime visit to tide pools during low summer tides can be an incredible experience—but remember to be careful of swiftly rising waters.

CONSERVATION: Rocky Coastline habitat is less threatened by coastal development than other nearshore habitats. It lacks the widespread draw of popular sandy beaches and is generally

Harlequin Ducks are a boldly patterned denizen of rough coastal waters. © JARED MIZANIN

poor to build on. Primary threats come from disruption to nearby marine systems, especially due to pollution and climate change. Oil spills are particularly devastating to this habitat. Overharvesting is also an issue, and several intertidal species of giant abalones (*Haliotis* spp.) are quite rare. Commercial harvest of many seaweeds for food or food production is also a potential threat.

DISTRIBUTION: Rocky Coastline habitat occurs throughout the Nearctic. It is abundant along the Pacific coast and is the most common coastal habitat from Alaska to Baja California. Rocky Coastline is less present on the Atlantic coast, found mainly from New England northward, and is absent from the Gulf of Mexico.

WHERE TO SEE: Big Sur, California, US; Kachemak Bay, Alaska, US; Acadia National Park, Maine, US.

Ne12F NEARCTIC PELAGIC WATERS

IN A NUTSHELL: Deepwater marine environments, generally beyond the continental shelf or along major deepwater canyons. **Habitat Affinities:** Pelagic waters all over the world. **Species Overlap:** SANDY BEACH AND DUNES; ROCKY COASTLINE; SEACLIFFS AND OFFSHORE ISLANDS; CORAL REEFS AND CAYS; KELP FOREST.

DESCRIPTION: North America is surrounded by the Atlantic Ocean to the east, the Arctic Ocean to the north, the Pacific Ocean to the west, and the Gulf of Mexico to the south. Deep pelagic waters vary widely in accessibility and proximity throughout the region. In places like Monterey Bay, California, deep canyons allow access to pelagic zones only a few miles offshore, while in other locations, this habitat may be well over 100 mi. (160 km) offshore. The pelagic and marine environments in the Nearctic are among the most well-studied in the world, but they remain relatively unknown compared to other environments.

Pelagic environments vary wildly throughout the Nearctic, with some holding shearwater flocks numbering in the hundreds of thousands and others being relatively barren. In these dynamic environments, the presence of marine life is driven by major ocean currents, cold-water upwellings, and seasonal migrations. The northern pelagic environments hold the largest concentrations of marine life in the Nearctic. The Gulf of Mexico is generally wildlife-poor, while canyons along the

Pacific coast tend to be the richest pelagic environments. The warm waters of the Gulf Stream in the Atlantic are also very productive both for feeding and as a migration route for birds, mammals, and fish. The habitat can be broken down broadly into **Pacific Pelagic Waters, Atlantic**

Sea ice provides an important resting place for pinnipeds, including Harbor Seals.
© PHIL CHAON

A breaching Humpback Whale is an awe-inspiring sight. © BEN KNOOT, TROPICAL BIRDING TOURS

Pelagic Waters, and **Arctic Pelagic Waters**. The Pacific and Atlantic waters have both tropical and temperate areas, though tropical areas are more widespread in the Atlantic. **Hawaiian Pelagic Waters** are part of the greater Pacific system but hold a different set of wildlife than Pacific waters around North America.

In Arctic Pelagic Waters, sea ice is an important feature. Sea ice forms in winter and can develop into ice sheets that cover most of the Arctic Ocean. During summer, large portions of the sea ice melt or break away from the mainland and form large floes. These are dynamic processes, and most sea ice lasts for only a single season. Old sea ice has survived multiple melting cycles and is generally thicker. With climate change, sea ice is rapidly disappearing, and the Arctic may soon experience ice-free summers.

WILDLIFE: There are major divides in the marine life of the three oceans and between warm and cold waters. Some widespread marine mammals like Humpback Whale, Fin Whale, Blue Whale, Common Bottlenose Dolphin, Orca, Risso's Dolphin, and Sperm Whale are found up and down the Atlantic and Pacific coasts. Regularly encountered mammals in Atlantic Pelagic Waters also include Common Bottlenose Dolphin, Atlantic Spotted Dolphin, Short-finned Pilot Whale, and Gervais's Beaked Whale. Some regularly seen Pacific Pelagic specialties include Gray Whale, Northern Right Whale Dolphin, Dall's Porpoise, and Pacific White-sided Dolphin. The tiny Vaquita is a critically endangered porpoise limited to shallow waters in the Gulf of California. Arctic Pelagic Waters and the far n. Atlantic have many fewer marine mammals but some great specialties, including the near-mythical Narwhal, Beluga Whale, Bowhead Whale, and pinnipeds like Walrus and Bearded, Harp, and Ribbon Seals. Sea ice is important as resting and pupping grounds for Arctic seals. Polar Bears rely on sea ice for hunting for at least part of the year. The best time for whale-watching in all three areas is the boreal summer and fall (June–September), though the Gray Whale calving season in late winter in the shallower waters around Baja California is well worth the visit.

The principal divide in pelagic bird species lies between the Pacific and Atlantic Oceans. Arctic Pelagic Waters are principally a summer feeding ground for birds of both the n. Atlantic and the

Above: **The Polar Bear relies on sea ice for hunting seals.** © KEITH BARNES, TROPICAL BIRDING TOURS

Below: **Black-footed Albatross uses dynamic soaring to travel effortlessly over great distances.** © DORIAN ANDERSON, TROPICAL BIRDING TOURS

n. Pacific. Pomarine, Parasitic, and Long-tailed Jaegers and South Polar Skua are most readily seen on pelagic waters in both oceans, though the jaegers can also be seen on tundra while breeding and on large bodies of water inland during migration.

Pacific Pelagic Waters have large seabird migrations in the fall, and August–October is the best time for pelagic trips, when typical species like Sooty (IS), Pink-footed, and Black-vented Shearwaters; Fork-tailed and Ashy Storm-Petrels; Northern Fulmar (IS); and Black-footed Albatross are joined by a wide array of less common species. Boat trips in Alaska produce the spectacular Short-tailed Albatross more and more regularly as numbers increase, and the Short-tailed Shearwater migration can number in the millions of birds. Another impressive migration occurs in s. California and off the coast of Mexico, where huge rafts of Black and Least Storm-Petrels occur in the fall and can number in the tens of thousands. The Pacific coast of Mexico has several localized endemics including Guadalupe Murrelet, Ainley's and Townsend's Storm-Petrels, and Townsend's Shearwater. Additionally, this a good potential area, especially off the coast of Oaxaca, to see a range of tropical petrels, including Hawaiian, Kermadec, Tahiti, and Juan Fernandez Petrels, as well as Galápagos and Christmas Shearwaters. The entirety of the world's population of Spectacled Eider winters in pelagic waters in the Bering Sea in small gaps in the sea ice called polynyas. Nearshore species in the Pacific include a variety of scoters and eiders; Brandt's, Pelagic, and Red-faced Cormorants; Black-legged Kittiwake; Blue-footed and Masked Boobies; and Brown Pelican.

Hawaiian Pelagic Waters are home to many more species from the w. Pacific as well as a few endemics. White-tailed and Red-tailed Tropicbirds, Wedge-tailed Shearwater, Laysan Albatross, Band-rumped Storm-Petrel, Hawaiian Petrel, and Red-footed Booby are among the most encountered species. During migration, White-necked, Black-winged, Cook's, Mottled, and Juan Fernandez Petrels and Christmas Shearwater also regularly occur.

In **Atlantic Pelagic Waters**, spring and summer trips out into the warm waters of the Gulf Stream produce the highest diversity of seabirds, and Cory's (IS), Great, and Audubon's Shearwaters are regularly seen alongside Black-capped Petrel (IS) and Band-rumped, Leach's, and Wilson's Storm-Petrels. The Gulf Stream, especially around North Carolina, is the best place to see the critically endangered Bermuda Petrel away from its breeding

Northern Fulmar is found soaring over cold waters in the Atlantic, Pacific, and Arctic Oceans.
© DORIAN ANDERSON, TROPICAL BIRDING TOURS

grounds. Warm-water species like Trindade Petrel, White-tailed Tropicbird, Red-tailed Tropicbird, and White-faced Storm-Petrel also occur here. Farther north in the Atlantic, Northern Fulmar and Manx Shearwater are common pelagic species, and Great Skua is seen rarely in winter. Nearshore areas are important for Surf, Black, and White-winged Scoters; Long-tailed Duck; Common Eider; Northern Gannet; and Great Cormorant. All the Atlantic alcids (members of the family Alcidae) are found in the pelagic zone for most of the year, and a winter visit is a great way to see Razorbill, Dovekie, Atlantic Puffin, and Black Guillemot.

The entirely pelagic Yellow-bellied Sea Snake is found in warm Pacific waters in the region. Sea turtles also spend large portions of their life in warm pelagic waters. Kemp's Ridley Sea Turtle is endemic to s. Atlantic and Gulf waters, and Leatherback and Loggerhead Sea Turtles are also more commonly encountered here. The other sea turtle species are widespread in both the Atlantic and Pacific Oceans. Green Sea Turtle is abundant around Hawai'i.

CONSERVATION. Nearctic Pelagic Waters cover a massive area and are relatively free of people. Despite this, there have been massive changes to this environment. Overfishing is a huge problem for the conservation of both the fish species and the birds and mammals that feed on fish. Vaquita and a wide range of seabirds are taken as bycatch on longlines and in gillnets. Declines in marine life are tied not only to direct exploitation but also to changing ocean conditions due to climate change. Disruption of vital ocean currents as well as warming surface temperatures threaten the viability of pelagic food chains and alter migration paths and nutrient availability. Warming ocean temperatures have also led to alarming declines in sea ice. The extent and longevity of sea ice in the Arctic has been decreasing annually, and ice-free summers may soon be a regular occurrence. Most Polar Bears rely heavily on sea ice for hunting, and without sea ice, extinction is likely.

Pollution is also a major concern. Agricultural fertilizers and other industrial runoff can lead to algal blooms that create oxygen-free "dead zones," especially in the Gulf of Mexico. Plastic waste is a recent epidemic. Ocean currents in the Pacific have created the enormous Great Pacific Garbage Patch, which covers more than 620,000 sq. mi. (1.6 million km²). Garbage, particularly small pieces of plastic, are often mistaken for food by sea turtles and seabirds. A survey of Laysan Albatross chicks found that 97% of dead chicks had plastic in their stomachs. Plastic accumulates in the stomachs of animals, causing lacerations and deadly impaction. Many pelagic bird species are also threatened on their breeding grounds on SEACLIFFS AND OFFSHORE ISLANDS. Endangered species found in pelagic waters include Newell's and Townsend's Shearwaters, Bermuda Petrel, and Townsend's Storm-Petrel.

DISTRIBUTION: Nearctic Pelagic Waters are found throughout the oceans surrounding North America away from the immediate coast. Many pelagic species occur only in especially deep water beyond the edge of the continental shelf or along underwater canyons. In the Bering Sea, the deep water beyond the edge of the continental shelf is over 300 mi. (500 km) offshore, while in parts of Oaxaca, deep pelagic waters are visible from the beach.

WHERE TO SEE: There are a number of good options for regular pelagic boat trips throughout the Nearctic. Some of the most diverse launch from: Cape Hatteras, North Carolina, US; Monterey Bay/Half Moon Bay, California, US; Cabo San Lucas, Baja California Sur, Mexico; Puerto Escondido, Oaxaca, Mexico.

Ne12G NEARCTIC CORAL REEFS AND CAYS

IN A NUTSHELL: An underwater ecosystem formed by stony corals, as well as associated small sandy islands, found in shallow tropical waters. **Global Habitat Affinities:** AFRICAN OFFSHORE ISLANDS; AUSTRALASIAN TROPICAL CAYS; ASIAN TROPICAL CAYS. **Continental Habitat Affinities:** SEACLIFFS AND OFFSHORE ISLANDS. **Species Overlap:** SANDY BEACH AND DUNES; PELAGIC WATERS.

DESCRIPTION: Just below the surface of shallow tropical waters lies one of the most diverse habitats on the planet. **Coral Reefs** form only in a zone extending from the equator to approximately 30°N and 30°S. Tropical corals need warm water and significant amounts of sunlight and do not grow at depths of over 160 ft. (50 m). The optimum temperature for most coral reefs is extremely narrow, 79–81°F (26–27°C), and few reefs exist in waters below 64°F (18°C). Most reefs are less than 10,000 years old and formed as sea levels rose after the end of the most recent glacial maximum. Depending on the underwater topography, Coral Reefs can form as nearshore fringe reefs; barrier reefs, which are separated by a deepwater channel; or isolated platform reefs.

Coral Reefs across the globe are formed from the skeletons and living biomass of tiny colonial cnidarians collectively called corals. Each coral colony is a cluster of numerous genetically identical polyps. Each individual polyp represents a saclike organism, usually just a few millimeters in diameter and a few centimeters in height, with tentacles encircling a central mouth opening. These polyps secrete a calcium carbonate exoskeleton close to their base. Over numerous generations, the colony develops a skeleton with structural qualities unique to that species. Typically, stony corals form mounds, large branching structures, or plates, all of which create unique microhabitats and structures for other animals. Mature coral colonies can reach dimensions of several meters. The growth of individual colonies transpires through the asexual reproduction of polyps. In some cases, corals engage in sexual reproduction through spawning: polyps from the same species release gametes simultaneously during the night, frequently around the time of a full moon. Once fertilized,

Coral Reefs are home to 25% of all marine species. © G. P. SCHMAHL, NOAA

the eggs give rise to an early mobile stage of the coral polyp called a planula. Upon maturation, these planulae settle down and establish a new colony. Living corals grow on top of dead coral skeletons and provide important structural habitat and food for thousands of other species of soft coral, bivalves, sponges, and anemones that are also important components of the reef.

As ocean waters transporting sediment cross a reef, they may deposit sand in leeward areas. If enough sediment accumulates on the reef, it may eventually form a small sandy island called a **Cay**. Cays are largely unvegetated, but over time, larger cays may develop soil and plant life, especially when assisted by large deposits of guano from nesting seabirds. These small sandy islets are a good, predator-free nesting area for tropical seabirds and share many wildlife characteristics with SEACLIFFS AND OFFSHORE ISLANDS.

Coral Reefs and Cays encompass a third habitat type, **Hawaiian Atolls**. Circular reefs that surround a central lagoon, atolls may be

Snorkeling around shallow reefs is a great way to encounter a Green Sea Turtle. © ANNA VARONA/WIKIMEDIA COMMONS (CC BY 4.0 DEED)

entirely submerged reefs or consist of rings of cays. There are two competing theories about atoll formation—the first posits that atolls form from barrier reefs surrounding volcanic islands. As a volcanic island becomes extinct, it slowly subsides below the ocean's surface, leaving only the ring of barrier reefs behind. The other theory holds that atolls are derived from large plateau-like reefs. Low ocean levels during the Pleistocene exposed these reefs, which then collected rainwater, eroding away the central portion of the plateau. Whatever the origin, the result is the same.

WILDLIFE: Coral Reefs and Cays are an area of incredible diversity and high levels of endemism. The popularity of this habitat as a tourism site makes access easy compared to other marine habitats, and a day of snorkeling or scuba diving is a great way to explore what the habitat has to offer.

Mammals are essentially absent from this habitat, though Hawaiian Monk Seals will utilize sand atolls as haul-out sites. A few larger cays also are home to introduced Black Rats.

The birdlife in Coral Reefs and Cays is restricted mostly to the cay section of the habitat, which can be home to tens of thousands of nesting seabirds during the spring and early summer months. Large seabird colonies found on cays in the Caribbean and Gulf of Mexico are dominated by Sooty Tern, Bridled Tern, Brown Noddy, Masked Booby, Brown Booby, and Magnificent Frigatebird. Laughing Gull, Least Tern, White-tailed Tropicbird, and Red-billed Tropicbird are present in smaller numbers.

The Hawaiian Atolls are an area of global importance for nesting seabirds, providing breeding habitat for 99% of the world's Laysan Albatrosses and Bonin Petrels. The tiny Midway Atoll is only 2.4 sq. mi. (6.2 km^2) but is home to 700,000 Laysan Albatrosses—75% of the global population. Black-footed Albatross, Wedge-tailed Shearwater, and Red-footed Booby are also present here.

The vast majority of species found in Coral Reefs and Cays are found underwater in the reef itself. A healthy reef is a kaleidoscope of shimmering colors as a mind-bending array of tropical fish move in and out of technicolor coral landscapes. The Mesoamerican Barrier Reef System (aka Great Mayan Reef) in the w. Caribbean Sea alone has well over 500 species of fish. In addition to staggering diversity, the reef also has some of the highest concentrations of Whale Sharks—the world's largest fish. Fish make up the most immediately evident fauna on reef systems (apart from the reef itself), but urchins, crabs, sponges, shrimp, bivalves, algae, anemones, and many other invertebrates also occupy the reef. Hawaiian Atolls and coastal reefs contain more than 7000 described species, including over 1200 species found nowhere else. The diversity is difficult to capture in a book focused on habitats, but most reefs have good field guides to the species found there—and even if you don't plan on visiting, it's worth investigating the staggering array of species.

Hawaiian Monk Seal uses exposed corals and cays as haul-out sites. © PHIL CHAON

Masked Booby breeds on small sandy cays in the Caribbean. © URS HUNGERBUHLER

CONSERVATION: Coral Reefs and Cays are a critically endangered ecosystem threatened by direct human activity and climate change. Mechanical damage has occurred to reefs from ocean trawling, dragging anchors, coral mining, and blast fishing with explosives. The most immediate and widespread threats come from climate change. Many species of coral are quite heat sensitive, and warming ocean temperatures lead to massive bleaching events, as the stressed corals release the algae that give them their vibrant colors and provide their food source. Bleached corals continue to live but are extremely vulnerable to starvation and disease. Other threats often exacerbated by climate change include disease, invasive species, and ocean acidification. Cays have also experienced extensive damage from climate change as sea-level rise and increasing storm severity threaten to destroy these tiny unstable islands. Cays and Hawaiian Atolls have suffered from introduced pests, especially Black Rats, which have decimated nesting seabirds. Widespread eradication programs have taken place over the past several decades, and many critical nesting islands are once again rat-free.

DISTRIBUTION: Coral Reefs and Cays are found in warm tropical waters on the continental shelf and ringing volcanic islands, generally in latitudes between 30°N and 30°S. There are very few reefs on the North American Pacific coast due to cold-water upwelling. The majority of reefs in the region are found in the Caribbean, from southern peninsular Florida west to the Yucatán Peninsula. The Florida Reef Tract and the Great Mayan Reef are of particular importance, with the latter being the second-largest barrier reef in the world. There are also significant coral reefs ringing the Hawaiian Islands. The Northwestern Hawaiian Islands are a series of atolls that hold some of the largest reefs but are largely inaccessible.

Tourism activities also threaten reef health. Chemicals in sunblock can damage corals, and movement between reef sites can spread disease. Taking proper precautions when snorkeling and diving is important to protecting the health of these ocean treasures.

WHERE TO SEE: Cozumel, Quintana Roo, Mexico; Dry Tortugas National Park, Florida, US; Kealakekua Bay, Hawai'i, US.

Ne12H NEARCTIC KELP BEDS

IN A NUTSHELL: A marine habitat found in temperate and polar waters dominated by dense "forests" of giant kelp. **Global Habitat Affinities:** None. **Continental Habitat Affinities:** None. **Species Overlap:** ROCKY COASTLINE; PELAGIC WATERS.

DESCRIPTION: From the shore, as we stare out over the ocean, this habitat is wholly unremarkable, appearing as a large mat of seaweed, just barely disturbing the water surface. However, just below the surface lies a towering forest of lush vegetation teeming with wildlife. Kelp Beds are considered one of the most productive environments on earth and are responsible for 1% of the planet's primary productivity despite occupying only 0.09% of the surface area.

Occurring in cold marine waters, this habitat is dominated by large brown algae in the order Laminariales. Brown algae are protists, a group of organisms that are not plants, animals, or fungi, which includes organisms like amoebas and slime molds. Despite their unrelated nature, kelps are considered marine analogues to terrestrial plants—where plants have stems, leaves, and reproductive organs, kelps have independently evolved stipes, blades, and sporangia. Kelp beds attach themselves to hard surfaces (usually rocks) with rootlike holdfasts. Gas-filled bladders

While unremarkable when viewed from above, Kelp Beds feel like a towering forest when viewed from the seafloor. NOAA/WIKIMEDIA COMMONS

called pneumatocysts form at the bases of the blades to help blades float close to the surface and keep the entire organism vertically stable. Ideal growing conditions for kelp forests include relatively shallow water, high light penetration, high levels of available potassium and nitrogen, and a water temperature in the range of 43–57°F (6–14°C). Under these conditions, some kelp species can grow nearly 2 ft. (0.5 m) per day and reach lengths of 250 ft. (80 m).

Most Nearctic Kelp Beds are dominated by a few species that create most of the structure for the wide array of organisms residing in these sheltered environments. On the Pacific coast, Giant Kelp (*Macrocystis pyrifera*) and Bull Kelp (*Nereocystis luetkeana*) are the

The rich underwater life of Nearctic Kelp Beds attracts many avian predators, including Brandt's Cormorant. © BEN KNOOT, TROPICAL BIRDING TOURS

two dominant species—and this habitat does not exist in the absence of Giant Kelp. Significantly smaller kelp beds occur in the n. Atlantic and are dominated by brown algae in the genus *Laminaria*.

This habitat is in constant flux and is subjected to many forms of disturbance. Annual die-offs occur naturally, especially during the winter months. Primary causes for die-offs include seasonal changes in day length, reduced nutrient availability, and increased intensity of storms. Kelp Beds are also subjected to intense predation by marine grazing species, which consume the stipes and dislodge and/or kill kelp. Snails and sea urchins are particularly voracious predators of kelp; in areas where populations of these grazers are unnaturally high, large, kelp-free "urchin barrens" will develop.

WILDLIFE: Kelp Beds are important sources of food and shelter for a variety of marine mammals such as California Sea Lion, Steller's Sea Lion, Harbor Seal, and Gray Whale. The Sea Otter (IS) is intrinsically tied to kelp forests. These important keystone predators spend their entire life in this habitat feeding primarily on urchins and mollusks. Sea Otters will use rocks to dislodge prey and

crack tough shells, making them one of the only tool-using mammal species. When resting, Sea Otters will anchor themselves to long strands of kelp to keep from floating away in the current.

Kelp Beds are also important feeding grounds for many nearshore bird species. Brandt's and Pelagic Cormorants; Snowy Egret; Brown Pelican; Pigeon Guillemot; Elegant, Royal, and Caspian Terns;

Sea Otters protect Kelp Beds by feeding on sea urchins, which can destroy kelp forests. © BEN KNOOT, TROPICAL BIRDING TOURS

Kelp Beds have a staggering abundance of fish, including the Kelp Greenling. © STEVE LONHART/ WIKIMEDIA COMMONS

Western, Glaucous-winged, and Heermann's Gulls; and Red and Red-necked Phalaropes are all commonly observed here. Terrestrial birds like Black Phoebe and Yellow-rumped Warbler will venture out to Kelp Beds to take advantage of the large numbers of flies concentrated above them.

The majority of species found in Kelp Beds are marine, and many of the 1000-plus species are endemic to this habitat. Kelp Beds provide important shelter for fishes at all life stages including many large and impressive species. Garibaldi, California Sheephead, Giant Sea Bass, Lingcod, Wolf Eel, Leopard Shark, Horn Shark, and many rockfishes (*Sebastes* spp.) are found here. Some rockfish species are incredibly long-lived—an individual Rougheye Rockfish was found to be 205 years old! This habitat is also home to a huge variety of invertebrates, including Pacific Sun Star or Sunflower Sea Star (*Pycnopodia helianthoides*), East Pacific Red Octopus, Bat Star, decorator crabs, and Gumboot Chiton. Charles Darwin once wrote, "I can only compare these great aquatic forests ... with terrestrial ones in the intertropical regions. Yet, if in any other country a forest was destroyed, I do not believe so many species of animals would perish as would here, from the destruction of kelp."

CONSERVATION: Kelp Beds are a habitat of critical conservation concern. In the Pacific, overfishing as well as the loss of Sea Otters to overhunting led to increased numbers of grazing invertebrates that destroyed swaths of kelp forest during the 20th century. Pollution, especially from agricultural runoff and sewage, is also responsible for large kelp die-offs near populated areas. Currently, rising ocean temperatures are the primary concern. In the 2010s, California lost 95% of its kelp forests during a series of El Niño–driven heat waves. Many species reliant on kelp have suffered similar collapses. Coinciding with these events was the appearance of sea star wasting disease, which has decimated sea star populations along the Pacific coast. The giant, spectacular Sunflower Sea Star is now critically endangered.

The recovery of Sea Otters is one of the few great conservation success stories from this habitat. Hunted nearly to extinction by the early 20th century, Sea Otters have recovered in many areas, and the global population is now estimated to be around 110,000 individuals. In areas where otters have recovered, sea urchin populations have dropped to natural levels, allowing the recovery of Kelp Beds.

DISTRIBUTION: Found in cold waters on the Pacific and Atlantic coasts, Nearctic Kelp Beds occur from c. Baja California, Mexico, north along the Pacific coast through the w. Aleutian Islands, Alaska. On the Atlantic coast, Kelp Beds occur from ˜36°N northward through Newfoundland and Labrador, Canada. This is a marine habitat of shallower waters, rarely found in water exceeding 150–200 ft. (45–60 m) deep.

WHERE TO SEE: Monterey Bay, California, US; Glacier Bay National Park, Alaska, US.

Ne12l NEARCTIC SEACLIFFS AND OFFSHORE ISLANDS

IN A NUTSHELL: Seacliffs and small offshore islands, often rocky, sandy, or poorly vegetated, that are important breeding grounds for oceanic wildlife and a small set of other animals. **Global Habitat Affinities:** AFRICAN OFFSHORE ISLANDS; INDO-MALAYAN OFFSHORE ISLANDS; AUSTRALASIAN TROPICAL CAYS. **Continental Habitat Affinities:** None. **Species Overlap:** ROCKY COASTLINE; SANDY BEACH AND DUNES; PELAGIC WATERS; TIDAL MUDFLAT.

DESCRIPTION: Off the coasts of North America lie an impressive number of small, isolated landmasses. In the northerly latitudes of the Nearctic zone, these islands are volcanic (e.g., the Aleutian archipelago in Alaska) or unsubmerged sections of the continental shelf, while farther south, many of the islands are formed from exposed ancient coral reefs or large accumulations of sand. Regardless of origin, one characteristic these small landmasses have in common is isolation. This habitat also includes steep, inaccessible seacliffs on the mainland that are often free of predators and with little disturbance from humans. Seacliffs and Offshore Islands serve as critical refuges for many pelagic species. Seasonally, many of these outcrops and islands teem with thousands of seabirds and seals along with a few hardy resident animal species.

This habitat is typically sandy or rocky with sparse vegetation—usually grasses and small shrubs. The island component is best discussed by region: Aleutian, Pacific, and Atlantic. Each of these regions has a unique set of breeding birds and occasionally accompanying wildlife. **Aleutian Seacliffs and Offshore Islands**, including the Pribilof Islands, Commander Islands, St. Matthew Island, St. Lawrence Island, Diomede Islands, King Island, Karaginsky Island, Nunivak Island, Sledge Island, and Hagemeister Island, comprise a long chain of volcanic islands in the Bering Sea formed along the subduction zone where the Pacific Plate slides below the North American Plate. This area has North America's largest concentration of offshore islands, most of which are covered with Aleutian SHRUB TUNDRA vegetation. The vast majority of the **Pacific Seacliffs and Offshore**

Rugged cliffs provide a predator-free refuge for nesting seabirds. © BEN KNOOT, TROPICAL BIRDING TOURS

Tufted Puffin nests in deep burrows on protected islands. © BEN KNOOT, TROPICAL BIRDING TOURS

Islands habitat is continental islands that sit relatively close to shore. They are covered in a variety of habitat types shared with adjacent mainland regions varying from TEMPERATE RAINFOREST to SONORAN DESERT. The volcanic Revillagigedo Islands are an exception, sitting several hundred miles from the Pacific coast of Mexico. Socorro is particularly diverse, with dozens of endemic plant species, most of which evolved from ancestors found on the Baja California peninsula. **Atlantic Seacliffs and Offshore Islands** are located mostly in the n. Atlantic from Massachusetts northward and are also typically continental islands. The vegetation here is found largely on adjacent rocky headlands and dunes. There are many small islets in the Caribbean, but most of these are associated with CORAL REEFS AND CAYS.

WILDLIFE: Offshore islands can host truly staggering numbers of wildlife during the breeding season. While mammals are less well represented on these islands than more mobile taxa, important rookery islands can hold pinniped colonies numbering in the hundreds of thousands. The Northern Fur Seal colony on St. Paul Island in Alaska's Pribilof chain once numbered over 1 million individuals. The Farallon Islands of California and Guadalupe Island off Baja California have significant colonies of the enormous Northern Elephant Seal. Apart from pinnipeds, the mammalian fauna on offshore islands is limited mostly to small mammals, including relatively small carnivores—Arctic Foxes have had great success colonizing northern islands, and Island Fox is endemic to the Channel Islands of California.

In far northern latitudes, millions of seabirds breed on offshore islands, and in the summer months these are fantastic locations to see a wide array of pelagic species on land. Typical breeding birds on Atlantic Seacliffs and Offshore Islands include Razorbill, Dovekie, Black-legged Kittiwake, Atlantic Puffin, Common Murre, Northern Fulmar, Arctic and Common Terns, Leach's Storm-Petrel, and Northern Gannet. Over 3 million Leach's Storm-Petrels breed on Canada's Baccalieu Island alone. There are few offshore islands or cliffs between Massachusetts and Florida, but the warm waters of the Gulf of Mexico and the Caribbean have a smattering of small sandy islets and coral atolls. These subtropical islands have a different set of nesting birds, including many pantropical species— Sooty and Bridled Terns, Black and Brown Noddies, Masked and Brown Boobies, and White-tailed Tropicbird—that are found in similar waters around the globe. The Bermuda Petrel was thought to be extinct for 300 years prior to its rediscovery in 1951. One of the rarest seabirds in the world, it currently nests on four small islets around Bermuda, and numbers have risen to 500 individuals.

On Pacific Seacliffs and Offshore Islands, an even wider diversity of breeding alcids can be found—Tufted Puffin; Pigeon Guillemot; Rhinoceros and Cassin's Auklets; Common Murre; and Ancient, Scripps's, and Craveri's Murrelets are joined by a diverse assemblage of gulls, terns, cormorants, and tubenoses. Offshore islands in the cool waters of Mexico's Pacific coast are home to several range-restricted endemics: Townsend's Shearwater, Townsend's Storm-Petrel, Ainley's Storm-Petrel, and Guadalupe Murrelet have breeding ranges restricted to Guadalupe Island and the Revillagigedo Islands. These islands also have several species of endemic land birds, including Guadalupe Junco, Socorro Parakeet, and Clarion Wren. Red-billed Tropicbirds, Red-footed Booby, and Blue-footed Booby are also common in these warmer Pacific waters. **Hawaiian Seacliffs** have a distinctive subset of breeding birds that includes Red-footed Booby, Red-tailed Tropicbird, Great Frigatebird, and some Laysan Albatrosses. The small Northwestern Hawaiian Islands are considered part of the CORAL REEFS AND CAYS habitat.

The Aleutian Seacliffs and Offshore Islands region overlaps broadly with the Pacific region but has some unique breeding species. Parakeet, Crested, Whiskered, and Least Auklets are endemic to this region. Red-legged Kittiwake is a breeding endemic on the Pribilof and Commander Islands. The Bering Sea islands of St. Matthew and Hall host few seabirds but are the sole breeding location for McKay's Bunting.

The herpetofauna of Seacliffs and Offshore Islands is fairly limited. Large numbers of sea turtles including Green, Loggerhead, Kemp's Ridley, and Hawksbill nest on warm-water islands around the Nearctic. Some of the islands near Mexico's Baja Peninsula have endemic lizards and snakes, including the rattle-less Santa Catalina Island Rattlesnake.

CONSERVATION: Small landmass, concentration of life, and relative isolation mean that Seacliffs and Offshore Islands are particularly susceptible to human exploitation and destruction. Historically, many seabird nesting colonies were targeted for commercial harvest of eggs and guano, while seal colonies were decimated for furs. Introduced animals have destroyed habitat and preyed on ecologically naive species. Goats, pigs, cats, rats, and mice have been the most detrimental of the introduced fauna, directly tied to several extinctions in this habitat. In recent years, valiant and often quite successful efforts have been made to remove these invasive species from Nearctic Offshore Islands. Guadalupe Island, Mexico; Nonsuch Island, Bermuda; and Santa

Red-footed Booby is a common sight around high cliffs in the Hawaiian Islands.
© PHIL CHAON

Red-legged Kittiwake nests only on the Pribilof and Commander Islands in the Bering Sea.
© BEN KNOOT, TROPICAL BIRDING TOURS

Cruz Island, California, are all sites that have had intensive eradication programs. The restoration efforts on Santa Cruz in the Channel Islands have resulted in the astonishing recovery of the endangered Island Fox from a low of 135 individuals in 2000 to over 1800 individuals today. After decades of ecological restoration, translocation of Bermuda Petrels to Nonsuch Island has resulted in a recovery and increase to 500 individuals.

Most Seacliffs and Offshore Islands are now well protected. However, stochastic oceanic conditions because of climate change mean that many species found in this habitat continue to decline. Collapsing pelagic food chains mean that, in many years, nesting seabirds do not have enough food to attempt nesting. While many of these species are long-lived and resilient to a few poor food years, continued scarcity may prove unsustainable. Black Rats are strong swimmers and may recolonize islands even after eradication. Continued monitoring is a critical part of restoration efforts.

DISTRIBUTION: Seacliffs and Offshore Islands are widely distributed throughout the Nearctic region, in the Pacific from the Bering Sea to s. Mexico, in the Atlantic from Nova Scotia to the Caribbean, as well as in the Gulf of Mexico. The largest numbers of islands are found along the Pacific coast from Alaska to Mexico and the n. Atlantic, while many small offshore islands also occur throughout the Caribbean.

WHERE TO SEE: St. Paul Island, Alaska, US; Witless Bay, Newfoundland, Canada; Channel Islands National Park, California, US; Kīlauea Point, Kauʻi, Hawaiʻi, US.

Ne12J NORTH AMERICAN PLAYAS

IN A NUTSHELL: Hard saline or alkaline pans formed in arid or semiarid basins that periodically contain shallow ephemeral wetlands. **Global Habitat Affinities:** AFRICAN SALT PANS AND LAKES; EUROPEAN SODA PANS AND INLAND SALT MARSHES; ASIAN SALT PAN; AUSTRALIAN SALT PAN; SALINE ANDEAN LAKES. **Continental Habitat Affinities:** VERNAL POOLS AND EPHEMERAL WETLANDS. **Species Overlap:** SANDY BEACH AND DUNES; TIDAL MUDFLAT; SALT MARSH; OPEN WATER; SEDGE AND GRASSLAND MARSHES.

DESCRIPTION: This type of wetland is found across the globe and goes by many names. Salt pan, salt flat, alkaline flat, dry lake, and salar are all words for the wetlands that in North America are called Playas. These brilliant white moonscapes can remain dry and barren for years at a time before bursting back into life during wet spells.

North American Playas form in low-lying basins and depressions in dry environments. Playas are found only in closed watersheds with mostly impermeable clay or caliche soils. Water from rain or snowmelt periodically fills these basins, bringing with it

When dry, North American Playa appears devoid of life.
© BEN KNOOT, TROPICAL BIRDING TOURS

dissolved minerals like sodium carbonate and borax from the surrounding landscape. Centuries of filling and evaporation have resulted in dense concentrations of salt and alkaline minerals, which form a hard crust over the clay bottom of the basin.

Playas are inhospitable to plant growth and are typically barren. Their margins are usually ringed with salt-loving or alkaline-tolerant plants, including several associated with coastal SALT MARSH. Typical plants found at the margins of Playas include shrubs like Shadscale Saltbush (*Atriplex confertifolia*) and Iodine Bush (*Allenrolfea occidentalis*) as well as herbaceous plants like seepweeds (*Suaeda* spp.), Saltgrass (*Distichlis spicata*), and Common Spikerush (*Eleocharis palustris*).

WILDLIFE: North American Playas typically exist in closed watersheds with little to no permanent surface water and no rivers. As such, Playas are incredibly valuable water sources for animals in the region. There are few mammals specifically tied to Playas, though the Chisel-toothed Kangaroo Rat is well adapted to eating saline vegetation. When Playas fill, large herds of Pronghorns congregate to drink.

A dry Playa is usually lifeless, but when filled with water, these wetlands can hold massive numbers of migrating or nesting waterbirds. During migration, these sites are

Right: **American Avocets are frequently found at the ephemeral oases, formed when playas fill with rainwater or snowmelt.**
© BEN KNOOT, TROPICAL BIRDING TOURS

Below: **Wilcox Playa in se. Arizona is a great place to look for migrating shorebirds from March through October (with peaks in April and August).** © BEN KNOOT, TROPICAL BIRDING TOURS

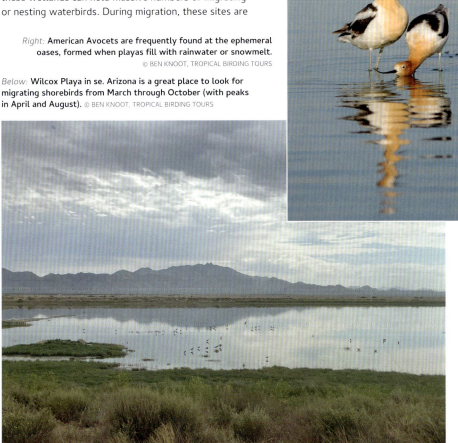

Dabbling ducks like Blue-winged Teal will nest at larger, semi-permanent playas. © BEN KNOOT, TROPICAL BIRDING TOURS

heavily used by a variety of shorebirds including Long-billed Dowitcher; Greater and Lesser Yellowlegs; and Stilt, Baird's, White-rumped, and Least Sandpipers. If water is present during the nesting season, many wetland birds will breed here, and Playas are important sites for American Wigeon, Northern Pintail, Blue-winged Teal, American Avocet, Wilson's Phalarope, Sandhill Cranes, Long-billed Curlew, and Black-necked Stilt. Interior populations of Snowy Plover are tied to this habitat and will nest here even when Playas are nearly dry.

As one of the few semipermanent sources of water in the area, Playas are critical to the survival of amphibians in the arid s. Great Plains. Great Plains Toad, Plains Spadefoot Toad, New Mexican Spadefoot Toad, and Sonoran Green Toad rely on these wetlands. During most of the year, desert toads are underground in burrows. However, immediately after the summer monsoon rains, they emerge from their burrows and can be heard calling from newly filled sites. When the rain is timely, there is a corresponding explosion in toad populations. It is possible to encounter over 100,000 toads around a single Playa. There are no reptiles closely tied to Playa wetlands.

CONSERVATION: Playas are a valuable wildlife resource, though they lack large endemic fauna, and many rare plants and invertebrates are associated with this environment. Roughly 80% of North American Playas have already been altered in some fashion, and virtually all remaining Playas are found on private lands. Playas are principally threatened by large cattle operations (especially when these are poorly managed), agricultural pollution, groundwater depletion, and sedimentation. In some areas, especially in the MOJAVE DESERT, mineral extraction—particularly borax and lithium mining—is common. Increasingly, climate change is driving severe droughts in the region, and many Playas are filled much less frequently than they formerly were.

Public-private partnerships, such as the Playa Lakes Joint Venture, based in the w. Great Plains, are working to conserve Playas on private lands. A recent expansion of the US Department of Agriculture's Conservation Reserve Program included Playas as wetlands eligible for funding as conservation easements.

DISTRIBUTION: North American Playas are found in noncoastal, nontidal locations throughout arid regions of the continent. There are some Playas in the Sonoran and Chihuahuan Deserts, but higher concentrations are found in the Mojave Desert and the Great Basin. The world's largest concentration of Playa wetlands occurs in the s. Great Plains in e. New Mexico, the Texas and Oklahoma panhandles, w. Kansas, and se. Colorado. Over 22,000 Playas are found in this region. Playas are typically surrounded by a matrix of SHORTGRASS PRAIRIE, CHIHUAHUAN DESERT, CHIHUAHUAN DESERT GRASSLAND, MOJAVE DESERT, or SONORAN DESERT.

WHERE TO SEE: Lordsburg Playa, New Mexico, US; Wilcox Playa, Arizona, US; Bonneville Salt Flats, Utah, US.

ANTHROPOGENIC HABITATS

Ne13A NORTH AMERICAN URBAN AND SUBURBAN ENVIRONMENTS

IN A NUTSHELL: Areas of dense human habitation, often with tall, multistory structures and little green space. **Global Habitat Affinities:** Towns and cities worldwide. **Continental Habitat Affinities:** None. **Species Overlap:** A subset of species from surrounding habitats.

DESCRIPTION: Anthropogenic features are an undeniable aspect of the modern landscape. These human-driven habitat changes are most comprehensive in the areas where we choose to live. From tiny villages to the urban sprawl of Mexico City (with 20+ million residents), more than 750 million people inhabit the Nearctic and have converted natural habitats into desirable areas to live. These areas are not sterile wastelands devoid of wildlife—in North America, human settlements have a wider array of fauna than most cultivated and grazing lands and sometimes even more than surrounding natural habitats.

Many suburban areas have a savanna-like structure of open grass with scattered trees.
© BEN KNOOT, TROPICAL BIRDING TOURS

On some levels we crave nature and have created simplified imitations—parks, reservoirs, and gardens—that host unusually high concentrations of flowering and fruiting plants that benefit wildlife. Many cities have larger numbers of trees than surrounding habitats and have even created islands of habitat that have permanently altered the ranges of some species.

In other cases, the draws to wildlife are less expected but no less real. Tall buildings imitate towering cliffs; sewage treatment areas mimic wetlands; rooftops and chimneys approximate barren ground and hollow trees, respectively. Trash dumps provide massive sources of food for adaptable scavengers, and many energy-production facilities use hot water that keeps bodies of water ice-free in winter and concentrates fish.

Areas of human habitation tend to vary along a gradient of density with urban areas on the higher end and suburban areas toward the middle. While the effects of human habitation are similar, there are some major differences for wildlife between urban and suburban areas. Urban areas tend to have larger buildings and fewer areas without buildings. The density of habitation is such that urban areas often have warmer microclimates, and in many cases, insect-eating birds can survive a winter in a crowded city at latitudes that would normally be fatal to them. In general, urban wildlife tends to be either migratory species or highly adaptable generalists. Suburban areas, on the other hand, tend to form a matrix with surrounding natural habitats as well as other managed landscapes. Suburban areas tend to have large lawns or other heavily manicured open spaces. Urban environments tend to be largely insular, but suburban settings can offer decent connectivity between remaining patches of habitat.

The residents of urban settlements are becoming increasingly aware of the importance of these areas for wildlife. Efforts to plant pollinator-friendly gardens are increasing, and people are making alterations to have their yards certified as valuable wildlife habitat. Backyard bird feeding is a common hobby, and there is even a competition that designates "America's Birdiest City."

WILDLIFE: A surprising array of large mammals can be found in Nearctic towns and cities. Among carnivores, Coyote and Red Fox have been particularly successful at moving into towns, while American Mink is common along waterfronts, and even Puma (aka Mountain Lion) and American Black Bear regularly enter urban areas, though the former remains largely unseen. Adaptable omnivores like Striped Skunk, Common Raccoon, and White-nosed Coati have elevated populations near human habitation. Herbivores like Eastern and Desert Cottontails, Black-tailed Jackrabbit, Groundhog, and White-tailed Deer thrive on lush grass lawns in suburbia. In Anchorage, Alaska, Moose are a common sight on city streets. North American Porcupine is abundant in the WESTERN RIPARIAN WOODLAND found in Albuquerque, New Mexico. Feral cats are a major problem in urban

and suburban areas, and while these areas can support relatively large mammals, native small mammals, reptiles, and amphibians are often quite rare.

While mammals have adapted well, birding around towns and cities can be truly

Coyote is an intelligent and adaptable predator, now found in many urban and suburban areas of North America. © DAVE SPANGENBURG

A flock of blackbirds migrating through New York City is presented with both benefits and obstacles by urbanization. © DOUG GOCHFELD

spectacular. Introduced species like European Starling, House Sparrow, Rock Pigeon, and Eurasian Collared-Dove are found primarily around human habitation. Additionally, dozens of species of pet birds—Rosy-faced Lovebird, Monk Parakeet, Red-crowned Parrot, Scaly-breasted Munia, Northern Red Bishop, and Red-whiskered Bulbul have become well established in urban areas. In large cities, green spaces act as migrant traps (see sidebar 6), concentrating huge numbers of migratory songbirds in spring and fall. Botanical gardens, cemeteries, and university campuses are other great locations for birding during migration.

Throughout the year in suburban areas, but especially in winter, the popularity of bird feeding has made yards the best place to look for many species from rosy-finches in Colorado to Mexican Sheartail in the Yucatán. Additionally, ornamental fruiting trees and shrubs host huge concentrations of frugivores and in some cases have turned migratory populations into residents. Fruiting trees are great locations to search for American Robin, Cedar and Bohemian Waxwings, and Gray Silky-flycatcher.

Reptile and amphibian diversity in cities tends to be relatively poor. Some cities like Miami host large populations of non-native herpetofauna. Small adaptable species like Western Fence Lizard and Red-backed Salamander do well in small urban yards. In less densely populated areas, wood piles and human debris can make excellent cover for herps, and searching these areas can be remarkably rewarding.

CONSERVATION: Urban and suburban development is a major cause of habitat loss in North America. Development is of particular concern in coastal areas where many habitats are rare and threatened. While urban and suburban areas have unnaturally high concentrations of resources, those resources are usually taken from the surrounding environment. This is especially true of water, as urban development in arid areas threatens the integrity of many surrounding freshwater habitats. Areas of high human population can also be a great opportunity for conservation. Many urban areas are protecting large remaining natural areas for people to visit—Rocky Mountain Arsenal National Wildlife Refuge in Denver, John Heinz

Bird feeding is a popular hobby in suburbia; a Blue Jay is pictured. © JARED MIZANIN

National Wildlife Refuge in Philadelphia, and Saguaro National Park in Tucson are just a few US federal reserves located very close to city limits. Such refuges provide opportunities for large numbers of people to be exposed to and educated about nature. Having many people who know and care about nature and wildlife is one of the best modern conservation tools available.

DISTRIBUTION: Urban and suburban areas are almost ubiquitous in North America, though larger cities tend to be clustered coastally or near major rivers.

WHERE TO SEE: Central Park, New York, US; Bosque de Chapultepec, Mexico City, Mexico; Tommy Thompson Park, Ontario, Canada.

Ne13B NORTH AMERICAN CROPLAND

IN A NUTSHELL: Areas devoted to intensive agriculture, often single-species row crops. **Global Habitat Affinities:** Temperate croplands worldwide. **Continental Habitat Affinities:** None. **Species Overlap:** Varies with cultivation type and location.

DESCRIPTION: Human activities have altered the landscape of North America for thousands of years, but few have had as much of an impact as modern agriculture. Croplands, or areas that are dedicated to the cultivation of specific species of plants for human use, are the largest form of land cover in North America. Croplands account for 45% of the terrestrial area of the United States and 60% of Mexico. The arable areas in Canada are much more restricted, due to high latitudes, soil type, and topography, accounting for only 7% of the country by area.

Land clearing, controlled burns, irrigation, fertilization, and other landscape-altering techniques that favor agriculture have been used in North America for thousands of years. While most commercially produced crops from the Americas originated with the huge civilizations found in c. and s. Mexico, hundreds of other species were cultivated across the continent, in small farms, in gardens, and through selective forestry. Beginning in the 18th century, Europeans began clearing huge forested areas for both timber and agricultural production. Areas of especially productive soils were nearly completely converted to agriculture, and prized land that was once TALLGRASS PRAIRIE and California Grassland (a subhabitat of CALIFORNIA OAK SAVANNA) is now almost entirely

Much of the Tallgrass Prairie has been replaced with cornfields. © RANDALL WICK/WIKIMEDIA COMMONS (CC BY 2.0)

cropland. Most farms until the 20th century were small and diverse, growing many species and cultivars on a single plot of land. These farms were often divided with hedgerows and woodlots that provided shelter for wildlife in agricultural settings. Since 1900, the trend has rapidly moved to fewer, larger, and less diverse farms. In the past century, the number of farms in the United States and Canada has fallen by 63 percent, while the average farm size has risen 67 percent. A similar trend has occurred in Mexico, though the number of small, diverse farms remains much higher.

The vast majority of cropland in North America is devoted to cereal crops—principally corn, sorghum, wheat, and barley. Soybeans, cotton, potatoes, beets, and rice also account for a large amount of the acreage in cropland. In Mexico, the diversity of climate and relatively warm temperatures mean most cereal production occurs on the Chihuahuan Plateau, except for corn, which is grown throughout. Mexico has a more diverse set of commercially produced crops including many orchard species like oranges, limes, mangoes, and avocados. Coffee is also a commercially important crop in Mexico and the Hawaiian Islands. Cropland varies wildly in terms of quality of habitat for wildlife. Many row crops like soybean and corn can be virtually devoid of animals. Others, like rice fields, can be filled with a variety of birds, especially when fallow. A few of the various crops grown on the continent are described below.

Corn, or maize (*Zea mays*), takes up more landmass than any other crop on the continent, with over 115 million acres (47 million ha) devoted to its cultivation. This freakish member of the grass family has been selectively bred to produce massive fruits made of hundreds of small kernels. Corn is typically planted in extremely tight rows, and mature plants grow to 10 ft. (3 m) tall. It is an annual crop, harvested once a year. Cornfields are generally fallow in the winter months.

Rice (*Oryza sativa*) is the most important cereal crop on the planet but is produced in relatively small areas of North America. A wetland species, rice is grown in paddies or flooded fields in low-

Rice fields often act as artificial wetlands and can benefit some wildlife. © BEN KNOOT, TROPICAL BIRDING TOURS

Coffee plantations are common in areas of former Mesoamerican Cloudforest throughout the tropics.
© ALVARO GUTIERREZ PHOTOGRAPHY

lying areas with mild winters. Most rice production on the continent occurs in the Central Valley of California, along the Gulf of Mexico, and in the Mississippi River valley. Rice is harvested once a year in most of the continent, and cultivation generally takes place in areas that were formerly wetlands.

Coffee (*Coffea arabica* and *Coffea robusta*) is an evergreen shrub that is grown at mid-elevations in c. and s. Mexico as well as Hawai'i. Traditionally, this small shrub was cultivated as an understory plant in the shade of remnant forest trees or planted shade trees. Starting in the 1970s, production largely shifted to coffee grown in open areas with full sun. In full sun, coffee shrubs grow more quickly, and the berries also ripen faster; however, the method requires more extensive forest clearance as well as larger amounts of water, fertilizer, and pesticide. Currently, about 25% of the world's coffee is shade-grown, though in recent years there has been a major push in favor of shade-grown coffee, as this form of production maintains some valuable wildlife habitat and is less environmentally damaging.

WILDLIFE: In general, intensive monocultures are poor habitat for wildlife. The row crops provide little cover or food for most species, and large pesticide inputs mean there are also relatively few insects. Less intensive forms of agriculture with hedgerows can provide good habitat for wildlife, especially small mammals and birds. The presence of these edge habitats is generally seen as negative, as rodents frequently feed on cereal crops, and frugivorous birds like Cedar Waxwing, American Robin, and European Starling will feed voraciously on fruit trees and other berries. However, there is recent evidence that having adjacent wildlife habitat can provide ecosystem services, primarily pollination and removal of insect pests.

Corn is a particularly desolate crop for wildlife enthusiasts and bird-watchers. Most studies have found zero birds breeding within cornfields while the crop is growing. The numbers are also dismally low for all other animals. These are biological deserts during the spring and summer months. After the harvest, some birds can be found in cornfields during winter, primarily foraging on waste grain, small amounts of corn left over from the harvesting process. During winter, cornfields can host huge flocks of Red-winged Blackbirds, Common Grackles, Rusty Blackbirds, and Brown-headed Cowbirds. Migratory flocks of Canada Geese, Cackling Geese, Snow Geese, Ross's Geese, and Sandhill Cranes can also be found in fallow cornfields. This habitat is also a good area to look for mixed flocks of Horned Larks, Snow Buntings, and Lapland Longspurs. With climate change, the areas best for corn production are shifting northward. This, combined with an increased demand for corn for ethanol production, is leading to a new wave of land conversion and the loss of lands in the US Department of Agriculture's Conservation Reserve Program. This shift is driving further habitat loss in MIXED-GRASS PRAIRIE and Prairie Pothole (see sidebar 14) regions.

Right: **Sandhill Cranes feed in huge numbers in cornfields during the winter months.**
© BEN KNOOT, TROPICAL BIRDING TOURS

Below right: **Snow Geese spend much of the winter in cereal-crop fields—especially corn and rice.**
© PHIL CHAON

Rice is a comparatively friendly habitat for wildlife. Within flooded rice fields, there are often fishes, frogs, and a variety of aquatic insects. These animals provide food for larger animals present during the summer months including several species of garter snakes and water snakes, Black-necked Stilt, Black Tern, Great Egret, Western Cattle Egret, Great Blue Heron, American Bittern, Sora, Virginia Rail, and other species associated with freshwater wetlands. During migration, many other bird species will use rice fields as stopover habitat, including a wide array of shorebirds, sparrows, and rails. Before and during harvest, rice fields on the Gulf coast are a great place to see Yellow Rail, King Rail, and LeConte's Sparrow. After the harvest, these agricultural wetlands are home to huge flocks of blackbirds, geese, ducks, and cranes. Many national wildlife refuges in California and on the Gulf coast have incorporated rice fields as part of managed areas. In Mexico, rice fields are a good place to look for Northern Jacana and occasionally even Jabiru. While there is no substitute for the preservation of natural wetlands and grasslands, rice fields do offer usable habitat for wildlife.

Coffee is grown primarily in the same climates that support MESOAMERICAN CLOUDFOREST. Replacement of this forest with sun grown coffee plantations provides little habitat for wildlife of any type. Shade-grown coffee is better, though not a perfect solution. Shade coffee plantations typically lack most sensitive understory birds like tinamous, antpittas, and wood-quail. However, for generalist and canopy species, the plantations are still usable as habitat. Wintering Neotropical migrants, especially, can be abundant in coffee plantations. Swainson's Thrush, Wilson's Warbler, Black-throated Green Warbler, Tennessee Warbler, Golden-winged Warbler, Summer Tanager, and many others can be found here in winter. Research in Jamaica has demonstrated that migrants like Black-throated Blue Warbler are valuable and effective removers of the Coffee-berry Borer, a destructive pest.

Wilson's Warbler is commonly found in Mesoamerican coffee plantations during the winter months.
© BEN KNOOT, TROPICAL BIRDING TOURS

With continuing habitat loss and shifts in agriculture, an important path for conservation is in developing agricultural systems that value wildlife and provide some sort of functionality.

CONSERVATION: As the most prevalent land use on the continent, Nearctic croplands are a primary driver of habitat loss. Habitat loss is especially prevalent in grassland ecosystems and wetlands. The heavy use of fertilizers, herbicides, and pesticides also threatens many aquatic ecosystems. Frequent plowing and soil erosion are major contributors to sedimentation in rivers. The demand for cropland is unlikely to decrease at any point, and finding solutions that allow wildlife to survive in this inhospitable landscape is important. Hedgerows and small forest patches provide important shelter for animals breeding in agricultural areas. Maintaining corridors between patches of suitable habitat also allows animals to move through fragmented landscapes and utilize small forest patches temporarily. Recognizing the value of wildlife species as pollinators and pest controllers is also one path for conservation. Recent programs in California have encouraged vineyards to provide nest boxes for Barn Owls, which are extremely efficient at controlling rodent populations. The US Department of Agriculture's Conservation Reserve Program provides direct funding for farmers to leave valuable habitat fallow or to allow grassland habitats to regenerate for a few years at a time.

DISTRIBUTION: Cropland is widely distributed throughout the North American continent, absent only from cold boreal and Arctic regions and some of the most arid zones. Even within arid zones, irrigated croplands are increasingly common, and large areas of the Colorado Desert (part of the SONORAN DESERT) are among the most heavily farmed parts of the continent. Other areas with high densities of cropland include the Great Plains, the Piedmont Prairie belt, California's Central Valley, and many large fertile river valleys.

Ne13C NORTH AMERICAN TREE PLANTATIONS

IN A NUTSHELL: A monoculture forest planted for wood production. **Global Habitat Affinities:** Tree plantations worldwide. **Continental Habitat Affinities:** None. **Species Overlap:** A subset of species found in surrounding forested habitats, especially EASTERN PINE SAVANNA; MONTANE MIXED-CONIFER FOREST; ASPEN FOREST AND PARKLAND; PONDEROSA PINE FOREST.

DESCRIPTION: Like all other aspects of the landscape, forests are all too often managed for anthropocentric purposes. Large swaths of forested areas in North America are tree plantations, planted for the rapid production of wood products, principally lumber and paper. In most cases,

Aspen plantations are used for paper production. © BEN KNOOT, TROPICAL BIRDING TOURS

Pine plantations tend to be uniform and lack structural variation. USDA

these plantations are monotypic, consisting of a single species of tree, with dominant species varying by region. Typically, tree plantations are created after an area has been clear-cut. They exist largely on private land but also in some publicly managed forests.

Tree plantations differ from naturally occurring forests in a number of ways. As already mentioned, most tree plantations consist of a single species and lack the diversity of natural forests. Tree plantations lack layers (no midstory or understory) and are even-aged, meaning all trees are of uniform height and spacing. Further, tree plantations are quite young ecologically, as most tree plantations are harvested every 10–60 years, depending on species and climate. Young forests lack many important structural features found in mature forests, especially large tree cavities, dead snags, and fallen logs. Tree plantations also lack variations in the forest like meadows and clearings caused by tree-fall. Often the understory of tree plantations is quite open and lacking in shrubs.

Many of the trees used in plantations are fast-growing hybrids, which are often disease-resistant. While tree plantations are often composed of native tree species, the industry preference for a single species can threaten habitats and forests dominated by less commercially desirable species. In the se. United States, most tree plantations comprise fast-growing and relatively straight Loblolly Pine (*Pinus taeda*) or Loblolly Pine hybrids. Farther north in the east, hardwoods are more common, and Quaking Aspen (*Populus tremuloides*) and hybrid poplars are planted for pulp and paper products, while oaks (*Quercus* spp.) and maples (*Acer* spp.) are used primarily for furniture. Eastern White Pine (*Pinus strobus*) and Red Pine (*Pinus resinosa*) are primary lumber trees. In the west, plantations are heavily dominated by Douglas-fir (*Pseudotsuga menziesii*), though Western Redcedar (*Thuja plicata*), Western Hemlock (*Tsuga heterophylla*), and Incense Cedar (*Calocedrus decurrens*) are also commonly cultivated. Tree plantations in montane areas of Mexico are generally dominated by pines (*Pinus* spp.), while lowland sites are often planted with teak (*Tectona* spp.) and eucalyptus (*Eucalyptus* spp.)—both of which are extremely fast-growing. Tree plantations are rare in the boreal zone due to the slow-growing nature of trees in this climate and the abundance of natural forests.

WILDLIFE: Relative to many other anthropogenic habitat types, tree plantations are good for wildlife. Plantations tend to have a reasonable subset of animals from adjacent forest habitats, especially if intact natural habitats are present nearby. For examples of mammals found in tree plantations, look at the accounts for MONTANE MIXED-CONIFER FOREST, PONDEROSA PINE FOREST, EASTERN PINE SAVANNA, LODGEPOLE PINE FOREST, MADREAN PINE-OAK WOODLAND, TEMPERATE MIXED FOREST, and ASPEN FOREST AND PARKLAND.

Many of the birds found in tree plantations also overlap with the habitats mentioned above. However, tree plantations noticeably lack species that need large tree cavities, dead snags, and fruiting plants. Woodpeckers are scarce in this habitat compared to other forests, as are small owls like Northern Saw-whet Owl, Boreal Owl, and Northern Pygmy-Owl in the nesting season. Larger raptors like American Goshawk and Spotted Owl also require mature, structurally diverse trees for nesting

Tree plantations often lack dead trees needed for nesting cavities used by birds like Black-capped Chickadee. © BEN KNOOT, TROPICAL BIRDING TOURS

and are unlikely to be found in plantations. In winter in e. North America, large conifer plantations often occur in areas where the natural forests are deciduous. This makes them attractive as winter shelter, and walking a pine plantation can be a good way to find Northern Saw-whet and Long-eared Owls.

CONSERVATION: Tree plantations are much better for wildlife than the complete loss of forest but are not the same as natural habitats. Depending on the tree species and location, plantations can, however, provide important habitat for birds and other wildlife. For example, Swainson's and Worm-eating Warblers have been found to adapt to young plantations in the American south, expanding available habitat for these rare species. Tree plantations are also popular as a tool for carbon sequestration in the fight against climate change. While potentially useful in this case, tree plantations can be made much more useful with careful planning and implementation. Planting a diverse array of trees, harvesting at different ages, and leaving some trees to mature are ways to make tree plantations more useful for wildlife. As with all agricultural habitats, finding methods to improve their value as wildlife habitat is an important step from a conservation perspective.

DISTRIBUTION: In North America, tree plantations are widely distributed in areas that are naturally forested and are generally poor for cultivation of food crops or as rangeland. Tree plantations are rare in the boreal zone, where most trees grow too slowly to be commercially valuable.

Ne13D NORTH AMERICAN PASTURELAND AND RANGELAND

IN A NUTSHELL: Areas used primarily for grazing livestock, including open range, managed pasture, and croplands dedicated to hay production. **Global Habitat Affinities:** AFRICAN GRAZING LAND; AUSTRALIAN OPEN GRAZING LAND; ASIAN GRAZING LAND. **Continental Habitat Affinities:** Often an altered or degraded form of existing grassland types. **Species Overlap:** TALLGRASS PRAIRIE; SHORTGRASS PRAIRIE; MIXED-GRASS PRAIRIE; CHIHUAHUAN DESERT GRASSLAND; MESOAMERICAN SAVANNA AND GRASSLAND; CALIFORNIA OAK SAVANNA; EASTERN GLADES AND BARRENS; MEXICAN BUNCHGRASS AND ZACATONAL.

DESCRIPTION: The majority of the land in North America is used for agriculture, and while not as obviously managed as NORTH AMERICAN CROPLAND, pastureland and rangeland accounts for a huge percentage of the continent. Generally, grazing lands occur in areas with poor soil or other conditions that are unproductive for growing crops. Despite the poor forage, grazing lands include many arid parts of the continent where low densities of livestock roam large areas. In North America, grazing lands and hay production account for 35% of the land area of the United States, 5% of Canada, and nearly 50% of Mexico. Almost universally, the livestock being grazed are cattle.

Grazing lands mostly fall in the category of rangelands, or areas of native or seminatural vegetation that are used for grazing. Rangelands are mostly grass- and shrub-dominated habitats and include SHORTGRASS PRAIRIE, TALLGRASS PRAIRIE, MIXED-GRASS PRAIRIE, HAWAIIAN GRASSLANDS, CHIHUAHUAN DESERT GRASSLAND, SAGEBRUSH SHRUBLAND, PONDEROSA PINE FOREST, CALIFORNIA OAK SAVANNA, MADREAN ENCINAL, and more. While these areas are not intensively managed or planted, grazing has drastically changed the landscapes. Intensively grazed grasslands tend to be overgrown with shrubs like Honey Mesquite (*Prosopis glandulosa*), Tree Cholla (*Cylindropuntia imbricata*), and Eastern Redcedar (*Juniperus virginiana*). Additionally, most of the major invasive grasses on the continent were introduced as forage for cattle. In many cases, these invasive grasslands have replaced significant portions of the native grassland habitats.

Large parts of North America have been heavily modified to accommodate grazing cattle. © DAVE SPANGENBURG

Pasturelands are carefully managed grazing lands that are actively seeded with grasses productive for livestock. These are enclosed systems where cattle are moved by ranchers instead of being relatively free-roaming. Pastures tend to be low in diversity with a few species of grasses often mixed with legumes, principally Alfalfa (*Medicago sativa*). Alfalfa and cultivated grass fields may mirror native grasslands but tend to look much more uniform and lack wildflowers. An unbroken sea of uniform green is almost certainly a pasture.

One of the most universal landscape features of grazing lands in North America is the barbed-wire fence. These low fences crisscross over 500,000 mi. (800,000 km) of open country and impede the movements of large mammals. Collisions with barbed-wire fences are a major concern for many low-flying birds including the endangered Lesser Prairie-Chicken and Gunnison Sage-Grouse.

WILDLIFE: Most native mammals from adjacent habitats are found in rangelands. The principal difference between rangeland and surrounding habitats is the active removal of unwanted mammal species. Gray Wolf, Coyote, and Brown (aka Grizzly) Bear have been persecuted for centuries as predators of livestock, and the loss of Gray Wolves in much of the west is directly attributable to grazing. Additionally, small burrowing mammals like prairie dogs, ground squirrels, and gophers can create potential hazards for cattle, especially in densely grazed pastures. Concerns about broken legs in livestock have left the country with a tiny fraction of the original Black-tailed Prairie Dog population. Historically, the Great Plains were heavily grazed by American Bison. By the beginning of the 20th century, bison were almost extinct, having been hunted to make way for cattle and as a form of warfare against Indigenous peoples. Recent reintroduction efforts have caused conflict, as bison and cattle are capable of spreading diseases to each other.

Pastureland can attract a subset of native grassland birds but lacks many more specialized species. For example, pastures in North Dakota may have Dickcissels and Lark Buntings but are unlikely to have Baird's Sparrows and Sprague's Pipits, which are found in intact MIXED-GRASS PRAIRIE. During cultivation, hayfields can be a good area to look for such bird species as American Kestrel, Northern Harrier, Short-eared Owl, Swainson's Hawk, Upland Sandpiper, Eastern and Western Meadowlarks, Horned Lark, Savanna and Grasshopper Sparrows, and Bobolink. However, due to early harvesting, these hayfields can be traps for many nesting birds. Nests, eggs, and chicks are often destroyed before fledging. In California, large hayfields host a significant percentage of the western endemic breeding Tricolored Blackbird, and conservation groups often raise money to delay the harvest of these fields during the breeding season. Grazing in rangelands also has negative impacts on birds, as the cattle deplete food sources, remove nest cover, and trample ground-nesting species. The critically endangered Worthen's Sparrow is mostly threatened by the conversion of native CHIHUAHUAN DESERT GRASSLAND to pasture and range. Barbed-wire fences provide good perches in open grasslands and are a good place to look for grassland birds, especially birds of prey.

Dickcissel isn't as picky as some grassland birds and will nest in overgrown pastures. © DAVE SPANGENBURG

CONSERVATION: Grassland habitats and grassland birds are among the most threatened in North America, and grazing has long been a driving force. Cattle can have a detrimental impact on native plants, soil health, and the stability of stream banks. They can also interfere with natural ecological processes and introduce fecal waste into water bodies. In areas with prolonged unsustainable livestock grazing, formerly vibrant streams and the surrounding wooded areas can be transformed into barren, arid expanses. The previously fertile topsoil can be degraded to the point of becoming airborne dust, leading to problems such as soil erosion and the accumulation of sediments in streams, causing

The bright, clear song of Western Meadowlark can be heard from great distances.
© BEN KNOOT, TROPICAL BIRDING TOURS

the disappearance of certain aquatic habitats. Additionally, the excessive grazing of native grasses that play a role in fire regimes may result in reduction in regular, low-intensity fires. The ubiquitous barbed-wire fence is also a major concern, as hundreds of thousands of birds die from collisions annually. Barbed wire is a major concern for endangered species like Lesser Prairie-Chicken and Gunnison Sage-Grouse. Vinyl markers can be used to increase visibility to low-flying birds and including an unbarbed lower wire can allow mammals like Pronghorn to move between fenced areas.

Historically, many natural areas were grazed by American Bison. Bison were highly mobile, and huge numbers would graze a small area intensely for a brief period before moving great distances. This type of high-intensity, low-duration grazing creates mixed-age grassland habitats that are especially suited for grassland birds. There has been a recent push among some ranchers to graze cattle in a way that mimics natural grazing regimes, called rotational grazing. In the absence of migratory bison, rotational grazing is essential to maintain habitats for many grassland birds. Mixed-intensity grazing and frequent movement of cattle is labor intensive but benefits both birds and the grazing land itself. By optimizing natural growing conditions for native grasslands, the land is more productive for both cattle and native birds. With huge amounts of land being used for grazing, changing practices to conserve ecosystems and benefit grassland birds is the only way to ensure continued survival of these habitats.

DISTRIBUTION: Pastureland and rangeland is widespread throughout the North American continent. Actively managed pasturelands are more common in wet temperate areas of the n. Great Plains and e. United States. Rangelands are mostly concentrated in the southern prairie provinces of Canada, the w. United States (especially the Great Basin, Wyoming, and Montana), and n. Mexico. Grazing lands are a mix of public and private holdings; most federal lands, including national forests, national grasslands, and Bureau of Land Management lands are leased for grazing.

Long-billed Curlew will often forage in heavily grazed pastures. © DAVE SPANGENBURG

INDEX

Page numbers in **bold** indicate an illustration.